Praise for *A Life in History*

"What is the true state of the once honorable vocation of research and teaching in History? David Kaiser is without question one of the leading scholars of his generation. His sober and totally candid memoir is absorbing reading that clearly and personally illuminates the ever more tragic collapse of authentic higher education in America."

—Arthur Waldron, Lauder Professor of International
Relations, The University of Pennsylvania

"David Kaiser's intriguing autobiography, *A Life in History*, captures a rare quality these days—the ability to stand for what you believe and base those beliefs on facts, not trendy opinions. If you want to learn how to live your own life, read this book and be inspired to be an upstanding rock in the stream of history."

—Morley Winograd, Senior Fellow, Annenberg USC
Center for Communications & Leadership Policy.

"David Kaiser's memoir, *A Life in History*, is a probing, sometimes searing, look at the professional life of an intellectual during the past half century. In the decades after he entered Harvard in 1965, Kaiser aspired to think, teach, and write in the best way possible, drawing on the assets and fielding the challenges of the American academy. He faced an uncertain job market, campus politics, and shifting intellectual fashions—at the same time producing a steady and provocative series of books on European and American diplomacy and politics. In these reflections, Kaiser offers a personal answer to how to sustain the life of the mind and to ensure a public presence for bold thinking."

—Anne Rose, Distinguished Professor of History and
Religious Studies, Penn State University

"David Kaiser is one of the few scholars to leave a lasting impact on the writing of both modern American and European history. His memoir offers a provocative account of how the historical profession and higher education have transformed in the last half-century. He powerfully elucidates how serious research can change the understanding of our world, and he critically examines the personal and political factors that too often get in the way. Kaiser's iconoclasm is insightful and entertaining, and it forces readers to think. This memoir will interest those who care about the writing of history. It also offers important ideas for the historical renaissance our society needs in an age of democratic crises."

> —Jeremi Suri, Professor, Lyndon B. Johnson School of
>   Public Affairs

"Reading this engrossing book took me back to my undergraduate days four decades ago, when Professor David Kaiser's brilliance in the classroom captivated me and completely changed my career trajectory. Kaiser's passion for the teaching and scholarship that energized him over and over again throughout his career makes this in part a beautiful love story. But he also pulls no punches in describing the changes in the historical profession that made it impossible for him to find a permanent home in a leading college or university and that have left little room for the teaching of international diplomatic history in the United States. This absorbing tale is a window into the inner workings of academia at our nation's premier institutions."

> —James Goldgeier, Professor of International Relations, American University

A
LIFE IN
HISTORY

DAVID KAISER

Published 2018 by Mount Greylock Books, LLC

ISBN: 978-1-7328745-0-3 (Paperback)
ISBN: 978-1-7328745-1-0 (Ebook)

Cover image credits: Photo of chair, Shutterstock © tharamust; building illustration, Michael Rohani.

Book design by DesignForBooks.com

Printed in the U.S.A.

"I guess I just ain't sensible," Prew said. "But I hate to believe that that's the only way a man can get along. Because if it is, then what a man is don't mean anything at all. A man himself is nothing."

"Well in a way," Stark said, "that's true. Because it's who he knows and not the man himself that counts. But in another way it's not true either, not true at all. Because listen: What a man is, sam, is always just the same. And nothing in God's world, no kind of philosophy, no Christian Morals, none of that stuff, can change it. What a man is just comes out in a different channel, that's all. Its like a river that finds the old channel dammed up and moves into a new channel where the current's just as strong, only it moves in a different direction."

—JAMES JONES, *FROM HERE TO ETERNITY*

"A scholar's real audience is not yet born."

—CAMILLE PAGLIA, "JUNK BONDS AND CORPORATE RAIDERS: ACADEMIA IN THE HOUR OF THE WOLF"

"And I am sick of your smart mouth too," Brewster said. He did his stare again. "Who is your superior?"

"I have none," I said. "I'm not sure I even have an equal."

—ROBERT PARKER, *A SAVAGE PLACE*

CONTENTS

INTRODUCTION

In real life and in fiction, some lucky men and women discover their vocation at a very early age—certainly before they are 20. Well before they reached that age, Ted Williams and Bob Feller had decided that they would be, respectively, the greatest hitter and pitcher of their generation, and were devoting every spare minute to making that happen. 25 years later, young Billie Jean Moffitt (later King) felt the same way about tennis. The same was true of musicians from Mozart to McCartney and Lennon, writers from Balzac to Hemingway and Roth, and soldiers like Napoleon Bonaparte, George C. Marshall, and many more. Their focus and enthusiasm gives them a head start, as Malcolm Gladwell argued recently in *Outliers*, and allows them to achieve remarkable things. Yet their impact varies for many reasons, including chance.

I have been one of those people. I had discovered my love and talent for history by the time I turned 11, and there cannot have been very many days since then that I have not, in one way or another, thought seriously about it. I was also a rather lonely middle child, and I was most at home, I discovered by third grade, in a classroom. From then until I finished graduate school, I had very few extraneous thoughts while sitting in class, and that habit stayed with me in 37 years as a full-time college and university faculty member. I also found that I loved archival research, and adding to the list of great works of western history. Meanwhile, I was continually re-evaluating the present and the past in light of new developments in the world around me.

This whole story, it seems to me, is well worth a book, not only because of what I managed to accomplish myself in the classroom and as an author, but also because my career coincided with profound changes in the historical profession and the content of university education, especially in the humanities. It took me some time to understand what was happening around me, but once I did—in the early 1990s—I began to comment on it and to do what I could to encourage the best traditions, as I see them, of my profession. These changes have had profound consequences. History occupies a much smaller place in colleges and universities today than it did when I began my college career in 1965, and partly as a result, it occupies less room in our national life as well. The crisis in history is part of the broader crisis in our national life, which, in the second year of the Presidency of Donald Trump, now raises the question of whether our institutions will continue to function as we have known them for 230 years, and especially since the era of the New Deal.

This is also a story of many other teachers and students. My contemporaries and I began our graduate education in the midst of a shrinking job market, but several of us managed to find homes in academia and made the most of our opportunities. I still have intense memories of the teachers who introduced me to history at Harvard, the best of whom showed me what being a professional historian is about. I have fond memories of many of the men and women I worked with in four different institutions of higher learning, as well as not so fond memories of others. They too are part of the story. Most of all, I am delighted that about a dozen former students eagerly accepted my invitation to contribute their own memories of working with me to the book. Some of them have remained friends for decades; others, remarkably, had not been in contact with me for many years, but still had very sharp memories—as I did—of our time in the classroom together.

I remain an emeritus professor at the Naval War College in Newport, but my active academic career is over. That has freed me to re-examine my experiences more clearly and without fear of what I might say. I hope this book will find its audience among all lovers of history, as well as active and retired academics. Some younger scholars, I am sure, have already had the same kind of lifelong involvement with the discipline that I have, and have great works within them to write and great courses to offer. I hope this book may encourage them to reach their potential, and to see their work, as I have seen mine, within a context of at least few centuries.

I

BEGINNINGS

I can date the beginning of my career as historian pretty precisely, sometime in the spring of 1955, when my family had moved from Bethesda, Maryland, to Albany, New York, because my father's career had come to depend upon the whims of the American electorate. I was in second grade and I had known for a year that I was an above-average reader but I think I had spent most of my time on fiction. I got off to a bad start with my new teacher, Miss Esmay. I was very angry and frightened by the move and I showed it by failing to hand in a few assignments during my first week there. She eventually read me out for it in front of the class. That did the trick, and I began performing on time and very well. I had also started reading books from the school library.

Landmark books were popular at that time. They ran to about 150 pages, and most of them dealt with episodes of American history, including wars, exploration, and inventors. We had one or two in our house for my older brother, but I had not read them. The one I seized on in the library was *The Monitor and the Merrimac*, by Fletcher Pratt, a serious historian who had written a lot of naval history for adults. The book began with extensive background about John Ericsson, the Swedish-American inventor who eventually designed the *Monitor*. After reading a couple of chapters I could see that the book was well above my grade level, but I was very excited that

I was having no real trouble with it. It combined the story of the *Monitor* and its battle with the *Merrimac* (which by that time had been renamed the *Virginia* by the Confederates) with a fairly thorough history of the naval side of the Civil War. I read it during slack periods in class and finished it, as I remember, within several days. I knew that I had passed a milestone.

Landmarks became my favorite companions, including ones on the Lewis and Clark expedition, prehistoric America, the Declaration of Independence and the Constitution (told through the eyes of a Philadelphia family), the Battle of Britain, and many more. I also read a number of another series, "Childhood of Famous Americans," which was usually pretty disappointing because it dealt only with their childhoods with just one chapter on what they later did. Meanwhile, like so many other historians, I was learning a sense of history through baseball. The first-ever baseball encyclopedia was published during the mid-1950s, and we had that too. We also had the World Book encyclopedia, which had a page devoted to the career of each President, describing the major events of his life and his tenure. It also had long articles on various wars. Last but not least, the family subscribed to *American Heritage* magazine, which was published quarterly in book form, complete with lavish illustrations. The articles were short enough to read.

My development took another big step forward in fifth grade, which I entered on schedule at age 10. My brother Robert, whose presence had loomed over me so far in my childhood, went off to boarding school, and I seemed to feel liberated by his absence. The school curriculum featured American history, for which we were issued two separate textbooks. One of them, I recall, had a distinctly left-liberal perspective on the past—the one I was also learning at home—and I read it by myself in class. In the midst of that winter, in early 1958, the Albany area was struck by a blizzard, and we missed an entire week of school while the snow was cleared. I sat down and began writing a history of the United States—and by the end of the week, I had finished it. Historians love archives—and I still have it in mine.

I wrote the history in careful longhand, single spacing on two sides of regular school notebook paper. It went very quickly over the period of European discovery and got going with a relatively detailed account of the early stages of the American Revolution, including the reaction to the Stamp Act, the Boston Tea Party, the outbreak of the war at Lexington and Concord and the Battle of Bunker Hill. The story of the revolution is very hard for even the brightest children to grasp. After a flurry of activity in New England and then in the Mid-Atlantic states, nothing happens for a while, and then suddenly, without warning, the British are "surrendering" at Yorktown. Then came a brief account of the failure of the Articles of Confederation and the writing of the Constitution, and then the real narrative began.

My most important source, probably, were the pages on each President in the World Book detailing their major accomplishments. I listed the candidates in each presidential election and, usually, the electoral vote count. I also gave the basic facts of every war, including the dates on which it began and ended. The whole narrative was firmly anchored in dates, including those of presidential assassinations (of which at that time there had been only three.) Another important source was a wonderful book by Roger Butterfield, *The American Past*, which told the story of the US with contemporary illustrations and short, pithy text, and which my family had acquired around that time. Thanks to Edward R. Murrow's *Here It Now* recordings, the narrative became considerably more vivid at the end of the First World War. I managed to cover the major events of the Second World War in a couple of pages (without mentioning the USSR, however), concluding with Roosevelt's death, the surrenders of the Axis powers, and the founding of the UN. I didn't do very well with the Korean War which I evidently hadn't read about in any detail. The last two paragraphs read as follows:

> "In October, 1957, the United States was shocked when Russia launched an earth satellite. Within two months another followed, this time with a dog in it. But in early 1958 the United States launched a satellite of its own.
>
> "Which brings me to the present. I wonder when I shall have to add something to this."

I don't remember doing any actual planning for how to write this history, but it's clear, reading it now, that I developed a clear sense of what belonged and what didn't. Presidents, elections and wars were critical, and their essential facts were given with care. That gave the history a rhythm, moving along in four-year chunks. Major issues, including the civil rights movement, were mentioned only as they affected electoral politics. And having found my rhythm, I finished the project in less than a week. That was a remarkable achievement in itself, and, I can see now, a real portent of what would turn out to be my greatest gifts much later.

That was not the only breakthrough I made during that fifth-grade year. Bruce Catton's history of the northern armies in the Civil War, *This Hallowed Ground*, was just out, and *American Heritage* printed a long excerpt dealing with the Tennessee campaign of 1863. I read it with great fascination—and got the whole book out of the public library. I had already, I think, done another major project that year on my own, working my way all the way through my older brother's Algebra I book, which he had left behind. I had also memorized the Gettysburg Address on a bet. Now I wanted to see if I could read the whole Catton book—and I did. I finished it one morning in bed at about 6:00 AM, reading the last paragraph aloud to myself in triumph. This was the first serious adult work of history I read. Within another year or two I had read Catton's more detailed three-volume history of the Army of the Potomac and acquired the Avalon Hill Gettysburg board game.

Meanwhile, contemporary history disrupted my life once again. From early 1955 through 1958, my father had worked as a close aide to Governor Averell Harriman of New York, who had served as Ambassador to the USSR during the Second World War and held various high positions under President Truman. Harriman (and my father) were hoping that he would win a smashing re-election victory in 1958, paving the way for a run for the White House in 1960. But although 1958 was the best Democratic year at the polls since 1936, Harriman was soundly defeated by a new face, Nelson Rockefeller. I began to cry when I heard that news on the morning after the election, because I knew we would be moving again. As it turned out, my father parlayed his connections and his experience as a delegate to the International Labor Organization into a new chair at American University's School of Foreign Service. We moved back to Bethesda in January 1959, although my parents passed up a chance to move back into our old neighborhood and school district. Our new house was on the border between Bethesda and Potomac. The latter town—now a millionaire's paradise—was in 1959 a rural hamlet full of horse farms and poor whites, and the elementary school represented a major step backward from the Albany area. But I spent only six months there before starting junior high in Bethesda.

North Bethesda Junior High was one of thousands of new schools that went up to educate the Boom generation, and it was only a few years old. Teaching, of course, was one of the few professions open to women in those days, and women made up most of the faculty. Nearly all were competent, and a few were truly outstanding. They included Doris Gazda, the young music teacher who led both the band and the orchestra, and Sheila Scanlon, who taught a very demanding geography course that was my next big intellectual experience. The geography textbook was based on climates, and we learned that California and the coasts of the Mediterranean, for example, had similar climates, and thus grew similar crops and encouraged similar ways of life. I also placed into the top math track, putting me on schedule to do Algebra I in 8th grade. (As it happened, I had already done Algebra I by myself in 5th grade, and I often wondered, in those days, how quickly a few bright math students might be able to progress if they got individual attention.) And meanwhile, I taught myself to touch type, using an instruction book that had somehow found its way into our house.

My own reading was branching out, too, and after my family saw a production of *The Caine Mutiny Court-Martial* at the Arena Stage theater, I read the novel upon which it was based. During and after 8th grade I also read *Exodus* and *Mila 18* by Leon Uris, as well as several books about D-Day and other campaigns in the Second World War. Eighth grade was less stimulating than seventh, partly because Miss Gazda (with whom I reconnected about ten years ago thanks to the web) had worn herself out and decided to step down. But it did feature a full year of American history, coinciding with a fateful election.

1960 was the first presidential election I was old enough fully to understand. I knew my father felt a great stake in the election, although I did not know exactly what it might mean for us. He originally favored Hubert Humphrey, the fiery liberal from Minnesota, whom he had come to know during the Truman years. After Humphrey lost to John Kennedy in the West Virginia primary and dropped out of the race, my father numbered among the thousands of Democrats who hoped that Adlai Stevenson might enter the race and win a third nomination to face Richard Nixon. That was the situation around July 1, when I went off to summer camp in Maine, a music camp where I played the clarinet and the piano, both of which had been part of my life for some time. While I was away, Kennedy was nominated, and when my parents picked me up after a month, my father was not only firmly in Kennedy's corner but showed no signs of ever having felt any differently. That was the attitude of a political professional, one which paid off for him and has continued to influence me all my life. I have voted for every Democratic candidate since 1968—albeit with varying levels of enthusiasm—and have always been shocked by liberals who found one or another excuse not to do so.

I was one of two members of my eighth-grade section who debated for Kennedy that fall. The class was well to do, almost entirely white, and, as it turned out, mostly Republican, and we lost the vote that followed the debate. I watched every minute of the four Nixon-Kennedy debates. Meanwhile I was also a member of the debate club, which was discussing whether Red China should be admitted to the United Nations. I was assigned to the affirmative, a position in which, as a good Democratic cold warrior, I did not believe. In fact the affirmative could never prevail in the climate of 1960–1. I was very much amused in 2004 when a *New Republic* story tried to argue that John Kerry's embrace of the affirmative in high school that year showed early leftist tendencies. I have no doubt that he, like myself, was simply assigned that side and tried to make the best of it.

Election night of 1960 remains the single most exciting night of my life, and I did not go to bed until about 4:00 AM, with the race still undecided. The emotional rollercoaster of that night was similar to what happened in 2016—but this one had a happy ending. Kennedy, like Hillary Clinton, began well and looked on his way to an easy victory. But his lead in the popular vote peaked around 10:00 PM at just under 2 million votes and began to shrink, and he was doing badly in Ohio and virtually every state west of the Mississippi, where religion was clearly playing a big role. As in 2016, a number of key states, including New Jersey, Illinois, Minnesota, Missouri, and California, were clearly going to be decided by razor-thin margins. When I awoke again and turned on the TV at about 7:30, NBC had just awarded California's electoral votes and the election to Kennedy. But within hours they had changed that call, and Illinois and Minnesota provided the margin of victory. Kennedy eventually beat Nixon by about 120,000 popular votes—but he had won the election. Decades later I had occasion to investigate the claim that Illinois had been stolen for Kennedy, and found it to be without foundation.

I think that I knew that my father would want a job in the new Administration, but I had no idea what that might be, and he certainly did not confide in me about it. As it happened, he had become involved in the fall campaign through Byron "Whizzer" White, a fellow Rhodes Scholar in the late 1930s who had met the Kennedy family during his time at Oxford, which my father, for whatever reason had not. White in turn had introduced my father to Robert Kennedy, who had been impressed by some very blunt warnings my father had given him about the Jewish vote. Many Jews distrusted Kennedy because they regarded his father Joe as a pro-Hitler anti-Semite—a true appreciation, as it happened—but RFK assured my father that Joe had given plenty of money to Jewish charities. (I later discovered that Bobby and Jack had been fighting this battle at least since Jack's first Senate campaign in Massachusetts in 1952.) Now my father found a role in one of JFK's strategies for governance.

Kennedy had campaigned on a promise of changing America's image abroad, and he announced in his inaugural that a new generation had taken power. To change America's image abroad, he appointed a number of new ambassadors from outside the Foreign Service. They were not, for the most part, major campaign contributors, but contemporaries who had made names for themselves in academia, journalism, or other fields. They included retired general James Gavin in France, John Kenneth Galbraith in India, Edmund Reischauer in Japan, William Attwood in the African trouble spot of Guinea, and, as it turned out, Philip Kaiser, my father, to the newly independent West African nation of Senegal. This news, conveyed to me by my mother, was a bombshell.

I can see now that the pattern of my childhood had taken shape. I was not very comfortable within my family, which was emotionally chaotic and suffered from a chronic lack of trust among its members. School had emerged early as my refuge. But I had now had to change schools four times between 2nd grade and 8th grade, and three of those changes had led to about a year of depression. Eighth grade had been a difficult year socially, but things were improving at the end of it. Now I was going to be torn out of my environment again for at least two years. Nor was this all. There was no American school in Senegal, and in October—only six months after we got the news of my father's appointment—I would be entering the French equivalent of 8th grade (4eme) at the Lycée in Dakar. In short, I had a few months to learn a whole new language. The first 14 years of my life had left me intellectually precocious but socially and emotionally somewhat backward. This new move was bound to accentuate both trends.

In the mist of that spring, I had an amazing experience when I brought the *Washington Post*, which I was delivering, into the house. On page 1, I learned that John Kenneth Galbraith had mentioned to President Kennedy that his son Peter—a few years younger than myself—was very unhappy about having to leave his school and friends in Cambridge, Massachusetts to go to India. My first thought was that my father would never have said anything like that to the President. Kennedy had written Peter a letter, saying that he thought he understood his feelings because his younger siblings had gone through the same thing in the late 1930s when his family went to Britain for the same reason. He also said that he regarded the sons and daughters of the people he was sending overseas as "my junior Peace Corps." That letter meant a lot—and not just to Peter Galbriath.

The experience of learning French so rapidly was mind-expanding. I became fascinated both with the sound of the language and the grammar, and indeed, came to understand English grammar much better because of it. My parents insisted on the four of us., including my younger brother Charles (my older brother was now in college) speaking only French at meals, and they hired a recent college graduate who knew French to live with us for a year in both the years that I was there to provide us all with help, The Lycée itself was a survival of the colonial era, during which it had been the only French public secondary school in the whole of French West Africa, of which Dakar had been the capital. The students were about evenly divided between French kids who had somehow found their way to Senegal, and native Senegalese, almost all of them boys. I never understood how the various faculty members—nearly all of them white French men and women—had wound up there, and their quality varied widely. The most important to me was Mdme. Damon, the French teacher in my first year, who took an immediate liking to me because she could see how hard I was working. While I never managed to earn a passing grade in dictation—transcribing a selection which she read to the class—I more than held my own in the discussions of French drama classics that we read in class. They included works by Corneille and Molière, the latter a true delight. Near the end of the year, in a moment of frustration, she remarked spontaneously that "Kaiser has made twenty times more progress in one year than the rest of you have made in your whole lives." Other classes included math (which was behind North Bethesda), history and geography (which in 4eme focused on medieval France), English, which I took as my first foreign language and whose teacher never enjoyed having me in the class, science, which was quite primitive—and first-year Spanish.

That was the additional challenge I faced. 4eme was the year in which French students began their second foreign language, which moved at a rapid rate. I had hoped to begin German—why exactly I am not sure—but my father talked me into doing Spanish instead. German was destined to play a bigger role in my life, but Spanish turned out to be my favorite class. The "prof," as we called them, a young woman, was a good one, and learning Spanish in French turned out to be quite easy, since Spanish is very similar to French, but much less complicated. Both the pronunciation and the grammar are more straightforward, and I ranked near the top of the Spanish class. By the end of that first year I could carry on a conversation. The second year my teachers were less impressive, and I was distracted by a good many other things, but I emerged from the experience in mid-1963 knowing French and Spanish.

The experience was broadening in other ways. Dakar was the gateway to all Africa from the US, and a steady stream of important visitors came through to check out the newly independent continent. The most distinguished and memorable was Edward R. Murrow, Kennedy's new head of USIA, who stayed with us for several days and was just as straightforward and approachable in real life as on the air. Others included Senators Kenneth Keating of New York and Allen Ellender of Louisiana, who got himself into trouble later in his tour of Africa with inflammatory remarks about the Africans' capacity for self-government. (Ellender hailed from Louisiana. After my father took him in to meet President Leopold Senghor, a distinguished scholar, and poet, Ellender commented that Senghor must have some white blood in him—"a pure black man couldn't be as intelligent as that," he said.)

We were almost completely cut off from American life. The Paris editions of the *New York Times* and the *New York Herald Tribune* arrived one day late, and we got *Time* and *Newsweek* every week, and intermittent reception from the Voice of America. Senegal had no television at all, and all American films were dubbed. The USIA did send us film of major presidential speeches, and it was thus that I saw, several days late, Kennedy's address to the nation about the presence of Russian missiles in Cuba. We obsessively read every word of *Time* and *Newsweek* every week, and I very much regretted not being able to see any of the great movies that appeared in 1962, except during a vacation we took that summer in London. I eventually made up for lost time.

The tiny handful of other American teenagers among the Embassy families included a few very serious readers. Several of the kids from Foreign Service families had learned and forgotten one or two foreign languages during their childhood. I also joined the Book of the Month Club (my parents must have allowed their subscription to lapse) while we were there. Through it I acquired, and read, *The Old Man and the Sea* and the complete Hemingway short stories, many of which resonated very deeply. And thanks to my contemporaries I also read *Look Homeward Angel* by Thomas Wolfe, and *From Here to Eternity* by James Jones. I was very conscious of my identification with Prewitt, the protagonist, in the latter book, very excited by the remarkable sex scenes it featured, and very moved by the intense, intimate conversations that punctuate it, but I had no idea how closely it was going to mirror the story of my own professional life. I also managed to read the current affairs novels that were dominating the bestseller lists, including two by Allen Drury (*Advise and Consent* and *A Shade of Difference*), *Fail Safe*, and *Seven Days in May*. We had also, as I recall, brought William Shirer's *The Rise and Fall of the Third Reich* with us, and I read that as well. Another book that arrived from the BOMC in the summer of 1962 was Barbara Tuchman's *The Guns of August*, her account of the opening month of the First World War. Another eager reader of that book was President Kennedy, who remarked early in the fall that he didn't want some future historian to write a parallel book called *The Missiles of October*.

I got some very real emotional support during those two lonely years from some of the younger Embassy wives from the Silent generation, who turned out to be kindred spirits. One such was Deborah Blair Waddington, who changed my life by lending me the first American edition of some of George Orwell's essays. I had already read *1984* and *Animal Farm* while in junior high, but now I was introduced to *Such, Such Were the Joys*, his harrowing account of his early school days, *England Your England, Inside the Whale* (about Henry Miller), and various others. I did not realize at the time that many of these pieces had received almost no notice when Orwell originally wrote them, but I must have noticed that he, like myself, had been a lonely kid who read a very great deal. His role in my life was only just beginning.

My immediate future was becoming a matter of debate in the first half of 1963. My father expected his tour to come to an end in the middle of that year, when he was due for a long home leave, but I wouldn't be remaining in Senegal in any case. I would be starting my junior year in high school that fall. Here family history came into play.

My older brother Robert, who was destined to have a long and distinguished career in journalism, had not had an easy childhood either. For reasons I have never understood, he had started elementary school a year early, and that probably got him off on the wrong foot academically. Never a particularly outstanding student, he had been an occasional disciplinary problem in school, and a source of some frustration to our parents, with whom he frequently clashed. Thus they had decided in 1957 to send him off to boarding school. He had been rejected by Andover and Exeter but accepted at Loomis (now Loomis-Chafee) in Windsor, Connecticut. While he had also had trouble academically there in his first year, as a sophomore, he had then turned his career around, largely through success as editor of both the school paper and the yearbook. In his senior year he had been turned down by Harvard but accepted at Yale, where by 1963 he was positioned to be an editor of the *Yale Daily News*. My father, who in 1962–3 was clearly annoyed by my continuing presence in the household, now believed that Loomis held the key to the future lives of all his sons, thanks to the relationship which he believed he had forged with the headmaster. He took it for granted that I would go there that fall.

I on the other hand did not *need* Loomis academically. I had been the top student in my class all my life, and my intellectual development had now taken another leap forward thanks to two years abroad. What I did need, as I knew very well, was a couple of years as a normal teenager within the innocent world which, ten years later, George Lucas captured so beautifully for posterity in the film *American Graffiti*. I would not have been unhappy to rejoin my old classmates from North Bethesda in Walter Johnson High School. But meanwhile, my mother, I believe, came up with another alternative solution, suggesting that I might live with my uncle Henry, a prominent attorney, and his family in Chevy Chase, and attend Sidwell Friends School. Already known as perhaps the best day school in Washington, it later became famous as the alma mater of Chelsea Clinton and Sasha and Melia Obama, as well as my older brother's two daughters. So I applied there, as well as to Loomis, and was accepted there as well. My mother later indicated to me that she had also told my father that if I were to go to boarding school, it seemed silly for me to go to Loomis instead of Andover or Exeter since I obviously could get in anywhere that I wanted. But he was unmoved.

I returned to the US before the rest of my family. Our Bethesda house was now vacant, and I lived there that summer with my older brother (who was holding down his first temporary job at the *Washington Post*) and a friend of his. My brother had now adopted the habits of so many oldest children, using the parenting techniques he had endured on his younger siblings. Since Loomis had been best for him, he was sure it must be best for me. I delayed the decision for as long as I could and until after my parents had returned on leave. Meanwhile, I worked in the office of Senator Hubert Humphrey, and attended hearings both on the Test Ban Treaty (which I heard Edward Teller oppose), and on the public accommodations provisions of the civil rights bill that Kennedy had introduced, (where I heard George Wallace argue that the 14th amendment was not a validly adopted part of the Constitution.) And in the end, on a fateful August day, I gave in and agreed to go to Loomis.

I regret that decision, but in many ways it worked out well. It did what my parents counted on it to do, getting me into the college of my choice—although I have no doubt that Sidwell Friends would have done the same. Academically, I would now rate it as a good, but not great, experience. Several years ago, an exact contemporary of mine, the filmmaker Kevin Rafferty, made a fascinating documentary about the Phillips Andover class of 1965. Rafferty is better known for two other films, *The*

Atomic Café and *Harvard Beats Yale, 29–29*, about the 1968 Harvard-Yale game. The Andover film is noteworthy for the recollections of many classmates about the most famous member of the Andover class of '64, George W. Bush. Rafferty's film persuaded me that Andover was well above Loomis academically. His classmates spoke in reverent terms about several of their teachers—terms I could not have used about any of mine. Several of them said that after Andover, their years at Harvard or Yale had been a breeze—a statement I certainly would never have made. Loomis's English department did teach its students to write concisely, and we were worked very hard and graded rigorously. At one time or another the class of '65—my class—had about 130 boys in it, but only 100 of them made it to graduation, the rest of them separated out, mostly because of academic difficulties.

The course I put the most into there, not surprisingly, was my junior year AP history course, into which I was moved after a few weeks. Our textbook was *The Growth of the American Republic* by Samuel Eliot Morison and Henry Steele Commager—a book whose focus on economic issues showed considerable influence from the older Charles A. Beard. We had to read a chapter of it for every class, and were frequently given a quiz on the chapter. I took notes on my typewriter, using a rule I carried into college: one sentence of notes per paragraph. As a result, my classmates were astonished by how many sheets of paper I could fill during a quiz. Morison and Commager focused in their second volume on the gilded age, the Progressive era, and the New Deal-the story of American history that I had learned at home, and one to which Lyndon Johnson was adding a new chapter. At the end of my junior year, the faculty awarded me the junior American history prize. As I remarked to my classmates at our 50th reunion in 2015, "they got that one right."

The strength of Loomis, in retrospect, was not academic, but social. The overwhelming majority of the students were not rich: they were the children of the New England professional class. A full 1/3 of them were day students from West Hartford. And the school still bore the influence of its first headmaster, Nathaniel Horton Batchelder, one of the many great educators of the Missionary generation, who believed, as some of his students later explained to me, that eccentricity was a virtue. *Regular Guys*, Rafferty's movie about Andover, spent a lot of time on the students' rigid social hierarchy. They went through a cafeteria line for all their meals, apparently, and the "cool" kids sat in one half of the dining hall while the plebes sulked in the other half. We could not do that. We were assigned tables for lunch and dinner for two weeks at a time, guaranteeing a broad exposure to every class and faction. While jocks ran the student government, the intellectuals had tremendous esprit de corps. I was angry to be there and got off on the wrong foot socially, but recovered very quickly and made a great many close friends. By senior year I was a recognized figure on campus and barely missed winning a special election to the student council. I wrote a regular political column for the school newspaper, and gave a piano recital late in my senior year. Meanwhile, I ranked in the top 5 of the class academically, which I knew would be good enough to get me into Harvard. I also finally discovered, by the end of my senior year, that I had some real ability as an athlete. Unfortunately I had wasted a lot of time playing the wrong intramural sports—the ones my brother had played. But I had immersed myself in the school history and culture, and I truly felt I belonged.

In the spring of my senior year I took three advanced placement exams, designed to certify that students had done college-level work in particular subjects. Nowadays, as I discovered when my own sons attended high school in the 1990s, advanced placement courses revolve almost entirely around what is expected to be on the test. We were given absolutely no information on that subject and never worried about it—in the same way, that neither I nor any of my classmates took an SAT prep course, or spent more than a couple of hours doing dry run questions for those tests. I received grades of 4 out of 5 in all three: American history, Math (really calculus), and English. That was to have fateful consequences too.

I knew I wanted to go to Harvard both because it was the nation's leading university, and because it was located in Boston. My mother's parents had met while attending Harvard

Medical School and Radcliffe, respectively—I never knew my grandmother, who died suddenly when my mother was 10—and both my father and older brother had been rejected for admission there. This would be the first decision I had managed to make about my own future. The college guidance adviser at Loomis, Robert Ward—one of the smartest of all the faculty members, and a brilliant politician who seemed to have every major admissions office in the palm of his hand—assured me that all would be well, and I did not apply anywhere else. On April 15, 1965, I was informed that I was admitted. On June 7 of that year, I turned 18. That, as it happened, was a very big day for the United States as well, marking the end of an era. Many years later I discovered that it was on that day that General William Westmoreland had cabled the Pentagon that he needed 175,000 men right away, and more in 1966, to defend South Vietnam. Two days later, I graduated from Loomis.

My father had now secured his dream job, the Minister—that is, Deputy Chief of Mission—to London, and I spent the next month in their palatial mansion in Kensington. Then I returned and spent about five weeks touring the country with a family from Westport, Connecticut, where another uncle of mine lived. I fell in love with the American landscape, and I have described the climax of that trip in my book, *American Tragedy*. I returned to my uncle's house in Chevy Chase in mid-August and for the first time in my life, spent several delightful weeks as a real American teenager, hanging out with a close friend from Loomis. We took full advantage of Washington's 18-year old drinking age for beer. I also stopped by the local draft board to register, but Vietnam seemed a long way away. In mid-September I took a bus to New York, and my uncle Jerry drove me to Harvard. I was finally where I wanted to be—and I remained there, with just one break of a year, for the next 15 years, the most formative and, at least until 1977, the happiest of my whole life.

II

HARVARD COLLEGE

1965–9

The Harvard that I entered in the fall of 1965 was at the climax of an era, one started by two Presidents of the university from the first half of the 20th century, Abbott Lawrence Lowell and James Bryant Conant. Lowell had created the house system in the 1930s, modeling it on the colleges of Oxford and Cambridge. Although the houses by no means dominated undergraduate education to the extent that their British counterparts did, faculty and graduate student tutors affiliated with them and they were the center of students' social life after their freshman year. As a sign of the times, the university made a fundamental change in the house system during my freshman year, deciding that house masters—some of whom were legendary campus figures—would no longer be able to compete for the students they wanted. Had it not been for that change, I would very likely never have met the classmates who have remained my best friends for life. Radcliffe still had its own campus and its own library, and Radcliffe students were barred from Lamont, the Harvard undergraduate library. That restriction was soon lifted and became less onerous in my sophomore year, when Radcliffe opened the new Hilles Library, a far more appealing facility than any of the older buildings. Radcliffe had no separate courses, and its students—who numbered ¼ of the Harvard class—received Harvard degrees. There were about 30 black (or as we would have said in 1965, Negro) students in my class, which was probably an all-time high. The student body mixed prep school graduates like myself (including several dozen entrants each from Phillips Andover and Phillips Exeter) with public high and day school graduates from all over the country. Yet there still was, as Jerome Karabel has shown in his remarkable book *The Chosen*, a fairly strict quota for graduates of three elite public high schools—Bronx Science and Stuyvesant in New York, and Central High in Philadelphia—whose graduates tended to be Jews. Today a similar quota limitsing the number of Asian Americans faces a challenge in court.

Conant's influence was more specifically educational. He had founded the General Education curriculum, requiring each freshman to take a full year course—chosen from about half a dozen alternatives—in Humanities, Social Sciences, and Natural Sciences. The program's most popular courses included Humanities (known as Hum) 2, Epic and Drama, taught by classicist and Master of Eliot House John Finley and playwright William Alfred; Hum 5, an introduction to western philosophy; Soc[ial] Sci[ences] 2, Western Thought and Institutions, an application of sociological theory to various great events in western history, taught by Samuel Beer; Soc Sci 136, Sociological Structures in America, taught by David Riesman; and Nat[ural] Sciences] 5, a biology course by George Wald, one of the pioneers in the study of DNA. The intellectual quality of these courses, the role they played in campus life, and the response they inspired among students, have no analogs, I think, in any American college or university today.

Many of these courses, to begin with, were extremely demanding, requiring thousands of pages of reading and substantial written work. But the most remarkable thing about them, in comparison to courses today, was that grade inflation had not yet begun. About 9% of the grades awarded during my freshman year were straight As (I received one of them, in Economics 1), and another 13% were A-s. The grade of B+ accounted for the next 16% of grades, Bs another 17%, and B-s another 15%. That totaled 70% honor grades, which in the most prestigious school in the country does not seem to be excessive. It also meant that a full 30% of course grades awarded were C+ or lower, and 5% were D or lower. What this meant was that nearly all of us took many courses with no expectation of getting an A—and often, we did not care. Final exams, lasting 3 hours, played an enormous role in grades, sometimes as much as 50% of the total. The best ones were written to require a full mastery of the course material, including essentially all the reading, and only exams that showed that level of mastery would receive an A. A B or B+—of which I received many—meant that you had clearly grasped a great deal of the course material—but not all of it. A C+ represented an adequate level of performance. I knew many people who had taken George Wald's Nat Sci 5 knowing full well that they would be very lucky to reach a B. But they had gotten an enormous amount out of it, and that, not the grade, was the point. We shall see in a moment that I had a similar experience myself. Grade inflation only amounted to about 5% during my four years as an undergraduate, but it took off in the following year, and by 1977, when I was on the faculty, about 38% of grades awarded were As or A-s, up from 29% in 1965–6, and only 9% of grades were below B-.[1]

As it happened, I experienced only ⅓ of a normal exposure to General Education, because I decided to take advantage of the opportunity to enter as a sophomore, which I had earned with my three successful AP exams. I had no intention of remaining only three years, but I suppose I welcomed the status of it. It also exempted me from the freshman swimming test (which I could have passed), the requirement to take freshman composition, and mandatory athletics (which in fact would have been good for me, as they had been at Loomis.) Under the rules, advanced standing sophomores had to take only one full Gen Ed course, and at least one regular course in each of the other two subject areas. Thus I managed to fulfill my Natural Sciences requirement (a field in which my high school education was already quite deficient) by taking one additional year of calculus in the math department. For

---

1 This data came from a story in the *Harvard Independent*, May 11–17, 1978, which I saved.

my one Gen Ed, I chose a course with a very particular reputation, Humanities 6, which was somewhat misleadingly entitled Introduction to Literature.

Like all the other great Gen Ed courses—and probably any great college course anywhere—Hum 6 was the brainchild of one teacher, Reuben Brower. He had begun his career as a junior Harvard faculty member in the 1930s, left for Amherst in 1939, and returned to Harvard 14 years later. He was an acolyte of the New Criticism, the school that insisted that all the meaning in a literary work was found within its text, and Hum 6 was based on that approach. Brower held a Guggenheim fellowship and spent 1965–66 in Britain, and I never met or even saw him in my years at Harvard. But the course was taught mainly by graduate students in section, and it fortunately continued in his absence. Not until the final exam in June did I really grasp the essence of the course, but it probably had more long-term impact on me than anything I took that year.

The reader may already have guessed that I have rarely thrown any intellectual productions out during my life, and I still have most of the sixteen papers that I wrote for Humanities 6, as well as the assignments themselves. This is I think the third time that I have reviewed them in the last 51 years, and certain aspects of them still shock me. On the one hand, the course forced us all to spend many hours on individual poems by Wordsworth, Robert Frost, and Yeats. We also read at least two Shakespeare plays, Jane Austen's *Persuasion*, and George Eliot's *Middlemarch*. Lectures in the course were rare and, by general agreement, not very valuable, and the real work occurred in sections, which met two or three times a week. The pastoral tradition was a major theme of the course that year, although I do not think it was ever sufficiently explained. The ability to focus on the specific language of a text, and to return to it again and again in the course of study, was, I think, the great value that I took away from the course, and it has been a key to my success as an historian. But reviewing the course materials and my section woman's comments on my papers, I can also see that the course was in many ways an example of how *not* to teach, and I am very glad that I eventually learned to do more or less the opposite of what I had been exposed to then.

New Criticism held that the meaning of a work was revealed through the reader's spontaneous reaction to the language of the text, not the surrounding historical context or a knowledge of the author's own life. Unfortunately, the committee that taught the course—who I must assume reflected Reuben Brower's own approach, even though he was absent—focused on inducing the students to have exactly the feelings they had about the texts they assigned. A typical paper assignment (I am holding one in my hand now) included about two dozen very specific questions about particular lines of the poem under review, worded in ways that leave no doubt that the answer was very clear to the instructors, and that the student's task was to read their minds. And my section woman (whose name I remember but which I see no need to repeat) commented in the margins of my papers at extraordinary length, again and again saying that while I had made a valid point, I had not quite said it in the right way— that is, the way that she would have said it. Her many questions in section followed the same pattern. She did identify one very real problem in my approach to literature, and I eventually managed to begin to overcome it. I had grown up in an incredibly judgmental atmosphere and I had a tendency to read moral judgments into literature. She seized upon this as the flaw in my character and approach and returned to it repeatedly during the term, even in cases where, as I look at my work now, I do not think it was at all warranted. In any case, she found most of my work wanting and most of my papers received grades of C or C+, grades which seem almost incredible when measured against the work I saw undergraduates turn out in later years.

So eager was she to turn us into mind-reading robots that she could not recognize or appreciate an instance of real learning. In the middle of the spring term, when the weather was lighting up my spirits, I grasped the tremendous emotional power of the conclusion of Wordsworth's *The World is Too Much With Us*, when the poet declared that as "a pagan suckled in a creed outworn," he might "Have sight of Proteus rising from the sea/Or hear old Triton blow his wreathed horn." I felt the power of the image and the mythic age it evoked. Then, a couple of weeks before the end of the term, we discussed Frost's poem *The Most of It*, in which the speaker, crying aloud across a New Hampshire lake, heard no response until there appeared "a great buck. Pushing the crumpled water up ahead,/And landed pouring like a waterfall,/ And stumbled through the rocks with horny tread,/And forced the underbrush—and that was all." Was the "all" ironic, I asked after a few minutes, was this force of nature indeed a more than fitting response? Rather than take any pleasure that a student had gotten the point—as I did so many times in later years—she looked at me and said, in the most patronizing tone, "Yes, that is the irony of the poem!" I had another "aha" moment on the final exam—which counted for relatively little—and wrote, at the bottom of it, "I finally caught on, didn't I," but I never received it back. But crucially, the lessons of the course have stayed with me to this day and I never once regretted taking it despite my C+ for the year.

My most successful course that year was the most popular course in the university, Economics 1, which showed the older generation at their absolute best. The reigning deity in university economics in the 1950s and 1960s was Paul Samuelson of MIT, whose first-year economic textbook had made him millions of dollars. Evidently somewhat jealous, the Harvard department had parceled out the major subject areas of economics—competitive markets, international trade, public finance, monetary policy, macroeconomic theory, and so forth—among its members, who had written short paperback texts published as a series. The theory, one fellow student of mine put it, was that six Harvard economists could equal one Samuelson. I took careful notes on all of them, using my one sentence per paragraph rule. That course, like Hum 6, was also taught mostly in section, and my section man was David Major, the best teacher I had that year. After the first hour exam—which was quite early in the term—he marked me down as the best student in the class. I had better than average math skills, and I had no trouble relating the graphs that made up so much of the instruction to the real world. Major tried to talk me into majoring in economics, but I was already on the history track.

The class was larger and smarter than my Hum 6 section. It also included the man who became the most famous member of the class of '69, Al Gore, Jr. I had met his father, the Senator from Tennessee, when he came through Dakar, and immediately realized my fellow student was his son. He looked like the most frightened and harried person in the class, and I do not believe that he ever opened his mouth in a class discussion. Several decades later at my brother Bob's house, I met his *Washington Post* colleague David Maraniss, who was writing a biography of Gore. I gave him my recollections of Gore in Ec 1, as we called it, and also gave him David Major's name. (He had a long career at Columbia.) Maraniss contacted him and discovered that he had had to enlist a tutor to help Gore get through the class.

The fall term dealt with microeconomics, which revolved around the theory of competitive markets. Major prepared himself well, and every class had a specific topic which he covered clearly and thoroughly. It was clear to me that in actual fact, most firms spent a lot of their time trying to make markets *less* competitive to give themselves an edge. But the course hit its stride in the spring, when we did macroeconomics. This was literally the climax of the Keynesian period in American economic policy. Since the 1930s economists had focused on the issues of cyclical depressions and maintaining employment, and under Kennedy and Johnson, liberal economists had a real chance to try their ideas out. They had produced steady economic expansion with remarkably low inflation since 1961. We did not know it, but that achievement was among the many that was about to go up in smoke as a result of the Vietnam War. The course never questioned the federal government's responsibility for the state of the economy—it dealt with how it could exercise it. Major, I remember well, spent about 20 minutes sketching out the ideas of a fringe right-wing economist named Milton Friedman, making clear that he was simply a curiosity to whom we should be exposed. Little did he know.

I had the biggest difficulty, that fall, choosing what course to take in my new major, history. I did not want to continue doing what I had done in 5th, 8th and 11th grade, and I passed up Frank Freidel's one year survey of American political history. (One of my roommates, Jonathan Hoffman, kept me posted on what Freidel was doing all year.) I listened to an excellent introductory lecture on colonial America by Bernard Bailyn, a young departmental star, but the topic did not seduce me. I also heard the first lecture by the social historian, Oscar Handlin, whose long reading list was composed mainly of his own books. The Confidential Guide to Courses, our bible—annually produced by the Harvard Crimson—argued that the course was more about Handlin than about history, and I decided to pass on it as well. I wanted to branch out into European history, but two surveys covering the early modern and modern periods were not being offered because the professors were on leave. Instead I wound up in the year-long History 142, the history of Britain from 1660 to the present, taught successively by two venerable faculty members, Elliot Perkins in the fall (1660–1815), and David Owen in the spring.

Elliot Perkins had graduated from Harvard in 1923, and one of the highlights of the term was his account of an hilarious exchange with his uncle at the Harvard-Yale game of 1922. "An era of good feeling then prevailed in our relations with our great sister institution to the south," Perkins said, "and the Harvard and Yale bands entertained each other's fans by playing *Boola Boola* and *Ten Thousand Men of Harvard*. But sitting beside me was my uncle, of the class of 1901, when feelings had evidently been very different, and as the Yale band marched towards us playing our song, he leaned over towards me and whispered in my ear, 'It's all very well, Elliot-but I hate the sons of bitches!'" Perkins looked and talked like the batty New England uncle Central Casting had sent over for a Hollywood production—slim, balding, squinting, and marked by a droll approach to life. Another legend had it that a particular Final Club (Harvard's substitute for fraternities) had in its files a paper on the Newfoundland fisheries, with a large drawing of a codfish on the title page, which one member after another submitted in Perkins's course every fall, always receiving an A. One year, however, the lucky student lost the first page and submitted a normal one instead. "The paper is as good as ever," Perkins wrote at the bottom of it, "but I miss the fish. B+." Perkins reputedly had never earned a doctorate, and to my knowledge he had no substantial publications. But he was a dedicated educator who loved his subject, late 17th and 18th century Britain, and although like many of his colleagues he had trouble covering the material he had planned to cover in an hour, he always held our interest and had a great feel for the issues and personalities of the era.

The lecture course was the foundation of a Harvard education in those days, although this was the only one I took my first year. (I took five of them in my second year.) They generally met three times a week, although some Tuesday-Thursday-Saturday courses were skipping the Saturday meeting. History 142 had no sections at all and I never even met the grad student who graded my written work. There was no hour examination in the fall, although we had to write two papers of about 12 pages each, based on substantial additional secondary reading. Perkins had selected the required reading carefully, giving us lots of options, and holding it to a relatively reasonable amount. The spring term reading was heavier. We were completely on our own when it came to doing it and making sense of it. As it happened, I had a lot of trouble establishing a good routine as an undergraduate and by the end of the fall term I was way behind in the reading. I took full advantage, however, of reading period, the three-week period in January during which most classes did not meet, and caught up. Reading period was a great institution, which taught me and thousands of others what they were capable of in concentrated effort, and I was very sad in the early 2000s to hear that the faculty had finally caved in and abolished it so that their students, like those at other universities, could end their fall term before the Christmas break.

Although the Harvard faculty included plenty of boring lecturers, lectures were supposed to be dramatic public events, both intellectually stimulating and entertaining—and I loved them. Everyone came to class with a Harvard notebook and took notes—something which 90% of my students at the Naval War College could never be prevailed upon to do decades later. I decided to take notes in complete sentences, turning the lecture into a writing exercise as well as a learning one. And thus, my notes for Perkins' second lecture (I had apparently been checking out another course during the first) begin as follows.

"Through this period, allegiance to the sovereign was allegiance not to the office but to the person of the King. As late as 1811, when George III was declared insane, it was expected that the Prince Regent could and would dismiss the whole existing government. The King's opinions were very important. At the time of the Restoration [1660] there was a strong personal and mystical element which gave the Stuarts tremendous moral ascendancy and prerogative powers. Charles II particularly enjoyed this moral ascendancy. Coming to power when he did he had some tremendous advantages. His subjects saw him as the lifeblood of the state, not the chief executive. His powers show how incredibly important he was. He was responsible for everything legally done in the Kingdom. He created peers to sit in the House of Lords, then the dominant house of parliament. He enfranchised the boroughs that elected the Commons. In religion he was the head of the established Anglican Church. In law he established all sheriffs and appointed or dismissed judges at his pleasure. All public offices were his domain. In foreign affairs his power was absolute. It was up to him to declare when parliament should be elected, summoned, be dismissed, or be dissolved. (This power was used importantly until cerca 1710.) Besides these powers there existed the royal mystique, which put supernatural powers in the King. This divinity was held through Anne." That paragraph represents about 20% of the notes that I took during that hour. Rarely if ever did I have an extraneous, unrelated thought during a lecture, and when I became a teacher, it hardly ever occurred to me that any of my students might be thinking about anything else either.

How Britain was ruled was the main subject of Perkins' lectures, and we were exposed to all the great political issues of the day. But we also learned a great deal about the international politics of the period, including the two great wars with Louis XIV between 1688 and 1713, the Seven Years' War, and the Napoleonic Wars. Late in the term he put on the board (and I carefully copied) a table of the various social classes of Britain

and their average income. He conveyed the dissolute character of 18th-century British life well, but also made sure that we
became acquainted with truly great statesmen like the elder and
younger Pitt and the great liberal Charles James Fox.

The final in late January was my introduction to humanities finals at Harvard, and I emerged with an A-. Perkins had
prepared us to expect documents upon which we would have to
comment, referring not only to their actual meaning but their
long-term importance. I chose a question on Charles II's Secret
Treaty of Dover with Louis XIV and discussed how it embodied
the issues of Catholicism, Charles's relations with Parliament,
and Britain's role in the coming struggle for the Spanish succes-
sion. Two other answers show remarkably detailed knowledge
of the politics both of the reign of Queen Anne and that of
George III. One of the fascinating aspects of the course was to
show how controversial George's early reign was in Britain as
well as across the Atlantic, and how many prominent English
politicians identified with the colonists. Having been brought
up to take American politics extremely seriously, I had no trouble with the readings, which treated British politics in the same
way. Because I had done poorly on one of the two papers, which
I had left until literally the last night before my departure for
London to see my family, I emerged with only a B+ for the fall
term, but I was more than satisfied with it.

David Owen, whose lectures had been legendary for about
two decades, was the author of a study of English philanthropy
to 1960, and he was more of a social and intellectual historian
than Perkins. He was certainly better organized and never failed
to do exactly what he had planned in a given lecture—complete
with a joke, which could reliably be expected to pop up with
about 10 minutes left. Neither Perkins nor Owen, I see now,
made clear the extent to which British politics had swung in a
far more conservative and repressive direction in the 1790s, in
reaction to the French Revolution. Owen also exaggerated, in
my opinion today, the rate at which the middle class achieved
political power. He seemed to enjoy discussing intellectual and
cultural changes more than anything else, and his most famous
lecture was a slide show about the Crystal Palace exhibition

of 1851. This exposé of Victorian taste had to be moved to Sanders Theater, the biggest lecture hall on campus, where it drew at least 100 extra students who were not in the course. He assigned more reading than Perkins and I again typed out careful notes. Because I had fallen behind in the reading, I couldn't get beyond a B+ on the hour exam, but the final went like a dream. My lecture notes on Owen carefully tell the story of the whole period from 1815 to 1939, when the course ended. This was not unusual: I can think of only one course, Freidel's American history survey, which tried to go up to the present day.

Last, but hardly least, I took sophomore history tutorial, a year-long half course that met, I believe, every two weeks, for which we had to write six short papers. Some weeks used selections from classic historians, including Herodotus, Thucydides (who was destined to play an important role in my life), Gibbon, and Francis Parkman; others dealt with current controversies such as the effect of the industrial revolution on British living standards and the role of ideology in 18th-century British politics. My tutor, John Ranlett—who began a long career at SUNY Potsdam the next year—was also an historian of Britain, and he liked me at once, pronouncing my first paper the best of those he had received on the topic. My last two papers, on a debate between Sir Lewis Namier and Herbert Butterfield about the motivations behind votes in the 18th-century House of Commons, and on Francis Parkman's views of the French and British colonists of North America, were both extremely succinct and based on cogent arguments. The year concluded with a sophomore essay, in which we had to write about 8 pages about one of six texts handed out, all of them from some of the great historians that were on the curriculum. I nearly failed to pass it, partly because of a poor design. Having done so well on Parkman, I decided to write on him again, but the passage from him that was selected was so outside the main themes of his work—it dealt with Chief Pontiac's conspiracy—that I had a terrible time finding anything to say. It was eventually returned with the minimum acceptable grade of C+.

I was well satisfied with an average between B and B+, which put me in Group III, the lowest rung of the Dean's List.

With the term over, I headed for Washington, D. C., to spend the summer at my uncle's house while working at the State Department—as it turned out, in the highly analytical Bureau of Intelligence and Research. I read classified cable traffic every day and was allowed to write two "intelligence notes" of my own. It was my introduction to bureaucratic infighting, and I was amazed when my superiors stood up me in a dispute with a mid-level Foreign Service officer from another part of the bureau. I also read quite a few of my father's own cables. Roger Pond, my old friend from Loomis, was again in the area, and his girlfriend fixed me up with a steady date. Meanwhile I managed to read through the Second World War memoirs of Winston Churchill, as well as several of Orwell's novels. I was definitely on a high when I returned to Cambridge in the fall of 1966. The new lottery for house selection had landed me in Eliot House, the domain of the legendary John Finley, who had long coveted the preppiest students for his manor. I and my roommate—an Andover graduate named Franz Schneider—might have qualified in the old days, but my six neighbors across the hall, whom I had not known as a freshman, would not have. Jim Davidson, from the Cleveland area, Eliot Quill from suburban Philadelphia, Bruce Frank—whom I had attended kindergarten with—from Bethesda, Wayne Barry from Chicago, and George Scialabba from East Boston, were all public school graduates, and Jon Rieder had attended Friends Central in Philadelphia. I have remained in at least some contact with all of them, and Davidson, Rieder, Quill and Scialabba remain very close friends. Jon Rieder became a fellow academic, a very productive sociologist who has become an authority on Martin Luther King, Jr.

For the whole of the 15 years (interrupted in 1969–71) that I spent at Harvard, I had no doubt that the undergraduate education in the university reached its peak in 1966–7, and I think the course catalogue would prove it. For anyone interested in contemporary history, modern literature, international relations and public policy, there were simply too many options to choose from. In the fall, I took an early modern Europe history survey, covering 1559–1648; a superb economics course on international trade; junior tutorial in history, focusing on

Britain; and lastly, one of the courses I remembered the most fondly, Comparative Literature 166, taught by a visitor from Chicago, a distinguished Russianist named Edward Wasiolek, in which a very large class studied the works of Fyodor Dostoevsky, Albert Camus, and William Faulkner.

The reading list for that course, in which as I recall the students were expected to know either Russian or French, was quite extraordinary. We read no less than three of Dostoevsky's four huge novels: *The Devils* (which became my favorite), *The Brothers Karamazov*, and, in reading period, *Crime and Punishment*, as well as one or two of his shorter stories. The Camus readings included *The Stranger*, *The Plague*, and *The Fall*, all of which I read in the original. Turning to Faulkner, we read *The Sound and the Fury*, *Light in August*, *Absalom Absalom*, and *The Bear*. Totaling up from the copies I owned at the time, I find 600 pages of Camus (and the pages of the paperback of *La Peste* were very long), about 1000 pages of Dostoevsky, and about 1300 of Faulkner, or 2900 pages overall. This was one course, I believe, in which I read everything.

Wasiolek was a well-organized and entertaining lecturer—sections only met two or three times during the term—and he held the class's attention. But his approach suffered from the biggest lack in the makeup of his GI (or "greatest") generation—an inability to engage with strong emotion. Even those among them who tried psychoanalysis—which included a number of Harvard professors—had learned only that their most powerful emotions were innate, having nothing to do with any particular experiences they had endured. Thus, he stressed that Dostoevsky believed that human beings were trapped in a cycle of hurting and being hurt by one another, and that the only solution was to surrender one's will to Christ. I am quite sure that he never made what seems to me now to be the obvious point, that Dostoevsky's characters are generally crippled by *shame*, which their families or culture seems to have heaped upon them. He cast Camus as a foil to Dostoevsky because Camus was an atheist who believed that our spontaneous reactions to nature and other men embodied a moral code. In the most provocative moment of the course, Wasiolek argued bluntly that we all had only three choices: to accept Camus's view, to become Christians as Dostoevsky wanted, or to commit suicide. This posed a problem for me, one that did not reach its climax for another year. I knew I was not religious and could never be, but I did not trust my own emotions sufficiently to rely on them as a guide to life. That was in a way what had given me so much trouble in Hum 6. I still felt I was trying to live up to some kind of code of behavior imposed from outside—the legacy, clearly, of my upbringing, and of parents who consistently gave the impression that nothing anyone ever did was ever enough.

The key to Camus, it turns out, was also emotional, but the evidence was not yet available in 1966. It emerged only decades later, with the publication of *Le premier homme*, the novel he was working on when he was killed in a car crash in 1960—an autobiographical novel of his childhood. Camus' father, a French settler in Algeria, had been mobilized for the First World War shortly after the author's birth in 1913 (coincidentally the year of my own parents' birth), and killed in the first month of the fighting. His mother spent the rest of her life as a charwoman, too depressed by life and work even to speak a word to her only son, evening after evening. Camus's life was saved by a teacher who recognized him as a gifted boy and encouraged him to pursue his education—an episode I could identify with myself. The great question of *The Stranger*—how Meursault could be so utterly indifferent to his mother's death—was suddenly answered. (Some critic may have made this connection, but I am not aware of it.) Camus's sensuality and search for meaning in life was a desperate struggle against the depression he had inherited from his mother, and the pain of never knowing his father. *The Plague* is usually interpreted as a parable of the Second World War, but Dr. Rieux was fighting death in life, as well as sickness, too.

Wasiolek also taught Faulkner, astonishingly, without any sustained attempt to come to grips with the pathologies of the South that play such a role in his books, and particularly in *Light and August*. But he did some brilliant analysis of the structure of that amazing novel, *The Sound and the Fury*, and in conclusion, he argued that Faulkner's heroes, black and white, were the ones who simply endured. (I also remember him remarking, with perhaps two weeks to go in the term, that he had evidently messed up the schedule and would not have time to discuss *The Bear*—"which is just as well," he added, "because I don't understand it.") Another professor might have gotten more out of the material, but the mere experience of reading those 3000 plus pages was more than worth the tuition money our parents paid for it. Using my Hum 6 tools, I wrote my paper on the novella *Old Man*, about a convict who escapes while working on a flood. It received a B- from another carping grader, and this remains the only piece of work in my academic career on which I thought I had, as the saying went, gotten screwed. Rereading it, I still think so. The paper focused on the themes of endurance and dignity in the face of absurd universe, two of the major themes of Wasiolek's discussions of both Camus and Faulkner—and the story of the convict, buffeted one way or another by the flooding Mississippi of 1927, foreshadowed my own tortured path through the absurd universe of academia. The final included about half a dozen relatively short questions and I emerged with a solid B in the course. I did about as well in the history of early modern Europe, in which we studied both the scientific revolution and the Thirty Years War, and I got an A in my junior tutorial on British history, where our tutor gave us very few written assignments, and I generally had the most to contribute in class. I got an A- in my economics course on international trade.

Unfortunately, a series of chance circumstances, and the gaps in my overall social and emotional development, were also catching up to me in what started out as the greatest year of my life, and the second half of the year, while still very valuable, was marred by some major difficulties. I still wasn't doing much of anything athletically, and I had also stopped playing the piano seriously, a dreadful mistake which I now regret. (It was corrected about six years later.) And the woman question, I can now see, still terrified me, and that fear stopped me from getting into what would have been a wonderful relationship with a Radcliffe junior I had met that fall. I treated her very unkindly and although we saw each other a few times on a friendly basis later on, I could never explain why, because I did not know myself. What filled some of the gaps in my life was a high-stakes poker game that I stumbled into midway through the fall term. I did learn the game, and still remember some remarkable hands, but it became much too big a part of my life and led to my missing a number of classes after playing all night. I lost more than I won, although not more than I could afford. Reading the quintennial Harvard College reunion books in the university archive in subsequent decades, I kept up with the fortunes of my fellow poker players, most of whom were graduating that year. They had had very checkered college careers, but most of them were outstandingly successful in later life, including two other academics. Meanwhile, having functioned at close to 100% academically in the fall, I fell to about 70% in the spring, but I still marvel at how much I got out of two of my spring courses, one of which was to shape my future career.

The first of those two courses, my first course in the French department, was ironically taught by one of the men who has contributed the most to the destruction of the humanities in American higher education. Fredric Jameson was a young assistant professor who had just been turned down for tenure. During the fall, he had taught a course on Jean-Paul Sartre and existentialism, his real specialty, which I heard about from Jon Rieder, one of my next door neighbors in Eliot House. He had taught that course in English, but both the lectures and the reading in his spring offering, French 184b, were in French. Determined to keep up my language skills, I continued taking notes in complete sentences—but this time in French ones.

The course fitted in beautifully with one of the elite Harvard undergraduate majors, History and Literature, where I might have found even more of a home than in history had I given it a try in my first year. The course studied left- and right-wing authors from the interwar period, including Louis Aragon, Louis-Ferdinand Céline, Louis Guilloux, Drieu la Rochelle, Robert Brasillach, Paul Nizan, and Sartre, While Jameson's sympathies, like those of the relatively small class, obviously lay on the side of the leftists, he was very far from the doctrinaire Marxist that he later became. His well-organized, rich lectures combined analyses of the novels' forms with elucidation of their historical significance. Every major plot line and every major character related to real events. Most of the major characters— many of them young—saw themselves at war with society, looking for a way to act. While the leftists wanted to act on behalf of, and in conjunction with, the masses, the right wing authors wanted a leader with whom the masses could identify. I never did all the reading this time, and I emerged with a B, but I doubt there is anyone else who remembers the course as well as I do, and I still think it was a great experience.

After leaving Harvard, Jameson eventually wound up at Duke, where he has become a distinguished faculty member and the leading Marxist critic in the United States. He seems to have modeled himself on his intellectual hero Sartre, who also managed to combine a great facility with words and a strikingly simple political creed of loyalty to revolutionary socialism. By the 1990s, another literary critic, John Ellis, described Jameson as the most cited and respected of American literary critics, and, since 1981, "in effect the patron saint of the 'race, gender, class' criticism that would dominate university departments of literature over the next decade"—and, indeed, still do 25 years later.[2] And Jameson's erudition—so dramatically in evidence in the spring of 1967—was now buried in endless jargon-laden sentences, all still at the service of the extreme revolutionary Maoist Communism that was just about to become fashionable when I heard his lectures. Even after the collapse of European communism in 1989, he remained a defender of both Stalin and Mao, arguing that the trouble with the Cultural Revolution was that Mao was persuaded to give it up too soon. He seemed to be driven, Ellis pointed out, by an extraordinary animus towards his own nation, the United States. Born sometime in the 1930s, Jameson, a brilliant scholar from the Silent generation, had begun by expanding upon the critical traditions he was taught, and I was fortunate enough to see the results. But like so many academics of his and my generation, he abandoned those

---

2 John M. Ellis, "Fredric Jameson's Marxist Criticism," *Academic Questions*, spring 1994, p. 30.

traditions entirely and went in an extraordinarily sterile direction in the wake of the Vietnam War. We shall return to this phenomenon and its enormous importance when the time comes.

Lastly, in February 1967, I stepped into one of the most popular and demanding of spring term courses that year, History 135B, International Politics, 1919–45. The professors were Ernest R. May, who at age 39 had been a full professor for at least five years, and newly appointed assistant professor Sam Williamson, who did perhaps half a dozen of the lectures. The great events of the 1930s were only three decades away, and everyone in the classroom had grown up in their shadow. The course was extraordinarily demanding. The reading included major monographs on the history or foreign policy of Germany, France, Great Britain, the Soviet Union, and the United States during this period, as well as a new book by a young scholar named Akira Iriye on the great powers and China from about 1919 to 1931, *After Imperialism*. It also included the highly controversial work by the British historian A. J. P. Taylor, *The Origins of the Second World War*, and a two-volume collection, *The Diplomats*, edited by Gordon Craig and Felix Gilbert. I did the great majority of the reading and listened to the lecturers carefully.

Ernest May was to play an enormous role in my life and career. A Texan whose father had been a lawyer and a major political figure in the 1930s, he had skipped a couple of years of grade school—as both Texans and New Yorkers in those days often did—and eventually earned his Ph.d. at UCLA when he was in his early twenties. He had already written books on the origins of both the U.S. intervention in the First World War and the Spanish-American War. He had a reputation as a power in the American historical profession, and he placed a great many graduate students in jobs around the country during the rapid expansion of American higher education in the late 1950s and 1960s designed to meet the needs of the Boom generation.

Tall and lean, with a crew cut, he bore a quite striking resemblance to the quarterback of the Baltimore Colts, John Unitas, and he was always impeccably dressed. What I did not know through all the years of our long association was that he, like my parents, was the victim of youthful trauma. His mother, who came from a leading Mexican American Texas family, had died in a car crash when he was a young child, and he had been sent to boarding school at a very early age. He had an extraordinary emotional reserve and often hesitated to commit himself in historical discussions, but he also had an incredible memory and a boundless curiosity about the history of virtually every part of the modern world. His lectures often managed to make sense of complex subjects and were always filled with interesting personal details about the historical figures he was discussing. Yet he had one great flaw as a lecturer: he could rarely if ever cover the material he had planned to cover within a single hour. I think that he had never been able to conquer the fear, so common to lecturers, that he would not have enough to say to fill up the hour, and he therefore piled detail upon detail, only to find, 40 minutes later, that he was nowhere near the end of the story he had planned to tell. This problem put a great deal of pressure on the junior faculty he sometimes used to share his lecture load. In 1967 that role fell to Sam Williamson; in 1976, it fell to David Kaiser.

I did a very large portion of the assigned reading and as always, took voluminous notes. May began the lectures with several on the Paris peace conference, which failed to set up stable "systems" of international relations in Europe, or the Middle East, or East Asia. He then announced that we would look at the establishment of such systems in the years that followed—and then at how each of them broke down. Thus we learned about the French occupation of the Ruhr in 1922–4 and the Locarno treaty, the Washington naval treaties of 1922, and the evolution of new relations in the Middle East. Since all this took much longer than planned, however, the development of German, Italian and Japanese aggression during the 1930s got relatively short shrift, and May eventually could devote just one lecture to the Second World War, finishing with a reference to the course on the aftermath of that war that he planned to give the next fall.

The most important part of the course for me was probably my term paper, which I consulted with Sam Williamson on. A Louisiana native who had, I believe, managed LSU's national championship football team in 1959, he was an extremely conscientious scholar who expected undergraduates to work as hard as grad students. His lectures were less entertaining than May's, but far more focused. I decided to write on the talks between the British, French and Soviets on a possible alliance against the Germans in the spring and summer of 1939. British documents on the talks had been published, and I tracked the talks carefully, my introduction to serious diplomatic history. There were no published French or Soviet documents available, and I did not follow Williamson's advice to check the German documents as well to get the reaction of the German Ambassador in Moscow. Rereading the paper, whose ground I covered in much greater detail years later, I see one key insight. Although the British government had guaranteed Poland in late March 1939, setting the stage both for the talks and the Second World War, it had hardly abandoned its hopes for peace, and indeed had done so to try to deter the Germans, rather than to prepare for war. Anxious not to provoke the Germans, the British government showed very little enthusiasm for an agreement until it was too late, and resisted allowing the Soviets to enter the states between the USSR and Germany, a concession the French were willing to make. The paper was quite thorough, but the style of the writing was unfortunately tentative, perhaps reflecting my somewhat confused emotional state that term. I was using the passive voice perhaps more than I ever did—both Loomis and Orwell had taught me to avoid it—and I wasted sentences explaining what I was about say, instead of just staying it. And unfortunately, I accidentally handed it in missing the next-to-last page, which included the bulk of my conclusion. Williamson made no attempt to contact me about that when he read it and gave me a somewhat disappointing B-, but I wrote a much better final, when I didn't have time to think about what I was doing, and received a B+ for the course. Despite my spring term slump, an A in junior tutorial raised my academic standing from Group III to Group II, the next-highest rung on the Dean's list. That summer, after visiting my parents in London during the Six Day War, I went back to my same summer job in Washington, but I was now, for various reasons, in a depression that lasted until the next spring. An extraordinary American league pennant race, ultimately won by the Red Sox in October, helped revive my interest in life.

That however was not all. Jeff Alexander—later to become a prominent sociologist—had become a friend of mine freshman year, when we both lived in Pennypacker. I had spent a good deal of time in his room sophomore year, when his roommates included Chris Wallace, one of my freshman roommates, and later, of course, a Fox News anchor. The antiwar student movement was growing by the spring of 1967, and Jeff, who also wrote for the Crimson, was becoming a revolutionary. Late in the summer he invited me to fly out to Los Angeles, where he lived, and help him drive his car back across the country. I accepted. Our stay in LA was noteworthy for a blind double date he arranged for me to make my first visit to Disneyland. It was the week after Labor Day—Harvard in those days started blissfully late in September—and on our way to Anaheim, we realized that Disneyland had gone on winter hours and had closed at 6:00 PM. So we decided to see a movie that had just opened, one that none of us knew nothing about, called *Bonnie and Clyde*. It was an extraordinary experience and, of course, our introduction to the film revolution that swept the nation that year, recently documented by the book, *Pictures at a Revolution*.

It was a good thing for Jeff that I joined him on the drive— his navigational skills were lacking, and without me I'm not sure where he would have wound up. In any event, we spent a good deal of the time arguing about politics. I remained a staunch supporter of the Democratic Party and President Johnson, although I had moved from support of the Vietnam war in my freshman year to agnosticism now. He believed in global revolution. Orwell had had far too much influence on me to ever embrace totalitarian revolution. I remember that he once asked me to confirm that I opposed terrorism as a means to social change, and when I did, he replied, "That means you are against all the social change going on in the world today." Jeff was sailing in the direction the wind was blowing among our most vocal contemporaries, and he continued his leftward drift for several years more. By 1972, however—when I saw him for the first time in three years—he defined himself once again as a liberal, and it is fair to say that I am probably to his left today. My evolution was far from complete, but it was never destined to take me that far from my roots in the New Deal and the New Frontier.

I cut a lot of corners junior year, but I did some serious work during the fall term, at least, and had another key experience, this time with Sam Williamson. My three courses for the fall, in addition to another round of junior history tutorial, confirmed that I was still broadening my horizons. For the first time I took advantage of another tremendous resource in the Harvard of the 1960s, the Government Department, Harvard's name for political science. The comparative government wing of that department was essentially an alternative history department covering most of the major nations of the world. It included distinguished scholars who had studied and published on Britain (Samuel Beer), France (Stanley Hoffmann), the USSR (Adam Ulam), China (Benjamin Schwartz), and Japan (Edwin Reischauer, whom Kennedy had appointed as Ambassador there.) The department also included one of the great big thinkers of his generation, Sam Huntington—most recently famous as the author of *The Clash of Civilizations*; a German immigrant named Henry Kissinger, whose path never crossed mine; and Richard Neustadt, an authority on the Presidency whom my father had known in the Truman administration, and who later became a close friend of mine. I signed up for Reischauer's course on Japan since the Meiji Restoration, which focused on the Japanese attempts to develop a democratic tradition—a story within which he viewed the Second World War as an interruption. The lectures were succinct and informative, I wrote an excellent hour exam and final, and I emerged from the course with only the second pure A that I had ever gotten. I also took a very popular new offering, Engineering Sciences 110, an introduction to modern data processing in which we actually got to program a mainframe computer. Math, like baseball, was always s refuge in tough times, and I enjoyed the course and got some kind of B.

Harvard was now facing student pressure for more direct faculty-student contact and fewer lecture courses. This was in my opinion a step backward, but the pressure grew over the years, and today most of the courses given by the history department—which has far fewer students than it did then—are of that kind. Sam Williamson decided to give one on his academic specialty, the origins of the First World War. I eagerly signed up.

Once again, Sam, who remains a friend, laid out the course with impressive thoroughness. We spent a week reading about and discussing each of the major European powers, with whose domestic and foreign policies we were expected to become familiar. Because in 1919 the victorious British and French insisted on assigning the responsibility for the outbreak of the war to Germany and its allies (mainly the then-defunct Austro-Hungarian empire), the war guilt question became the source of a prolonged historical debate during the interwar period. Many historians, including the American Sidney Fay—whose two-volume book was the text for the course—argued that Germany had been judged too harshly. Williamson had already written his dissertation about the Anglo-French Entente from 1904 through the outbreak of the war, and he was now working on a book about the key role of Austria-Hungary. Although Sam eventually turned to administration, first as provost of the University of North Carolina and then as President of the University of the South, he eventually brought out a book on that topic as well. Seven years earlier, in West Germany, the historian Fritz Fischer had exploded a bombshell with his book, *Griff Nach der Weltmacht* (Grasp at World Power), arguing not only that his own nation had played the critical role in unleashing the 1914 war, but that it had done so specifically to create a great European and colonial empire. That book, which aroused the hostility of the whole German historical profession, had just been published in Britain in English in 1967 but we did not use it. Williamson also introduced us to the remarkable three-volume work of the Italian Luigi Albertini, *The Origins of the War of 1914*, which had also been translated, but because the American edition cost 50 1967 dollars—2–3% of our tuition and fees—he could not bring himself to make us buy it and read it as the text.

The latter part of the course examined the prewar crises in the Balkans and Morocco, and then turned to a day-by-day account of the crisis of July 1914 Meanwhile for our first short paper assignment I volunteered to review a new account of the assassination of the Archduke Franz Ferdinand, *The Road to Sarajevo*, by the Yugoslav historian Vladimir Dedijer. That book detailed not only Franz Ferdinand's key role within the Austro-Hungarian government, but also the origins of the conspiracy within Serbian intelligence that killed him. Years later, I paraphrased Dedijer's title in a long work about another critical political assassination. My final exam was the best piece of work that I did that year. The key question asked why various peace proposals during the July crisis had failed, and I argued that all the powers had made decisions in the early stages of the crisis that made war certain, since they embodied irreconcilable goals. I detailed the argument with a day-by-day account of the crisis from the time of the presentation of the Austrian ultimatum to Serbia on July 23 through the outbreak of war in the first few days of August. Williamson did us a great service by emphasizing the importance of Eastern European issues—an aspect of the crisis that Barbara Tuchman had completely ignored in *The Guns of August*. As it happened, I would return to this topic again and again during the next 20 years, both in teaching and scholarship, and I owe Sam Williamson a great debt for introducing me to it.

The course had another aspect as well. Williamson had written his dissertation for Ernest May, and he was now part of an informal faculty seminar called the May group, which was exploring different ways to study how governments functioned. They were beginning to reject the idea that governments could be viewed as unitary actors making rational decisions to achieve their aims. Instead, they thought that bureaucratic routine and conflicts among leading governmental thinkers resulted in compromises that might or might not serve the nation's interest. The May group's seminal work had not yet been written—we shall come to it in due course—but we tried the new approach out in our analyses of European powers. This was, for me, the beginning of something very big.

The course catalog was very weak in the spring of 1968, and I did by far the least work of any term. I finished the year in Group III, but not by much. I finally got myself back in athletic action, doing quite a bit of skiing that winter, and joining pickup basketball games in the gym on many afternoons. But the first half of 1968 saw a series of extraordinary political events, and started a revolution in my own mind that turned me into an independent thinker on crucial issues.

The general atmosphere both at Harvard and in our political life in 1965 had already been described rather brilliantly by another Harvard man. W. E. B. Du Bois , with reference to what he found when he arrived in Cambridge in the 1880s. "When I was a young man," he had written in the late 1930s, "so far as I conceived, the foundations of present culture were laid, the way was charted, the progress toward certain great goals was undoubted and inevitable. There was room for argument concerning details and methods and possible detours in the onsweep of civilization, but the fundamental facts were clear, unquestioned and unquestionable."[3] In the mid-1990s, for reasons that will become clear, I came to understand that that kind of consensus resulted from great events like the Northern victory in the Civil War, and the United States' victory in the Second World War. But by early 1968, my fellow Boomers and I were now rebelling against the overwhelming certainty of our parents about politics, our obligations, our need to prepare for our future careers, and our personal and sexual habits. (The latter, of course, caused particular consternation among millions of families with daughters, of which mine was not one.) Fortunately for me, I think, I was so firmly grounded in the older generation's world that my own rebellion, while significant, did not go as far as many others.

By the summer of 1967, however, it was becoming harder and harder to believe in the wisdom of the older generation because of the apparently endless war upon which it had embarked in Vietnam. My depression had many sources, but

---

3 W. E. B. DuBois, Dusk of Dawn, in Du Bois, *Writings* (New York, 1986), p. 572.

one was the obvious shipwreck of the Johnson Administration, which in 1965 had seemed—like me and my family—to be on top of the world. The Republicans had won a sweeping victory in the 1966 Congressional elections. By the summer of 1967 my faith in the Vietnam war was increasingly shaken by on the scene reporting, and particularly by some extremely trenchant columns by the great humorist Art Buchwald. But the revolution in my outlook did not take place until the first three months of 1968, beginning with the Tet offensive and ending with Lyndon Johnson's withdrawal from the Presidential race.

The Vietnam War ultimately became a subject on which I could claim authoritative standing, both because of my book, *American Tragedy*, and my supervision of the unit dealing with it for about 20 years at the Naval War College. Revisionist scholarship has claimed that the Tet Offensive was a dreadful defeat for North Vietnam, and that it could have led to a US victory if Johnson hadn't lost his nerve. The offensive did not, in fact, achieve its objectives, but it drove home a critical and very true lesson that was confirmed, we later learned, by an intelligence appreciation written about a year later for incoming President Nixon. Nearly three years of American involvement had *not* reduced the enemy capability to fight. It developed in the weeks after Tet that General Westmoreland now wanted 200,000 more troops, further proof that the balance of forces had not shifted in our favor. Much of the older generation had also lost faith in the war. I had not dared hope that Senator Eugene McCarthy's candidacy could get anywhere, but in early March, he nearly won the New Hampshire primary. Senator Robert Kennedy, who had earlier declined to challenge Johnson, now did so. That decision divided many of my best friends, and I was among those who remained faithful to McCarthy. But no one was prepared for Johnson's withdrawal from the race at the end of March. The establishment appeared to be on the run.

I had accepted the rationale for the Vietnam War that had grown out of the 1930s, that aggression had to be stopped in order to prevent further aggression. I did a great deal of thinking over the next few years about those assumptions and gradually concluded that while some areas, such as western Europe and

Japan, had to be defended, it was simply impossible to apply the same rule to the whole world, and especially to the densely populated Third World. Years later that evolved into a multi-front view of the Cold War, which I will come to in due course. Although the opening of the archives on the origins of the Vietnam War was decades away, evidence began to leak in the early 1970s that many of those involved in the decision to intervene had understood from the beginning how unlikely it was that we would succeed. I did not, like so many of my contemporaries, now begin to feel that the whole enterprise of cold war foreign policy was evil, that the United States was hopelessly imperialist, or that our whole society was evil, as well. That, more than anything else, was destined to divide me from my contemporaries within my chosen profession in the decades to come. Meanwhile, however, I felt the same kind of intellectual and emotional liberation that Du Bois underwent in the first decade of the twentieth century, and like so many of my contemporaries, I was never the same again.

These events did not lead me into radical politics, but rather re-invigorated my interest in electoral politics. In another turning point, I did not, for the first time, return to Washington for the summer, but spent it in Cambridge where I had gotten a good summer job within Harvard. I lived with four other students near Fresh Pond and realized that Cambridge was now my home. Several of my roommates were political junkies, and our patron was an administrator at the new Institute of Politics—part of the equally new John F. Kennedy School of Government—named Barbara Harris. We realized by July, after Robert F. Kennedy, as well as Martin Luther King, Jr., had been assassinated, that Hubert Humphrey was going to win the Democratic nomination, but we hoped that he could beat Richard Nixon and change policy as President. In an effort to move his position on Vietnam before the Democratic convention, we drafted a letter on behalf of our fellow college students and got several campus leaders to sign it. I contacted John Stewart, one of Humphrey's leading aids whom I had worked with in the summer of 1963, to try to get attention for it. Unfortunately, Humphrey played it safe on Vietnam and stood by the

President until midway through the campaign, and we received no reply. Yet we followed the dramatic events of the Chicago convention in the greatest detail. Alas, the turmoil in the country, including hundreds of urban riots, anti-war protests, and university demonstrations, pushed almost 60% of the electorate into the arms of Richard Nixon and George Wallace, and Nixon won the election and put an end to the New Deal coalition.

School began again in the third week of September. The most noteworthy development of the fall was the beginning of my first serious relationship, with a Radcliffe junior named Sue Elliot, which lasted for about a year and a half and had some important consequences for my life as a whole. That was certainly all the remaining cure for depression that I needed, and it helped get me fully back on track academically, too. The major focus of my attention in the fall term was one of the best courses I ever had, Social Relations 138, Intergroup Relations, taught by a real American original, the social psychologist Thomas Pettigrew.

Two years earlier, in the fall of 1966, I had heard an enormous amount about Pettigrew from my neighbors Jim Davidson and Jon Rieder, who were taking his course on race relations in America, as well as Government professor Banfield's course on urban America. Pettigrew was a liberal and Banfield a conservative, and several dozen students were in both classes at once. In the fall of 1968 Pettigrew's course filled the largest lecture hall in Emerson Hall on Tuesday and Thursday afternoons, and he was the most charismatic lecturer I had as an undergraduate. Pettigrew was a very proud representative a species that has become almost extinct politically in the last 50 years, the white southern liberal. The 39-year old Virginia native knew and had worked with many leaders of the civil rights movement and had made research trips to the scene of some of the early civil rights crises, including Little Rock. He was caustic about the white political leaders of his own section, but he was never more energized than when he had an opportunity to identify a northern racist. I still remember his reminder that Simon Legree, the brutal overseer in *Uncle Tom's Cabin*, was specifically identified as a Yankee from Vermont. Pettigrew was very approachable, and I saw him in office hours more than once. Above all, the intellectual design of his course was the most brilliant of any that I took at Harvard.

The Social Relations department combined sociology and psychology, but Pettigrew did not stop there. As he explained in the first lecture, the course would successively study race relations in America from six different perspectives. He began with an historical approach, an economic and legal history of race relations in America. Then came a sociological approach, in which he analyzed the situation of the black population in American cities, surely the most urgent domestic question dominating the news in the United States at that moment. This one took the most time, and dealt separately with employment, housing, and education. Pettigrew remained a strong believer in integration and a skeptic about black separatism. The third part of the course, which started in mid-November, was the "situational approach," which studied actual interactions between black and white Americans, and held out the hope, in many ways, that more contact between the races would improve race relations. The fourth, "personality" or psychodynamic approach, studied the psychology of prejudice, the specialty of Pettigrew's own teacher Gordon Allport, author of *The Nature of Prejudice*. The fifth, the "phenomenological" approach, contrasted many commonly held beliefs about race and race relations with reality. And the last, the "stimulus object approach," focused on the Negro himself. (Pettigrew at one point defended his continuing use of "Negro," rather than the newly fashionable "black," on the grounds that polls showed a majority of black Americans still preferring "Negro.")

Pettigrew had in fact written *A Profile of the Negro American*, a work which no white academic would probably dare write today. The book was on the course reading list, and it was essentially a careful and sympathetic analysis of what slavery and segregation had done to black Americans, economically, medically, with respect to crime, and, more than anything else, emotionally. As I think about this today, when racial issues are again at the forefront of national discourse, and I am in frequent discussions of them with young black Americans on Facebook, it can seem patronizing that Pettigrew did not let black people speak for themselves. But the personality traits he saw in Negroes— especially men—were the same ones which black men often complain about having to project today—an unaggressive, non-threatening persona. And ironically, the bulk of the course, in its own very different way, echoed a frequent complaint of black people today: that our real racial problem involves white people, not black ones. Pettigrew was speaking for the liberal white and black consensus that had evolved over the course of the twentieth century when he argued that white prejudice was the source of our racial problem and that overcoming prejudice was the key to solving it. He did not talk about "white privilege," but he spent much of the course on white attitudes.

The organization of the course had another critical aspect as well. Rather than simply begin with the historical approach, Pettigrew took two specific case studies and analyzed *them* from all six different perspectives in two lectures apiece. One of those was apartheid in South Africa, where he had spent a year as a visiting professor. The other was the subject of lynching, and that one I found particularly fascinating.

I am not quite sure why, but I had become very interested, and somewhat knowledgeable, about lynching in America during the early 1960s. I was particularly struck in the summer of 1963 or 1964—I am not sure which—to see a reference in the *Washington Post* to a lynching in Princess Anne, Maryland, on the Eastern Shore, as recently as 1933. At Loomis we had to write a long senior essay, and I had planned to write it about lynching and perhaps even to drive over to Princess Anne and try to talk to some people about that one. But my father was very hostile to the idea. That certainly did not reflect any lack of support for civil rights on his part, but he was thinking like the American Ambassador that he was. The topic was "dated," he said—which was only half true—and he clearly felt such a paper would be a useless embarrassment to the United States, even if it was only read by one Loomis teacher. I had given up the idea.

Pettigrew's survey of the subject was thorough and fascinating. I remember one incident from the Q & A that was typical of him. "Were women ever lynched?" asked a white Radcliffe student. He paused in thought. "Occasionally, yes," he said. Then he brightened up. "What was much more common," he continued, "was for women to *participate* in lynchings." He traced the prevalence of lynching, its triggers, the long, unsuccessful effort to pass a federal law against it, and finally, the disappearance of it in the 1950s thanks to political pressure. I decided to make lynching the topic of my term paper for him— with a particular focus.

More than thirty black citizens had been killed during the great Detroit riot of 1967, the event that started the terminal decline of that city. Three of them were black teenagers who were shot by three white police officers in the Algiers Motel— and these were execution-style shootings that could not possibly be justified by anything the victims were doing. In the year following the uprising, the novelist John Hersey—whose novels included one about the Warsaw Ghetto that I had read in Senegal—had gone to Detroit and interviewed everyone he could about the incident, including at least two of the accused officers. His book on the subject, *The Algiers Motel Incident*, had become a best seller, and I used Pettigrew's scheme to analyze it as a lynching. My section woman liked it and I received an A- for the course. I got another A- in a history course on Tudor England, and a B+ in the next-to-last economics course I took. Meanwhile I was working on my senior thesis.

Although Sam Williamson was now the faculty member I knew best, I decided not to write my senior thesis about diplomatic history. Instead, I chose my first intellectual hero, Orwell. I had now read all of his novels and several published collections of essays. Coincidentally, in that very fall of 1968, four volumes of his collected journalism and letters were published both in Britain and in the US. I decided to write on the evolution of his thought from childhood through 1940, leaving out his most famous works, *Animal Farm* and *1984*. My adviser was a grad student named Simeon Wade.

My analysis of Orwell's thought, as it developed, combined evidence about his personal and emotional life with the evidence of his writings. I argued that his concern for the integrity of every individual dated at least from his school days, described in the famous and harrowing essay, *Such, Such were the Joys*, when every boy's status was determined by his parent's income, and Orwell (then Eric Blair) was terrorized by staff and fellow students alike because he was on scholarship. His accounts of his subsequent life as a policeman in Burma—*Burmese Days* and the essay *Shooting an Elephant*—stressed how the role of imperialist determined one's personality and acts. Then came *Down and Out in Paris and London*, in which Orwell purposely shed all the trappings of education and privilege and spent a couple of years living literally at the lowest depths, washing dishes in Paris restaurants and tramping about in Britain. By the mid-thirties Orwell had published several works and was doing some left-wing journalism but he was almost unknown. He became a socialist after investigating conditions in the mining town of Wigan and then going to Spain to fight in the civil war. But because he belonged to the dissident militia the POUM, as he described in his classic *Homage to Catalonia*, he saw the effects of Soviet totalitarianism and developed a hatred for it that he never lost.

Returning after being wounded in Spain, and subsequently coming down with tuberculosis, Orwell by 1939 was completely disillusioned with both the literary and political scene in Britain. He felt any new war would serve only the ruling elite, and even wrote an antiwar pamphlet that as of 1968 had not survived. He expressed his disillusion in a number of writings, including his remarkable essay about Henry Miller, *Inside the Whale*. But the actual outbreak of war in 1939 completely changed his views. England he decided, was indeed worth fighting for, in large part because of the English respect for individual life. In the essay *The Lion and the Unicorn: Socialism and the English Genius* he looked forward to a different England, sketching out a vision that did foreshadow the achievements of the postwar Labour government.

Senior history theses were supposed to be about 80 pages long. Mine came in at 97, and I was very happy with it. The grading took place, as I shall explain amidst one of the most turbulent eras in the history of Harvard. The outcome—a grade of magna cum laude—was entirely satisfactory to me, but the details were interesting.

Each Harvard undergraduate thesis was assigned to two readers, neither of whom could be the tutor who had advised the project. Two graduate students split on mine, giving it a summa cum laude minus and a magna cum laude minus. The department always assigned a third reader when a split of that magnitude occurred. That honor fell to a full professor, John Clive, the departmental authority on British intellectual history. Clive said some nice things about it, but he complained about the length, said there was "too much familiar ground," and suggested that "perhaps the author did not have time enough to tighten up and cut." He too gave it a magna minus. I did not know it, but I had been introduced to the standard academic reaction to my work. The writing of the thesis was far superior to most of my earlier efforts and I regret that I have never found a way to get it into print, even though Widener Library still has a copy.

I took yet another economics course in the spring, but the rest of my last term had a French flavor. A new faculty member, Jean-Jacques Demarest, taught a course on twentieth-century French literature. It introduced me to André Malraux and Georges Bernanos, and revisited Camus, while adding more experimental writers as well. He was not a particularly difficult grader, and I did very well. More of a revolution was the second term of Stanley Hoffmann's course on modern France, Soc Sci 117, covering the period from 1871 to the present.

Hoffmann, like Pettigrew, turned just 40 in 1969, but he was already a massive presence on the campus. I learned much later that he was the illegitimate child of an Austrian Jewish mother and an American father, neither of whom had ever married. His mother had fled Austria during the 1930s, and he had spent the war in southern France, quite fortunately escaping the holocaust. No one combined the best of humanities and social sciences at Harvard better than he. On the one hand, he had an encyclopedic knowledge of literature and film, to which he was utterly devoted; on the other, he had helped found the elite undergraduate major Social Studies, which studied Marx, Weber, Tocqueville, and Durkheim. (I shuddered in the 1990s when I learned that Foucault and Habermas had now been incorporated as well.) His full-year course on France, which I was entering in the middle, alternated between political history, diplomacy and war, and trends in thought. A paper and a final made up the entire grade.

I do not remember how I got to know Hoffmann a bit during that term. This was the beginning of the most lasting friendship I made among the permanent faculty, and I do know that by the middle of the term, I was one of the students he often looked at during his lectures to gauge my reaction. He used careful outlines and was always well-organized. He was a liberal and moderate social democrat and traced the largely unsuccessful efforts of men like Jean Jaurès and Léon Blum to get France on a more left-wing track. The theme of the course was the long series of revolts against the relatively sterile bourgeois orthodoxy of the Third Republic (1871–1940), coming from both the left and the right. Jameson had prepared me well for this. But also had a tremendous appreciation for Charles de Gaulle, who in 1958 had put an end to the Fourth Republic, ended the Algerian war, faced down serious revolts from senior military officers, and created a new state based on a popularly elected President. As it happened, de Gaulle had just survived the last great crisis of his presidency—the revolt of May 1968—and he stepped down after losing a minor referendum late in the spring of 1969.

For my paper I decided to write about the break between Albert Camus, whom I had come to love, and Jean-Paul Sartre in the early 1950s. That had been occasioned by the publication of Camus's major non-fiction work, *The Rebel*, a critique of twentieth-century totalitarianism and a study of its origins. I read it with tremendous concentration. Sartre's acolyte Francis Jeanson had reviewed it negatively in Sartre's own periodical, *Les Temps Modernes*, rejecting its implicit and explicit criticisms of Stalinism. That in turn provoked a rejoinder from Camus, and then a violent contribution from Sartre himself, publicly announcing the end of the two authors' friendship. While Camus began *The Rebel* by affirming the value of life and ultimately rejected any philosophy that denied it, Jeanson and Sartre argued that history was a struggle, and that men had an obligation to pick a side. My paper benefited from long arguments with Jon Rieder, who had studied Sartre with Jameson and was always willing to take his side. While only about ¼ of the length of my thesis, I think its quality was just as high, and the section man's comments were very gratifying.

My undergraduate career was coming to an end in triumph, but my immediate future was entirely uncertain. Richard Nixon was clearly not about to end the Vietnam War any time soon, and my student deferment was going to lapse after graduation. I heard about an Army reserve unit in central New Hampshire with a remarkably short waiting list from a friend, and I got the process of applying for enlistment underway. But I was not prepared to join just yet, cherishing my freedom. I explored the possibility of teaching high school, which in theory would entitle me to an occupational deferment, but my draft board secretary in Bethesda informed me that the board was not inclined to grant those deferments. Meanwhile, my girlfriend—working, as it happened, with my parents—had arranged a summer job in New York city that she thought would help her prepare her senior thesis the next year. I had agreed to accompany her. My intense involvement in academics that last term was probably a way to avoid facing the choices before me.

Meanwhile, all hell had broken loose at Harvard. The Students for a Democratic Society chapter had grown in strength, and it now included a Progressive Labor Party faction, who were avowed Maoists dedicated to a "worker-student alliance." Building occupations, which had begun at Berkeley in 1964, had spread to Columbia in the spring of 1968, and Cornell and elsewhere during 1969. In April, the SDS chapter—whose members included my friend Jeff Alexander—met and rejected a motion to occupy a building, with the PL faction voting in the minority. The next day, typically, the PL faction occupied University Hall, the seat of the Dean's office, on its own. They demanded an end to ROTC on campus (for which the faculty had voted earlier in the year), the formation of a Black Studies Department, and an end to the expansion of the Harvard campus in the community. The Dean of the Faculty—an historian, Franklin Ford, whom I later came to know—acted quickly, and by dawn the next day a large force of policemen had assembled outside University Hall. After the students refused to leave it, the police cleared them, violently, and made several dozen arrests. As so often happened on campuses in that era, the police action turned the bulk of the student body against the administration and towards the occupiers.

A student strike and a huge meeting in Harvard Stadium followed. Motions to continue the strike until all demands were met failed by the narrowest of margins, and the students voted for a three-day strike instead. The strike collapsed after the three days, but the university was never the same. The faculty voted to create a department of Afro-American studies. Pettigrew, whom I spoke to, had opposed this. He was deeply offended by the idea that the new department was needed because no one had been interested in black studies heretofore. He felt he was one of several scholars who had spent their whole life in that field. Attempts to "restructure" the university to give students more power did not conciliate the revolutionaries, and I attended a famous meeting in which grievances were aired. The problems continued through our graduation, where the SDS asked for, and eventually secured, the right to add a speaker of their own to the program. He attacked Harvard's role in the military-industrial complex in biting terms, ran over his allotted time, and was led from the podium pronouncing the commencement "an obscenity." I felt like Orwell watching the Communists of his era at work, and I was no more sympathetic than he was.

I feel incredibly fortunate to have entered Harvard when I did. The institution not only took undergraduate education seriously, but understood that great individual faculty members held the key to it. The faculty required enormous amounts of work, but punished us only mildly—with Bs instead of As—if we completed only 75–80% of it. (There were also notorious "guts," or easy courses, but I never took any of them.) We wrote an enormous amount. The lecture format suited me to a T. I do not think that the history department had the overall quality of either the economics department or the government depart-ment, but it provided some very solid instruction. But I got as much from Hum 6—despite its instructional problems—from Wasiolek's course on Dostoevsky, Camus, and Faulkner, from

Jameson, from Hoffmann, and from Pettigrew as I did from any history course. Meanwhile, May and Williamson had taught me how to study governments. Writing my thesis was a great experience. That I remember so much of my undergraduate experience, the books that I read, and the lectures I heard—and that I have carefully kept nearly the whole record of that experience to this day—shows, I think, how much I got out of it, even if, for much of the time, I felt guilty about not doing more.

The commencement brought that phase of my Harvard career to an end. In New York, I received notice that I had been reclassified I-A, although I was in no danger of being drafted until I had had my pre-induction physical, which would take several months to arrange. But in New York, I investigated employment opportunities, and wound up with an entry-level job at Bell Labs, a major defense contractor, in northern New Jersey. My Harvard degree and my two computer science courses were enough to get them to take a chance on me. Bell Labs employees customarily received occupational deferments. I decided this was a good solution to my short-term problems with the draft board, and I went to work with them.

The time I spent from Bell Labs, from August 1969 until late June 1970, was interesting and remunerative, but not especially important to my intellectual development. I acquired more computer skills and enjoyed some of the work I did, but I knew it would be temporary. My draft status did not improve as a result of the new draft lottery in December, because I drew the number 85. And in May 1970, almost on the day of the Kent State shootings, I found I would *not* be receiving an occupational deferment. Some fancy footwork, and my earlier contacts with the New Hampshire reserve unit, got me into the Army Reserves before I could be inducted. It would however take quite a few months before I could go off for four months of active duty for training. I moved back to Cambridge.

Jim Davidson, one of my best friends, was living in a four-bedroom apartment on Trowbridge St, about a half mile from Harvard Square, and invited me to move in with him. He was marking time career-wise and driving a cab, and within a couple of months I was doing the same. I was now 23 and this was the first year I had spent without academic obligations. I loved being a cab driver and learning the ins and outs of Cambridge and Boston, and I spent enormous amounts of spare time talking baseball with Jim—the first MacMillan encyclopedia had just appeared—and going to the movies. There were now three art houses in Cambridge alone, and film was busting out all over. I also went skiing whenever I could, and I was starting to learn tennis. My first girlfriend and I had broken up before I returned, and this also turned out to be my most active year for exploring the woman question. Among others, I met Cathy Moody in July 1970—at a Wednesday afternoon Harvard summer school tea. She had one more year of college to go at Mills in Oakland, and she came back for a visit the next January She was to become my wife.

I also knew, by this time, what I wanted to do—to go to grad school in history. I applied to Stanford, Michigan, Yale (I think), Harvard, and Brandeis. I remember writing in my Harvard essay that I hoped to study Orwell, Bernanos, and other twentieth-century European intellectuals. The schools announced their decisions in March. I was rejected by Stanford and Yale, but admitted by the other three. The only one that offered financial support was Brandeis, but I knew I could get help from my parents if I went elsewhere. I consulted a tutor I knew, one I had not studied with. "Go to Harvard," he said. I did. More than anything else, I was thrilled to be staying in Cambridge, which I knew was now my home. Cathy, meanwhile—a French major—was admitted to a comp lit program at Brandeis.

I spent early April through early August of 1971 at Fort Leonard Wood, Missouri. To my own amazement and to the horror of my old friends back in Cambridge, I enjoyed my army experience very much. It was somewhat similar, of course, to boarding school, and I loved going in on an equal footing with everyone and showing how I could perform. My company was about evenly divided between draftees—many of them poor whites from Arkansas and Missouri and black Americans from urban centers—and guardsmen and reservists like myself who had been to college. I kept a diary, and got into serious trouble about two weeks into basic training when some of my drill sergeants broke into my locker and read it. They did not appreciate some of things I had said about them, and I was called into one of their offices, where three of them screamed at me for an hour. The next day, however, both the company commander—a captain in his twenties—and the first sergeant made it clear to me that they disapproved of what had happened and assured me that I would have no more trouble. I didn't. To my surprise, I became one of the best shots in the company on the rifle range—but I have never fired a weapon in civilian life.

When the summer was over I flew to San Francisco, and Cathy and I drove back across the country, arriving just before it was time to start school. On the trip, I read an extraordinary historical novel, *Once an Eagle* by Anton Myrer, which I had learned about in the Army thanks to the journalist Ward Just. The novel's hero, Sam Damon, enlists in the US Army around 1916, wins a battlefield commission in France in 1918 (and is eventually wounded), serves long and difficult peacetime years between the wars, and eventually rises to major general in the Second World War. A man of absolute integrity, he is thwarted at many turns by more political officers, but dies in the early 1960s well satisfied with the path he has taken. Once again—as with *From Here to Eternity*, which Cathy read that summer at my suggestion—I did not realize how prophetic all this would be for me. I moved back into Trowbridge St. with new roommates, since Jim was now living with his future wife, Evalinn Welling, also a very close friend of mine. Already there were rumors that the college job market was tightening up and would get worse, but I didn't care. I knew I was where I wanted to be. In fact, the happiest period of my life was about to begin. I trusted the universe.

III

THE MAKING OF AN HISTORIAN

1971–6

I moved into the biggest bedroom in the Trowbridge St apartment. Not for about four decades did I learn that a college classmate of mine whom I did not yet know, Bill Strauss, was also living in that building while he attended Harvard Law and the JFK School. After a couple of months I managed to switch from my New Hampshire unit to a very flexible one that met at the Boston Navy Yard. Cathy got a room in an apartment in Watertown, and both of us had cars. That first year was another extraordinary one for movies, including *The Last Picture Show*, *The French Connection*, and *The Godfather*. But I was more focused on my studies.

My parents were covering my tuition, but I was determined to take care of my expenses myself. I borrowed $1000 from the federal government from a program established by the National Defense Education Act, the only loan I ever took out. I also got licensed to drive a cab in Boston, rather than Cambridge, and drove one day a week on weekends all fall. With rent of only about $60 a month, I managed quite well and found in December that I had used very little of my loan. I continued to do some typing to raise more spending money through the end of that year, but I gave up the cab during the spring term.

First-year grad students, like undergraduates, were expected to take four courses. The colloquium for first-year graduate students in European history counted for two of them. It met on Wednesday afternoons for two hours, and on that first Wednesday I met my fellow graduate students. There were fifteen of them, three of whom became particularly good friends. One was Nancy Ryan, who had just graduated from the first Yale undergraduate class to include women. She was extremely intelligent—so much so, perhaps, that she left graduate school after one year and went to Yale Law instead. She went on to a very distinguished 35-year career in the Manhattan District Attorney's office, leading the 2010 reinvestigation that cleared the five men who had been convicted of the rape of the Central Park jogger. I haven't seen or spoken to her since 1972 but she has surely confirmed my high opinion of her.

A second was Diana Pinto, Radcliffe '70, who remembered me from at least one undergraduate course at Harvard but whom I had somehow managed to miss. Of Franco-Italian descent, she was an extremely poised and striking young woman, a leftist who had written her undergraduate thesis about Antonio Gramsci. She was my most frequent study partner. During our first year, she fell in love with a French grad student in government, Dominique Moisi, and eventually married him. She finished her doctorate in French history but never held an academic position in France, where she and her husband become leading lights of the Paris intellectual scene. Both, eventually, wrote autobiographies of their own.

It took me longer to get to know Tom Childers. He had graduated from the University of Tennessee in 1968, done some army service in ROTC, and spent a year in Germany on a Fulbright researching the resistance to Hitler. Our first sustained conversation, I remember, took place in his stall in the stacks of Widener—we all had one, where we were encouraged to keep our books and study—and it dealt mainly with football. It turned out that Tom had been a big-time high school quarterback in East Tennessee. He talked about the experience entertainingly, but as if it had taken place on another planet—as indeed, in a way, it had. We spent a great deal of time watching baseball and the NFL together over next five years, and he even got me mildly interested in his real passion, college football. Tom had a great future as a historian ahead of him. He has remained one of my closest friends.

The remaining 11 students included one, the scion of a famous publishing family who had obvious hippie tendencies and left school after a semester. Another, a leftist graduate of the University of Wisconsin, talked incomprehensibly and at great length, and was invited to receive his MA degree and leave Harvard after a year. I have often thought that he might have done just fine had he come along 10 or 20 years later, when opaque prose styles had become the norm. A third person who departed early—actually after only one term—was a student of Russian history, Adele Lindenmeyr, who had been put into the (mostly western) European colloquium. She eventually completed her doctorate at Princeton and became a colleague of mine at Carnegie Mellon, and then, a professor and dean at Villanova. Another colloquium member was an army officer who eventually became a lieutenant general, and at least two others gave up academia after getting their degrees and had careers in banking. Another, a Cambridge native named Chris Stribakos, eventually earned his degree and became a professor at the Massachusetts College of Art and Design. To my knowledge the only 5 who had careers in history departments were Childers, Lindenmeyr, Stribakos, myself, and Todd Endelman, who studied Jewish history and had a long career at the University of Michigan. For the last decade, higher education had been massively expanding to meet the needs of our own Boom generation, and the leading grad schools had fed a steady stream of Ph.Ds. onto faculties. Demand for faculty was already dropping drastically.

My first year presented me with another problem, language qualification. Any doctoral candidate in European history had to pass proficiency exams in two different European languages, and Spanish, as I recall, could not be one of them. In Senegal I had originally wanted to begin German as my "second foreign language" at the Lycée, but my father, showing a frequent prejudice of American Jews of his generation, had talked me into doing Spanish instead. Knowing what lay in store, I had started working on German in the army the summer before grad school, and my old interest in languages revived. I kept doing some work during the fall and took the exam, I think, In January. It was a straightforward translation exercise which (appropriately) used historical texts, and I passed. It is always easier to learn a new language when reading about a subject one knows something about, and I think I managed to make my way through a couple of short German texts that year. My real immersion, however, lay in the future.

The colloquium was designed to introduce us to major topics in modern European history, and essentially to teach us to read like professionals. A week's reading often amounted to about 1000 pages although we were expected to learn how to distill the book's "argument" without ever reading every word. That was a habit I never really wanted to acquire, and while I certainly didn't read everything (and there was no test to find if we had), I paid very careful attention to a number of the books. Two faculty members shared the lead of the seminar. In the fall, the senior man was Franklin Ford, the former dean of the faculty who had had a minor stroke and stepped down in the middle of the 1969 student strike. Ford had established important credentials in both French and German history, and Germany was his specialty on the faculty now. He was joined by an assistant professor in his early thirties, Steve Schuker, who had written a thesis on European diplomacy in the early 1920s, one that became the book, *The End of French Predominance in Europe*. In the spring, Ford was replaced by the intellectual historian H. Stuart Hughes, whom I had meanwhile gotten to know while auditing his lecture course in the fall.

Ford had written a groundbreaking book about the 18th-century French aristocracy, *Robe and Sword*, which, not coincidentally, was on our reading list for the first week of the term. He had followed that up with a narrower book on Strasbourg, and he had written a general European history as part of a series. But his decision to become Dean of the Faculty—a full-time job—in 1962 must have been significant. In later years I became suspicious of academics who became administrators. Giving up the classroom and the library for an administrative position seemed to me an admission that one's life heretofore had been a mistake. I personally was determined never even to become a department chairman, and that was one ambition that I realized in full. Ford was no longer dean, but he had another major problem that led later in the decade to some embarrassing situations. He had become an alcoholic, and that showed occasionally, in minor ways, in the classroom contacts I had with him in my first two years. While he had plenty to say in some sessions of the colloquium, he often sat back and let Schuker take the lead.

Schuker did not hesitate to do so. Along with another assistant professor, Charles Maier—whom I did not meet until later—and Williamson, he was one of a long string of junior faculty who had studied modern European or American diplomacy during the previous twenty years, most of whom had gone on to fine careers elsewhere. Steve, who became a friend of mine, was a ferocious researcher and a fine writer. He had ambitious plans for two additional books on interwar diplomacy in Europe. After being turned down for tenure at Harvard he landed jobs at Brandeis and then at the University of Virginia, where he eventually retired. But his projected great works never appeared. He enjoyed being argumentative, and he had very strong views on almost every topic, especially when the colloquium reached the twentieth century in the spring term. Every colloquium session began with two 20-minute presentations by students, and he sometimes followed them up with a presentation of his own. The combination of Ford's highly reserved style and Schuker's abrasiveness left many students feeling somewhat at sea that fall.

The very first week introduced me to the atmosphere of graduate education and came as something of a shock. It dealt with 18th-century France and Britain, and by far the most important work of the required reading, as I saw it, was Tocqueville's *The Old Regime and the French Revolution*, which I had enjoyed so much in Hoffmann's course as a senior and reread with interest. But the discussion focused on the nature of the French nobility and bourgeoisie, and particularly on a book a couple of people had read that was not even in the syllabus. It was about 2/3 of the way through that I opened my mouth for the first time, mentioning my surprise at how the discussion had gone, and suggesting that the issue of why there had been a revolution in France but not in Britain—one very much on Tocqueville's mind—deserved some discussion. My interest in the big questions foreshadowed the course my career would take. Despite the enormous debate on the French Revolution that had been raging for decades, we approached it only indirectly, spending two weeks on the intellectual response to it.

We also spent two weeks on 18th-century power politics, the first on the elder Pitt, Britain's leader in the Seven Years War, and on Frederick the Great of Prussia, and the second on Napoleon and Metternich. I gave my first presentation in the first, preparing very carefully and making a good impression. The following week, which my old friend Sam Williamson attended, fell very flat. Very few of the students had any interest in war and diplomacy. The term concluded with three weeks on the emergence of industrial society, including one on the hot new field of demography. I was not especially well versed in those topics and did not particularly desire to be, but by the end of the term, as Ford and Schuker noted in comments that they distributed, I had clearly established myself as the most active participant in class discussions. I was flabbergasted by some of the students—especially the women—who week after week did the reading more conscientiously than I did, but sat through the class without saying a word. There wasn't a great deal of written work in the colloquium, and I performed only adequately in it.

The most important part of the first year were the two research seminars each student had to take. In the fall I found myself in Ernest May's, entitled peacemaking. In the first meeting it was not clear whether we would focus on the aftermath of the first or second world wars; in the second, we settled on post-1945. We all needed to find a specific topic for which primary sources were readily available. Somehow, relatively early in the term, I stumbled upon an interesting fact. At the end of 1944, with war still raging, opinion in the U.S. Congress had reacted negatively and almost unanimously to a British intervention in Greece, designed to forestall a leftist revolution and perhaps restore the Greek monarchy. A little more than two years later, in the spring of 1947, however—as my own birth was nearing—the Congress had overwhelmingly voted to support Harry Truman's decision to replace the British presence with American assistance to the regime that the British had installed. I began intending only to analyze the 1944 episode, but as I began to work through the Congressional Record, I decided, as I reported in a seminar meeting some weeks later, that I could go all the way through the spring of 1947. I was glad that I did.

This was, as it was supposed to be, my first experience with really intense research, and it turned out to be a labor of love. The U.S. Congress was filled with names I had grown up with, many of whom were still very much with us, including Mike Mansfield, J. William Fulbright, Claude Pepper, Everett Dirksen (who had died in 1969), and Lyndon Johnson (who actually spoke only once on any subject during the whole period I looked through the Record.) I was trying to keep my eye on Greece and foreign policy, but I couldn't help but get fascinated by various domestic pieces of legislation as well. But in addition—and for reasons I did not understand for another 25 years or so—the climate within Congress was unlike anything I had ever seen. Opinion ranged from white supremacists and vicious anti-New Dealers on the one hand all the way to a few vocal black representatives and several actual Communists or fellow travelers on the other, and they were not shy about expressing themselves. On one occasion in the summer of 1945, James Eastland of Mississippi read at length, with great distress, from reports of black American soldiers consorting with German women during the occupation. "Someone has told these boys they can cross the color line," he said ominously. The next day Senator Robert Wagner of New York defended the black soldiers in no uncertain terms. Another exchange has stayed with me all these years. In the midst of a long colloquy between the venerable progressive Burton Wheeler of Montana and the arch-racist Theodore Bilbo of Mississippi, Bilbo referred to "the voters of my state." "Will the Senator yield?" asked Wheeler. "What percentage of the people in the Senator's state vote?" (With Negroes barred from the polls, the figure was between 10 and 20%). "All the qualified people vote," replied Bilbo. "But what percentage of the people vote?" Wheeler repeated. After a couple of more iterations of the same question and answer, Wheeler had had enough. "That is why the state of Mississippi has such excellent representatives," he said. "That's right," said Bilbo. "We get the cream of the crop."

As usually happens in the midst of sustained research, patterns emerged. To begin with, I found that the Atlantic Charter which President Roosevelt and Prime Minister Churchill had issued in August 1941, before the US was in the war, calling for a world of free nations that would choose their own form of government, was the template against which nearly all legislators measured actual events in occupied Europe, including Greece. My paper identified four different strains of Congressional opinion and differentiated their reactions to the British intervention in Greece (as well as related developments in Belgium, Italy, and Eastern Europe.) Mainstream internationalists called on FDR to reassert the principles of the Atlantic Charter in opposition to various British and Soviet moves, while mainstream isolationists argued that these events proved that Roosevelt's foreign policy could never work in the postwar world. At the fringes, two other smaller groups simply took sides in the Greek civil war. On the left, two Congressmen from Washington state and Senator Glenn Taylor of Idaho—later to become Henry Wallace's running mate in 1948—supported the leftist resistance against the British intervention because they thought it was fighting Communism, just as they felt they were doing within the United States itself.

During 1945, I showed, a growing distrust of the Soviet Union and its intentions largely replaced the more impartial skepticism towards the postwar aims of both London and Moscow in most of the Congress. Discussion of foreign affairs faded somewhat during 1946. The Congressional elections of November 1946 gave control of the House and Senate to the Republicans and eliminated some of the most left-wing Democrats from the Congress. When President Truman called for aid to Greece and Turkey to defend against Communism on March 12, 1947, moderate Republican and Democratic Congressional supporters stressed that this policy fitted the goals of

U.S. war aims in the Second World War. But on the other side, conservative Republicans and southern Democrats—some of whom had been skeptical about the application of the Atlantic Charter to the world back in 1944—voted overwhelmingly for Greek-Turkish aid on the grounds that Communism was now a tremendous threat that had to be resisted. In particular, 18 out of 22 southern Senators and 101 of 103 southern Congressmen voted aye. (Two decades later, researching my book *American Tragedy*, I found a remarkable *lack* of enthusiasm among southern Democrats for the Vietnam War.) The only opposition came on the one hand from extreme conservative Republicans who refused to take the Truman Administration's anti-Communism seriously, and the remnant of leftist Democrats, including Senators Glenn Taylor and Claude Pepper of Florida and Congresswoman Helen Gahagan Douglas of California, who felt the US was stepping into the British imperialist role. None of their careers in Washington, as it turned out, lasted much longer.[4]

Focusing on one specific issue—policy towards the Greek civil war—I had managed in 31 pages to show how the postwar cold war foreign policy consensus had developed. I had been very interested to note—although I did not put this in the paper—how closely the arguments of leftist Senators and Congressmen against intervention in Greece paralleled the arguments I had been hearing for six years against the US intervention in Vietnam. May rewarded me with an A–, and my career was fully launched. Several months later, in the spring, the department endorsed my application for financial aid, and I was granted tuition and $2200, as I recall, on which to live. It would no longer be necessary to call on my parents for help or to keep driving cab one day every weekend and do some typing to earn my keep.

The spring term in Cambridge, marked by longer days and eventually by warm weather, was always far more enjoyable than the fall, and this year was no exception. H. Stuart Hughes

---

4 Pepper, defeated for re-election in 1950 by George Smathers in a primary, returned as a Congressman in the 1960s. Douglas lost badly to Richard Nixon in the California Senate race of 1950 and left politics for good.

replaced Franklin Ford as the senior faculty member in the colloquium, and the tone immediately changed.

Hughes, the grandson of the U.S. Chief Justice and barely failed Republican Presidential candidate Charles Evans Hughes, was another Harvard original. Tall and handsome, with almost white hair at the age of 54, he was about as left wing as an academic of his generation could safely be. Hughes had earned his doctorate from Harvard on the eve of the Second World War, writing about the European economic crisis of 1812. Commissioned in the Army, he joined a cadre of some of the greatest historians of the GI generation doing intelligence work, including Gordon Craig (of Princeton and then Stanford), Carl Schorske (Princeton), and Franklin Ford, all working under the giant of the Harvard department, William Langer. He had become a Harvard assistant professor after the war, initially failing to earn tenure but returning after some years at Stanford in the 1950s. In 1962, he had run an independent campaign for Senate on a peace platform against young Ted Kennedy and Republican George Lodge, emerging in November with 2.4% of the vote. His first wife had been French, but he had been divorced from her sometime in the 1960s and had married a graduate student named Judith who had now become an assistant professor. That turned out to be a fateful move for both of them—and, in a way, for me.

I had audited Hughes's course on the intellectual history of the 19th and 20th centuries in the fall term. Hughes was not a great scholar. The two books he had written, *Consciousness and Society*, on major European thinkers of the early twentieth century, and *The Obstructed Path*, on 20th-century French intellectual history, were uneven to say the least, and it was clear that he had not read some of the works he discussed in the latter. But Hughes was in his way a great intellect, and I learned more from him about how to lecture than from any other faculty member. He spoke in perfect sentences with very few notes, he always had a clear point to make, and he always finished on time. One early lecture that I remember well traced Catholic social thought by looking at four papal encyclicals over a period of about 80 years. An early lecture on Marx and Engels did a remarkable job of making sense of the evolution and complexities of their thought. A lecture on democratic socialism moved easily from the Fabian society in Britain to the German Social Democrats, and thence to Jean Jaurès in France and Orwell in Britain. The Orwell lecture gave me the opportunity to introduce myself and give him a copy of my undergraduate thesis to read. He was obviously impressed and asked me to come see him in his office hours to talk about it.

Essentially, Hughes's lectures presented a century-long conversation among the great thinkers of the past—revolutionaries, philosophers, sociologists, and even novelists. Thomas Mann, he explained, was trying to resolve dilemmas defined by Erich Fronm and Nietzsche. His two heroes were Max Weber and Sigmund Freud, both of whom got plenty of attention, and he referred proudly to his own four years of psychoanalysis. He also had a great knack for working the news of the day into his lectures, another tactic that I copied. Most Harvard professors got a round of applause after their last lecture, but Hughes got at least a sprinkling every morning in his newly remodeled classroom at Harvard Hall. Hughes saw himself, like his subjects, as a player in an extraordinary drama of western thought and action. And because he was interested in individual lives, he had also developed a sense of generations. Beginning a lecture on Keynes, he remarked that economics thrived in periods of crisis and depression like the 1930s, while history thrived in periods of restoration, such as after 1815 or 1945. I had lost touch with him by the time William Strauss and Neil Howe's books appeared in the 1990s but I think he would have enjoyed them. And indeed, the last words of his last lecture still ring in my ears. "At any rate," he said, "we are in a new era. A whole generation has grown up for which the Second World War is not even a memory. I leave this to your reading and your reflection in the years ahead." That got the biggest hand of all. I have taken him up on it.

Auditing was, in fact, a huge part of my graduate experience. Despite the centrality of the German experience in the late 19ᵗʰ and 20ᵗʰ centuries, the History Department did not at that time have a full-time professor specializing in modern Germany, and was trying to fill the gap with visiting professors.

In the spring of 1972 that role was filled by a German, Hans-Ulrich Wehler. Wehler had spent some of his childhood in the US, as I recall, and his English was completely fluent. While class analysis played a big role in his lectures, they showed a thorough mastery of the history of politicians and political controversies, and I and several fellow students regularly sat in. Wehler dressed modestly and lectured with fierce concentration and charisma. From him first learned the basics of the rise of Bismarck, the foundation of the German empire, the growth of socialism and the rise of German imperialism—none of which I had studied in my undergraduate experience at all. And meanwhile, a notebook shows, I was also taking in lectures by the sociologist Daniel Bell on Marxism and young Professor Patrice Higonnet on 18ᵗʰ-century France. Today, scanning the course offerings of the Harvard history department, I do not see a single lecture course on the modern history of any major European nation, including Britain, with the exception of one on the Soviet Union. More general lecture courses have such extraordinary chronological reach—in one case, as long as 4 centuries in a single term—that it would be quite impossible for them to address anything in any detail.

Most of the faculty were liberals, not Marxists, but most of them were working on the same broad problem: the development of modern economies and political systems, a drama of capitalism and socialism, revolution and democracy, and Communism and Fascism. For men born in the 1910s, 1920s, and 1930s, as most of them were, these questions had shaped their world and much of their lives. They had lived through one of the most turbulent and creative periods in the history of western civilization, and were eager to explore it with us. There cannot have been many more exciting times to study history.

When the colloquium began again in February with a week on the revolutions of 1848, Hughes immediately set a new tone. He rebuked one presenter for having brought too many notes. There were, he said, only two ways to lecture: to read verbatim, a technique that demanded real theatrical skill, or to have just a few notes as reminders, as he did. He also immediately urged us to use more active verbs and to avoid the expression "you have" as a substitute for "there is" or "there are." The spring term syllabus focused much more on the intersection of politics, economics, and diplomacy in the major European nations. It included weeks on Italian and German unification, imperialism, pre-1914 socialism, the origins of the First World War, the domestic effects of that war, the impact of the Depression, Nazi Germany, and resistance movements during the Second World War. (It was in the spring of 1972 that the magnificent documentary *The Sorrow and the Pity* came to the US, although it did not open in Boston until the following fall.) I gave my first presentation on the outbreak of war in July 1914, drawing on what I had learned from Williamson four years earlier, and supplementing it with some reading in the great classic by the Italian newspaper editor Luigi Albertini, *The Origins of the War of 1914*. My presentation emphasized that all the major powers had made decisions that were certain to lead to war. Schuker immediately tried to divert the discussion, arguing that the real problem was Germany, or, as he put it with his usual outrageousness, "a leading race—in some sense a master race—at the heart of Europe." Two weeks later, I gave another presentation on the failure of the British, the Germans under the Weimar Republic, or the French to react to the Depression with Keynesian policies. David Landes, the department's leading economic historian who attended the colloquium as a guest that week, complimented me on it. We finished the year with a session on the vocation of history.

Hughes was also giving a graduate seminar that spring, and I toyed with taking it and writing a paper about Proust's great novel as a piece of history. But instead, I left intellectual history behind, and took a seminar on Vichy France, given jointly by Stanley Hoffmann and a young history faculty member, Patrice Higonnet. I was, of course, renewing my acquaintance with Hoffmann, and I had attended most of the lectures in the first half of his course on France—the half that I had not taken in college—during the fall. Higonnet, who had been born in France and grown up in Cambridge, was one of three assistant professors from the Silent generation who had been given tenure in 1970. All of them had only one book to their credit at that time, and of them all, only one ever managed to write more. In 1972 he was at work on a textbook on 19th century Europe, but I don't think it was ever published. He had broad interests, liked students, and was very easy to talk to. The Vichy seminar was held at the Center for European Studies on Frances Av east of the campus, just a couple of blocks from where I lived. That center, along with the Social Studies major, was one of Hoffmann's biggest contributions to Harvard, and it was the scene of many social and intellectual gatherings throughout the year. The blackboard of our classroom featured an inscription, "Nous sommes Marxistes tendance Groucho," which no one, apparently, could bring themselves to erase. The first presentation I gave in that course dealt with the diplomacy of the 1930s and the fall of France. I worked hard on it and delivered it smoothly, while Hoffmann, who was as engaged in the classroom as anyone I ever saw, nodded vigorously at the main points. "You have an enormous subject!" he said respectfully when it came to an end.

I decided to write my seminar paper on the political thought of a conservative Vichy critic, the Catholic novelist, and polemicist Georges Bernanos. I had been introduced to him in a French course in the spring of my senior year, in which Prof. Jean-Jacques Demarest had us read his masterpiece, *Journal d'un Curé de Campagne* (*Diary of a Country Priest.*) Although Bernanos came from a tradition with which I was utterly unfamiliar, the power of his language and thought had impressed me, and I knew that he was both a conservative Catholic monarchist and a violent anti-Fascist. My paper, which ran to over 50 double-spaced pages with about 100 footnotes, had pretty much passed out of my consciousness after I wrote it and I was pleasantly surprised in 2012 when I packed up my last office to find a copy. Rereading it has awakened a lot of ideas.

The paper put Bernanos, who was above all his own man, in the context of various French right-wing thinkers—including Charles Maurras, the editor of the *Action Française* and the French William Buckley of his time—and of French politics. It showed what a unique individual Bernanos was. Maurras believed above all in order and saw the Catholic Church as one of its foundations, but he was not himself a believer. Bernanos was a devout Catholic who found virtue only in the common people and in individual heroic figures who would risk literally everything for their beliefs. His Catholicism was intensely personal, and he could be violently critical of the Catholic hierarchy. Bernanos was a disciple of one of the founders of French political anti-Semitism, Édouard Drumont, but he actually hated the French bourgeoisie far more than the Jews. Like so many Marxists of that era he was a rebel against bourgeois society, whose materialist values he rejected. He was also a passionate nationalist who thought France had to stand for something, and he had left France for Brazil after the Munich agreement both because he foresaw France's defeat by Germany and because he thought France had dishonored herself by abandoning an ally. At the end of the paper, I made an important discovery. In *The Obstructed Path*, H. Stuart Hughes, of all people, had written that Bernanos had never recanted his anti-Semitism. But it turned out that he had, in an unpublished introduction to a book about the Warsaw ghetto uprising, in which he paid tribute to the Jewish people's struggles for their beliefs and their existence, not only in the Second World War but in the whole of their history.

The paper, I see now, was about Bernanos's response to the great Atlantic crisis of mid-century (he died in 1948), what I would now call, following Strauss and Howe, a fourth turning. As I write these words on January 20, 2017, the United States and the world are entering the critical phase of the next fourth turning, with a most uncertain outcome. The example of Bernanos, who called upon us to stand by our political beliefs without regard to the consequences, has become highly relevant to us all. The paper also showed that Hoffmann, Higonnet, Jameson, and Demarest—combined with my Lycée education—had turned me into an honorary citizen of the Third Republic, quite at home amidst its writers, its politics, and its military history.

Cathy, meanwhile, was completing the first year of her comp lit program in Brandeis, focusing on French literature. She read all of Proust's great work and finished the year with a very original paper about it. On my 25th birthday—June 7—she presented me with my own new copy of Albertini's three-volume classic on the origins and outbreak of the First World War. It remains one of my most cherished possessions. Higonnet and his wife Ethel had the whole seminar over to dinner in their Cambridge apartment. After doing my two-week summer camp, we went off to Europe, visiting my parents in London, backpacking through Norway and Finland, and making our way to Moscow to visit my older brother, stationed there as a foreign correspondent, and his wife. I spent a lot of that summer reading books I had run into during the year without time to go through them. The trip to the USSR moved me to read Solzhenitsyn's *The First Circle*, partly because in Moscow, we met Lev Kopelev, a fellow camp inmate of Solzhenitsyn's and the model for the character Rubin, and also *Dr. Zhivago*. I would return to both again and again. Hughes had given an excellent lecture on Thomas Mann, and I had read *The Magic Mountain* during Christmas vacation and *Dr. Faustus* that summer. None of this kept me from improving my tennis game, going to the movies at least twice a week, and keeping up with baseball, the NFL, the NBA, and the very exciting and tragic Munich Olympics. Looking back, I would have to rate that year as perhaps the most intense, intellectually, that I ever spent. I had some great teachers and great friends, I was in love, and I loved every minute of it. The collapse of George McGovern's presidential campaign and Nixon's massive re-election were not inspiring but even they could not really dampen my spirits.

I think that it was also during 1972 that I read perhaps the most important book to come out of Harvard in that era, Graham Allison's *Essence of Decision*. As a graduate student in political science Allison had sat in on the May group, an interdisciplinary faculty seminar that explored different ways to study how policy was made. Using the Cuban missile crisis as a template—an event about which we knew much less then than we do now—he put forth three models to explain American policy during the crisis. Model I postulated that nations acted as rational actors, and thus that their actions had to be explained as proper ways to achieve particular goals. That was, and often remains, the most common form of analysis of governments, but the rest of the book was really designed to debunk it. Model II, organizational process, highlighted the ways in which the bureaucratic routines of the Soviet and American military and American intelligence agencies had determined what the two sides did at critical points. Thus, American intelligence identified the Soviet missile sites in Cuba because they looked exactly like similar bases in the USSR and Eastern Europe, and the American military proposed a huge air strike followed by an invasion of Cuba to deal with the problem because that was the plan they had in their file cabinet. Model III, governmental politics, viewed policy outcomes as resulting from a struggle among leaders. This book was a blindingly illuminating experience for me, as it became for many of my students. I never used its specific concepts explicitly, but its approach informed my own works on the European great powers in the 1930s, the origins of the Vietnam war, U.S. policy towards Cuba in the early 1960s, and finally the US response to the Second World War in 1940–1. It has never let me down, and I am very disappointed that its influence has if anything faded over the decades.

The second year of graduate study in history at Harvard was a strange one. It was devoted entirely to preparation for one two-hour *oral* examination, testing the student's proficiency in four chosen fields of history. In theory, the four fields were supposed to cover three of the defined periods of history: ancient, medieval, early modern, and modern. One could also, however, do a field in a subject from another related department, and substitute it for one of the three periods. There was no way, however, to get out of one field in ancient or medieval history, for which some prior coursework was usually required.

To prepare myself for a medieval field, I had taken a full-year survey of medieval history from Giles Constable in 1971–2. This was not, as it turned out, an efficient use of my time, but I learned a lot, and was introduced to one of the half-dozen greatest works of 20th-century literary criticism, *Mimesis* by Erich Auerbach. Using texts from the Bible to Proust, Auerbach brilliantly traced the changing nature and role of western literature. Yet rather than do medieval history with Constable for my generals, I found I could do English social history in the Middle Ages with another classic Yankee type, Professor George C. Homans. That turned out to be reasonably interesting and undemanding. I then decided to do modern Germany, supervised by Franklin Ford, and modern diplomatic history, supervised by May. The fourth field was modern French government, taught by Hoffmann. These choices, except for the first, reflected my keenest interests, but they also embodied my strategy for getting a job. I now anticipated writing my thesis on some European diplomatic topic for May, but I wanted to be able to put myself forward for jobs in French or German history too.

To prepare for generals we met with our supervising professors about once every two weeks for an hour or two to discuss what we had read. We were of course expected to familiarize ourselves with both standard and newer, more fashionable works on various subjects, but it seemed to me there was more emphasis on being able to discuss the major historical problems than on being able to refer to the trendiest names. That suited me to a T, and I used the reading to fill in more gaps in my historical knowledge. Hoffmann was a part-time historian as well as a political scientist, and there was very little difference in my discussions with him than those with Ford or May. Tom Childers was also doing modern Germany and modern international relations and we spent a lot of time together. We were joined in the German history group by Charles Skinner, who had had to interrupt his grad school career with two years of service in the U.S. military. He eventually had a distinguished career in the Foreign Service, and teaches today at the University of Pittsburgh.

My teaching career began early that fall. Patrice Higonnet was once again teaching his course on the French Revolution that fall—the one I had audited the year before. I asked him if he needed a grader, and it turned out that he did. His course had an interesting structure. The reading list began with a readable text covering the whole 1715–1815 period, and students were required to read it all before the hour exam, ensuring that they would have a good factual background before the discussion of the revolution itself began. The remainder of the list was split into about half a dozen topic areas with several books in each, and the students had to pick, as I recall, just one. Grading the hour exams was pretty straightforward: the question was designed to see if the students had read the whole text. If they had they generally earned at least an A-; if not, some sort of B. We got along splendidly and were good friends, I felt, by the end of the term. At that point he left to spend a term in Paris.

Meanwhile, Cathy and I decided to get married that June. Early in the 1972–3 school year she had decided graduate school was not for her. Given what has happened to literary studies since then, that was undoubtedly a wise decision. She landed a job teaching French in a northwest suburban high school. We arranged to hold the ceremony in the Harvard faculty club, and it was a great occasion. Late in the afternoon of the wedding, after the reception was over, Secretariat won the Belmont Stakes and the Triple Crown. We had already found our first apartment, on Mass Ave about 2/3 of the way to Central Square from Harvard Square.

In the spring of 1973, about a month before my generals were scheduled in May, the incumbent Dean of the Faculty stepped down. Franklin Ford was tapped as a temporary replacement, and he withdrew from helping us to prepare for generals or from giving the exams. He was replaced by a bright young—but temporarily, fallen—star of the department, Charles (or Charlie as he has always been called) Maier. Like Steve Schuker, who was something of a rival, Maier was about 10 years older than I was, and had become an assistant professor in the late 1960s. His dissertation, a study of France, Germany, and Italy in the years immediately following the First World War, was not nearly as thoroughly researched as Schuker's, but it was built around an original concept, "corporatism," to explain how those nations were governed in the turbulent early years of the 1920s. In the fall of 1971 both Maier and Sam Williamson had come up for tenure, and both had failed to get it. Williamson had almost immediately decamped for North Carolina, while Maier, who was finishing his contract, I believe in 1973, had signed on at Duke, while continuing to live in Cambridge. His dissertation was published as *Recasting Bourgeois Europe* and won several prizes.

I read a great deal that year, but I don't think I learned nearly as much as the year before. "Do you know the Langer books?" May asked me when I saw him for the first time in the fall of 1972. He was referring to *European Alliances and Alignments, 1871–1890* (500 pages), and *The Diplomacy of Imperialism* (800 pages), which continued the saga from 1890 to 1902. Within two or three weeks I had read and taken notes on both. May was both fascinating and frustrating in small groups. He hated to teach by rote, and he was always fascinated and enthusiastic about any new idea. He also had a great aversion to stating a definite opinion about almost anything. I also did more auditing. Peter Stanley had been a May student in the early 1960s, writing his thesis on the US and the Philippines, before going to the University of Illinois at Chicago Circle. In 1972 the department persuaded him to abandon his tenure-track job there to become an assistant professor and teach a course on the Progressive Era. The course was excellent, and I audited it along with Diana Pinto and, occasionally, my friend Evalinn Welling. Stanley and I became good friends, but the decision to return to Harvard brought his career as an historian to an end. When his contract was up he had to go into administration, and 25 years later he had become the President of Pomona College when my son Daniel attended it from 1997 to 2001.

The general exam obviously induced a good deal of anxiety. By the time I took mine the Watergate hearings had just begun. Both I and my four examiners alluded to the similarity of the process as we got started that sunny afternoon in May. I began with Homans and didn't do very well with him at all, for some reason botching some relatively simple questions. Then, I turned, I believe, to Charlie Maier for Germany.

Maier began with a brilliant question. "Supposing," he said, "that you were going to give a series of lectures on German history from 1871 to 1933 focusing on something *other than* the origins of Nazism—what would it be?" "I would discuss the development of parliamentary government," I said, and we were off and running. I had committed the major changes in coalitions, laws, and controversies between the parliament and the executive to memory, and we had a very high-level discussion for most of our half hour. Near the end, I remember, he asked me to comment on the significance of German expressionism in the 1920s—a clear allusion to the book *Weimar Culture* by Peter Gay. Instead of answering simply and honestly that I hadn't read that book, I tried to fake a brief answer with poor results. It was absolutely critical in generals not to waste any time talking about things one did not know. Hoffmann surprised me because his questions nearly all related to the structure of the government, not historical events, but I did fine. May presented no problems, and we did go over some well-traveled ground about the outbreak of the First World War and other issues. He called me that evening to say I had been given a "Good minus," because of trouble with Homans. But I knew no one would ever care about anything but that I had passed.

My thesis remained to be written.

In the fall of 1972, I believe, I had purchased an Avalon Hill board game entitled *The Origins of the Second World War*, and played a round of it with several fellow students. Although officially a diplomatic rather than a military game, it worked rather like Risk, with Britain, France, Germany, Italy and the USSR competing for influence in the smaller states of Eastern Europe. If either Germany or the USSR reached a certain level of influence, the war was presumed to have begun. This obviously recalled the paper I had written in my sophomore year for Sam Williamson, and I suddenly thought that I might write my thesis on the same topic: the competition for influence among the great powers in Eastern Europe during the 1930s. May, who was now the only diplomatic historian on the faculty and who had advised dissertations on European and East Asian topics as well as American ones, was the logical adviser, and I spoke to him about it sometime that spring. It was one of the pivotal conversations of my life.

That topic, I knew even then, was enormous by normal dissertation standards. Three current junior faculty members—Williamson, Schuker, and Maier—had written dissertations involving at least two countries, but Williamson's was more narrowly focused and Schuker's and Maier's had covered only a few years each. I was proposing to examine the policies of three great powers—Germany, Britain, and France—towards no less than nine new nations: Austria, Czechoslovakia, Hungary, Rumania, Yugoslavia, Poland, and the Baltic states of Estonia, Latvia and Lithuania. I knew the work would have a big economic as well as a political dimension, and I hoped to write about an entire decade. Many professors, I am sure, would have suggested—or demanded—that I scale it back drastically. But May did not. He was enthusiastic from the word go, as he always was when anyone proposed to do anything new, and he encouraged me to go ahead. Whatever else happened between us in the years to come, that was a gift of inestimable value.

Dissertations depended on sources, and mine would have to come from German, British and French archives. Schuker, while writing his dissertation, had persuaded the Harvard documents center at Widener to buy microfilms of the British cabinet deliberations and cabinet memoranda for the 1930s, and that was an excellent place to start. The diplomatic papers of the foreign office were now open for the 1930s, but they sat placidly in the Public Record Office at Portugal Street in London, and I would have to spend an unknown amount of time there. The Germans, meanwhile, had paid the price of their defeat in the war. The allies had photographed and microfilmed virtually the entire archive of the German foreign office, and the Boston Public Library, which along with Widener belonged to a local consortium, had bought the full set of thousands of reels of microfilm. (They had not been much used, and I remember one of the librarians nearly fainting from shock when I showed up and asked to see them.) The French archives, on the other hand, remained closed, but Schuker assured me that I might be able to see some material from the Finance or Commerce ministries. All of this was of course rather daunting, but somehow I had already imbibed into my consciousness the first rule of research, stated brilliantly by the King of Hearts in Alice in Wonderland: "Begin at the beginning, and go on until you come to the end: then stop." And so I did. Before getting into archives or published documents, however, I read through the *Economist* of London for the entire decade, looking for material on Eastern Europe. There was plenty there, and this exercise immersed me in the period that I was going to write about. I have tried to do something similar for every subsequent book.

Having passed my generals, I assumed new teaching responsibilities in the 1973–4 school year. Dissertation students could assume a 2/5 load—giving sections in a lecture course or teaching tutorials. I did both. Stanley Hoffmann was giving another legendary course, a full year survey entitled War. The first half was very theoretical and introduced me to Clausewitz; the second was essentially a history of the Cold War. Hoffmann met regularly with the TAs, who included Tom Childers and one of Hoffmann's own students, Michael Mandelbaum, who has had a very distinguished career in political science. In May 1974, I remember, Hoffmann ended his last lecture reading the last paragraph of Camus's *The Plague*, which anticipated the day when rats would once again emerge from the catacombs to die in a happy city. He apologized for his pessimism—which I found quite unwarranted—but more than three decades later, in 2007, I had occasion to email him and congratulate him on his foresight.

My second fifth was a junior tutorial in European history, and for the first time, I put together my own syllabus from the French Revolution to Nazi Germany. I attempted to give my students a sampler of the best historical writing on s series of critical topics. I was realizing the real joy of university teaching: getting smart young people to read some of one's favorite books. The topics included the French Revolution, the Napoleonic era, the 1848 revolutions, German unification and the introduction of real democracy in Britain and France, imperialism, the origins of the First World War, and Nazi Germany. For comparative purposes I also threw in a week on the US from the 1830s through the 1850s. My best student defected to Social Studies halfway through the year, but the others worked very hard and enjoyed it thoroughly. So did I.

On Thanksgiving weekend of 1973 the Harvard community was devastated by a horrible crime. On Saturday evening, while walking home from the library, Ethel Higonnet, the wife of Patrice Higonnet and herself a history grad student, was accosted and murdered near Brattle Street in Cambridge by an unknown white male. At least one passerby saw the beginning of the incident but apparently thought that the two people knew each other and made no attempt to intervene. Harvard eventually staged a performance of Mozart's requiem in her honor. A couple of weeks later, I knocked on Higonnet's door at CES and asked him if he had a moment. "That depends on what you want to talk to me about," he said, "About history," I replied. We sat down, and I raised a general issue that was coming up in my tutorial. He responded eagerly, and we parted warmly. I had already written a letter of condolence, and two years later I received a moving handwritten reply.

Months later, as the school year wound down, the Hoffmann connection paid off when the Center for European Studies provided me with a grant that enabled me to spend the summer of 1974 in London and Paris to plunge into the archives. Although my father had had to leave government service in 1969 after Nixon's election, he had remained in London in the private sector, and my mother helped find us a convenient apartment that we could afford. I had now become a serious tennis player and a fanatic fan, and Wimbledon took place not long after I got there. I did spend a few days on the scene with family members, but meanwhile, I established my research routine.

Like retirees, as I now know, grad students can have trouble establishing a good routine, because their time increasingly becomes their own. I added an anchor to my life right after my marriage, when, for the first time since high school, I resumed regular piano lessons. I plunged into them with enthusiasm and was soon beginning every day with an hour at the keyboard from about 8:00 AM to 9:00 AM, but I didn't do nearly as much research during that first post-generals year as I had planned. In London things changed. The archive was open from 9:00 to about 4:30 and every minute was precious. I spent the whole day there with an hour break for a sandwich and a half pint of beer at a local pub. (To this day I drink every day at lunch in

Europe, but almost never in the US.) I had my own uniform—sandals, jeans, and a sweater. This was of course long before the invention of the laptop computer, and we took notes in pencil. I found it very easy to pour all my concentration into the large volumes of documents the archivists brought out, three at a time. Researchers who planned carefully, as I did, almost never found themselves with nothing to do.

The British Foreign Office, I discovered—and confirmed in later researches—had the most brilliant filing system of any comparable institution. Rather than maintaining a prescribed set of files for every country, they started a file any time a new agreement had to be negotiated, or a diplomatic demand ushered in a new crisis. Everything related to that episode went into the same file, and when the crisis or negotiation was over the file died as well. Each document was passed up the departmental ladder from the desk officer to the department head, and thence to the Permanent Undersecretary and at times the Foreign Secretary himself. One after another, every one of them wrote minutes on the document. Within two weeks they had become close friends of mine. I did very little copying, focusing on reducing the documents to their essential meaning in my notes. I had no idea when I began how much of the 1930s I would be able to manage, but within a couple of weeks it seemed possible that I might get to the outbreak of the war by mid-September when I would have to return home. As it turned out, I did just that.

I took about a two-week break in August with Cathy to do some research in Paris, and then to visit Tom Childers and his wife who were spending some time in Berlin, where he was doing research. With introductions from Steve Schuker, I did get to see some important documents about trade and loans in the French finance ministry, and a few from the Ministry of Commerce as well. Nixon resigned while we were in Paris and I will never forget the sight of the headline from *Le Figaro* when we came down for breakfast in our hotel. A month later, back in my parents' apartment in London—Cathy had already had to return—I was watching the European track and field championships on TV when the announcer said the broadcast would shift to Washington for a special announcement. This could obviously mean only one thing. Ford had pardoned Nixon.

Back in Cambridge, I fulfilled my teaching obligation with two junior tutorials instead of one. One of them, I remember, included Tyler Stovall, a very fine student who eventually became an historian at UC Berkeley and recently served a year as President of the American Historical Association. Another had John Savarese, who decades later won fame, if not fortune when he defended Martha Stewart. Stage II of my research began that fall, in the microfilm room of the Boston Public Library, an easy T ride from our Central Square apartment. The German Foreign Office microfilm was often difficult to read, and it was only in the course of my work that my German reading skills really blossomed. To this day I can read anything relating to a topic I know something about pretty easily, although I still can't carry on a conversation in that language. The German Foreign Office filing system was as bad as the British was good. The Germans did keep a set of required files for every country, and there were so many of them—political, economic, and financial—that it was never easy to figure out into which one an individual document should go. I was now using notecards to take notes, and it was only after I put the notecards from different files in chronological order that a coherent story emerged. Trade, particularly trade in agricultural products, had become the main focus of the thesis, and I spent some hours in the basement of Widener copying trade statistics from League of Nations documents as well.

By the end of 1974–5, I had completed going through the relevant German microfilm—a very big but rewarding task— but I knew I had to go back to Europe for a few weeks at least, both to view some unfilmed items in the German archive in Bonn and to fill in a gap or two in Britain, including the recently released letters of Neville Chamberlain. The History Department declined to fund my request for support for the trip, so Cathy and I financed it. Things went smoothly in both places. My stay in Britain once again coincided with Wimbledon, and although I never actually attended the tournament, I saw virtually all the key matches, including Billie Jean King's epic victory over Chris Evert in the semis on her way to her sixth title, and Arthur Ashe's stunning defeat of the heavily favored Jimmy Connors. I flew home the next day. I was ready to write—and to enter the job market.

The story I had to tell had fallen into place. The new nations of Eastern Europe, particularly the agrarian ones, had never gotten off the ground economically during the 1920s, and the Great Depression had hit them hard. For two years, in 1931–2, the Germans, British, and French had debated some schemes to help the new states, but without the slightest result. Hitler's coming to power in 1933 had changed the situation for several reasons. Hitler planned to conquer much of Eastern Europe on the way to a climactic war with the Soviet Union that would make Germany a world power. But in the short run, he tightly controlled German trade, cut Germany off from the world economy, and overheated the economy with public works and rearmament. Germany had never been self-sufficient in food and Hitler would not spare the necessary foreign currency to buy the cheapest grain available from overseas. But Rumania, Hungary, and Yugoslavia had no choice but to accept German Reichsmarks—which could only be spent in Germany—in exchange for their grain. Beginning in 1936, these nations filled a critical gap in the German food supply, allowing rearmament to continue.

The British and the French, meanwhile, had adopted an entirely different policy, favoring imports from their respective empires. The British Foreign Office took note of what the Germans were doing, but declined to compete with them for most of the Eastern European market. Indeed, by the late 1930s some British officials thought of Eastern Europe as a good outlet for German expansionist tendencies, economically if not politically. Both the British and French foreign offices included one official who called for resistance to the German initiative, but they remained isolated and unheeded. In separate chapters I dealt with political issues, including half-hearted attempts by the French to form a tighter alliance system in Eastern Europe, and, finally, the Munich crisis of 1938. A great deal had been written about that, of course, but I managed to contribute something new, arguing that the outcome of the crisis was inevitable given decisions which the three great powers had reached earlier. Dealing in my last chapter with 1939, I argued that the Germans were no longer able to solve their economic problems by trade, and had to either give up their expansionist goals—which Hitler would never do—or begin war then and there. The Nazi-Soviet pact, which provided them with grain and oil, allowed them to begin the war with the British and French that Hitler had shied away from in the previous year.

My research taught me something else. Among the documents I studied were two of the most analyzed of all Hitler's rule: his memorandum for Hermann Göring on the economic Four Year Plan of 1936, and the so-called Hossbach conference in 1937. In both cases I saw things that no one else had, simply because I was looking at them in a somewhat different context and had new knowledge about the German economic situation. One reason historians now write so little of lasting value is the belief that too many important topics have already been thoroughly covered. That, I am convinced, is not true, as anyone who does thorough research on almost any topic will surely discover.

Essentially, I had shown how one apparently peripheral area of policy—trade with Eastern Europe—shed light on the overall goals and strategies of all three of the great powers. That, I believe, is what most dissertations should try to do, and I helped at least one grad student do the same later in my career. May reacted very favorably to the early chapters, and I was on my way. Meanwhile, I applied for several jobs.

I certainly had no idea that I could stay at Harvard, and there were many institutions at which I would have been happy to work. Two opportunities that I recall that fall were at the University of New Mexico, asking for someone in a field in Europe after 1939, and at Notre Dame, which was seeking an historian of modern Germany. I was immediately eliminated from the first search, for which I wasn't qualified, and I had an interview at the convention of the American Historical Association—the profession's annual meat market—in Atlanta with a Notre Dame professor, but nothing more. But the best chance seemed to be at Emory, in Atlanta, which I believe wanted a historian who knew something about imperialism. I also had a fortunate connection there, because one of their senior professors had been a fellow Rhodes Scholar of my father's in the late 1930s. The whole department interviewed me in Atlanta as well, briefly and rather cursorily. I did not give a presentation but I supplied them with chapters from my dissertation.

One day, reading the AHA job bulletin in the History Department office in Robinson Hall, I saw a one-year lectureship in European history—at Harvard. May had said nothing to me about it, but I spoke to him, and he encouraged me to go ahead and apply. May had now begun a four-year term as department chair, but he was due for a half-time leave in 1976–7. Rather than take a term off, he had talked the department into hiring a junior faculty member to split his teaching with him over the whole year. He was to embarked upon a big research project in Washington, a study of the arms race that had been commissioned by Secretary of Defense James Schlesinger. Schlesinger's firing in the midst of that year by President Ford was a big shock to him, but the project continued and eventually bore some fruit.

Another story rocked Harvard in 1975. H. Stuart Hughes, certainly a leading light among the historians of Europe, announced his departure for the University of California at San Diego. The reason, he frankly told the *Crimson*, was that the department had failed to tenure his second wife Judith, whom he had met when she was beginning graduate school. She had written a slim book on the origins of the Maginot line, and he claimed that she would have been chosen for tenure if the standards of recent years had been applied—an apparent reference to the 1970 promotions of Professors Higonnet, Keenan, and Womack. I was naturally sad to see him go and stopped by his office to say goodbye, but I didn't realize that his departure might have some subsequent impact on myself.

In February or early March, on a Tuesday—I remember it was the day of several Democratic primaries—I returned to our apartment one evening and Cathy informed me that Emory had rejected me. There was no explanation. Suddenly, the whole question of whether I would be an historian at all was up in the air. Harvard had not yet made any decision on their position, and the next day I told May what had happened. That afternoon, I believe, his secretary, a young woman named Carol Glassman with whom I had become friendly, nudged me in the History Department library across the hall from the main office and told me that I evidently would get the offer for the lectureship. May had asked her to make some copies of my c.v. for a department meeting. Cathy and I celebrated at Durgin Park in Boston. My career was launched—however uncertainly.

Shortly thereafter, we found a new apartment in a high rise in Medford, much closer to Cathy's work, but still accessible by public transportation from Harvard. I was still writing chapters and made steady progress on the manual typewriter I had used since Loomis. May, frequently traveling to Washington, lost interest in my thesis as soon as I had been hired, and it was well into the summer before I made clear that he had to read the rest of what I had done so that I could meet the September 1 deadline for a November degree. He finally did. The second reader was Franklin Ford, but I doubt that he ever read it. The Harvard history department did not require dissertation defenses. To have completed a thesis on the scale of mine in three years was in retrospect a remarkable achievement. While it was not unheard of for people to finish theirs in only two years, most graduate students took longer—and wrote on narrower topics. I didn't feel that I had been hurrying, but I had done it.

On May 19 of that year I found a surprising note waiting for me in the office I shared from one of the students in my junior tutorial. When he came to see me the first time the previous fall he had left rather abruptly, as if he had something to say which he could not quite get out. He had been a relatively quiet student in class and an adequate performer in his written work, and he had contributed more late in the year. He now explained that he had originally planned to major in economics, but that the "general" in his family—his father—had insisted that he switch to history or English. He said that he had felt very unprepared for his first-in-class presentation in the fall and that he had nearly changed majors then—but "I stuck it out!" He had made a great effort to prepare more carefully in the second semester. "What I'm really trying to say<' he wrote, "is, I learned more this year than in any course I've ever taken. Of the 20 topics we covered I had previously dealt with one, and I feel much more at home now in dealing with the other 19. . . . Please don't take this as anything other than a statement of respect for your knowledge and my recognition that I should have gone into economics but that the same [sic] I learned a hell of a lot in history."

By a happy coincidence, it was that summer that my six-year military obligation in the Army reserves came to an end. The small medical headquarters unit to which I had belonged since 1972 was open with a skeleton staff every day, and they allowed us to come in and make up drills at our convenience during the year. That was how I had been able to travel for weeks or even months at a time. They also had an informal policy of refusing to allow soldiers to take the 4 unauthorized absences a year to which we were entitled—if we missed a drill, we had to make it up. Without saying anything to anyone, I simply skipped my last four drills, and received my discharge in the mail. For six years, while everyone else's hair had been long, mine had been short. It was months before I got a haircut now.

In the fall term May and I would combine to teach a course on international politics from 1815 to 1970. I would give two sets of lectures lasting two weeks apiece. We would teach a small group course in the spring together as well. For the rest of my teaching load, I chose to advise about 8 undergraduate theses. I wanted to be able to focus on the lectures. My relationship with May took a new turn that summer when we began playing tennis together. He was as dedicated as I was—although 19 years older—but I had a lot of pent-up frustration as I completed the last of 21 years of formal education, and I beat him the first few times out.

The unique cultural features of Cambridge had contributed enormously to this, the happiest period of my life. It was a small city several of whose neighborhoods were dominated by students of all kinds—and Harvard Square businesses and restaurants catered to those students. There were perhaps a dozen used bookstores in the immediate area and during the early 1970s I constantly scoured them as I built up my library of historical works, many of them out of print. By the early 1970s Cambridge was a world-class film center with about six separate theaters (or screens) showing art house movies and, increasingly, classic movies that in those pre-VCR days could not be seen in any other way. The Harvard Coop had an enormous record section. I continued my lessons at Longy where my teacher, David Bacon, gave me far more pieces and far more difficult pieces than I ever would have imagined I could do. Cathy and I both had as much fun getting a double hamburger special for $1.50 at Charlie's Kitchen as we would have eating in a fancy restaurant. Today the used bookstores are gone, records and CDs are a curiosity, and most of Harvard Square is fully yuppified with upscale chain stores that one can find in any major city. Never have I been such a part of a community that shared my tastes in so many things.

I have never been religious, but the Greek scheme of things has always appealed to me. Not one god, but many, lived on Olympus. Every mortal seemed to have won the favor of a couple of them, while others were determined to screw him over. Life depended on which gods were looking at one on that particular day. In 1976 I felt I had generally been very fortunate for more than ten years, and I genuinely believed that this was only the beginning. That, it would turn out, was only half true.

IV

HEAVEN AND HELL

1976–80

As soon as I was hired, May introduced me to another project of his. He was now doing some of his teaching at the JFK School of Government, and he and the political scientist Richard Neustadt were beginning a graduate course on the uses of history in policy making. I had met Neustadt when I first came to Cambridge since he was both a long-standing friend of my father's from the days of the Truman Administration, and the father of a classmate of mine. I had even briefly dated his daughter in my junior year. He was older than May—a member of the GI generation—but warmer, and this began a friendship that lasted until his death in 2003. Neustadt, most famous as the author of *Presidential Power*, took his teaching very seriously, and we met for an hour or two every week to plan the class, which I continued to help teach for the next four years. He firmly believed that policy outcomes could improve if policy makers learned more history and ways of using it. I was always more skeptical, but the subject was interesting. Eventually May and Neustadt turned the course into a book, *Thinking in Time*.

My lecture course with May, International Politics, 1815–1970, began in September. He did the first two weeks of lectures, on the Congress of Vienna, spending lots of time on portraits of the leading figures, and falling well behind where we had planned to be. Then I had two weeks in which to do four lectures of my own, roughly on the period 1840–1870. We all learn from our experience, and I was determined to cover what I set out to do in each.

The topic of the first lecture was the Eastern Question, the relations among Russia, the weakening Ottoman Empire, and the other European powers, roughly from the 1820s thorough the Crimean War in the mid-1850s. I read in about five different books to prepare. After some general background, I remember, I split it into three parts on three different crises. When I showed up, I was quite surprised to see May in the classroom. He explained that it was his only chance to hear me. Borrowing techniques I had learned from him, from Stuart Hughes, and from many others, I used the lecture to introduce the class to key figures such as Mohammed Ali of Egypt ("a remarkable man, with an equally remarkable modern-day namesake"), Lord Palmerston, and Adolphe Thiers of France. I also put the story in the context of the general problem of intervention in distant lands, which, with the end of the Vietnam war only 18 months previous, was very much on everyone's mind. To the delight of the students, I finished on time. "Splendid!" May said. My next three lectures covered the unification of Italy and Germany, the latter focusing the interplay of domestic and foreign policy.

A second set began with wartime diplomacy during the First World War and dealt with the 1920s and 1930s. I spent the last third of the wartime diplomacy lecture on US entry into the war, and I felt something new come over me as I did. The Vietnam War had re-opened the question of America's appropriate role in the world. I had discovered writing my first seminar paper five years earlier that a substantial body of left-wing opinion had opposed US policy in the early stages of the Cold War on roughly the same grounds that my contemporaries had opposed Vietnam: that our government was fighting legitimate revolution and supporting the status quo, at least in part out of economic interests. And in one of our planning sessions for the uses of history course, May had introduced me to the 1948 isolationist classic by Charles A. Beard, *President Roosevelt and the Coming of the War 1941: A Study in Appearances and Realities*. Beard, the most influential American historian of the first half of the twentieth century, had been a confirmed anti-imperialist since 1898 and clearly believed that even in the Second World War we might have let the rest of the world take care of itself. I did not agree with respect to Europe, but I did wonder, as did he, if it had been necessary to contest Japan's attempt to conquer China, which had helped lead to Pearl Harbor. In the lecture on 1917, I briefly reviewed the arguments against war then: that the Europeans must work out their own quarrels, that a wartime United States would create a more powerful state dangerous to liberty, and that we were as likely to make things worse as to make them better. In our time, I said, we had seen many of those things come true, and it was hard to read those debates without wondering whether the isolationists had been right. "But Wilson," I concluded, "decided to go in. That is the decision we have been living with ever since, and that is the decision we will be living with for the rest of our lives."

My last lecture on appeasement and the outbreak of the European war finished with the conclusion of Churchill's magnificent speech in the first week of June 1940, when he promised that Britain would fight on "until, in God's good time, the New World, with all its power and might, sets forth to the rescue and the liberation of the old." May gave the last few lectures and got the customary hand at the end of the last one. When it began he gestured at me, sitting in the front row, and when I stood up, the applause got louder. The exams, most of which I read, turned out well, and I was encouraged. I told May I would give the course again if I had the chance.

May was now talking about keeping me around a bit longer, and trying to make this as budgetarily easy as he could. 1/5 of my salary would be paid by the JFK School if I taught Uses of History with him and Neustadt. For a second fifth, he asked me if I might like to teach a freshman seminar. This was a famous part of the Harvard experience that I had missed because of sophomore standing—an opportunity for a small group of students to work with a faculty member. I accepted at once, and proposed one for the next fall on the origins of the First World War.

Another upheaval shook the history department that year. The American historians—of which May was one—were benefitting from a separate institution within the department, the Charles Warren Center, which had its own endowment. It turned out that they were paying themselves summer research stipends of perhaps $5000 each out of its funds, without any real accounting of the research they were, or were not doing. (Some of them, like May, Bernard Bailyn, and David Donald, published regularly; others, like the intellectual historian Donald Fleming, did not.) The economic historian David Landes, one of the most distinguished historians of Europe in the department, found out about this practice and evidently complained vocally about it in a department meeting. One morning May came about an hour late to one of our class prep sessions with Neustadt and explained that he had been conferring with a colleague and could not break away. It turned out that Landes was announcing that he was re-affiliating with the Economics Department. In a single year, the department had lost its two most eminent European historians, Hughes and Landes. Both of them had thought highly of me.

In February, May and I began teaching our second class together, a small group conference course. He had not designed it especially well, and we attracted only three students. Meanwhile, I had applied for a couple of French or German history jobs at Stanford, I believe, and Oregon, but neither seemed to be going anywhere. I asked him about my future at Harvard as we were walking across the yard. "I think I can persuade the department to turn your appointment into an assistant professorship," he said. That would mean a six-year appointment, including at least a term of leave—plenty of time to get going on a second book. Cathy, who was wearying of her teaching job, was thrilled and started scanning real estate ads. Everything seemed to be going astonishingly smoothly.

A couple of weeks later May told me he was meeting with the department and asked me to stop by afterwards. I did, eagerly. "Well—no," he said, with a somewhat embarrassed smile. The department, he explained, was not willing to make a decision quite so quickly, and was going to announce two junior positions and solicit candidates. I was encouraged to apply. There was no way to know what would happen, but I remained optimistic. Meanwhile, I had taken the first steps towards getting my dissertation published. I sent it to the Princeton University Press, where an editor named Joanna Hitchcock replied that while she thought "you have the makings of a book here," she thought it needed a substantial cut. Unfortunately I wasn't quite prepared to hear that yet. Eventually, I sent it to the University of North Carolina Press, where Steve Schuker had just placed his book on the French occupation of the Rhineland.

I was feeling more and more tension that spring, and beginning to have some trouble sleeping. On the one hand, the most likely outcome seemed to be that I would be solidly established, right where I wanted to be, for some time. On the other, I as yet had no formal security even for the forthcoming year. Finally, in the last week of May, I believe, May called me into his office again. Once again he was cordial.

"We couldn't make a final decision on the appointments because too many of us had already left town!" he exclaimed. They were offering me one more year, and a year to a Princeton Ph.D. named Tom Baker, who did Spanish history. They would revisit the whole issue next fall, complete with another search, he said. Breaking this news to Cathy was particularly difficult for another reason. A year earlier, in July, she had announced that she wanted us to have a child. After giving it some thought, I had asked if we could wait another year, since I wanted to enjoy the first year in which we had both worked full time. She had agreed. Now, obviously, going ahead with an uncertain future was risky. But I felt so badly about letting her down that a few days later, I suggested that we stick to the plan—and we did. She quit her teaching job on the assumption that she would be pregnant within a month or two. As it turned out, it took a little longer. Our son Dan remains today one of my two best friends (his brother is the other), and I certainly have never regretted that decision, but a year later it would look like a highly questionable choice. On June 7, 1977—about a week after May gave me the news—I turned 30. I remember thinking that I would have enjoyed the milestone a lot more if the assistant professorship had come through.

I eventually came to understand what had really happened. To begin with, the remaining European historians, whose resentment towards the Americanists had surfaced during the Landes affair, did not like the idea of May—another Americanist—filling a European history slot with one of his students, no matter how well qualified. And the key player, it would rapidly emerge, was Patrice Higonnet, whom I had regarded as one of my best friends in the department and whom I had graded for a few years earlier. The departures of Hughes and Landes had elevated his stature, and he had plans for his favorite student, Matthew Ramsey. Ramsey was a college classmate of mine—I had not known him then—but he had not had to go into the army for some reason and had started grad school a year earlier than I. He was now six years into his graduate education but he had not finished his dissertation, on medicine in 18th century France. Higonnet, I believe, wanted, first of all, the prestige of picking the two new junior faculty members, and secondly, to make Ramsey one of the choices. To do so, he had to postpone the search for a year until Ramsey could be eligible. When the fall term began, he emerged as the chair of the new search committee, and it was clear from a brief contact I had with him that he was no longer a friend. He also began his work by eliminating a host of candidates, including Tom Baker, the historian of Spain who had been hired along with me for one year, and who had been assured when he arrived that he could plan his teaching for the long haul. Baker, informed that his Harvard career was over with a brief typewritten note in December, went into banking after that year.

Two noteworthy jobs appeared in the AHA job bulletin that fall. One was at Michigan, which was looking for a German historian. I wrote in for it and got a pro forma response. The second really caught my eye: it was at Reed College in Portland, Oregon, which in those days at least was known as one of the half-dozen best liberal arts colleges in the country. The author of the ad, Professor Owen Ulph, specified an historian of early modern Europe but said that the department was flexible and that they were more interested in finding someone who understood the nature and importance of teaching at a place like Reed. I was beginning to think that my real gift was for teaching, rather than writing, and I wrote an enthusiastic letter, but nothing much came back.

I was now in the midst of perhaps the most intense teaching experience I had ever had. My idea for a freshman seminar on the origins of the First World War came, of course, from Sam Williamson's conference course in the fall of my junior year, but I gave it a new twist. The course description announced that each student would be assigned a county to follow for the whole of the term—Germany, Austria-Hungary, Russia, France, or Britain. (As it turned out, nearly every country had two people, not one, assigned to it.) My first job was to pick my students.

I was born near the beginning of the Boom generation in 1947. The freshmen in the fall of 1977 had mostly been born in 1959, near the end of it. Most of their parents now came from the Silent generation, not the GIs, and they had, therefore, had a much easier time with them growing up. Freshman seminar moderators had to interview everyone who signed up, and I think I had about 30 who had. The program was run by Susan Lewis, one of the administrators who actually had their finger on the pulse of the educational process at Harvard in ways that virtually no faculty member ever did. We got along very well from the beginning. It wasn't until later that I realized how fortunate I had been in the students who showed up wanting to take the seminar.

I saved the applications for all nine of the students I accepted. The two most qualified were men I have remained more or less in touch with ever since. Matthew Diller, a New Yorker, was one of two graduates of Stuyvesant High School, one of the competitive schools in the New York system, who joined the seminar. (Many years later I discovered that another of their classmates had been Stacy Nelkin, who had had a very youthful affair with Woody Allen and served as the model for Tracy in *Manhattan*, which did not even appear for two more years.) As he explained in his application, Matthew had spent several years working at Simulations Publications in New York, designing board games based on wars. I had some experience with them myself, and in his interview, I mentioned that I had been struck by how often the games seemed to produce the correct historical outcome. He explained that when someone designed and tried out a game and a different outcome resulted, they would immediately manipulate it to bring it more in line with history. Matthew has remained a lifelong friend. He eventually went to Harvard Law and became a law professor and then a dean at Fordham University in New York. Stephen Biddle also had a gaming background and had a vast knowledge of military history. He went into an academia and became something of an expert on warfare, in the 1990s and 2000s as a public commentator on the wars in Iraq. One young woman, Melissa Scott, had graduated from one of the most famous high schools in America, Central High in Little Rock. I found out later that her parents had never owned a television. Another student, James Mann, was a graduate of Walter Johnson High School in Bethesda, where I might have gone myself had we remained in Washington in 1961. Most of them were public school graduates. All of them were very eager and enthusiastic.

Because the students were responsible for five different countries, I had to make up five different reading lists every week. It was a labor of love. We began with presentations on each of the countries' general state and moved on to some of the earlier prewar crises. Then, about halfway through, they all read Allison's *Essence of Decision*. They also spent one week reading historical novels, including *Dr. Zhivago*.

Jude Hammerle

David Kaiser's seminar on the Origins of the First World War changed me in many interesting ways.

I was a Boston kid, the second-ranked student from a Catholic high school with a very narrow but reliable path to the College. I say reliable because a number of past graduates had done well in Cambridge, including Bill Fitzsimmons, who was

Harvard's Director of Admissions when he kindly interviewed me. We Massachusetts residents are three to four times more incident in the Harvard population than in the national population, so a majority of freshman rooming groups include at least one of us, and we serve as an annoyingly-accented mastic that binds the class together. Like others I'm sure, I hopped the T into the Yard in the fall of 1977 feeling fairly entitled to my Harvard sweatshirt, but I was not a scholar.

When I recovered from the shock of learning I'd need to pick my own courses from a perfect-bound book as thick as my fist, printed on thin Bible stock, and with no help, I gravitated to the seemingly safe section headed *Freshman Seminars* and resolved to apply for Dr. Kaiser's offering on Origins. I say "apply" because the seminar required an application and a personal interview with the Professor.

Heading to the interview, I planned to major in Government. In fact, my college application had served notice to potential rivals that I intended to be the President of the United States. Given this career path and a soft "A" in my high school class on American diplomacy, I felt I had a good rap for the interview. Of course, I did not know that American diplomacy played absolutely no role in the origins of the Great War, and proceeded immediately to display my deficit, mentioning submarines and the Lusitania in my interview. Somehow I made the waiting list.

By a compound equation of miracles, an accepted student demurred, Dr. Kaiser offered me the vacancy so created, and assigned me to the vital Austria-Hungary desk. Growing up reading the World Book encyclopedia on rainy days, I'd learned that another Kaiser—Wilhelm II, adorned in a devilish *pickelhaube* helmet—had been declared the villain of the tale by cringeworthy posters of the period. I knew no reason to doubt these posters. And while I had learned about Austria and Hungary from my boyhood hobby of stamp collecting, the old Emperor Franz Joseph and Austria-Hungary itself were utterly unknown to me. In academic terms, I was as clean a slate as there ever was.

The course and students were ingeniously organized. One pair of students represented each country, and together in weekly meetings, we relived all the pre-war crises in chronological order. We read broadly, coming to understand that the topic was among the most thoroughly researched in the field of History. But Dr. Kaiser would not waste our time, we knew, so we enthusiastically turned all the old stones again. He was an appealingly unusual figure in my freshman experience, which centered around venerable professors lecturing to big rooms in detached, theatrical style, with students as the laugh track. In contrast to these, Dr. Kaiser possessed the elite street cred we accorded to members of the daring rebel Class of 1969, was just twelve years removed from us in age, and demonstrated substantial, gentle skills of personal engagement. Most importantly, he knew what he was looking for: something everyone else had missed. And in the end he found it, or better, inspired us to find it.

The research guidepost for the Austria-Hungary desk was the relentlessly methodical three-volume work by Luigi Albertini, *The Origins of the War of 1914*. In particular, the work excelled for its integration of long passages of original diplomatic correspondence within the narrative text. Flipping through my own copy today I still marvel at the author's willingness to lead with his scholarship rather than his prose—clear, original and insightful though that is. I'm sure it's even better in the original Italian. I still remember Dr. Kaiser's reaction ("Oh, that's good") when the group's discussion exposed that Bethmann-Hollweg was the only player in the drama who simply could not live with the status quo in Europe, as shown by certain of his actions around the time of the Austrian ultimatum to Serbia. Six years after the class, Dr. Kaiser wrote each student a letter of thanks and enclosed a copy of the article in *The Journal of Modern History* presenting his new synthesis.

In conclusion, I must say that Dr. Kaiser's class changed me in many interesting ways. Before (and probably during!) the class, I read uncritically, taking each author at her/his word and giving equal weight to each in my consideration. Working through and with Dr. Kaiser, I learned to read with an eye to what each author missed, and so have come to view the literary tradition on every subject as a set of tantalizing gaps that need to be filled. I became a History major immediately after the class, graduating four years later with *Magna* honors and a proud inch of shelf space in Widener Library where my senior thesis sits. I have since pursued a rebel career path, relentlessly challenging the conventional wisdom in my field (business strategy), viewing virtually everything as an exercise in benevolent espionage, and working whenever I can to perfect and advance a new model of the deep structure of human nature, which I frame as a challenging yet thoroughly orderly game of strategy.

~

When we reached the crisis of July 1914 itself, two readings made the course truly state of the art. First, I realized that the various Harvard libraries owned enough copies of Albertini's great work, *The Origins of the War of 1914*, for me to require it. That book runs to three volumes and 2000 pages, and the last two volumes begin with the Sarajevo assassination. The second was the publication of a wonderful one-volume documents collection, *July 1914: The Outbreak of the First World War*, edited by the German historian Immanuel Geiss. We were able to do an almost hour-by-hour account of the critical days, and when at one point I asked each of them to name their country's ambassadors in all the other major capitals, they all could do it.

For the final meeting of the course, I invited them all to submit a possible alternative scenario that might change the outcome of the crisis. The two students doing Britain—Lizzie Leiman and Steve Harris—produced telegrams in which the British government essentially ordered all the other powers to cooperate in a peaceful settlement of the dispute between Austria-Hungary and Serbia, on pain of having Britain intervene on the other side. Only I had seen them before the class met on the top floor of Hilles Library, and we handed them out to the others then. I then shuttled from room to room, listening as the teams role-played their government's leading figures and serving when necessary as a diplomat or tie-breaker. In the climax I was closeted with the two German representatives who were playing the Chancellor, Bethmann Hollweg, arguing for peace, and the Chief of Staff, von Moltke, pushing for war. I was playing the emperor, and at the critical moment I decided that he, as usual in crisis, would have caved in and opted for peace. I did, and within ten minutes war had been averted. It was probably the most intense hour of teaching that I ever did.

I had an unfortunate setback that fall, when I heard from the University of North Carolina Press about my book manuscript. Following the usual procedure, they had sent it out to a distinguished scholar for a confidential reading. When I saw it, I strongly suspected that the reader was Gerhard L. Weinberg, an authority on Nazi foreign policy who was now teaching at UNC. Eventually that was confirmed to me through the historians' grapevine. Weinberg had already written the first volume of a history of Nazi Germany's foreign policy and was at work on the second, which appeared around 1980. Later he wrote a huge history of the Second World War.

While working on his book, Weinberg had adopted a revisionist view of Neville Chamberlain, the British Prime Minister and the architect of the appeasement policy towards Hitler. A number of scholars, mostly British, were now arguing that Chamberlain had done the best he could in a bad situation. Chamberlain's policies were relevant to my book because he clearly was not disturbed by any peaceful gains that Germany might make in Eastern Europe, and indeed, of course, had collaborated in the truncation and emasculation of Czechoslovakia at Munich. In his review of my manuscript, Weinberg was very positive towards my analysis of German policy in the 1930s but declared that I had gone "haywire" because of my "animus against Chamberlain" in the second half of the book. He pronounced that portion to be without merit and recommended against publication, and the editor regretfully had to accept his opinion. I showed it to May, who initially did not think Weinberg had written it. "Let me put it this way," he said, "it's a lot more gracefully written than anything he's ever gotten into print." In the wake of this setback, however, I had another conversation with Joanna Hitchcock of the (more distinguished) Princeton University Press, and she agreed to send a slightly truncated version of the manuscript out for review. It was some months before it came back.

Weinberg's admiration for Chamberlain had an ironic consequence in 1983, when *Newsweek* contacted him to authenticate a sensational new document: the diaries of Adolf Hitler. Like his equally distinguished British colleague Hugh Trevor-Roper, he yielded to professional vanity and did not realize, as he really should have done, that this was a job for document experts, not historians. Weinberg allowed a newspaper to fly him to Europe to make a very brief inspection of the diaries. Turning to the entries about Munich, he found Hitler describing Chamberlain as a "cunning fox" who had imposed worse terms on him that he would have gotten from Mussolini or French Premier Daladier. Weinberg, as he evidently admitted at the time, was impressed, since this was very close to what he thought himself. He gave the diaries a qualified endorsement—a judgment that blew up in his and Trevor-Roper's faces when the diaries were exposed as forgeries a few days later.

Meanwhile, as I later came to understand, the Harvard search had taken a new turn—one that reflected one of the most unfortunate aspects of American academia.

For centuries, educated Americans have felt politically superior, but culturally inferior, to Great Britain. By the second half of the twentieth century Oxford and Cambridge had the reputation as the best universities in Europe largely because Germany, which had rightly enjoyed that honor before 1914, had damaged and discredited itself in so many ways. Certainly in the 1970s the United States had a more versatile historical profession than the British and boasted very distinguished historians of every major European country, as well as of our own. Yet then, as now, American academics had a weakness for British accents—one which British academics remain well aware of to this day.

British faculty, meanwhile, were expected to work very hard for their living, teaching many individual tutorials to undergraduates at Oxford and Cambridge colleges, and waiting decades to achieve the esteemed title of professor. They understandably saw American history departments as pots of gold at the end of a transatlantic rainbow. Two rising stars, both destined for fame and fortune, had applied for the assistant professorships at Harvard. They were Tony Judt, who had already written two books on the French socialist party, and Geoff Eley, whose dissertation focused on the political role of the German Navy League before 1914. Higonnet had arranged to interview them sometime over Christmas vacation. While both of these men were indeed strong candidates, as we shall see, I felt then, and I still do, that with the American job market shrinking to the vanishing point, it would not have been too much to expect American departments to give preference to United States citizens who had had the courage to devote their lives to history.

The job market, indeed, was very much on Ernest May's mind, but he was thinking of an entirely different solution. Working with a friend from the Rockefeller Foundation, he was putting together a program to channel Ph.Ds. from the Humanities into management positions in private business. May and I, I felt, were now good friends, and there was no question that he had great esteem for what I had done. But in a number of remarks, he made it clear that he did not believe that *any* young historian could now expect to land a job at a major university or liberal arts college, and that we all had to have other alternatives in mind. In my own case, I signed up to take the Foreign Service exam during that year and eventually passed it and had an interview. Yet in my heart, I knew that I was not in the least interested in that career.

Sometime during that winter, the search committee interviewed me. On the European side, it included Higonnet, the historian of Russia Richard Pipes, and Wallace McCaffrey, who studied early modern Britain. May and Frank Freidel, who was in the midst of a never-to-be-finished multivolume biography of Franklin Roosevelt, filled out the committee, giving it a 3–2 European-American balance. The interview was a blessing: after a year of waiting for a decision that seemed never to come, I at least had an hour to do something to help my cause. May began with a good question: how would my dissertation help a lecturer preparing some lectures on the origins of the Second World War? I talked about how the great powers' policies towards Eastern Europe reflected their broader objectives. The conversation was lively, and everyone enjoyed themselves thoroughly—including, clearly, Patrice Higonnet. "We don't have to ask you what you would teach," he said at one point—"you'd teach what you are teaching now!" I replied that there were other things I would like to do, including a general history of twentieth-century Europe that was now planned. May told me the next day that it had gone very well, but in a tone that clearly questioned whether it would matter. Decisions still lay ahead. Had Stuart Hughes or David Landes been sitting on that committee things might have been quite different, but they were both gone from the department for good.

And then, on February 1, 1978, I started my own lecture course, History 1961, International Relations, 1871–1975. It met Monday, Wednesday, and Friday at 9:00, in a classroom, as I remember, in Sever Hall. The time (never a popular one) and the amount of reading scared quite a few students away, and I wound up with about 20, including 4 graduate students. One of those was Eliot Cohen, a Government student, who has become a prominent academic, sometime public servant, and public intellectual, most recently as a violent critic of the Trump Administration. Two of the most enthusiastic students were studying the Middle East. Their names were Joanie Garrett and Geri Cohen, as I recall, and I do not know what happened to either of them. Cohen was a very attentive lecture auditor and became the student I looked at most often for feedback from the podium.

I planned the course carefully, taking advantage of everything I had learned about Harvard courses since 1965. The scheme for the reading list, I am proud to say, came from the Higonnet course I had graded for. I have never turned away from an idea, a discovery, or a conclusion simply because of who happened to have conceived of it. The reading list had three parts. Part I included three general texts covering the whole period of the course, finishing up with Adam Ulam's *The Rivals,* a rather informal but remarkably perceptive history of Soviet-American relations during the Cold War. (I was now getting to know Ulam in the Senior Common Room, or weekly faculty watering hole, of Eliot House, where I had re-affiliated as a non-resident tutor.) Part I in its entirety was required before the midterm to ensure that the students were broadly familiar with the whole sweep of the course by then. Part II was divided into fourteen sections on various specific topics, and each student had to pick two. The final examination would include one question based on each. The topics were German unification; the Eastern Question and the Crisis of 1875–8; Imperialism; the origins of the First World War (for which the reading included an entire volume of Albertini); the United States and the First World War; the relationship of socialism, Communism, and wartime diplomacy during the First World War; the Versailles Treaty and its consequences; the interwar diplomacy of the Soviet Union; Nazi foreign policy; the crisis in the Far East that led to Pearl Harbor; the U.S. entry into the Second World War; the early stages of the Cold War; and lastly, a more unusual section entitled, "The Individual in International Relations." As usual, the whole list included many of my favorite books, and the last section was no exception. It began with a wonderful short story set in the Franco-Prussian War by Guy de Maupassant, *Boule de Suif,* and continued with a choice of British novels about imperialism; Remarque's *All Quiet on the Western Front*; Orwell's *Homage to Catalonia*; and John LeCarré's first masterpiece, *The Spy Who Came in From the Cold.* The reading period assignment was Allison's *Essence of Decision* which I was now proselytizing at every turn. The course also required a substantial paper, and I wrote some general guidelines for what it might be. Looking back on it I can see why a good many students were scared away. The ones who were not, however, did not regret it.

The lectures got off to a good start. The course, and the search committee deliberations were briefly interrupted in the first week of February by the great blizzard of 1978, which stranded several thousand cars on Route 128 and nearly covered our own car in the parking lot of our Medford apartment building. I knew when the key search committee meeting was, but May—once again on his way to Washington—did not call me after it. I reached Higonnet late that afternoon from my office.

"Ernest May said he would speak to you," he said. I said that he had not.

"There are three people on the list," he said. He then described Judt and Eley, referring to each as a "phenomenon." "You're the third."

Although later in the conversation he referred to "two jobs," I innocently understood this to mean that we were the three choices for the two positions and that therefore, I would be hired if only one of them turned Harvard down. I labored under that misconception for at least a couple of weeks, but then I heard that Matt Ramsey, Higonnet's student, had been hired for one of the jobs. Investigating, I found that I was simply the third choice for *one* of the jobs.

Cathy was now pregnant and due in mid-August. I had no immediate prospect of employment, having heard nothing from either Michigan or Reed. A year earlier I had felt that my life was everything I could want; now it was collapsing all around me, and it looked as if I might have to start it over. I toyed with the idea of going into business with a new friend of mine. He was William Young, a rare book and art dealer who lived in Wellesley. I had met him about a year earlier, I think, through a mutual friend, Steve Flink who was establishing himself as one of the country's leading tennis writers for the magazine *World Tennis*. Bill was a marvelous eccentric. He had met his wife Dot at an AA meeting—at this point, neither of them had had a drink in many years. He was very successful in the art business and had his own tennis court. He didn't have to work very hard any more, and he spent most of his time dong three things: playing tennis, watching tennis, and researching the case of Sacco and Vanzetti. I knew something about the case, having read Francis Russell's book *Tragedy in Dedham*, which argued that Sacco was guilty. Bill violently disagreed, and during 1977, I think, he had developed a brilliant argument about the evidence in the case tending to confirm Sacco's innocence. He made a further great discovery later that year when Governor Michael Dukakis gave Sacco and Vanzetti a kind of half-pardon and opened the State Police archives on the case. Bill's house and court were a refuge during this terrible year, but I realized the idea of working for him probably wouldn't go very far. Cathy and I also considered buying a Maine country store. In the fall of that year the whole situation had driven me, for the first time, to seek a psychiatric appointment at the University Health Center, and by the spring I was taking a sleep aid. I was frequently exhausted.

I called Professor Ulph, the chairman of the search committee at Reed. He clearly understood where I was coming from but made it clear that the job was for a historian of early modern Europe, which I was not, and that would make me a very tough sell. Hanging up, I decided to offer to show I could do the job. I wrote him a letter declaring that if I were invited out to interview, I would give a talk covering the last few centuries of European history. I decided that it would deal with periods of general war, going back to the Thirty Years' War, which I had studied in the fall of my sophomore year. I did some reading and made some preliminary notes for such a talk. I never was invited out to Reed, but I found myself fascinated by the successive attempts of the Hapsburgs, Louis XIV, Napoleon and Hitler to dominate Europe.

The lecture course was going very well. Every lecture did just what I had hoped. I knew I was doing exactly what I wanted and I knew how good I was, but it seemed my career was nearly at an end. At some point late in the term, two students from the Committee on Undergraduate Education came in to administer questionnaires that would be the basis for an entry in their course guide. It didn't look likely that the course would be in the catalogue the next year, or that any review would appear. In April, I think, May told me he had had a talk about me with Adam Yarmolinsky, an old New Frontiersman now working for the Arms Control and Disarmament Agency of the Carter Administration. I had a talk with Yarmolinsky about working for him in Washington, which seemed to be the most likely possibility to allow me to remain employed and feed my soon-to-be-growing family. But I felt no enthusiasm for it. But then, May gave me a remarkable piece of news. Tony Judt, the first choice for my job, had taken a position at Berkeley, instead, with a promise of early tenure. Eley, no. 2, was also not ready to commit. It was suddenly possible that I might get the appointment after all. Then, I heard from a fellow grad student that Higonnet was talking about someone else as a third possibility. His office was on the same small corridor as mine on the second floor of Robinson Hall, and I went in and confronted him. He assured me that there was no new third choice for the job.

Suddenly, at this point, I got a phone call from Clarion State College in western Pennsylvania. They had advertised a job in European history in the fall, and although I had completely forgotten about applying for it, the department chair now informed me that I was "one of our leading candidates" and invited me to come out an interview—at my own expense. I shared this news with a new friend of mine. Abby Thernstrom was the wife of Stephan Thernstrom, a social historian who had rejoined the department with tenure in 1973. I had met her because she was also giving a freshman seminar, and Cathy and I had begun socializing with them. They were still garden variety liberals at that point, although this was about to change, and they were both clearly taken with me. "If you get it," she said, "go ahead. You'll write yourself out of there." In another staggering development, Princeton University Press forwarded me the manuscript review they had received. It was extremely enthusiastic, highly recommending publication, although it also suggested that the manuscript might be cut by as much as a third. My career was suddenly back on track, except that I was just a couple of months away from unemployment.

My father, who had been a major figure in Democrats Abroad through eight years of Republican rule, was now back in government service, appointed Ambassador to Hungary by Jimmy Carter. He was home on leave as these events took place, and I made the mistake of mentioning the planned trip to Clarion. He had of course been very proud to boast of a son teaching at Harvard, all the more so since both his other sons now held excellent jobs in journalism, but he could not apparently bear the shame of having a son teaching at a Pennsylvania state college. During the next 48 hours he not only harangued me to give up the idea completely, but enlisted my favorite uncle—who was usually far more understanding—to do the same. They thought of me as their brilliant son or nephew destined to bring credit to the family. I thought of me as a historian and every friend I had understood why I was going.

I had a bad cold, I remember, when I took the trip a couple of days later. I was also affected by what my family had put me through. Clarion was in a very pretty and very remote spot. The teaching loads were heavy. Not a single faculty member, I was informed, was working on anything for publication. They were all very cordial. As the chair left me at the airport, I tried to impress upon him that I was serious about the opportunity. Then I flew home.

The next day I went into my office at Robinson Hall and walked down the hall to the main history office. Carol Glassman had left town a year earlier, but Nancy Cramer, the departmental secretary, saw me. "I need to talk to you," she said. "Let's go to your office."

We sat down. I remember that it was a sunny spring day.

"Eley," she said,"is worried about health insurance for his wife, and wants to delay coming for a year. May checked with the department, and you can be reappointed for another year."

My body reacted in two parts. My head and shoulders felt relief, because my family was safe and my career would continue. But my gut felt despair because the nightmare was going to continue.

In succeeding weeks I had the presence of mind to call the Committee on Undergraduate Education and assure them that although it might be too late for History 1961 to be listed in the 1978–9 catalogue, it would be given in any case. I had my oral exam for the Foreign Service and was failed, largely, I suspect, because I told the examiners that I had been renewed for a year and they knew that I wouldn't be joining anyway. Clarion wrote me one sentence telling me that I had not been selected, and I had a last talk with Professor Ulph at Reed. They had hired someone else. I gave my last lecture to an enthusiastic hand, and spoke to several students. "You were wonderful wonderful wonderful!" said Geri Cohen. Last but not least, I submitted a new course proposal to the department for the spring of 1979.

Entitled, "The Problem of Domination over Europe, 1555–1945," it grew out of the several days' work I had done on the talk I had hoped to give at Reed. It was approved.

In the midst of that horrible spring, I had also written a note to one of Harvard's most distinguished faculty members, David Riesman. Not only was he known for his devotion to teaching—James Bryant Conant had hired him to teach in the Gen Ed program—but he was also an authority on American higher education. I sketched out my situation and asked him what he thought I could do to find a job. He replied that he found my situation appalling—for academia as well as myself—but that there was little he could do. He did ask me to come see him, however, and we became friends.

Then Cathy and I took off for Budapest to visit my parents for the better part of a month. That month coincided with most of the World Cup in Argentina, which I watched alone, late at night, with total concentration. I had been introduced to the tournament four years earlier during my dissertation research in Britain when it took place in Germany, and the Germans beat the Dutch 2–1 in the final. We flew home on about June 19, when the tournament was nearing its climax.

The next day, another beautiful late spring day, I took the bus into the office and checked my mail. There was a note from the History Department at the University of Michigan, where I had applied for a German history job many months before, with no result. The note thanked me for my interest. "We have offered the position to Geoffrey Eley of Cambridge University," it read, "and we are delighted to report that he has accepted."

The next few minutes may have been the last unreservedly happy ones of my life. I had the job, I had six years to write another book, and my future was assured. I called Cathy. Then I literally ran down the hall to look for May in the history office. Nancy Cramer told me he was in Washington, and I told her what I had. Then she gave me the number to reach him there. I went back to my office and called him.

"Hello," I said. "I've just received this letter." I began to read it to him, and he cut me off. "Yes, I know about that!" he said.

"Then I'm all set?" I said.

"No," he said. "Patrice wants to have another search."

"WHAT?"

"Yes," he said. "Apparently he only listed you as the third choice because he thought it would please me."

I made it clear that I felt I had had a firm commitment to receive the job under these circumstances, and that the department had not kept that commitment. "You're entitled to feel that," he said. But he said nothing about reversing the decision. I had to call Cathy again.

I know that Ernest May had genuine esteem and affection for me, but there were hidden depths to him that no one could plumb. Carol Glassman, his secretary, had been deeply disillusioned a couple of years earlier by a very troubling incident in the history office. The departmental secretary—that is, the leading permanent administrator—was another lovely young woman whom we all felt very lucky to have. Bernard Bailyn, who was both the department's most distinguished scholar and one of its more difficult personalities, had asked her to discipline one of the secretaries in the Charles Warren Center, the Americanists' private preserve. She had refused on the grounds that it was none of her business. Bailyn had apparently demanded that May fire her—and he had done so. When dealing with lesser humans such as administrators or junior faculty, Harvard professors had an unhealthy respect for one another's feelings. I had been treated far more fairly during my brief service in the US Army than I was in the Harvard history department.

There were, however, exceptions, and I was not without friends. I immediately called Steve Thernstrom. Somehow, he had not realized what had happened at the critical department meeting, but now he was furious and urged me to fight. So did Peter Stanley, who was stuck in assistant professorial limbo himself. I wrote a calm, careful, detailed letter to May, repeating that both he and Higonnet had assured me that under these circumstances the job would be mine, and asking the department to make good on those assurances.

This was the great crisis of my professional life, and my reactions were heightened. On the Wednesday of that week the last three World Cup games before the final were being screened on closed-circuit TV at one of Boston's downtown movie palaces. I went with two British friends even though I had to finance the three $25 tickets. (They eventually repaid me.) Holland beat Italy 2–1, Brazil beat Poland 3–1, and Argentina, needing to beat Peru by 4 goals to reach the final, beat them 6–0 in a match now widely thought to have been fixed. It was one of the most exciting sporting days of my life. It let out around 5:00, and I took the T to Harvard and drove home to Medford. I had a minor accident in the parking lot. Unfortunately I did not get to see the final for many years, because one of my favorite cousins got married that weekend in Connecticut. Had I done so the symbolism might have overwhelmed me. The Dutch, whom I was rooting for, came from behind to tie the game in the last few minutes, just missed a chance to score the winning goal when a shot hit the post in the last minute, and lost in extra time. 40 years later, they have never won the World Cup.

A day or two later I went out to Bill Young's to play tennis and get a break. Two phone calls came for me, both from Harvard, referred by my wife. One was from the general counsel of the university. At some point in my conversations about the situation, the idea that I might sue had come up. I certainly hadn't decided that I would, but the rumor had reached him and he wanted to intimidate me out of such a thought. The second call was worse. It was from a woman in the Dean's Office.

"One of the students in your freshman seminar," she told me, "has died."

Every one of those students had meant a lot to me, but some had meant more than others, and they flashed through my head. "Which one?" I asked.

"Steven Harris," she said. Steve was from Florida, an Andover graduate. He had been one of the two students doing Britain, and he had written the mock cables threatening the other powers that had enabled us to avoid the outbreak of war in 1914 in our simulation. He had died in a car crash. Two days later I wrote a long letter to his family, eventually receiving a printed card in response.

About a week after I had written May—still the chairman—I received a brief reply. Too many full professors were again away from Cambridge for the summer, he wrote, and the matter would have to be taken up in the fall. That, unfortunately, meant that Thernstrom would not be there for the meeting. When I showed the letter to the psychiatrist I was still seeing intermittently he expressed his astonishment. He could not believe that I had not yet exploded, after two full years of twisting slowly in the wind. As it was my emotions were so bottled up that I had to force myself to put music on the record player.

Then, however, occurred something extraordinary and revealing. In the long run publication would determine my future, and my book could be published by Princeton Press—but first, it had to be severely cut. Despite the insanity all around me, I went into my office in the last week of June and began doing what had to be done. Now I learned something about myself: that the past, in the form of my research and writing, was such a source of endless fascination that I would nearly always be able to immerse myself in it, no matter what might be happening in my life. The manuscript had over 500 pages and 100 single-spaced pages of footnotes, and the era of the personal computer and Microsoft word was years away. Yet working on my rusty Hermes manual typewriter, I completed those revisions by early fall, and the book went back to the original reviewer and out to a new one.

Meanwhile, sometime in August, the new edition of the CUE Guide appeared, and I turned to the entry for History 1961. It read as follows.

Despite its absence from the catalogue, History 1961 will be given this Spring. Although Harvard has a plethora of excellent courses which deal, to some extent, with international relations (e.g. Gov 40, Gov 112, Hist 1643, Hist 1333), History 1961 is at least the equal of any of them. History 1961 is a detailed, thoughtful, interdisciplinary survey of international relations in the last century. Dr. Kaiser approaches the historical phenomena from a political science perspective. Although some students feel that the scope may be too broad, most agree that if a survey of such an extensive period is possible, then this course accomplishes the feat. Several students state that, because the course moves so quickly, some background is extremely helpful.

Dr. Kaiser is almost unanimously praised, both as an individual and as a lecturer. Students find him easily approachable and appreciate his relaxed attitude. He is open-minded and willing to listen to and present differing opinions. This quality becomes particularly evident in the optional biweekly sections, which he personally conducts.

In his lectures, Dr. Kaiser presents a great deal of well-ordered, enlightening information in a fascinating way. Each lecture is a case study of the actions of some major actor or country at a particular time. At the end of the course, with each case study in mind, the student must try to create his own overview or synthesis.

Students find that, although a great deal of reading is assigned, all of it need not be done to succeed in the course. Nonetheless, many students do most of the reading because they enjoy it. Respondents suggest that the reading be used to develop themes and organize principles. Lectures provide more than enough factual information.

Dr. Kaiser is praised for his overall organization of Hist 1961. The readings are divided into fourteen categories. Although the student must have some familiarity with each category, he is expected to know two parts extremely well for the final. Students praise the hourly as being fair and thought-provoking.

Although everyone benefits from Hist 1961, the students who seem to find it least productive are those who want more structure and synthesis. Students who wish to think and actively create their own framework for the diverse and abundant material, with the guidance of a thoughtful professor, find the course of the best of their academic careers.

Twelve years earlier, young, innocent, and all ears, I had sat in a Harvard lecture hall for the first time. Almost from the first moment, and certainly from the first term, I had had an extraordinary sense of what a good lecture could do, Wasiolek, Jameson, Hoffmann, Pettigrew, Stuart Hughes, Wehler, and, on his best days, May, had shown me what was possible. Now I had managed to put what they had given me together in my own way, and I was continuing a great tradition in undergraduate education. And the students knew it.

I already knew very well that elite academic opinion viewed teaching—especially undergraduate teaching—as a necessary annoyance that took professors away from their real work of writing, and that therefore should be allowed to take up as little time as possible. Even those professors who obviously loved it and put their heart into it—like Hughes or Hoffmann—did not let their feelings show outside their classrooms. But I could not fall in line with the prevailing unwisdom, not only because I had found my true calling in the classroom, but also because I think that the intellectual demands of good teaching are at least as important as those of research and writing. One cannot teach at the highest level without a thorough grasp of one's subject, the ability to express one's self simply and clearly, and above all, the ability to put events in larger perspective. Those are the skills that have almost vanished within the historical profession in the last thirty years, with terrible consequences.

On August 24 my son Dan was born. School started about a month later, featuring a reprise of the freshman seminar and another round of sophomore history tutorial. Meanwhile, I lobbied a couple of senior faculty—Franklin Ford and the Americanist David Donald, whom I had worked with on a department committee—regarding the coming department meeting about my appointment. Both were sympathetic, and Ford said he regretted not having been involved in the search.

The day finally came and I found myself in May's office again. "I am authorized to offer you a three-year contract as an assistant professor," he said, "starting this year." He paused. "I was instructed to tell you that renewal is unlikely." I am not aware of any other assistant professor who did not serve for six years.

"Was there any unhappiness about this—other than the obvious?" I asked, referring to Higonnet.

"He wasn't there," May said. The man whose duplicity had caused the crisis had skipped the meeting rather than try to defend himself. "But yes, there was plenty of unhappiness." The message was clear. I had three years to find another job, a quest that so far had proven fruitless.

Cathy now insisted that we spring into action on the real estate front. These were the inflation-ridden 1970s, and mortgage interest rates had gone to 9%. We had saved quite a bit of money the previous year. By Christmas we had found our property: an ancient, almost unimproved Victorian just off College Ave in Medford. We immediately had to spend $5,000 that we got written into our loan on a new roof, a new fireplace, and some new plumbing. We became adept do it yourselfers and actually rebuilt the kitchen as well. The next two years were, in addition to everything else, the toughest ones financially that we ever had, and really the only time in my adult life that I had to watch my checking account carefully to see that it did not run out by the end of the month. The house was large, although the third floor was unfinished, and it would have made a wonderful long-term home.

Having sent the manuscript off, I plunged into teaching again. The freshman seminar, alas, was a big disappointment. The students I managed to attract simply did not compare to the ones the previous year, with the exception of Michael Levitin, a Virginian whom I unfortunately assigned to Great Britain instead of Germany or Austria-Hungary were he would have contributed the most. He is the only one of them with whom I have remained in touch. But my sophomore tutorial was another matter entirely.

I had been switched to sophomore history tutorial in the previous year. It was a very different experience from what I had been through in 1965–6, consisting of six one-month units on various topics of current historical interest. A committee made up the reading lists. There were units on Marx, on Martin Luther, on the Cold War, the Chinese Revolution, and on North American slavery. Most of my students in the tutorial came from Eliot House where I had affiliated, and they were an amazing group.

Michael Stern, a graduate of the Dalton School in New York, announced himself as the roommate of Matthew Diller, whom I had taught the year before in my freshman seminar and who was now majoring in government. It was not until several weeks afterwards that another faculty member in Eliot House dropped it that he was the son of the famous violinist Isaac Stern. Michael was enthusiastic, if a bit manic, and reminded me a bit of myself 10 years earlier. He was struggling to define himself while remaining very much in the aura of his family. He eventually succeeded and is now the Music Director and conductor of the Kansas City Symphony. We have never lost touch. An equally remarkable personality was Vada Hill, a black graduate of Cincinnati's elite Walnut Hills High School. Vada had some motivational problems that year, but he always had very intelligent things to say and was never shy about saying them. I lost touch with Vada after leaving Harvard but reconnected with him in 2008. He has been very successful in the corporate world. In tutorial he clashed frequently (if cordially) with Joe Triebwasser, a middle-class New Yorker with a far more elitist temperament than any of the others. Sanity came from Jenny White, a lovely young woman from Watertown who seemed to be one of the world's nicest people. "Jenny is the most together person in the whole tutorial," Vada once remarked, and I could not disagree. I also lost touch with her but reconnected in 2007. She is now a clinical psychologist. Last but not least was a Californian, Arturo Velasco, who was generally quiet (Stern, Hill, and Triebwasser took up the time just fine), and eventually told us that he hoped to be a monk. And in the spring they were joined by Matthew Diller, who decided to move from government to history. I never had a class that I looked forward to more.

Matthew Diller

I took three classes with Professor David Kaiser during my first three years at Harvard College—a freshman seminar on the origins of the First World War in the 1977–78 school year; a seminar on the struggle for hegemony in Europe in 1978–79 and a sophomore tutorial in history during the same year.

David had a profound influence on my college career and no doubt beyond, especially because I first encountered him during the fall of my freshman year. The First World War seminar was organized in a novel way—each student was assigned to specialize in one major power for the course of the semester. The structure made for particularly engaging class discussions as students each brought something different to the table. Of course, the narrative leading up to the First World War is immensely gripping, and the War itself is one of the great fascinating puzzles of history—how could Europe plunge itself into such a catastrophe over matters that in retrospect seem hardly worth the candle? I believe for all of us in the class it was an incredibly absorbing academic experience. For me, it helped cement a love of the study of history that continues to this day.

The seminar on Hegemony in Europe was similarly novel in that it examined three major attempts by a single power to establish domination over Europe—Spain in the 16th Century, France under Napoleon and Germany in the first part of the 20th Century. Thus it covered different nations in different periods. In an era of specialization, it is rare to see a course like this offered as it demands tremendous knowledge that spans time and place.

Finally, the sophomore tutorial for history majors was a curriculum pre-set by the History Department. It also spanned the centuries and the globe. I remember the conversation as particularly lively.

So here are some observations about seminars taught by David Kaiser in the late 1970s at Harvard:

1. They reflect David's wide-ranging curiosity about history and his intellectual ambition. He always focused on big-picture

questions and got students engaged with the grand questions of history.

2. Discussion in a David Kaiser seminar had a level of animation, passion, and engagement that I have rarely seen in a classroom (I say this as someone who has been an academic and teacher for 25 years). Classes often followed a pattern. Students would go around the room offering their interpretation of views of the subject matter. It would be interesting and respectful, but tame. David would then interject his own opinion which was generally unexpected and often shockingly out of the box. The class would then erupt in reactions—people both agreeing and more often disagreeing with David, and then engaging each other. The time flew by, and by the end of the session, the students were generally in a calamitous uproar.

3. David would come to know each of the students well—how we would react to a given argument or issue, what our leanings were. This would enable him to bring students into the conversation by drawing on how he would predict each of us would react to something. Equally important—he cared about what we had to say. It was always he clear he was open to learning from us, as well as imparting information and ideas.

The bottom line is that classes were hugely fun and the history itself leaped off the page—the debates were filled with energy. He taught us not to be afraid to form our own views and not to worry if those views were dramatically different than received wisdom. We could evaluate and form arguments as well as anyone.

He also impressed us with the idea that nothing is inevitable and that things could have gone differently if the individuals involved had made different choices—he was a great believer in human agency. Looking back we can appreciate the context and pressures that led to various decisions, but the history of world events is ultimately about people and decisions they made. This is not to say that he neglected larger social and cultural backdrops, far from it, but David's interest was principally in how individuals responded and how looking back, we should view these responses.

I am grateful to at David for the passion and energy he brought to bear in the classroom but also for his intellectual honesty and fearlessness.

～

My lecture course resumed in the spring, and thanks to the CUE guide, more than 60 students signed up and I moved into Harvard Hall 201, one of the best remodeled medium-size lecture halls on campus. The atmosphere was electric almost from the beginning: the students expected something great and were not disappointed. Meanwhile, I debuted my new conference course on attempts to rule all Europe. Looking back at its reading list, I am rather astonished by the breadth of view that it embodied.

Four leaders had attempted to achieve some form of domination over Europe from 1559 through 1945: Philip II of Spain in the late 16th century, Louis XIV 100 years later, Napoleon in the early 19th century, and Germany from 1914 through 1945 in the 20th. I did not think one could do justice to all four in a term, and in the two iterations the course was destined to have, I dropped Louis XIV from the first, and Philip II from the second. Like the freshman seminar, the class met weekly for two hours. Each one-month unit began with general reading on the period and its most important leader. Then, however, each student took over responsibility for a particular topic area. Here is where I am retrospectively impressed by my creativity and ability to find the necessary readings.

The topic areas were key personalities and their motivation for conquest; the role of ideology; the economic basis of hegemony; the administration of conquered territories; the sources of resistance; military factors; naval factors; the role of Britain; the role of the Americas; and the role of decision-making processes, an attempt to extend the Allisonian approach to earlier periods. After the first week of each term, the classes were mostly taken up by presentations by the students who had taken responsibility for these topic areas. The topic areas also became the basis for their final papers. The initial cohort of students for the class included Matthew Diller, Steve Biddle and Melissa Scott from the freshman seminar. Matthew wrote a wonderful paper about decision-making processes under Philip II, Napoleon, and Hitler, and Steve did a great job on military factors. I, meanwhile, had decided that I was going to turn this course into a book. Like *Economic Diplomacy and the Origins of the Second World War*—the new title Princeton Press and I had settled on for the book we were preparing together—this was a huge undertaking whose outcome I could not predict, but I was determined to give it a try. By the next year, 1979–80, I was reading whatever I could find on the era of Louis XIV, and taking careful typewritten notes as usual. I still thought that works of great scope offered the best chance of distinguishing myself from the great mass of young historians competing for very few jobs.

Eventually, as we shall see, the course did become a book. Nearly 30 years after I gave it, in January 2009, my wife and I were guests at an inauguration party held by my student Vada Hill in Washington. Also there was a law professor named Tony Perez, who had written his paper on Philip II, Napoleon, and Hitler in 1979 and still remembered the course very well. He had also read the book that it had become in 1990.

During these years the history department began having annual one-day retreats for all faculty. At one of them, someone began talking about how historians were now writing relatively narrow monographs rather than broad synthetic treatments. I raised my hand during discussion and suggested, I think, that synthesis remained a key part of the historian's task. John Clive, a senior professor, responded. "But what are you going to do?" he asked. "Get up in your last lecture like 'Frisky' Merriman in History 1 [a western civilization survey during the inter-war period]? He used to take his pocket watch out and hold it swinging back and forth like a pendulum, saying that one side was 'liberty' and the other was 'authority!'" The whole room burst out laughing as if on cue at such a naively simplistic view of the past. When we next broke, I approached Jim Wilkinson, another junior faculty member whose teaching career, as it turned out, was coming to an end. I told him that in my opinion, the flood of monographs should allow us to do what Merriman had done—only better. I can still see the shock on his face. I learned more about Merriman four decades later, writing *No End Save Victory*, about US entry into the Second World War.

I remember one job that was offered that year: a position in German history at Georgetown. Although technically my specialty was European diplomatic history, Germany played such a big role in my forthcoming book, and I had now done so much teaching in modern Germany that I felt fully qualified. I attended the AHA convention that year—I can't remember where it was—and had a very cordial interview with a Georgetown committee. One of them wanted to know why I was applying since I was now a Harvard assistant professor, and I explained that Harvard assistant professors were advised not to expect tenure. None had received it now since 1970, and it was going to be a number of years more before anyone did again. But a few weeks later I called the chairman and was informed that I had been eliminated from the search because I was not an actual specialist in Germany.

That was, I see now, a prophetic episode that explained why I was never destined to hold a permanent job in a major university history department. My job market strategy was a failure. That was the only time, I believe, that I ever got to the point of an interview for a job in French or German history, either one of which, I am quite sure, I could have taught very effectively. Every job a department advertised had a very specific description, and with dozens of candidates, departments invariably gravitated towards the men and women whose interests fit it most exactly, rather than look for the most promising or intellectually ambitious scholar. Breadth of interests, I eventually realized, reduced, rather than increased, one's marketability.

In 1978–79, two episodes confirmed that I was certainly one of the leading educators in the Harvard history department. Joe Triebwasser, the smartest student in my remarkable sophomore tutorial, won the History Department prize for the best essay written in sophomore tutorial, a comparison of

Marx and Tocqueville. Meanwhile, I advised the senior thesis of a senior from Chicago, Jonathan Alter, on the overthrow of Ngo Dinh Diem and the advent of the Vietnam War. Jon was a Crimson reporter who had found his way into the Uses of History course with May, Neustadt and myself in the previous year. His thesis was by far the biggest academic effort he made at Harvard, and he did a great job. We had long conversations about it in my office as his thesis evolved, and he interviewed several surviving figures in the story, including a key CIA agent, Lucien Conein, and Averell Harriman. He received two summa minus readings and a magna minus reading. The latter particularly irritated me because it came from a fellow graduate student whom I did not like. I had played tennis with him a few times, and although he was a somewhat better player than I was, he made sure of his victories by cheating at crucial moments.

I was serving that year on the department's Board of Examiners, which supervised the awards of prizes and degrees. One such prize was annually awarded to the best undergraduate thesis that year. Because of the magna minus reading, Jon's average grade was not quite the highest, but at least two of my colleagues on the board thought that his thesis was, in fact, the best. I don't think I have ever shared this with Jon, who remains a friend, but I could not bring myself to join them in trying to get the prize awarded to him. Fairness has been an obsession with me all my life—the effect, probably, of being a middle child—and I didn't think Jon should benefit from having his adviser on the Board. In addition, while I thought the magna minus reading was wrong, I knew how random the grading process tended to be, and I thought everyone had to be prepared to live with it. In the end Jon did not get the prize, but I knew that I had probably advised the best senior thesis written that year and the best sophomore essay, all the while teaching a very successful lecture course and a groundbreaking conference course.

Jonathan Alter

I first met David when I was a junior at Harvard in 1977–78. That year, as an undergrad, I took a course at the Kennedy School of Government on the uses and misuses of history, taught by the legendary political scientist Richard Neustadt and distinguished historian Ernest May. We met in that class, and the next year, David became my thesis adviser.

My senior thesis in the history department was about U.S. policy in Vietnam in 1963 and 1964 and how it moved from a counter-insurgency effort to a more conventional military intervention. David was an extremely attentive thesis adviser who gave me personal attention that I never would have received had I convinced a full professor to advise me. I did go to Ernie May partway through for advice; May was helpful. He was— if I remember right—the one who suggested I use Robinson and Gallagher's analysis of how the client state calls the tune (they were scholars of British imperialism in Egypt) as a frame for my analysis of the relationship between Washington and Saigon in the wake of the Diem coup. But it was David who worked with me regularly and helped me make my 100-page thesis good enough to receive a summa cum laude. (Unfortunately my grades outside the history department were such that I cascaded from summa all the way down to plain cum laude at graduation).

I didn't always take David's editing well. I remember that he met me a couple of times in tennis clothes and told me he was a line judge. I thought that captured his personality perfectly— fastidiously ruling things I wrote in and out of bounds. At age 21 I might have preferred someone cool—like Jim Thomson, head of the Neiman Foundation, who used to take me out for liquid lunches—but I also knew my thesis would be much better for David's efforts and that I was lucky to have him. It started as a burden for me and became the best experience of my four years at Harvard because, with the exception of one David Donald class on the American Civil War, it was the only thing I put all of my energies into. It also prepared me for the analytical approach—with plenty of historical context—that I brought to my Newsweek work and for writing books.

One of my thesis readers—an Asian-American woman scholar—advised me to prepare my thesis for publication but I never did. Had I done so, I might have beaten David to the punch since his book *American Tragedy* covered much of the same ground some years later, though by that time with much greater access to documents from the period.

I remember meeting David at the Harvard Club in NYC to talk about it. He later footnoted me for some help I gave him in the Newsweek archives, but I remember being a bit disappointed not to be in his acknowledgements. I learned later that David had no copy of my thesis and thus no access to rare interviews on the subject with Lou Conein, Michael Forrestal and Averell Harriman—key players from the Vietnam era who were dead by the time he wrote what turned out to be a first-rate book.

We were out of touch for long periods, but I remember feeling he got a raw deal in academia. It reminded me of why I made the right choice in becoming a journalist, though even in college I knew that academia wasn't for me—that "academic politics are so bitter because the stakes are so small," as Kissinger said.

I was delighted to resume our own friendship after so many years and grateful to David for his sage advice on George Marshall when I was considering a biography of him. (I'm writing a biography of Jimmy Carter now instead). I've been influenced and informed by much of David's writing over the years, and it's impressive to see him soldiering on despite career setbacks. He is a good example of how a dedicated scholar can make a great contribution even if he doesn't scale the heights of the greasy pole of academia.

~

In the fall of 1979 the penultimate year of my contract began. Fearing that the deterioration of the freshman seminar might continue, I dropped it—but I added a whole new lecture course. In the previous year, I had offered to fill the still-vacant slot of History 61, the projected 20th-century Europe survey, but May had replied that these courses were being reserved for senior professors. I was rather shocked later that year when an old friend of mine from another university department interviewed for an assistant professorship and told me that he had been asked whether he wanted to teach it. Instead, I decided to venture into territory I did not know as well, and added a term on international politics from 1740 to 1871, focused on Europe, to make a two-course sequence with my existing course. That involved a lot of work, and many was the day that I spent in my office putting an entire lecture together for the next day. I lectured on Frederick the Great and Maria Theresa from the 1740s through the 1760s, on Britain and the American Revolution, and, over a span of a couple of weeks, on the wars of the French Revolution and Napoleon. Then came the Congress of Vienna, Metternich, Europe and the American Civil War, and Bismarck. It was many years before I learned about the impact the course had on one student.

James Goldgeier

I arrived at Harvard as a freshman in 1979 preparing to be pre-med. For the most part, my freshman course load was pretty standard: freshman writing, economics, and chemistry.

I was looking for a 4th course and was talking to a junior I met through a friend to get advice. He suggested I take European Diplomatic History 1740–1870 from Professor David Kaiser.

I had taken American history in high school, but that was it, much to the chagrin of my mother, who taught ancient and medieval as well as world history at another high school. I was a little intimidated at the idea of taking a course that wasn't an intro, but luckily Harvard lets you shop around for classes, so I figured I would sit in the first week and see what it was like.

I was hooked from the moment I walked through the door. Professor Kaiser brought to life extraordinary figures I had never heard of, like Maria Theresa and Frederick the Great. He would walk slowly back and forth across the front of the classroom, explaining the European state system of that period and discussing the diplomatic prowess or lack thereof among the different figures. I wouldn't have known Metternich from Bismarck when I started. But I was enthralled by these larger-than-life figures and their machinations. Compared to chemistry, this seemed much more fun! I dropped pre-med (that too, was to my mother's chagrin) and never looked back.

A year later, I went to the history department to learn more about the major. What I learned was that Professor Kaiser had left Harvard, as had another popular young professor, Molly Nolan. I was furious, especially because the 1870-present European diplomatic history course wasn't being taught that year. (I finally was able to take it the spring of my senior year.) I wandered over to the government department and signed up for that major, ultimately pursuing my Ph.D. in political science and becoming an academic. But I never lost my love for diplomatic history, and the love for the subject that Professor Kaiser instilled in me has stayed with me through my academic career and shaped the work that I do to this day.

Whenever I teach, I aspire to inspire my students as Professor David Kaiser inspired me.

∼

I did sophomore tutorial again, and the class included Michael Levitin, who had been the star of the freshman seminar the previous fall. It also included a young man named Jim Hershberg, who confessed that he was suffering from severe motivational problems, but who eventually parlayed an undergraduate thesis on Harvard President James Conant into a fine career as an historian. Money remained very tight in the Kaiser household in the midst of inflation, and I had taught a summer school course in the summer of 1979 and turned my lecture courses into university extension courses, teaching two evenings a week, during this academic year.

Michael Levitin

I first met David Kaiser forty years ago, in September 1978, when I was a freshman at Harvard and David was an Assistant Professor of History. The world was different then: the most advanced technology we had was the stereo and the electric typewriter. Without smartphones and ear-buds, students talked to each other as they crossed the Yard. But bliss it was to be a college freshman, as it ever was.

Harvard's freshman seminar program allows first-year students to work directly with faculty members. David offered a seminar on the origins of the First World War. There were 8 of us in the seminar, each focused on one of the principal countries: Germany, France, Russia, Italy, Austria-Hungary, the Balkans, and England. (Two students covered Germany. England was "my" country.) The seminar progressed chronologically, from the Balkan crises of the 1870s through August 1914. Although the seminar focused on international politics and diplomacy, we also spent a week on domestic politics, social movements, and cultural developments. (The readings on England for that week included articles and book-excerpts on the suffrage movement and H.G. Wells.) And David dedicated a session to Graham Allison's *Essence of Decision*, which laid out three conceptual frameworks for understanding the behavior of national governments. Allison's models—"organizational process" and "governmental politics"—sharpened our analysis of decision-making and the impending crisis. Each week, David provided study questions to guide our reading and shape the discussion. We met at Hilles Library on Wednesday afternoons beginning in mid-September. As the semester and seminar progressed, the days shortened—the lights going out across Europe—and the world moved ineluctably towards catastrophe.

David was an extraordinary seminar-leader. Some of this is evident from the design of the seminar, which reflected David's remarkable knowledge of the material. In class, David asked probing questions and encouraged vigorous discussion. The readings allowed each student to contribute at multiple levels and from multiple vantage points, from the broadest to the country-specific. More notable was David's ability to ask the right question, at the right time, of the right student. It was my first semester in college so I had no perspective, but even now, after many years of college and graduate school, and having been an adjunct professor (and seminar-leader) myself, I have never seen better.

Unlike most faculty members, David also taught a section of the sophomore tutorial in history. In my sophomore year—1979–1980—David was my sophomore tutor.

Sophomore tutorial was a full year course for 10 students. Each 4-week cycle examined a particular topic, or multiple aspects of a topic, from different perspectives. The topics David had selected for the sophomore tutorial included the Cold War, Martin Luther and the Reformation, American slavery, the French Revolution, and Marx. For example, for the American slavery cycle, we read Fogel and Engerman's *Time on the Cross* and one of its principal critiques, *Reckoning with Slavery*, as well as non-quantitative materials, including *Roll, Jordan, Roll*. At the end of each cycle, David assigned a paper. For the Cold War cycle, David asked us to assess whether the Cold War had ended, and if so, when. (The Reagan era had not yet begun!) The goal of the tutorial was to introduce students to the core skills of professional historians: reading primary and secondary sources critically, analyzing evidence and arguments, and presenting conclusions persuasively in writing.

David showed a lot of skepticism about the use of American military power. Even to a college freshman, it was clear that the war in Vietnam had influenced David's thinking. (With the passage of time, Vietnam's influence on David's approach has become even more obvious.) In the seminar, we studied the Anglo-Russian entente of 1907. While the 1907 agreement did not resolve all differences between England and Russia, David observed that two nations—previously antagonists—had set aside some of their differences and reached an understanding that allowed each country to focus on interests of greater strategic importance than Afghanistan and Persia. Military power, David thought, should be deployed only in service of vital interests.

Although the tutorial and seminar were both small-group courses that emphasized reading and discussion, they differed in significant ways. The tutorial had a broader scope and students with different levels of interest in the topics. And the tutorial offered more opportunities to write and learn from comments on one's writing. David was an outstanding writer and critic. (Reader, you can only imagine what it is like to prepare this reminiscence for *his* book.) And David was an outstanding tutor for all the reasons he was a great seminar-leader, this time displaying his small-group teaching talents across a wide range of topics and methodologies.

May had finally stepped down as department chair, replaced by Wallace McCaffrey, an authority on the reign of Elizabeth I. Despite what May had told me only a year earlier—that I was "unlikely" to be renewed—things were going so well that I asked McCaffrey about that possibility. He replied, in a manner suggesting that he had already thought about it, that while I could *not* be renewed, I could be considered for promotion to non-tenured associate professor. It turned out that four other assistant professors were coming up for that promotion. One, Molly Nolan, a Marxist, taught a popular European history survey. (It was not altogether comprehensive: a student who had taken it once told me that she had not realized, when she finished Nolan's course, that Austria-Hungary had been in the First World War.) Two others, a married couple, were sharing an appointment in Iranian history, and the fourth, Fred Cooper, who had the office next to mine, was just completing his second work in African history. I submitted the manuscript of my book, now scheduled to appear the next year, and several professors showed up unannounced one morning to hear a lecture on Britain and the Napoleonic wars. Steve Thernstrom, however, told me that the department had had a preliminary discussion of these promotion cases and had decided that such promotions would take place only in the most exceptional circumstances—whatever that meant.

Sometime late that fall, McCaffrey in his study on the top floor of Widener library informed me that "the Department decided not to make a promotion, in your case." It turned out that of all the candidates only Fred Cooper had been raised to associate. He left for the University of Michigan a few years later. Steve Thernstrom later told me that no one had said anything negative about me at the decisive meeting. Among the senior faculty, David Donald, a civil war historian with whom I had served on the Board of Examiners, was the only one to talk to me about the vote. He told me that he had voted for my promotion, in part because he knew what a "good citizen" I was. I appreciated that very much. I do wish, now, that I had asked McCaffrey to explain exactly what I might have done that I had not done to secure the promotion.

It took a couple of months for the *Crimson* to discover what had happened. McCaffrey told them that the qualifications for promotion to non-tenured associate were "to be tenurable at a major American university." It was clear that the criteria remained very vague. The story noted that with the departure of Molly Nolan and Mangol Bayat—one of the two Iran specialists—the department would not have a single woman faculty member. In the months that followed a small movement grew up on Molly Nolan's behalf, in particular, arguing that she had been denied promotion because she was a woman. Since I too had been denied despite qualifications that were at least comparable to hers, I did not appreciate this. But throughout the controversy I said almost nothing to the *Crimson*. I wish I had.

Rutgers, meanwhile, was offering a job in European history, and I had applied. I had spent much of 1969–70, as it happened, in northern New Jersey, the only time since 1965 that I had been away from the Cambridge area. I was not enthusiastic about returning, but the Rutgers department had an outstanding reputation. I interviewed with them at the AHA convention—I can't remember where it was—and the interview turned into a wide-ranging discussion that seemed to go very well. I sent them my book manuscript. The historians whom I consulted regarded this as a prestigious possible appointment and I certainly wanted it, but I also wanted congenial surroundings. My dream all along had been to catch on somewhere else around the Boston area, but nothing along those lines ever opened up in the late 1970s.

The write-up in the CUE guide for History 1961 for 1979–80 had been nearly as enthusiastic as the one the year before, and 100 students signed up for it in the spring. I was assigned two graders, both May students: Melanie Billings Yun, who eventually joined the Foreign Service, and Tom Schwartz, who was writing his dissertation on the US occupation of Germany and who has taught American diplomacy at Vanderbilt for many years now. The crowd filled Harvard 201 and included a good many auditors, and again, applause broke out at the end of every lecture. Two freshman, Clare McHugh, and Lisa Mihaly sat front-row center. I had had a friend as an undergraduate named Mark Mihaly, and when I asked Lisa about him, she confirmed that he was. . . her uncle. I was still only 32, and that came as a bit of a shock. What I did not realize until many years later was that those freshmen were the leading edge of Generation X and that a contemporary of theirs named Barack Obama had started school at Occidental College that fall.

Clare McHugh

I attended a private girls high school in Baltimore called Bryn Mawr. It was a pretty academic, traditional place, once headed up by the historian Edith Hamilton (author of *The Greek Way* and *The Roman Way*). Many of my classmates were encouraged to go on to women's colleges, but after visiting Harvard College with my family as part of the 25th reunion of the Harvard Class of 1952 (my father's class) I was determined to enroll at Harvard. Once there, I flirted for a week with some pre-med classes, but quickly reverted to my high school interest in history and in the first semester of my freshman year, the fall of 1979, I took two history courses, one on the early years of the Christian church and another on the history of Germany, both of which I found quite dry.

I heard from some upper classmen that David Kaiser was a more dynamic lecturer, so in late January 1980 I went with my roommate Lisa Mihaly to the first day of his class on diplomatic history on the second floor of Harvard Hall. I remember that Professor Kaiser was surprisingly young and he talked in a very intense and passionate way, a contrast to his older, somewhat formal colleagues I had been taught by in the fall term. From the first lecture, I was engrossed and entranced. This was history taught more ardently than I had experienced before.

Professor Kaiser was the best kind of storyteller, the kind that makes you think about the consequences of actions, how personality determines choices, how chance plays a role in every person's—and every nation's—fate. But he brought the rigor of scholarship to all verdicts about why things turned out the way they did, and he left space for the things we can't, and might never, know. Now, upon 35 years reflection, I realize his teaching was brilliant training for a journalist, who only writes the first draft of history, but needs to constantly assess the different factors that lead to certain outcomes. But at the time I thought nothing of the future utility of this course, only about how entirely absorbing it was to trace the development of modern Germany, the causes of both World Wars, the poignant inter-war period, the aftermath of Europe's collapse. Because Professor Kaiser made the subject so alive and consequential in his lectures, with the readings to amplify the themes that he pointed out, I also learned that it's the quality of the teacher that makes a subject meaningful to the student. That's the key, far more so than the specifics of the material.

Lisa and I became the junior-most groupies in a lecture room full of Kaiser fans. He attracted a very articulate crowd, and he was available after class to further the discussion of the day's themes. He expressed admiration for some of his students' ideas, and he clearly fed off their reactions to the material, but he was always out in front, leading, challenging, and question-ing. It was stimulating and fun to be around him, and I worked hard to keep up. Why study history I was asked some years later by some high-schoolers I was coaching for their O-level exam. The pat answers—so as to better understand the world, so as to be a better citizen—only take you so far. If you studied it the way Professor Kaiser taught it, you were hungry to know and express ideas the way he did, with restless intensity, some impatience with theory, and great relish for the telling details, the quirks of personality, the articulate witnesses who pass their testimony into the future to be interpreted with clarity and generous insight.

~

Eliot House was again the center of my social life at work. The system of resident and non-resident tutors and affiliated faculty had been started to promote student-faculty contact, and I was allowed to eat as many as five meals a week in the dining hall. Matthew Diller and Michael Stern were the nucleus of a group that gathered frequently for lunch. The group also included Amy Wax, a resident adviser who was finishing her medical training, but who eventually decided to become a lawyer instead, and Alan Brinkley, son of the famous newscaster, a history graduate student who was writing his thesis on Huey Long and Father Coughlin, the demagogues of the 1930s. Today Amy is a rather conservative law professor at Penn while Alan has had a very distinguished career as a historian and provost at Columbia. Music was another huge bond among us all.

In early December 1979, I believe, I called my Wellesley Hills friend William Young, the art dealer and intrepid Sacco and Vanzetti researcher, whom I had not seen much of that fall. His wife Dot answered. She had just left him at Mass General for a thorough checkup. He had been complaining of various things for months, she said, and they had to look into it. Bill was eccentric and had always been something of a hypochondriac, and it seemed to me that Dot was not at all sure there was anything wrong with him.

A few days later I called again, and she answered. Bill had just come home from the hospital, she reported.

"So I take it they couldn't find anything wrong with him?" I ventured.

"No, he has terminal cancer," she replied bluntly. He had tumors in his pancreas and his liver. Bill was 53. He was at that time one of my best friends, and their house had been a great refuge in a very difficult time. I was stunned. I asked about coming to see him, but she said he wasn't seeing anyone just yet.

I began thinking. I was convinced that Bill had made very important discoveries about Sacco and Vanzetti, discoveries that should not die with him. I called Dot again and suggested that he might give me his research archive and that I might try to turn it into a book at some point. She obviously was interested. A few days later I called again, and Bill answered. I asked him if I could come visit and he said yes. The next weekend, I did. He was in excellent spirits and determined to remain upbeat. "Dot told me what you said about the book," he said. "I think it's a great idea, and if anything comes of it, you can share the royalties with her." I spoke to him on the phone a few more times but that was the last time I ever saw him.

Sometime that winter I was contacted by Prof. Rudy Bell of Rutgers about the job there. He made it clear that he was very impressed by my book manuscript and that he regarded me as a leading candidate. He indicated that he had run into trouble because the departmental historian of Germany, whose name I cannot remember, had not wanted someone with my level of German history expertise in the department, but when I arrived on campus for an interview he assured me that the man was now on board. He spent most of his time trying to sell me on Rutgers, the academic atmosphere there, and the department's commitment to research. He took me around, meeting various faculty members, and then I gave a talk.

It is one of the horrors of academia that one is always judged, in theory at least, on one's next project, rather than one's last one or on the whole body of ones work. Bell had advised me not to talk about *Economic Diplomacy and the Origins of the Second World War*, my forthcoming first book, since they already had the manuscript. Thus I talked instead about my projected work on eras in which one power had tried to dominate Europe, then tentatively entitled "Instability and Hegemony in Europe, 1559–1945." The argument, which was at a very early stage of development, was that Philip II, Louis XIV, Napoleon, and Hitler had taken advantage of widespread political instability to increase their power and influence. The project impinged upon the interests of Herbert Rowen, a very distinguished historian of early modern Europe in general and the Dutch Republic in particular. He was the author, editor, and translator of several rather broad works on the topic. In an earlier private meeting, he had vented his feelings about the sad state of the European side of my own department. "Higonnet doesn't exist, as far as I can see," he said, referring to his poor publication record, and he said similar things about a couple of others. But Rowen did not like my talk. "You haven't got anything new here," he said, and I dissented. As a matter of fact, my thinking on the project was not nearly as sophisticated as it later became, but I would have hoped that my ability to bring *Economic Diplomacy* to a successful conclusion would have inspired confidence that I could do the same for this one. In his case, apparently, it didn't. Afterwards, Bell complimented me for having dealt with his criticism without losing my equanimity. As he drove me to the airport, he said that one of the most satisfying things about running the search was to have read as fine a manuscript as my own.

A week or so later, I think, he called to tell me that I had not gotten the job. I honestly cannot remember who did. He was clearly depressed and remarked that "in a rational world" things might have turned out differently. That was, as far as I knew, the last job on the table for me that year. As an alternative to academia I had now pretty much settled on teaching in a private school. I had met with history chairs at both Andover and Exeter over the previous two years, but neither one had ever actually had a position. I was registered with an agency that handled such appointments and got one or two calls, but I was not prepared to leave academia until I had to. Then, chance took a hand.

Tom Childers, my best friend in graduate school, had finished his dissertation, which became the book *The Nazi Voter* at the same time that I had finished mine, in the spring of 1976. He had been ready to give up on academia then and in fact, was negotiating for a government job in Washington, but suddenly, Franklin Ford, his dissertation adviser, had suggested him for an assistant professorship at the University of Pennsylvania. Within a week the job was his. He remained there, as it turned out, until his retirement in 2016, keeping the lecturing tradition he had imbibed at Harvard alive in two extremely popular courses on Nazism and the Second World War. Since his college days Tom had been friendly with Walter MacDougall, whom he had met in a summer study program in Germany. MacDougall had earned his Ph.D. at the University of Chicago and published his dissertation as a book entitled *France's Rhineland Diplomacy, 1914–1924*. His career had been having its ups and downs.

MacDougall had begun very well, securing an assistant professorship at Berkeley. But his book had had a very mixed reception, including a scathing review from a professor at Rhode Island College named Sally Marks and a violent attack at an AHA panel, which I witnessed sitting next to Childers, by none other than Steve Schuker. He did not in 1980 expect to get tenure at Berkeley, and he was looking around for other jobs. What Tom told me, perhaps in March 1980, was that MacDougall had just interviewed for a job at Carnegie-Mellon University in Pittsburgh (as it then was) and that they had turned him down.

I do not believe that I ever admitted this to anyone at the time, but Carnegie-Mellon was really not on my map. I had been aware of Carnegie Tech, but I had never heard of the Mellon Institute, an art school, nor did I know that they had merged and were trying, in their own way, to turn themselves into a full-fledged university. Nor had I taken any notice of their ad in the AHA bulletin. When I checked it I could see why. It offered a joint appointment in the departments of history (actually history and philosophy) on the one hand, and social sciences on the other, and the wording certainly did not refer specifically to diplomatic history. But now I contacted the chairman of the history and philosophy department, Ludwig Schaefer, and sent them my ms. A few days later I received an enthusiastic call from him—"we like what you do," he said— and we arranged to fly me to Pittsburgh. By a great stroke of luck, Jim Davidson, one of my best friends in college and my roommate for a year after college, had just gotten a job as a reporter for the *Pittsburgh Press* and moved there. Evalinn Welling and their young daughter had not yet joined him. He met me when I arrived.

Carnegie Mellon (to use the name that it subsequently adopted) was working very hard to put itself on the map. Its most distinguished faculty member, the psychologist and computer scientist Herb Simon, wrote years later in his memoirs that the administration had a plan for the school and expected faculty to fall in line with it. The school had about half a dozen major parts. The Mellon College of Art—the former Mellon institute—included one of the nation's best drama programs. The Graduate School of Industrial Administration, Simon's home, doubled as an economics department. The engineering school—the descendant of Carnegie Tech—was also one of the nation's best, and it included the computer science department, which was also very strong. The School of Urban and Public Affairs was CMU's equivalent of the Kennedy School at Harvard. Last but hardly least, the College of Humanities and Social Sciences had descended from the women's branch of Carnegie Tech, the Margaret Morrison College of Home Economics, named after Andrew Carnegie's mother. The university president, Richard Cyert—an economist—had turned the H&SS, as it was known, over to another economist, Pat Crecine, as Dean, with the mission of building it into a world-class school—in a particular way. Cyert and Crecine did not believe that any of the departments in H & SS, including history, could compete with major departments across the board, but they charged each of them with selecting a subfield or two in which they could be as strong as anyone. That—in a strange way—was what opened the door to me.

The main subfield within history was the relatively new and now burgeoning field of social history. A few years earlier, CMU had landed one of the leading figures in the field, Peter Stearns, who was in the midst of a long and turbulent career and life. Born in 1936, Stearns, like me, had earned his B.A. and Ph.D. at Harvard by 1963. He had then earned tenure at the University of Chicago, but left to go to Rutgers, by which time he was married to his second wife. That marriage had also broken up, and at Rutgers, he had married a graduate student named Pat Branca. Using the same gambit that Stuart Hughes executed when he left Harvard, Stearns had then landed both himself and Branca jobs at CMU. That situation had become difficult when their marriage also broke up. As I learned before long, the department was now faced with her tenure review a couple of years down the road, but a potentially difficult situation was averted when she decided to quit both CMU and academia. Stearns had recently married his fourth wife, a historian who had decided to switch careers and become a psychiatrist. They had a daughter the exact age of my son Dan. Stearns's goal was to turn the department into a leading center of social history, that is, the history of ordinary people whom history books to this date had tended to leave out. He was an extraordinarily prolific writer, with a highly developed SOP for plunging into a subject, doing some reading, and turning out a quick book.

Stearns, together with another historian of approximately his age, Joel Tarr, had a secondary interest: applied history. This was essentially what I had been teaching with May and Neustadt at the JFK School, and Tarr knew May. And this was the departmental specialty to which I was expected to contribute.

The Social Sciences department, meanwhile, was a mix of political scientists, economists, and sociologists without a very clear mission. They wanted to add faculty with expertise in strategic studies, which was certainly related to the diplomatic history I did, although not the same thing. I was not convinced that I could find a real home in that department, and Pat Crecine, when I met with him privately, indicated that if it ever developed that I was not a good fit I could move full-time to history. That, as it turned out, was what happened—rather rapidly, indeed.

The chair of the History Department, Lu Schaefer, was an original whose attitudes reflected his German-American roots. He sincerely loved history and was a very effective teacher, but he had never published anything substantial. He was notoriously cheap, carefully controlling the departmental budget, and jealously guarding his authority. That had led Joel Tarr to quit the department and move to Social Sciences just as I arrived. Tarr had started life as an urban historian, and had now become a policy specialist. He was very skilled at the real job of Carnegie Mellon faculty—attracting grants to fill up the university's covers. I shall return to that aspect of the job.

This time I gave my presentation, with Schaefer's encouragement, about *Economic Diplomacy*. It went very well. A few days later, Schaefer called to say that the two departments had met and agreed to make me an offer. The salary—$20,000—represented a raise of a few thousand from what I was making. In subsequent negotiations, I agreed to go on a lengthy tenure clock—another 7 years. The full clock was 9 years, and Schaefer refused to count my first two years at Harvard because I had been only a lecturer, not an assistant professor. He assured me, however, that I *could* come up earlier, and I interpreted that to mean that I might get it as soon as I had another substantial achievement to show. We reached agreement. I called Bill Young, who had heard all about my job travails for the last three years, to tell him the story had a happy ending. He was very weak, but appreciative. It was our last conversation.

The combination of a new baby, a new fixer-up house, and my struggles at work had inevitably taken a big toll on Cathy and me as well. A few weeks later Cathy and I discussed putting our house in Medford—to which I had become quite attached—on the market with some realtors. But another realtor leafleted the neighborhood looking for a house to buy, and we contacted her. Within a few days we had an offer for our asking price—proof that it had been too low. Then, we traveled to Pittsburgh together to check things out there. We could not hope for anything nearly as good, but we found a nice house in Edgewood, a small suburb in the East End of town, in a mixed middle- and working-class section. Our house sat at the corner of two dead-end streets, and the street was full of young children. The town also had a tennis and swimming club a two-block walk away.

In the first week of April, my office phone rang. It was Dot. She began with small talk, but I didn't have to ask why she had called. "Well, Bill died," she said. She invited me to a memorial, where a neighbor—another tennis partner—spoke well. I had also gotten to know her daughter Pat. On the way back to our car I sobbed in Cathy's arms, not just for Bill, but for the whole life that I was leaving behind of which he was such a part. Dot had us out for dinner once more, and I left with all Bill's archive on Sacco and Vanzetti, including the five thick volumes of the transcript of their trial and appeals.

Things were winding down. Various faculty members congratulated me on the job. None that I can remember commented on what my loss would mean to Harvard. That was left to students. At the least meeting of my sophomore tutorial my students presented me with a coffee table book, *Tennis, Game of Motion.* "Thanks for a great year," they inscribed it, and signed it individually. I remember six of them—there were eight—very clearly.

And with all that going on, I see, I started a new phase of my career as well. For the better part of a decade the *New Republic* had been edited by Marty Peretz, who had a dollar-a-year contract, reputedly, with Harvard that allowed him to teach a famous freshman seminar. Richard Nixon had just written one of his periodic books, *The Real War*, and I wanted to review it. I found Peretz on the phone, called him, and identified myself.

"I know about you," he said. He seemed pleased to hear from me. He quickly commissioned the review, and it appeared in April. Nixon had evidently fallen in with the emerging neo-conservative movement, and the book was a blunt plea for the use of maximum force, everywhere, as well as a violent attack on Democrats for "losing" Vietnam. I reviewed a few more books for them in subsequent years.

And then came my last lecture.

Clare McHugh

I can't remember exactly when I learned that David had been denied promotion and would be leaving Harvard, but I recall how incredulous I was. Why would they let go of one of their best, a teacher and scholar who embodied what Harvard represented? Someone who took students along with him on a search for truth? His last lecture was excellent of course, but I sensed how hard it was for him, to be saying goodbye to this joint enterprise. And I felt sorry that Harvard undergraduates coming after me would never have the experience I had had.

~

Harvard 201 was even more packed than usual, because the class had been designated as one that alumni visiting for reunions might attend. The audience also included Michael Stern, Matthew Diller, and Cathy, who heard me lecture for the first time. The topic was the future of Europe and the possibility that its division might ultimately end. I do not have my notes, alas, but I remember speculating that the US, the USSR, and the Europeans would all have to agree upon a new solution. I certainly did not foresee that the Soviet Union might collapse within less than a decade, but I did not believe that the existing situation would last forever. I remember that I copied Stuart Hughes' wording about their thoughts in the years ahead in the last sentence, and the room exploded as everyone rose to their feet. A freshman in the front row handed me another gift, a watch, on behalf of himself and a friend. I was overwhelmed and didn't wait for the applause to finish as I walked out. What I should have said, to conclude was this.

"As you all know, this will be my last lecture here. That is very sad for me, and I know that it's very sad for many of you as well. Other people made that decision and bear the responsibility. They made the same decision in several other cases as well—more or less on the principle that young people simply shouldn't be promoted. That decision makes no sense to me, if only because I don't know what else I could have done that I have not done over the last four years.

"Few, if any of you, will stay around here as long as I have. When I sat out there where you are 15 years ago I was transfixed, and I know I couldn't help thinking, gee, it sure would be something to stand up there and do that. And it was. But whether you are here for four years, seven years, or longer, you will experience some joy and some great frustration. Get what you can out of it. I don't think anyone ever got more out of it than I did. And above all, no matter what may happen. . . . don't ever forget what a privilege it is to study or to teach in the only institution I know where a class is supposed to be something to cheer about."

More than 35 years later, I can see my experience at Harvard in a number of different perspectives.

I am overwhelmed, to begin with, by my review of the intellectual environment of which I was lucky to be a part. The historians who taught me and whom I taught with had very mixed records when it came to publications, and more than a few of them, I can see now, had some form of Asperger's or autism which made them extremely difficult to deal with personally. Some of them, too, had a very irresponsible attitude towards their duties. Only weeks before my departure I got a rude shock involving the reading of a most inadequate senior thesis. I had been tapped as the third reader, indicating that the first two readers had differed widely. The thesis was handwritten, very cursory, and contained important misstatements of fact. I gave it no distinction, meaning that the author would not graduate with honors. On the day the theses were returned I was in the history office, as were many others, looking at all the grades, now on file. The first reader of this particular thesis had been another May student, Zach Narrett, who had also awarded it a no distinction. The second reader had been a distinguished senior faculty member who was known for spending as much of his time as he could in Washington. (He has hardly figured in this account to date.) He had given it a magna cum laude. I stared at it in amazement and showed it to Zach, who stared back. Then the same thought occurred to us in unison. "He didn't read it," I said, and Zack nodded.

But for all that, I sat through hour after hour of lectures and wrote hundreds of pages of papers and exams about great questions of modern civilization. They centered on the politics, the economics, the diplomacy, the warfare, and the great ideas of the last two or three centuries, the centuries that have given us our modern world. I read, and acquired, a tremendous amount of great history. The long and still-continuing controversy over the origins of the First World War which I learned about initially from Sam Williamson; the extraordinary explosion of great books about the origins and impact of National Socialism, most of it written by Germans who had been children during the war; the efforts of many Frenchmen to imagine a just society; and the drama of the early Cold War years were only some of the many gigantic questions in which I had been immersed, on which I had lectured, and to which I still always enjoy returning. At the moment that I departed in 1980, no one could have imagined that within another 30 years, that tradition, within the universities of the West, would be almost entirely dead. We shall look at its long agony in forthcoming chapters.

I also had the extraordinary good fortune to begin my teaching career with very bright, highly accomplished students who were accustomed to doing a great deal of work. Harvard, I now realize thanks to Jerome Karabel's extraordinary book, had never attempted to fill its ranks with the 2000 or so smartest 18-year olds in the country, and the student body still included graduates of certain smaller prep schools, athletes in certain sports, and sons and daughters of the rich and famous whose academic qualifications were undistinguished or worse. But the bulk of the student body was dedicated and very smart, and some remarkable intellectual talents were scattered among them. In short, they enthusiastically took advantage of what I had to offer, and it was a very long time before I got a crack at a similar student body again.

My professional experience, alas, foreshadowed the rest of my career all too closely. I had a somewhat unusual background which had given me a bit of a head start, and I had been a child prodigy as a historian. I had trained myself as broadly as I could, I had chosen a dissertation topic which could easily have been broken down into half a dozen different dissertations, and I had completed it in just three years. I had then put my creativity, breadth of interests, and above all enthusiasm to work in the classroom, with spectacular results. Yet the men who judged me had no algorithm that would allow them to distinguish me from the average bright graduate student or form some idea in their minds as to what I was likely to become. Worst of all, in my opinion, they simply did not value my most important skill: my ability to think big, to ask, and answer, very broad historical questions. I was the kind of scholar whom, decades earlier, James Bryant Conant had sought out to teach general education courses, but there was no more explicit demand for such a person either at Harvard or anywhere else.

I cannot resist comparing my subsequent career to those with whom I competed for slots at Harvard. The two Englishmen who so fortunately decided to join the faculties of UC Berkeley and Michigan, where tenure was on offer, had distinguished careers. Tony Judt, who was ready to bring out two books on the French Socialists, moved from Berkeley to NYU where he was able to form his own center for European studies. His dissertation was his last piece of major archival research, but he wrote several more important books, including *Postwar*, a survey of postwar Europe from 1945 to 2005, and he turned himself into a leading public intellectual. Judt, who was a year younger than I am, was horribly stricken with ALS in his early 60s and died in 2010. He discussed the disease in the *New York Review of Books* and I wrote him an email (I had only met him once or twice) describing our "interaction" back in 1977–8 and thanking him for his good sense in turning Harvard down and thereby allowing me to have a career. He replied warmly.

Geoff Eley is another matter. Having written *Reshaping the German Right*, a trendy history of the German Navy League before the First World War, he became deeply involved in new, postmodern trends of academe in the 1980s and 1990s. That was also his last piece of archival research, although he has written a series of essay-type books in subsequent years. In 2002 he published *Forging Democracy: The History of the Left in Europe, 1860–2000*. A European version of Howard Zinn's *People's History of the United States*, it argued that the whole European movement towards democracy could be traced to various leftist movements. Let me simply say that I do not feel that my own output, which includes four works involving very extensive archival research and a synthetic work of greater scope than anything they attempted, is in any way inferior to theirs. As for Matthew Ramsey, Higonnet's student, he published his dissertation on 18th-century French medicine as a book in 1982, was not promoted by Harvard, and spent the rest of his career at Vanderbilt. He never wrote another book.

I left Harvard knowing that I would probably never return, and arrived at Carnegie Mellon quite doubtful that it was where I wanted to be in the long run. Essentially, although I had not yet arrived at the formula that I eventually did, I knew now what I wanted: to teach in an institution that I might have wanted to attend. That broad umbrella included the Ivy League, the major state universities around the country, and many of the liberal arts colleges where I was very confident that I would feel at home. But sadly, I also left a very different person than I had been just four years before. During the fall of 1979, while I and four others were up for promotion, I had remarked to one of them—accurately—"You see, I go through this every year." The experience of waiting, month after month and even year after year, for decisions meaning professional life or death, made by men who evidently lacked any empathy for what they were putting younger people through, had traumatized me in ways that affect me to this day. I had swallowed a lot of rage during my childhood, and I had done the same for the last few years. My trust in the universe, which had peaked in 1976, was gone forever. Worst of all, as I eventually realized, my unconscious had become convinced that any really good news was only the prelude to something terrible just around the corner. My love for history, however, has continued to sustain me.

V

AT CARNEGIE MELLON

1980–86

The university and the department that I joined in the middle of 1980 had unique histories, and found themselves at a real turning point. The whole College of Humanities and Social Sciences of which History and Philosophy was a part, had been created only seven years earlier, in 1973, replacing the Margaret Morrison College of Home Economics. The senior faculty in history were mostly middle-aged members of the Silent generation (b. 1925–1942). They had earned their doctorates from prestigious universities in the 1950s and early 1960s when the job market was booming—but the Margaret Morrison College had evidently offered the best job they could find. Most of them had only one book to their credit, and at least one had less. But several had adopted the new CMU credo and secured grants for sponsored research. They expected younger colleagues to do the same.

I never knew exactly how the college and department secured new resources at that moment, but they were in the midst of a major expansion, which was most unusual in those days. I was only one of about half a dozen very bright and accomplished young junior faculty who were added in the early 1980s. W. Andrew "Andy" Achenbaum already had a book to his credit and was a rising authority on aging in America. Kate Lynch was another Harvard Ph.D., a student of David Landes, who had finished a book on historical demography and came from a stint at the University of Utah. Adele Lindenmeyr, who had spent one term in my first-year graduate colloquium at Harvard before moving to Princeton, had written her dissertation on charity in late Imperial Russia. Within the next couple of years, we added Anne Rose, the author of a major book, *Transcendentalism as a Social Movement*, who came from Cal Tech, and Andrew Barnes, a freshly minted Ph.D. from Princeton who studied religion in early modern France. And in the mid-1980s we added Lizabeth Cohen, a rising star from UC Berkeley who had written a long dissertation about ethnic groups and the New Deal in Chicago; her husband Herrick Chapman, who wrote on the French aircraft industry in the 1930s; and Mary Lindemann, an eclectic and productive historian of early modern Europe. All of them were put on some variant of the university's interminable tenure clock. From the beginning, many of us regularly ate lunch together, and within a few years we were also teaching together in a required course. We were often joined at lunch by three older colleagues, Gene Levy, Dick Schoenwald and Donald Sutton. Levy, who ran the undergraduate program, had published nothing for many years, but taught creatively and effectively. Schoenwald, who had published a biography of the young Freud, taught an introduction to western art to the students in the art school, changing the reading list almost every term. While he never finished another book, he was a genuine intellectual with ideas about almost everything. Sutton was a British historian of China with a very strong publication record. These three men had something else in common: none of them belonged to the inner circle among the senior faculty.

Coming from four inspiring and traumatic years at Harvard, and initially given very little scope for my talents, I did not get off to a good start in the classroom. My only course in the fall was two sections of The Origins of the Modern World, the western civ course—taught mainly from a textbook—which we provided for the engineering school. I tried to make it interesting, but evaluations suggested that I did not succeed. In the spring I did a scaled down version of my old international politics course that was much better received. My other department, Social Sciences, had me down for a course in the origins of the First World War, but its chair neglected to cross list it under history, and the signup was too small to allow it to proceed. Meanwhile, I continued my new project on eras of European hegemony.

The facilities at Carnegie Mellon for the humanities were mediocre at best. The library was very small and made no real effort to stay current. The University of Pittsburgh library was only a few hundred yards away, and its collection was stronger, and I immediately established a close relationship with our interlibrary loan department, which must have secured at least 100 books for my massive new project over the next seven or eight years. But in another key field—computers—CMU ranked near the top. We did not yet have PCs, but a room containing about 20 monitors attached to a mainframe was just up the long hallway from my office. (Our buildings, made of stone, had been designed to hold machine shops in the Carnegie Tech days) I began writing a section of my new book on the reign of Louis XIV and learning to write on a computer. It was a liberating experience that turned me into an even faster writer. Mistakes suddenly were so easy to correct that I lost any remaining inhibitions about writing full sentences quickly. It was only a few years later that full-scale word processing programs became available, ones that would handle abbreviations, footnotes, and even multiple windows. My attitude towards new technology, formed then, has never changed. It has enabled me to do what I was already doing, only far more efficiently.

My association with the Social Science department never went smoothly, and it came to an end by mutual agreement, as Pat Crecine had foreseen that it might, after only two years. That department also had some bright young faculty, including Bob Coulam, a student of Richard Neustadt's at Harvard who had written a book on the development of the F-111 fighter plane, and Greg Fisher, a political scientist who became a friend. It had a monthly meeting to discuss hot social science articles—articles which I often had a great of trouble understanding because they had so little to do with data. I was rather astonished to discover the kind of article that could be published in economics or political science or sociology nowadays—arguments based on a data set that was never laid out in detail, even though the selection of data points was obviously key to the conclusion. I had been taught that human behavior could only be explained with the help of detailed research in primary documents, but they were trying to explain it by modeling. Meanwhile, these faculty members faced unremitting pressure to write proposals for grants from the National Science Foundation. The grants were designed to support their salary or part of it, for a designated time; to fund a graduate student or two; and to contribute about half their proceeds, as I remember, to the overhead of the University. Such grants, therefore, had become a necessity rather than a luxury for the school. I had no basis for applying for one of those, but I did begin an annual ritual of writing applications for year-long fellowships from the National Endowment for the Humanities, the Wilson Center in Washington, the Guggenheim Foundation, and one or two other funding sources for my new book on periods of general war in Europe. The first round was unsuccessful.

Late in 1980 *Economic Diplomacy and the Origins of the Second World War*—the book version of my dissertation—was published by Princeton University Press. One of the first reviews to appear, in the *Political Science Quarterly*, was probably the most gratifying. A well-known historian, Michael Hogan, spent his first two paragraphs doing exactly what reviewers should do: summarizing what I had said, first about German policy, and then about French and British. He concluded as follows, showing that he perfectly understood and approved of what I had tried to do.

> "There is much more to Kaiser's book than can be summarized here. It is chock-full of insights on a range of subjects: the motives influencing Soviet diplomacy, the thinking behind Chamberlain's policy of appeasement, the reversal of Anglo-French policy in 1939, and the economic origins of the war. The book is impressively documented with British, French, and German archival materials. Kaiser is especially good at delineating bureaucratic rivalries and the linkages between political

goals and economic diplomacy. One sometimes wishes for a little information on the American side; but this is a small complaint against an excellent monograph."

A few months later, a British historian, Alan Milward, published his review of the book in the premier historical journal in the United States, the *American Historical Review.* Milward was a leading authority on the German war economy and its relation to the economies of some of the occupied territories. He had visited Harvard and given a talk during my last year on the faculty. He had looked at the manuscript of the book that was then sitting in the History office, but he had said nothing about it to me. He now took his revenge upon me for having failed to mention an article he had written (and which I cannot now locate) about changes in the terms of trade between Germany and Eastern Europe—a subject of only very marginal relevance to what I had to say. Milward's review took me to task for ignoring certain literature (which he did not identify), argued that I was not economically sophisticated, and made a truly incomprehensible argument about the limitations of my analysis of German policy. Of the chapters devoted to Britain and France he said nothing, and he concluded by suggesting that I should have written a different, narrower book. When I sat across a table from Milward at a conference about 8 years later, he looked at me with a hatred that suggested he could not forgive the survival of my career. He also talked briefly to the table about nationalism as a trick employed by governments to secure the allegiance of their people—an argument that would come as a surprise to British, German, and other European politicians today. Together these two reviews illustrate the rewards and punishments of tackling an ambitious subject, especially when young. Open-minded colleagues may be entranced; jealous ones will take their revenge.

Two other reviews reflected the ambitions of younger scholars. Wally MacDougall's failed candidacy for my job at Carnegie Mellon had led Tom Childers to alert me to the job in the first place. Although MacDougall was still at Berkeley, his future there was doubtful, and he evidently resented that Carnegie

Mellon had preferred me to him. He reviewed *Economic Diplomacy* for another leading journal, the *Journal of Modern History*, and I later learned that the review had been the subject of some intense discussion between him and its editors. It began with some boilerplate praise, but spent most of its time arguing that I had vastly exaggerated the significance of the story I had to tell, concluding that this was another tale of a dog that did not bark in the night. A couple of years later MacDougall did secure tenure at Berkeley, and a few years after that, he joined Tom Childers at Penn.

Across the Atlantic, Paul A. Kennedy, a rising British star then teaching at the University of East Anglia, reviewed *Economic Diplomacy* for the prestigious *Times Literary Supplement*, together with the second volume of Gerhard Weinberg's *The Foreign Policy of Hitler's Germany*. Kennedy dealt with my book fairly briefly and amicably, but then turned to Weinberg's massive tome. He showed it proper respect but proceeded to criticize it based upon three important points that Weinberg, he argued, had failed to mention. Every one of those points came straight out of *Economic Diplomacy*—but Kennedy made them sound like his own. Given that Weinberg had singlehandedly blocked the publication of my book at another press, I would very much have appreciated proper credit for those insights.

While attempting to plug away at my next big book, I was also doggedly pushing ahead with the book on Sacco and Vanzetti that my late friend Bill Young had bequeathed to me. I was studying certain key areas of the trial transcript myself, and was more and more convinced that Bill really had discovered the key to the case: evidence that the critical firearms exhibits against Sacco were not genuine but had been substituted by the prosecution. At some point, I began reading the entire trial transcript, an almost mesmerizing experience. And during that first year, I mentioned the project to the History Department chair, Lu Schaefer, which led to a characteristic example of the joys of working at Carnegie Mellon.

Schaefer had real intellectual curiosity, and he had grown up in eastern Massachusetts and was probably old enough to remember the execution of Sacco and Vanzetti in 1927. He was immediately excited when I told him what I had and had me give a presentation about it to the department at his house one evening. He even said that it sounded like a good project for the department to fund—the ultimate praise from a man who so zealously guarded his budget. I welcomed the support. When however Lu discussed the matter with the departmental power behind the throne, Peter Stearns, Stearns evidently commented that this "wasn't the kind of thing we hired him for," and Lu returned to me to caution me "not to spend too much time on it." But the money was enough to fund a trip back to Boston, and also to hire one of my former students, Michael Levitin, as a research assistant. There was a trove of documents on the case at the Harvard Law School library, and at some point Michael began going through it for me and making some critical discoveries.

I also gave a presentation about the project to the social sciences department, with striking results. Jay Kadane was a statistician in that department who was interested in criminal justice issues. I mentioned that one of the challenges of writing about the case—as with any other complex series of events—was that it involved a number of independent issues, all of which bore heavily on guilt or innocence. Sacco and Vanzetti had been convicted of a payroll robbery in broad daylight in South Braintree, Massachusetts, carried out by five men, in which two guards had been killed. About ten eyewitnesses had placed Sacco or Vanzetti at the scene of the crime, but their testimony had been called into serious question. One bullet claimed to have been taken from one guard's body, and one shell claimed to have been found on the ground had later been matched to the automatic found on Sacco several weeks later on the night of his arrest. Years after their conviction, but before their execution, a criminal jailed for another robbery and murder had confessed to participating in the crime and pointed his finger squarely at the Morelli gang of Providence, Rhode Island, the leading organized crime family in New England. Kadane explained to me that a branch of statistics—Bayesian analysis—could be used to relate each of these issues to the overall probability of innocence or guilt. Eventually he and a colleague became sufficiently interested in this project to embark on a full-scale analysis of the case based on these principles themselves.

I cannot remember exactly when I began writing what became *Postmortem: New Evidence in the Case of Sacco and Vanzetti*, by William Young and David Kaiser. (Although that book was in the end drafted entirely by myself, I had no compunction about listing Bill first, simply because I knew that it would never have been written at all without him.) But I remember two extraordinary "aha" moments that made it what it was. The first is too complicated to explain; the second related to Michael Levitin's most remarkable discovery, bearing on the question of whether Bullet III—the bullet taken from the dead guard Berardelli and later matched to Sacco's pistol—was a genuine exhibit.

It was because the other five bullets removed from the bodies of the two guards came from an entirely different weapon, never recovered, that bullet III had always been somewhat suspicious. Bill's great contribution had been to match up the testimony of the very distinguished medical examiner, Dr. George Burgess Magrath, about the paths of the various bullets in Berardelli's body with the testimony of the best eyewitnesses. They had seen a bandit stand over Berardelli, who had already sunk to his knees on the ground, wounded, and fire downwards into him twice. And indeed, Magrath identified the tracks of two bullets that had gone downward through his body—including Bullet III. It seemed impossible that it could have been fired by a different weapon from the others.

Michael's most dramatic find was nothing less than the testimony before the grand jury in the case, which no researcher had ever seen before. Among other things, that testimony discredited the identification evidence of key eyewitnesses even more thoroughly than it had been undermined in the past. But it also included testimony about the bullets by Magrath—and the District Attorney, Frederick Katzmann, had asked Magrath if, in his opinion, the four bullets from Berardelli's body had been fired from the same weapon. While stating that he had no proof, Magrath had affirmed that he thought that they had, and added the chilling words, "they looked exactly alike." This was dynamite, because the difference between bullet III and the other bullets was, in fact, obvious to the naked eye to anyone with knowledge of the marks left on bullets. The grooves in the other bullets all slanted to the right; those in bullet III slanted to the left. And as Bill had noticed, when Magrath took the stand many months later, Katzmann's assistant Harold Williams took great care not to let him view bullet III and the other bullets at the same time while he identified them.

Michael Levitin

As I reflect on the last forty years, several of David's characteristics deserves additional emphasis.

The first is his integrity. In both the seminar and the tutorial, David emphasized that a historian is obligated to read the sources fairly and accurately. I had a vivid example when working on *Postmortem*. At the time, David was finalizing his first book, *Economic Diplomacy and the Origins of the Second World War*. One afternoon, David showed me a couple pages from the draft. Another author had interpreted a document inaccurately, to support the author's point. This was the historian's greatest sin, David said. One was obligated *not* to fit the evidence to one's conclusion. Integrity required historians to read all documents fairly and accurately, to present the facts objectively, and even to commend (or criticize) individuals fairly in light of the historical record.

The second is his thoroughness, his dedication to examining all relevant sources. David stressed that the best historians read everything relevant. They also read many things that might ultimately prove less useful, because in advance one might not know what was relevant.

The third is David's insight. Here are two examples, both delivered not as the central point of the seminar or tutorial but as casual observations during class. Some applicants of decision-theory assume that military leaders seek opportunities to use military power. David observed that Admiral Tirpitz, the politico-military leader of the Imperial German Navy, sought to avoid conflict with Britain and that what Tirpitz really wanted was a naval law guaranteeing him three new capital ships every year. And in the American slavery portion of sophomore tutorial, we read interviews with former slaves conducted in 1936–1938 by the Federal Writers' Project. David observed that, even when a former slave thought life on his or her own plantation had been tolerable, all former slaves could recall at least one instance when a slave on a neighboring plantation had been treated cruelly. The implication was unstated but obvious.

Since 1984, David and I have stayed in touch, connecting regularly to discuss current events, David's latest project, baseball, and the most recent post on David's blog.

When I think back on my own life and consider those distant hours in Hilles Library and what came after, it is clear that David had a significant influence on me. I am lucky to have had David as a teacher and even luckier to count him as a friend.

~

In June of 1982, I believe, after our term was over, I took a trip to the Boston area to pursue some leads myself, staying with my cousins Tema and Mark Silk, who had also been there through most of the 1970s. Dropping into the Harvard Coop, I found a book that would change my life: *The Bill James Baseball Abstract 1982*. James, I knew from a previous article in *Sports Illustrated*, was a young man from Lawrence, Kansas— a few years younger than I was—who had developed his own approach to baseball statistics. Since 1976 he had been privately publishing a baseball annual, and the *Sports Illustrated* piece had enabled him to sell it to Ballantine Books. It was a sensation. James was, very simply, the most original thinker in my own generation that I had yet discovered. He had a knack for cutting through the bs that dominated the mainstream sports media, and he had new ways to measure both offensive and defensive performance and to understand what made particular teams successful. Two years later, in 1984, I convinced the *New Republic* to let me review that year's Abstract for them, and that led to some brief correspondence with James—who, for all his other virtues, is not an easy man to get to know. I began playing around with various statistics myself, using our new pcs and lotus 1–2–3 software. Jim Davidson, who was now a reporter for the *Pittsburgh Press*, and who I had poured over the Macmillan Encyclopedia with back in 1970, sometimes joined in.

It must have been around 1982 or early 1983 that I finished a draft of *Postmortem* and began shopping it around. It was at times the most nerve-wracking work I had ever done. Perhaps because the issue of guilt or innocence weighs on us all in one way or another, researchers can really agonize over this kind of project, and my sleep was troubled on numerous nights by weird dreams about the evidence. Fortunately I eventually learned to cope with these issues, and when I embarked twenty years later on a similar project of even greater moment they did not bother me much at all. Meanwhile, in December 1981, my second son Tom had been born. I had taught one course that fall and was teaching three in the spring term that started in January, I remember, and early in 1982 I developed ulcer symptoms. For some reason, the doctor I consulted at our HMO did *not* simply prescribe tagamet, which had recently come on the market, but told me to control the symptoms with diet instead. I struggled with those symptoms off and on for a couple of years before a friend gave me one Tagamet pill in a moment of great distress on a ski trip, and it cured my symptoms on the spot.

In 1981–2 I taught a discussion course on one of my favorite subjects, the origins of the First World War. That got me thinking about the whole subject in depth again, and I decided to write an article about it, and specifically about Germany's responsibility for the outbreak of the conflict.

That topic, as I have mentioned, had vaulted onto the center stage of German historical scholarship in 1960, when Fritz Fischer, a well-established German historian, had published *Griff Nach der Weltmacht*—grasp at world power, but published in English as *Germany's Aims in the First World War*. That book dealt mainly with the extravagant expansionist war aims that the German government pursued nearly from the outbreak of the war until its collapse in 1918. But Fischer also took another look at the July Crisis and concluded, in effect, that Germany had triggered the world war in order to realize those grandiose plans. For four decades, nearly all German historians had argued that Germany was not responsible for the outbreak of the First World War—as the Treaty of Versailles had insisted that it was—and they had held to that view even more firmly since 1945, while acknowledging responsibility for the Second World War. The outcry against Fischer had been so intense that in the early 1960s, when he planned a trip to the US to discuss his work at various major universities, his own West German government interceded with the State Department to make sure that he did not get a visa. Fortunately, a group of courageous American historians, led by Gordon Craig of Stanford, sent their own protest to the State Department in return and Fischer got his visa.

In the 20 years since 1960 several of Fischer's students had written monographs substantiating his main points, and he had published a second book *War of Illusions*, focusing on the years before the war. Both he and various other authors had pushed the argument a step further, arguing not only that Germany was responsible, but that the German government had started the war as a *domestic* strategy, a means of warding off the increasing threat of socialism. In introductory paragraphs, I listed no less than thirteen relatively recent new works that touched on one aspect or another of these questions. I was convinced of German responsibility, but I was not convinced that the government had undertaken the war for domestic reasons.

My eventual article, "Germany and the Origins of the First World War," covered a lot of ground in relatively few pages. The introduction of *Weltpolitik*—"world policy"—in 1897, I argued, did not imply a plan for an actual war, or any particularly specific foreign policy goals. Bernhard von Bülow, who took over German foreign policy in 1897 and remained in charge until 1909, understood the need to score cheap triumphs in distant lands but did not believe a new European war would serve Germany's interests. Most other leading statesmen were similarly cautious. He also understood that even a victorious war would create more, not fewer, problems at home. Bülow gave way to

Theobald von Bethmann Hollweg in 1909, and I could see no real evidence that he was primarily concerned with the threat of socialism either. But he had convinced himself that Germany needed a much larger colonial empire, even at the risk of war.

My experience with Sam Williamson and with my own seminar at Harvard had taught me that the origins of the war could not be ascribed to one country alone. After Serbian military intelligence had orchestrated the assassination of the Austro-Hungarian Archduke Franz Ferdinand, the Vienna government had decided to attack Serbia, and I argued that the history of previous crises suggested that Berlin would never have unleashed war on its own. But Bethmann did unleash it, I argued, by backing the Austrians against Russia, supported by France, even at the risk of war. "The war Bethmann unleashed was indeed a grasp at world power," I wrote; "in that essential sense Fischer is entirely correct."

The shadow of the Vietnam War and its consequences hung over my article, since it was now clear, nearly 20 years after it had begun, what a catastrophic mistake it had been and what dreadful consequences it continued to have. "Since the late nineteenth century," I wrote,

> the enormous potential power of the modern state has fascinated statesmen, publicists, and historians. Yet the exercise of that power has frequently been thwarted by other characteristics of modern states and societies: the difficulty of coordinating their numerous institutions, the inevitable fragmentation of authority from which they suffer, the tendency of bureaucratic routine and inertia to undercut changes in policy, and the enormous political strains that inevitably accompany any drastic reallocation of resources either at home or abroad. In subsequent years the dilemmas of Bülow, who recognized bureaucratic inertia and political conflict as useful checks upon unreasonable ambition, and Bethmann, whose attempt to cut an imaginary Gordian knot ended in disaster, have proven to be characteristic of the twentieth century. Imperial Germany was the first but not

the last modern state to succumb to the fascination of its power while ignoring the constraints upon its use.

I doubt that I have ever written 34 better pages than I did for that article, and I have received many compliments for it over the years. It appeared in the *Journal of Modern History*, which had been started at the University of Chicago during the interwar period specifically to address the controversy over the responsibility for the Great War. But it remains my only explicit written foray into the controversy over 1914, and it has never appeared in any anthology on the outbreak of the war, or secured me an invitation to participate in a conference on the subject. I was shocked, too, in the 1990s, when after the reunification of Germany the pendulum swung back against the Fischer thesis, first within Germany and then elsewhere. By 2014, when a spate of new books appeared to commemorate the centennial of the war's outbreak, the idea that all the powers more or less equally shared the blame came back in fashion. Recently, I happily discovered that J. C. G. Röhl, the author of a massive three-volume biography of the Emperor William II, reaffirmed the clear finding of German guilt for the world war in the introduction to a new condensed version of his work.

When the article appeared in the fall of 1983, and I received 100 reprints, I contacted the Harvard alumni office, got the addresses of the 8 surviving members of my first freshman seminar, and sent them each a copy. Nearly all of them replied warmly. I also inscribed copies for Sam Williamson and for Fritz Fischer, whom I had never met, telling them both that the article would never have been written without them. And with Sam's help, I organized a proposed panel for the AHA convention in December 1983 that would discuss the outbreak of the war. To complement me I recruited two other relatively young historians, Douglas Porch, who had already written books on French imperialism, and William Fuller, an authority on Russian civil-military relations before the First World War. In a harbinger of things to come, the AHA rejected our panel. When I asked for an explanation I was told that committee members thought there was nothing new to be said about 1914.

Several years later I was in Washington in December when the AHA convention was held. It featured a panel on the First World War, and Fritz Fischer was one of the panelists. I attended with great interest. Fischer was now in his seventies. He was short and stocky—shorter even than I (5' 7")—and showed no trace of arrogance over what he had to say or the enormous role he had played in his profession. Twice he apologized on the podium for his difficulty finding the right English word. He began talking with a group of acquaintances when the panel finished, and I approached him and simply handed him another copy of my article. He glanced down at it, his face instantly broke into a broad smile, his head shot back up, and he pointed at my chest, as if to say, "that's you?" I nodded. Outside of the classroom, that was the greatest moment of my career.

Yet another new interest with long-range consequences opened up in 1983. My brother Bob was now the editor of the Sunday Outlook section at the *Washington Post*, commissioning articles every week on all sorts of topics. In the late summer of 1983, I believe, he called me to say that he was preparing a special edition to commemorate the 20th anniversary of JFK's death and asked me if I knew of any historians who were particularly well versed in the controversy over his assassination. "Just your brother," I replied. The assassination had interested me from the traumatic day that it occurred and I had read several books on it and followed the work of the House Assassinations Committee (1977–78) with great interest. My brother was always understandably reluctant to use his position at the *Post* to help family members, but a couple of days later he called again to say that he wanted me to do the piece.

I jumped in with both feet, reading the HSCA report and establishing contact with the committee's chief counsel, G. Robert Blakey, who was now a law professor at Notre Dame. We had a series of long telephone conversations in which Blakey elaborated on his belief that while Oswald had indeed fired the fatal shots, organized crime was behind the assassination. My eventual piece, published on November 20, 1983, examined three theories in detail: the lone assassin theory, the idea (which I rejected) that Cuba was behind it, and the mob theory. But I reached no firm conclusion and focused on how so many key figures in 1963–4 had been too afraid of what they might find to investigate key issues very thoroughly. Late in the 1980s I thought about doing a book about the case, but Blakey at that point advised me against it. New developments lay ahead. I also took advantage of the 20th anniversary to write a piece for the *New Republic* on JFK entitled "President and Politician," which concluded with a comment on the deterioration of our political life since his death. A comment in the *Boston Globe* found my piece superior to one by Arthur Schlesinger, Jr., that led the issue. But many years later, when TNR published an anthology covering its whole history, it was Schlesinger's piece that was included.

I was meanwhile marketing *Postmortem*, on Sacco and Vanzetti. Several authors over the last half-century had written very successful books about the case, including Francis Russell, the advocate for Sacco's guilt, who was still very much alive. But several general publishers refused to bite on ours. I contacted Harvard University Press, where Aida Donald—wife of my former colleague David Donald—was enthusiastic. She sent it out for two readings, but they were simply not quite favorable enough. It then occurred to me to approach a Harvard classmate named Bruce Wilcox who was now the lead editor at the University of Massachusetts Press. I had not known him, but Jim Davidson was a mutual friend. He was immediately excited by the book, and although he made the mistake of sending it out to an amateur researcher who didn't want anyone else bringing out anything on the case, he eventually accepted it in 1984. I now had two books and a major article to my credit and felt that my future was quite secure.

I had been raised to the level of non-tenured associate after two years, in 1982, but I still was not scheduled to come up for tenure until 1986, when I would be 39. One morning in the fall of 1984, I believe, Lu Schaefer called me into his office and offered to move my case up a year, until the next fall. I was delighted. The reason emerged only gradually. The department was interviewing another candidate for a job: Joe Trotter, a junior faculty member at one of the University of California campuses. Like Kate Lynch, Anne Rose, Andy Achenbaum, and myself, he had one book out—a short work of social history—and did not yet have tenure. Yet he wanted to be hired as a tenured associate and Schaefer, and other senior faculty indicated that he would be. The reason, they frankly admitted, was that Joe Trotter was black, and therefore more desirable. "He's in a different market," they said. Schaefer called all the junior faculty members together to put this to them. All but myself assented, although Andrew Barnes—now a close friend of mine, and also black—seemed to me quite embarrassed to do so. I however said that I did not think it would be good for the department to have one person walking around with a sign on his back reading, "I got tenure immediately while you all had to wait years and years because I was black." The appointment, however, went ahead. Trotter was a rather quiet, gentlemanly man who, like me, spent most of his time on his own work. He never became a member of our lunch group. I have to admit that I didn't make much of an effort to get to know him after he was hired although I always respected him. I'm sure the difference in our status was the reason.

My teaching situation had also changed. My contemporary Kate Lynch had taken over the leadership of the Origins of the Modern World, the required course for engineering students, and had improved it enormously. The reading now included several major books, including *Montaillou* by the French historian Leroy Ladurie—an account of life in a medieval French village—*The Family, Sex and Marriage in Britain*, by Princeton's Lawrence Stone, and my old favorite, Tocqueville's *The Old Regime and the French Revolution*. Most of the best young faculty, including Adele Lindenmeyr, Andrew Barnes, and myself, were teaching sections along with her. At some point I developed a course on the Second World War. And in the middle of the decade, I picked up a thread from my old lecture course at Harvard, designing a course on the history of twentieth-century Europe based on historical fiction and autobiographical materials. The reading list included Pasternak's *Dr. Zhivago*, Malraux's *Man's Fate*, several works by Orwell, *Bread and Wine* by the Italian socialist Ignazio Silone, and Solzhenitsyn's *The*

First Circle, the story of an elite labor camp for engineers that had become one of my three or four favorite books. I also arranged for the students to see *The Sorrow and the Pity*, about occupied France. The course really dealt with the dilemmas of living under tyranny and the pitfalls of political activism.

I added another dimension to the course with an author I had learned about elsewhere, the European therapist Alice Miller. Miller, who was then acquiring a following in the United States, was best known for *The Drama of the Gifted Child*, a study of how children learn to orient themselves around their parents' needs, but I used another book with explicit historical implications, *For Your Own Good*. That book began with at least 50 pages of hair-raising excerpts from 18th- and 19th-century German child-rearing manuals that consistently focused on breaking the child's spirit. Miller was convinced that many leading Nazis had had such an upbringing, with two critical effects. On the one hand, it left them with enormous pent-up rage against their parents that had to be vented against others—particular others, like concentration camp inmates, who were as helpless as they had been. On the other hand, it left many men and women unable to feel anything consciously, and therefore capable of doing almost anything without any pangs of conscience about it. This was a variant of Hannah Arendt's famous argument about the banality of evil which she developed reporting on the Eichmann trial in Jerusalem. Miller thought that children could develop healthily if they were simply given the right to their own feelings, including very nasty ones, and I was increasingly influenced by this in raising my own sons. Initially I included a short paper in which the students used Miller to analyze a character of their choice from one of the books. It took about three years for me to take the logical next step.

I had learned to understand Carnegie Mellon students. While their average level was well below Harvard both in ability and preparation, there were very bright exceptions. Some of the engineering students were all-around brilliant kids who could have succeeded at anything. And some of our own H & SS students were also very bright and had somehow found their way into our institution. One such was the single best student I ever had there,

Heather Newton, who arrived a year after I did. A North Carolinian, she was a natural intellectual whose mother wrote juvenile fiction. Carnegie Mellon had recruited her by mail, and she had responded. She was a type of student I always liked: generally quiet, although clearly engaged, in class, and simply outstanding in every piece of written work. She was a student of mine in origins of the modern world, and then took a pair of mini-courses I taught on McCarthyism and on Vietnam. The last assignment in the latter course invited students to write a memo to any President at any point in the war, and she wrote one for Nixon on the eve of his inauguration. She argued so brilliantly that he could blame the Democrats for the war, announce that he had received new information, and wind it up then and there that I wished he could have received it in real life.

Heather was also in the inaugural class of War and Revolution and wrote a great paper in the form of a 2020 letter to an imagined child in college who had decided to become a revolutionary. She also asked me at one point for some career guidance, and I advised against going to graduate school in history, even though I knew she could be a brilliant student. I was now convinced that no one should not go who was not so determined that nothing could stop them—like myself.

Heather Newton

*"He felt himself at last beginning to be a teacher, which
is simply a man to whom his book is true, to whom
is given a dignity of art that has little to do with his
foolishness or weakness or inadequacy as a man."*

—John Williams, *Stoner*

I entered Carnegie Mellon in the fall of 1982, one of the few students from below the Mason-Dixon Line, shy with little confidence in my intellect. I planned to major in writing and dreamed of becoming a Southern novelist. I had never taken a real History class. The focus of the CMU History department was on social history—an approach that appealed to my love of story. My first History class with David Kaiser was a mandatory freshman survey course: Origins of the Modern World. David taught my small section. The professors took turns lecturing each week to a crowd of some two hundred students. When David lectured on the French Revolution that spring, his passion brought the subject to life. When he finished, ducking his head so that his signature forelock covered his eyes, the lecture hall broke into a spontaneous ovation. I never witnessed any other professor get that response in my four years at CMU.

The Origins readings, and David's teaching, converted me to a love of History. The next semester, I took his class on Vietnam, and at the end of the semester he wrote an invitation on my final to come by and talk about my plans for a major. Over my four years, I took whatever class he happened to be teaching, and he served as my honors thesis advisor. Things I loved about his classes: David's excitement and energy, his incorporation of novels (or non-fiction books that read like novels) into the curriculum, our mutual fascination/revulsion towards Richard Nixon, and the privilege of listening to someone so intelligent think out loud and engage me as if I deserved a seat at the table.

Two favors David did me: First, when I was a senior, having shelved the Southern novelist plan, I was trying to decide between law school or graduate school in History. David, based on his own frustrating experience, warned me away from academia. Second, when I wrote to him my first year of law school to tell him that I had done well—good grades and Law Review—he wrote back with words I needed to hear and finally internalized, "I'm glad your grades turned out well, but I'm not surprised. It's about time you started worrying about something more problematical than your ability."

My favorite assignment under David, in his War and Revolution class, was to pretend I was a middle-aged mother whose son had just written that he was dropping out of college to join a revolutionary movement. I am now the middle-aged mother of an 18-year-old. I found "A Letter To Junior" in a dusty box recently and was struck by how prophetic both the assignment and my response had been. In his comments on the paper, David wrote:

"I honestly don't think I've ever had a paper that ended on such a frank note of uncertainty. It's actually more impressive than any neatly tied up conclusion would have been. You always seem to me a very level-headed person, but even you want to believe it's possible. Well, for a long time, so did I.

"Thinking about it now, I suppose I feel it's more important politically to resist evil than to try to create paradise So perhaps I would say, Junior, anything you can do to stop the war in Peru is OK, but stop there . . . As for hoping that his generation can 'do it right'—most of us have the feeling of wanting to make something go really well, to be part of something that's making us and others happy. But it doesn't have to be a whole society! Indeed, trying to transform a whole society may well be an escape from solving problems closer to home. I honestly don't feel that at 37 I've lost any of my idealistic temperament, but it's just channeled differently. I don't expect to ever see the perfect (or even near-perfect) socialist revolution. . . .

"To have faced these questions and faced your own lack of a consistent answer is a very rare achievement. Understand that you are different from most people, but try not to be scared by it. And with time, some answers may seem clearer. Some, but not all. That's what makes it fun."

After a long detour, I did become a Southern novelist. As a novelist, regret fascinates me. So few of us arrive at middle or late age without our share. David's regrets seemed to include not finding a permanent teaching home at his beloved Harvard or a comparable institution, and frustration with the lack of appreciation he found for himself and his tangible body of work in the academic setting. As his former student, however, I see only success in his teaching me and my peers to see the world in a new way, and affirming our place in that world.

~

I spent the summer of 1983, I believe, writing a draft of the section of my new book that would deal with the era of Philip II of Spain. I had done a great deal of reading on his reign in the Iberian Peninsula, the religious wars in France, and other related matters. But the draft I produced was a relatively standard narrative of events similar to many found in general histories of Europe. When it was nearly done, I finally had the key breakthrough that made the eventual book, *Politics and War: European Conflict from Philip II to Hitler*, what it became. The breakthrough, like the British invention of the *Dreadnought* battleship, made the 100 pages I had written obsolete, but I didn't mind. Here, a certain intellectual patience had allowed me to reach a new intellectual level.

Both the late 16th and early 17th centuries were marked by huge conflicts in nearly every part of Europe: the Iberian Peninsula, France, Germany (during the Thirty Years War, 1618–1648) and Britain (the civil war of the 1640s and 1650s.) What I suddenly realized was that all these conflicts grew out of attempts by monarchs to dominate their aristocracies. Again and again they failed to do so because they lacked a real governmental structure, and because the great aristocrats were laws unto themselves who freely sought and obtained the assistance of foreign monarchs. Since the 19th century, the western historical profession had been fascinated by the emergence of modern states, but I was convinced that they had read too far backward from the present and imagined the emergence of such states centuries before it had actually taken place. The great wars of the years 1559–1659, I concluded, reflected the nature of aristocratic politics during that turbulent century.

A number of historians had written about the "general crisis of the 17th century," a term coined by the British historian Hugh Trevor-Roper, but I eventually entitled this first section of *Politics and War* "The General Crisis of the 16th and 17th centuries." And in the introductory section of that chapter, I argued that the same patterns of conflicts that Trevor-Roper and others had identified persisted until about 1660, and that called the very concept of "crisis" into question. Another fine British historian, J. H. Elliott, had already written that the "crisis" that Trevor-Roper had located in the 1640s was not dissimilar to the decade of the 1560s. I argued that one could say the same about any decade from the 1560s through the 1650s, with the exception of the 1610s. "This leads to a further conclusion," I wrote: "that the persistence of conflict over this chaotic century does not reflect a 'crisis,' in the sense of a temporary breakdown of European political or institutional arrangements, but was rather the *natural consequence* of the key social, political, economic and religious aspects of European society, which made conflict inevitable and its lasting resolution almost impossible." I had now become very familiar with the major literature on this period, and my footnotes showed that several others had had similar insights at one time or another. No one else, however, had fully developed them.

When an academic—particular a young one who has not yet secured a permanent position, as I still was—begins a large research project (like *Economic Diplomacy*) or a great synthetic work (like *Politics and War*), colleagues, search committees, fellowship committees and editors immediately want to know what the argument will be. This is most unfortunate, because it can take years—literally—of scrupulous research and thought for the underlying patterns in the material to emerge. I had been thinking about eras of general war in Europe for about five years when this insight occurred to me in my office, but once it had, I realized that the other eras could be addressed in a similar fashion. Even now, as at the age of 70, with 8 books under my belt, I find that when I propose something on the Kennedy assassination or Franklin Roosevelt and US entry into the Second World War, editors want to know "what will be different about this book" long before I can tell them. The answer, actually, is that it will be different because David Kaiser is going to write it, and if they want some idea of what that means they should spend a couple of hours with any of his earlier books. *Politics and War* is not my favorite among my books, but I do think it was my most remarkable achievement.

Progress had also been slow because I was teaching four courses a year all through this period. I had become a firm believer in Parkinson's Law, and if my next class was at 11:00

tomorrow, I did not start preparing for it until I got to the office around 9:00 on that day. I continued to use spare hours to read in the voluminous and inspiring literature on early modern politics, war, and diplomacy—most of it secured via interlibrary loan—but I couldn't write during term time. Every year for four or five years in a row, I wrote four or five fellowship applications for a year's support to the NEH, the Guggenheim Foundation, the Wilson Center, and other places that I cannot recall. I remember that I was once turned down by the Davis Center at Princeton even though their topic for that particular year, war and society, was exactly what I was writing about. This became a source of increasing frustration, and finally, one year, I took up the NEH on their offer to supply the committee's comments on my project. They were most illuminating. One reviewer noted the extraordinary scope of the project, but declared that he was "willing to gamble" both because of my excellent record and because he thought the profession still needed works like these. But two others dismissed it as hopelessly ambitious and clearly refused to vote for it. That episode, I know now, embodied my experience within the historical profession. Even now it includes some individuals who have not given up their freedom of thought and who can still be excited by someone who refuses to be bound by prevailing orthodoxies and prevailing boundaries. *But there is never a majority of such people on any committee with the power to make decisions.* As we shall see, I owe the only good things to happen to me in the second half of my career to two men in two different institutions who luckily had the power to put their ideas into effect. And neither one of them had even met me personally when they chose to contact me and offer me a job.

By the end of academic year 1984–5 I must have finished a draft of the first part of *Politics and War*. *Postmortem* was published that fall by the University of Massachusetts Press and received rave reviews in the *Washington Post* and in the *Times Literary Supplement*. Francis Russell, who had been arguing for 25 years that Sacco was guilty, also published a new book on the case himself that year, and we were written up (although not formally reviewed) in the Sunday *New York Times* book review.

According to the promise I had received from Lu Schaefer in the fall of 1984, when Joe Trotter was hired, I was supposed to be reviewed for tenure that fall, and with two books under my belt I did not see how I could miss. But suddenly, early that summer, Schaefer called me into his office, showed me a memo from the President cautioning against attempts to bring junior faculty up for tenure "early," and reneged on the deal. I was furious enough to discuss the situation with an assistant dean, Tony Penna, who was always honest and forthcoming. He was clearly depressed by the story, and commented, "History and Philosophy needs new leadership." He also said, discussing my tenure prospects, that *Economic Diplomacy* "didn't count," because I had written it before I had gotten there. *Postmortem* would have an uncertain bearing on the case as well, because it was, as Peter Stearns had put it years earlier, "not the sort of thing I had been hired to do." My case would depend on my progress on *Politics and War*. During the next year (1985–6) Peter Stearns was tapped to replace Lu Schaefer as department chair. He remained determined to make the department a leading center of the study of social history.

Social history, which had begun as an attempt to *supplement* traditional political history with accounts of how people actually lived, had received a big boost from the politics of the late 1960s and early 1970s. My own generation of academics had grown up largely convinced of the corruption of the elite and the fundamental injustice of modern society. Virtue was to be found only among the lower classes. As I have discussed with reference to the controversy over Germany and the outbreak of the First World War, it had been fashionable even to argue that great wars were mainly conspiracies by the ruling class to hold down the working class. In 1980, Howard Zinn had published the first of many editions of *A People's History of the United States*, arguing that only popular agitation, not leadership, had ever led to any of the changes for the better in the United States. I had been too busy with my own work, teaching, and family during the first half of the 1980s to pay close attention to the changing balance of power within my profession, even though the rejection of my proposed panel at the 1983 AHA Convention had been something of a fire bell in the night. In the spring of 1985, however, a remarkable two-part article by the historian Theodore Draper in the *New York Review of Books* sounded an alarm more loudly. More than thirty years later, those articles stand as a milestone in American intellectual history.

Draper—a member of the GI generation—was the author of a standard history of the American Communist party. He had belonged to it as a young man before leaving, as so many people did, when he discovered that the party was always first and foremost a tool of Moscow. His articles, which were later published as part of a book, focused on several new historians of American communism.[5] These men—including Maurice Isserman, Roy Rosenzweig, and Gary Gerstle—were all from the Boom generation as we now define it, and they had self-consciously founded a new school dominated by a new approach to studying American communism. Re-reading his careful characterization of their school, I am very struck by the enormous influence not of their conclusions, but of their methods and tone.

These new historians, to begin with, explicitly linked their work to their own lives and their identity, specifically to their college involvement in the New Left. They wore that affiliation, Draper noted, like a badge of honor, and implied that their youthful views allowed them to see American communism with different eyes. Secondly, they were writing *against* something very specific: traditional approaches to American communism, of which Draper himself had been the leading exponent. Those approaches had emphasized—inevitably—that the CPUSA was a subsidiary of Moscow and the Comintern, and that it followed party discipline quite slavishly and carried on public campaigns against any members who either refused to do so or who symbolized a line that had now been discarded. Anyone who remained a party member very long learned to put Moscow's interests first. That, the new historians argued, was traditional "political" history, while they were writing the "social" history of the

---

5 Theodore Draper, *A Present of Things Past* (New York, 1990), pp. 117–53.

Communist party, focusing on the lives, thoughts, and feelings of ordinary party members. This approach led to a greater reliance on memoirs and interviews conducted decades after the fact—sources which good historians had understood to be less reliable than contemporary documents for well over a century. In reaction to history's traditional focus on decision-makers (including party leaders), a kind of fetishism of the ordinary person had developed, leading one new historian to argue that studies of Communism should pay attention to "who stopped over at one's house after dinner to play cards, listen to a ball game, sit on the porch drinking a beer, discussing the news," or "whom one could depend on to take care of the kids, lend one money, go shopping." "Everything about everyone,' Draper commented—one might have though unnecessarily—"is not necessarily significant or relevant, even in social history." But in fact, younger historians were rapidly deciding that everything about ordinary people *was* important, if only because most history, until then, had dealt with the extraordinary people who made decisions that changed the lives of millions.

These new perspectives and new methods led to new conclusions. (Again one might have thought that an alarm bell might have gone off: methods and perspectives that invariably lead to similar conclusions are obviously biased.) The major conclusion of many of the new works on communism was that the ideas and behavior of American communists reflected "authentic American radicalism," rather than simply Moscow's instructions. They specifically put this thesis forth as a contrast to Draper's earlier view, and their most vociferous attacks were directed against Harvey Klehr, a young historian who had written a history of the CPUSA in the 1930s that echoed Draper's conclusions. But repeatedly, when Draper looked carefully at the evidence presented for this, it turned out not to validate the conclusion, and sometimes it clearly undermined it. The new historians were arguing that black was white, simply because it made them feel better to see it as white. A decade later, when related new approaches had infected my own field, I discovered the same thing again and again. When I ran down the footnotes of articles featuring "innovative" approaches to diplomatic history, the source often seemed to undermine, rather than to support, the point the author was making.

The reader may be asking himself whether this new revisionist school really differed fundamentally from other new schools in history, and whether this controversy was qualitatively different from, let us say, the bitter interwar debates over the responsibility for the outbreak of the First World War. The answer, I believe, is yes, but I will defer a full explanation until I come to further controversies in the 1990s. Draper wrote succinctly about the generational aspect of the shift he was documenting and even compared the "yuppie" left-wing professoriate to "yuppie" neoconservatives, who had in the 1980s been attracting much more attention. While the former ensconced themselves in universities, the latter were more at home in "corporation-subsidized foundations and institutes or [in] job openings in Reaganite Washington." "The post-New left academics are, of course, far from having taken over the universities. An influx of them into a single specialized field can, however, make a considerable difference." What neither Draper nor I understood in 1985 was that these historians were simply one vanguard of a much larger revolution that would achieve at least parity during the 1990s and nearly absolute supremacy by 2010, when the oldest Boomers reached retirement age. And the neoconservatives and the leftist academics had one thing in common: a blunt rejection of the ideals and practices of our parents and grandparents, who had created the world in which we had the great fortune to grow up.

I got another insight into current intellectual trends about a year later, when I was invited—somewhat to my surprise—to attend a conference at the University of Virginia organized by a law professor, John Norton Moore. Entitled "Vietnam: A fresh look at the arguments," it turned out to be a neoconservative conclave featuring Norman Podhoretz, Robert Turner (then head of the US Institute of Peace), Harry Summers (author of the recent book *On Strategy*, blaming military mistakes for the loss of the war), and David Horowitz, a Red diaper baby and 1960s leftist who had swung wildly over to the other side. I had no idea how I had come to be invited and by the second day I was sure that whoever was responsible would be loath to admit it, because my contributions to the discussions were so out of sync with the prevailing wisdom. Led by Podhoretz, speaker after speaker explained that the war had been won on the ground at the time of the Tet offensive but lost because of a stab in the back from liberal intellectuals, the media, and the Democratic Party. I enjoyed the conference even though by then, in October 1986, I was on anti-depressant medication, coping with the worst emotional crisis of my life.

By the summer of 1986 I had completed half of *Politics and War*, the sections on 1559–1659 and 1789–1815. The latter section, about the formative period in modern European history, had been a constant joy to research and write, and I had related the revolutionary and Napoleonic wars, and the French successes and failures, to the political changes that were sweeping Europe. I had gotten excellent feedback on the first section from Geoffrey Parker, an authority on the period, and on the second from Simon Schama, who had joined the Harvard department as a full professor late in my years there after writing a long history of the Netherlands during the Napoleonic era. Both were British. A draft of the Louis XIV section already existed—although I knew it would have to be extensively rewritten now—and I did not think that the section on the two World Wars would take too long because I was already so familiar with the material. I had shown these sections to Peter Stearns, now chair, and he had reacted very favorably to them, particularly to the first. My long-awaited tenure review was now at hand, and at the end of the summer of 1986 I did not see (at least in the conscious part of my brain) how anyone could question my right to promotion, based on my two books, the article on Germany and the origins of the First World War, and other short pieces including those in the *New Republic* and a couple of op-eds in the *New York Times*. My long struggle, I thought, was over. It turned out that my unconscious felt otherwise.

One morning early in the term, when deliberations had not yet begun, I reached my office getting ready for my course, War and Revolution, which I believe was in its second iteration. I was missing a key book and had to run to the library to get it. I went from there to class, which went perfectly well and headed for my office. In the hall I ran into a friend from another department, Granger Morgan. An engineer, he studied the implications of science for public policy, and he had become interested in the currently hot topic of nuclear winter. He was writing a grant proposal about it and had found a role in that proposal—I can't remember exactly what it was—for me. When I ran into him in the hall, he told me that we had to have material fully prepared within a week. At that moment, I felt something go off inside me.

I got into my office suddenly feeling quite anxious. I sat down with a customary antidote, the day's *New York Times*, which I had picked up at the bookstore. It didn't work. I was overwhelmed by the worst bout of anxiety I had ever felt in my life, a genuine panic attack. Eventually I went down the hall to the office of the most sympathetic senior faculty member, Gene Levy. It was hard to explain what was happening to him since I didn't really understand it myself. He wound up calling Cathy, who was now working in public relations at the Carnegie Library and Museum, just a few hundred yards away. She came over and eventually escorted me to our local HMO. I eventually left with an Ativan prescription, and a day or two later I was put on an early anti-depressant, amitriptyline. It took a few very difficult weeks for it to kick in, during which my situation became considerably more alarming.

Although Peter Stearns was on campus, he was also on leave, and a temporary chair, John Modell, was handling the case. John had written only one book, but he had already had tenure elsewhere when CMU hired him a few years earlier, and thus had come as a full professor, an honor that lay years in the future for me, since I would remain an associate if and when I was tenured. Modell had also managed to procure a new academic plum, a spousal appointment for his wife Judith, an anthropologist. She was placed in the Department of Social and Decision Sciences but was not doing well there for the same reason that I had not—she had very little in common with the other people in it. Simultaneously, Anne Rose—Annie to all her friends—was up for promotion to *non-tenured* associate, even though she too had a substantial book to her credit when she arrived at CMU and was now well into a second one, a study of the impact of the Civil War on the generation that fought it. One reason I had thought my case was so solid was that Peter Stearns had once commented to me that he knew the current promotion process was unfair, and that it had been particularly unfair to two people, Annie and myself. I could only agree. Annie, as it happened, was also in the late stages of her second pregnancy at the time.

After my panic attack I began spending as much time as I could at home, and I was watching a VCR in our third-floor tv room one morning when the phone rang downstairs. It was Annie. "David," she said, "I am not going to be reappointed. They have turned me down." She was, as always, totally calm and professional, although clearly very angry. Annie was one of my real peers among the junior faculty and was always a joy to talk to about any of her varied interests. I was also, of course, deeply shaken, and the rest of the junior faculty were as well.

And I was more so after Modell and I had a brief conversation about how my case was going. Yes, I had two and a half books to my credit, but *Economic Diplomacy*, as Tony Penna had already explained to me, "didn't count" because I had written it before I had arrived, and *Postmortem* had been "not the sort of thing we hired him to do," and thus "didn't count" either. Everything stood or fell, apparently, on the half-finished *Politics and War*. I was now doing very well in the classroom, but under CMU tenure rules, a faculty member had to be scored a 3—outstanding—on either publications or teaching, *and it was a corollary that a 3 in teaching could not be awarded merely based on what one did in the classroom*. It was only later that I realized who the biggest problem was. When I had arrived in 1980, Joel Tarr, a senior professor, had just moved from History to Social Sciences because he could not stomach Lu Schaefer's dictatorial leadership. I had been a great disappointment to Tarr because he had expected me to devote myself to "interacting" with colleagues—that is, doing collaborative articles—and writing grant proposals, like himself. I had been too busy being David Kaiser to do that. Now, however, with his friend Peter

Stearns in charge, Joel had come back into history, and he was no friend of mine.

I was now walking around with the same feeling that I had had at Harvard for four full years, waiting for an ax to fall on me from behind. Despite everything I had done—and I was now just months away from my 40th birthday—my fate was entirely out of my own hands. The strain inevitably carried over to my home life, although neither of my sons, now 8 and 5, had any idea of what was happening. In November I got a call from my old friend Tom Childers's wife, inviting me to a surprise 40th birthday party for him on December 10. Tom was now tenured at Penn, where he was keeping the Harvard lecturing tradition alive in courses on Nazism and the Second World War. I desperately wanted to get out of town, but in the end I decided not to go because I could not face an evening surrounded by historians, most or all of them tenured.

Finally, in mid-December, I got the call from Modell telling me that I had passed the departmental vote. I never asked him or Peter Stearns what the vote was, although Peter at one point indicated that there was something we should discuss. Ten years, hundreds of students, two and a half books and a number of shorter pieces after earning my degree, I finally had a secure career as a historian, albeit in a university and a city in which I knew I would never really feel at home. I had carved out a place for myself in the community, but my heart was elsewhere. A few years earlier I had been alerted to my true feelings when one of my favorite cousins, Rebecca, came through town on a brief visit with her husband. They had been living in California but now announced that they were moving to Boston. For a split second on our front porch, I wanted to kill her.

And with all that going on, that fall was also the occasion of one of the greatest teaching experiences I ever had. I was doing War and Revolution, the Experience of the Twentieth Century—my favorite course now—and one day I got an office visit from a dark-haired, petite young woman named Lisa Ann Deutsch. She had not as I remember opened her mouth in class, but she turned out to be a ball of fire one on one. She told me a good deal about herself—her parents, like so many of the parents of these Xer students, had divorced long ago—and also wanted to know more about me. "You want to be a Harvard professor," she said. "Well, I was a Harvard professor," I replied. I did not think then and certainly do not think now that she was making a pass at me, but I got the distinct impression that she hoped to flirt her way to an A. But her first paper had been a run-of the-mill B. (One of the few things I liked about CMU was that we were not allowed to give pluses and minuses.)

Her second paper, a few weeks later, posed a real challenge for me. The topic was the meaning of heroism, based on the books we had been reading by Pasternak, Orwell, and others. She wrote a good paper but it was written, it seemed to me, according to a formula, and it parroted a lot of what had gone on in class. Other papers were better. After some thought, I commented that while some people would probably give it an A, I couldn't, because I didn't see enough originality there. For her final paper she chose a topic based on a quote—one which, like so many such quotes, I had written myself:

"Probably no generation has suffered more than the European men and women born between 1880 and 1920. Threatened by death throughout their lives, they also repeatedly faced almost impossible moral choices in their struggle for physical and emotional survival. Many were easily seduced by the promise of utopian ideologies—both Communist and Fascist—which promised heaven on earth, but instead robbed them of their humanity and implicated them in horrible crimes. Viewing the history of the period, it is difficult to feel any confidence in the future of the human race or the real purpose of life on earth."

The paper follows.

> The generation of Europeans born between 1900 and 1920 suffered physically, morally, and emotionally because of the history which occurred during their lives. Often, in order to survive, these people had to make impossible moral choices. They were also tempted by the ideologies of communism and fascism, which

promised them a solution but in reality made them less humane and often implicated them in crimes. Though the history of this period may be grim, a lot can be learned from the people who lived through this turbulent period. Yuri Zhivago in Boris Pasternak's *Doctor Zhivago*, Christian de la Maziere in Marcel Ophuls' *The Sorrow and the Pity*, and Clara Makarygin in Aleksandr Solzhenitsyn's *The First Circle* lived in various times of instability in Europe in the first half of the twentieth century, and much can he learned from their experiences. The most important lesson which survived the destruction and the turbulence of this fifty year period is that we can be confident in the future of the human race and in the purpose of life on earth.

Pasternak's *Dr. Zhivago* is set in one of the most violent and terrible periods of twentieth-century European history. At this time, the whole country of Russia was mesmerized by Lenin and the ideology of the Reds. Both the man and the ideology promised a solution to the oppression and misery which existed under the Czarist regimes. It is true that the embracing of ideology in this revolution made many less humane and implicated many more in crimes. However, from Pasternak and his character Doctor Zhivago, there is a light of hope and purpose which glows in this dark and terrible human tragedy. There is a lesson to be learned from Doctor Zhivago, the man—we can have confidence in the future of the human race and in the purpose of life on earth. Yuri's strength, his realizations and understanding of life, his writing, and his love for Lara all serve to embody hope and to teach the present generation that there is a purpose of life and confidence for the future of the human race.

Zhivago's strength and his attitude toward the revolution are important facets of his personality. Once, he was briefly tempted by the ideology of the revolution. However, he was strong enough to resist the temptation. Yuri realized that what the revolution was aiming to achieve and the means designed to achieve that end were wrong. Pasternak's own view of the revolution is presented through Doctor Zhivago—the revolution went wrong, but someday Russia will be resurrected. Yuri never lost his hope that Mother Russia would triumph sometime in the future. His ability to resist the temptation of revolutionary ideology and his hopeful attitude toward the future when his own period was so devastating are inspiring for the future of humanity.

Yuri's philosophy of life is an important part of the novel but is also important in providing the present generation with confidence in the purpose of life. Yuri advocated, as did Pasternak, that life should be lived and cherished. He treasured life and the experiences which it offered to him. He reveled in nature and proclaimed its beauty. Yuri's view of death is an essential component in his philosophy. He believed that people are immortal because they live on after they die through those whom they loved in their lives. The purpose of life, as Doctor Zhivago viewed it, is to live it to the utmost, to delight in its experiences, to bask in the nature which surrounds the living, and to remember that our soul lives on in those whom we love after we die. Doctor Zhivago's philosophy is awe-inspiring and beautiful. His philosophy expresses the purpose of human life in the most fundamental terms for the past, the present, and the future.

Yuri also expresses the purpose of life because in the midst of one of the most turbulent and brutal periods of history he was able to fulfill his life-long dream of writing poetry. It was Yuri's dream to write, and he lived his dream. Yuri states that "Every man is born a Faust, with a longing to grasp and experience and express everything in the world" (p. 285). Yuri accomplished this Faustian goal through his writing. Despite everything, he turned his situation into an inspiration for the future of humanity. He was inspired to write, and he wrote. He was able to find the peace to create in a world in which there was no peace. Yuri fulfilled a desired purpose in a time in which dreams were shattered and destroyed. Man's ability to live his dreams under the most dire circumstances provides a good feeling of confidence in humanity and in the purpose of life.

Finally, the ability of man to love another in any time during any situation is an inspiration for the future of humanity. Zhivago and Lara's love managed to transcend the Russian Revolution, their separations from each other, their marriages. They experienced a beautiful and pure love which must be admired. Pasternak describes their love: "Oh, what a love it was, utterly free, unique, like nothing else on earth! . . . They loved each other because everything around them willed it . . . " (p. 504). Yuri and Lara's love is a source of confidence in mankind. Love can flourish even under the worst circumstances. Man's ability to love provides the faith for his future and gives purpose to his existence.

Doctor Zhivago was able to resist the seduction of revolutionary ideology, but Christian de la Maziere fell victim to the seduction of fascism. Though he was a fascist and a member of the Waffen S.S., in his later life he has realized how dangerous an ideology and a promise that fascism was and truly regrets his support of and involvement in fascism.[N.B. Maziere is the one-time young Fascist and Nazi soldier interviewed in the second half of *The Sorrow and the Pity*.)

Maziere, a French aristocrat who grew up in an atmosphere of anti-Semitism, became a fascist for two reasons. First, fascism was the only revolutionary choice for members of his social class. To Maziere, fascism represented a promise to change the world. Second, Maziere desired to rebel against his family. Many people in Europe during this time period joined radical, ideological parties in efforts to rebel against their families and the established order. However, Maziere admits that he became a fascist without knowing the meaning of fascism. This is probably true of many who joined these radical parties—they were unaware of the actual meaning of and implications of the ideologies advocated by these groups. Instead, they were enticed by the promise of heaven on earth which was emphasized by these seductive ideologies.

It becomes evident that Maziere's reasons for joining the Waffen S.S. and becoming a supporter of National Socialism were similar to those of other people. However, Maziere realizes that he made a mistake, and he truly regrets that mistake. Maziere's realization is encouragement for having confidence in the future of the human race. When asked in the interview about his feelings toward his former association with National Socialism, he replied:

Only fools never modify or change their opinions. I take responsibility for myself only, of course. I have changed, but that's another story . . . . Young people ask me what I think about commitment, about their own sense of commitment today. It's always attractive, commitment, fascinating because it is a change, but sometimes it also has dramatic consequences. So I must admit . . . . I advise caution (p. 153).

It is not possible to determine how many fascists and Nazis of the twenties, thirties, and forties truly take the responsibility for their actions and their commitments. Also, it is not possible to determine how many of these people truly regret having belonged to and supported them. Maziere and others like him are an indication of the feeling

of confidence in the human race. People make mistakes, and many never realize or regret them. This is a source of feelings of despair about the human race's future. However, people like Maziere provide us with confidence in humanity. It is comforting to know that people can realize when they have been wrong and can take responsibility for such actions. This in itself indicates that the future of the human race is one in which to have confidence.

Aleksandr Solzhenitsyn's novel, *The First Circle*, permits our generation to view the future of humanity with confidence. Solzhenitsyn's novel itself is a source of optimism, and his character Clara, who although she plays only a minor role in the book expresses a message which is loud and clear.

Solzhenitsyn's novel itself and his themes are important sources for confidence in the future of the human race and the purpose of life on earth. Simply, the novel is about the scientists and technicians (zeks) who are prisoner in the Soviet GULAG after World War II. These men are imprisoned for being alleged enemies of the Soviet State. Solzhenitsyn himself was in such a prison, and his own personal experiences are described through Nerzhin.

Solzhenitsyn wrote The FIrst Circle in efforts to protest the tyranny and the abuses of the Soviet State. The book, however, is optimistic because it illustrates that the oppressive Stalinist state with its fear and terror tactics was unsuccessful. Also, when Solzhenitsyn was writing the book, he knew that these camps had been closed down and the prisoners freed. This story serves to document that a society based on terror and fear cannot survive.

Though Solzhenitsyn writes this novel knowing that these camps have been closed and with his own experience from being in one of these prisons, the novel can convey and does convey a sense of hopelessness and despair and can make one doubt the ability of his fellow man to endure. However, although there is grimness and despair, Solzhenitsyn punctuates this with signs of hope. For example, the deep and close friendship between Nerzhin and Rubin again illustrates man's ability to love another man and the comforts which love can provide. The fact that humans can find solace in other human beings under the most inhumane and dire circumstances illustrates that there is a purpose to life and that humanity, as long as men love men, cannot ever reach a state of total despair.

Solzhenitsyn further encourages his reader with the words that Nerzhin's wife wrote in his confiscated book of poems: "And so it will be that everything lost will return to you" (p. 653). It can be inferred from these words that the freedom which the prisoners lost in exchange for oppression and brutality will be returned to them. Also, these words signify that there is hope that whatever a human being loses can be regained. Devastation and destruction, whether physical or emotional, can be overcome.

Another facet of the novel which provides the reader with confidence in the human race is the setting of the novel over Christmas. In this sense, the novel can be seen as a parallel with the life of Christ—a series of struggles. All of the characters are confronted with struggles and must make choices. However, Christ was resurrected, and this fact is the provision of hope for the characters as well as for mankind. The characters will be resurrected from their imprisonment and their hell. Mankind will triumph in the future as in the past.

Confidence in the future of human life can also be found in the character of Clara, Prosecutor Makarygin's daughter. Though she is not a major character, Clara's message makes a major impact within the novel and life in general. Clara suffers because she is aware of the injustices within her society. She knows that some of the prisoners are innocent, and she knows that her father is responsible for condemning innocent men to prison. Clara possesses a wonderful and keen insight into life and the Soviet system. She knows that something is seriously wrong. She is tormented by the contradiction which she views her father to be. Clara finds many faults with communism, the Party, and the Stalinist regime. She rebels against all that her father and the system stand for. Her awareness of the world around her is inspiring as is her ability to see the injustices and evilness of the communist state which surrounds her.

Our present society stresses the existence of generation gaps and usually the negative and detrimental effects which they have on society. In the relationship between Clara and her father, the reader witnesses a generation gap and a youth in rebellion.

Makarygin even states with respect to his daughter and her views: "Again, the eternal impossibility of explaining the wisdom of the older generation logically and clearly to the-foolish young" (p. 426). Generation gaps existed in postwar Russia, and they exist in present day society. In all periods of history, younger generations rebel against older ones. This is the story of life and its cycle. Solzhenitsyn views this youthful rebellion as hopeful for the future. He sees it in a positive light. Solzhenitsyn believes that the struggle between truth and untruth makes life worth living, and this can be a meaning of generation gap. Changing attitudes among generations give life a purpose and confidence in the future of humanity.

Though the generation of Europeans born between 1900 and 1920 did experience a great deal of devastation and destruction and suffering and though they were challenged by extremist ideologies and the tasks of mere survival and rebuilding their lives, they prove that we should have confidence in the future of the human race and in the purpose of life. Pasternak's concluding paragraph in Doctor Zhivago, which descibes a scene with Gordon and Dudorov ten years after the revolution, is a beautiful, timeless passage which summarizes a feeling of confidence in mankind and a sense that life is worth living:

"To the two old friends, as they sat by the window, it seemed that this freedom of the soul was already there, as if that very evening the future had tangibly moved into the streets below them, that they themselves had entered it and were now a part of it. Thinking of this holy city and of the entire earth, of the still-living protagonists of this story, and their children, they were filled with tenderness and peace, and they were enveloped by the unheard music of happiness that flowed all about them and into the distance. (p.522–3)

If history teaches us anything, it teaches us that there is a purpose of life-on earth and. that we must have confidence in the future of the human race.

This was not the most elegantly written paper that I ever received in that course, but it was the most moving. Lisa had engaged two great novels and a great documentary intensely and emerged with a genuine, heartfelt answer to a difficult question. Two years later another student wrote on her evaluation of this course, "It is what education should be," and the paper bore that out. And although this thought has never occurred to me until now, I was probably finding hope in the wake of my own long private ordeal, too. In the Harvard tradition I came out of, an exam that showed real mastery of the course usually earned at least an A- in the course as well as an A for itself. Following that tradition, I wrote an enthusiastic comment and gave her an A for the paper and the course. When she came by to pick it up she was one of the most excited students I had ever seen. I had set a high bar, and she had gone over it. I reached out and gave her a half-hug with one arm as she went out, and she returned it with interest. I never saw her or spoke with her again.

VI

THE FORK IN THE ROAD

1987–91

After the 1986 Christmas holidays, I began to feel an enormous sense of relief and a renewed ability to enjoy life. Everything seemed to get quite a lot better over the next three years. Both my sons were now in school and Cathy was back at work, and eventually struck out on her own in public relations. Carnegie Mellon (as it was now known—the word "university," apparently, did not suit the powers that be) was four miles away from my house, and I began commuting by bike. I had been deeply involved in our small town's youth soccer program since it began, and I was also a referee in another local town with a much larger program. And although I had never resumed regular piano lessons since moving to Pittsburgh, I was now playing more and more and better and better.

My teaching role became more important during the next two years. In addition to War and Revolution, I was now teaching the junior course for history majors and minors, of which there were eventually about 30. The best history students in it always seemed to have some odd story behind their finding their way to Carnegie Mellon, and my biggest problem working there, from start to finish, was that I could not imagine why any talented kid interested in liberal arts would want to come. Initially I had the students write substantial research papers, and I remember one from a pre-med student named Craig Denny on the security case of J. Robert Oppenheimer that would have done credit to anyone anywhere. But for several years, a considerable portion of the class simply couldn't manage the assignment, and I changed course. The class became a course on how to think historically, assigning several pairs of books on the same topic, with conflicting interpretations. The topics included Jacksonian democracy and whether the controversy over the U.S. Bank actually had a real effect on the American economy; the question of whether slaves really responded to economic incentives, as Robert Fogel and Stanley Engerman had argued in *Time on the Cross*; and the issue of Franklin Roosevelt's leadership on the eve of the Second World War. Every student had to write a short paper for each unit.

I was also teaching on another front, one which in retrospect is even more interesting.

The Carnegie Mellon history department and the applied history program that was part of it had graduate programs. I was somewhat taken aback by the seriousness with which they were taken when I arrived, because the students covered a very broad range in quality, and I had just seen myself and many Harvard contemporaries struggle, usually without success, to establish themselves in a job. But some of my senior colleagues were very proud of the program and their right to grant Ph.Ds. This had led to a minor disaster early in my career when a man in his mid-30s who had started grad school at an Ivy League school 15 years earlier—and never earned a degree—had managed to impress Joel Tarr to the extent of getting him to award a year of fellowship support. He was writing on a topic involving European war, in theory, and he was turned over to me. Not surprisingly given his track record, he got nowhere during that year. Tarr obviously thought that that was partly my fault, but I did not think that anyone who could not motivate himself should be pursuing a graduate degree

Subsequently I had taken on a few students from the applied history program. One, Xiao-Bing Li, was a Taiwanese immigrant who had graduated from Carnegie Mellon in 1985. The Chinese government, remarkably, was now making some primary sources about the first decades of Communist rule available to scholars—something that the USSR never did. He took advantage of this to write a very interesting thesis about the Taiwan Straits crisis of 1954, which began by showing that China in the wake of the Korean War was actively seeking détente with the West. After receiving his degree in 1991, he was eventually hired by the University of Central Oklahoma, where he has been a prolific author and editor of books on Communist China, including its involvement in the Korean War. He has also edited international oral histories of both the Korean and Vietnam Wars. He would rank as a very productive scholar at any university in the country.

A second was Harold Scott, who wrote his dissertation on covert action under the Eisenhower Administration. Although the available source material was not as plentiful as it later became, he did a fine job, incorporating a number of different cases, including Cuba and the Congo. He was initially hired by the public policy school at the neighboring University of Pittsburgh, but later moved to Howard University, where is he now the director of the International Affairs center. The field of American diplomatic history was becoming increasingly polarized between neoconservatives on the one hand and revisionists on the other, and I once kidded him, years after he had finished, that I was sorry not to have planted him firmly in one of those two schools. He laughed and said that my approach was more intellectually stimulating, which I appreciated.

I was fortunate that all my grad students had real intellectual ambitions, and they were fortunate, I would like to think, that I wanted to encourage them. I am astonished in retrospect that an actual majority of my Ph.D. students went on to careers in academia—a percentage that I suspect very few of my contemporaries at major universities could match. I have no doubt that I could have advised some extremely interesting theses had I ever worked in a major graduate program, but we shall never know how my students would have fared in the job market.

In my adult life I have generally reached my major intellectual turning points by accident. In the late spring of 1987, I was invited to a weekend conference at the Ditchley Foundation in Britain, bringing together a "new generation" of academics and civil servants to discuss the state of the world. I enjoyed the conference thoroughly, but its most important moment, for me, came on my second night when I went into the library looking for something to read and emerged with *The Education of Henry Adams*. Ernest May in lecture had once touted Adams's *History of the United States during the Administrations of Thomas Jefferson and James Madison*—a 9-volume work—as a very great book, and I had spent $35 on a used four-volume set at one of Cambridge's best second-hand bookstores. But I hadn't gotten around to reading it, or anything else by Adams. Within just a few pages, however, I realized that I had discovered one of the people to whom I would always feel the closest.

The parallels between Adams and myself were quite striking. While I certainly could not boast of such a distinguished lineage as the grandson and great-grandson of Presidents, I too had spent my childhood among the great, the near-great, and the would-be great of the world of politics. Our lives had revolved around the same two geographical poles, Boston and Washington—and both of us ultimately preferred our adopted home to the one where we had been born. His father Charles Francis Adams had been Minister to the Court of St. James during the Civil War, while mine had held the same title exactly a century later, during the Vietnam War. (By 1964, however, the position was not so exalted, since the American mission now included an Ambassador as well.) And both Adams and I had been Harvard undergraduates—and Harvard assistant professors. But Adams, like Arthur Schlesinger Jr., had quit Harvard's history department because he preferred to live in Washington. That I would never have done. In the *Education*, written decades later (like this book), Adams's enthusiasm for his subject—medieval history—and for his students shone through anyway. One student, when asked what use he planned to make of his Harvard education, replied, "The degree of Harvard College is worth money to me in Chicago." Consciously or unconsciously I am sure that many of mine had felt the same, but they had taken plenty of joy in learning as well.

When I got home, I read Adams's novels, led by *Democracy*, his classic political novel of 1880s Washington. The hero of the novel, Silas P. Ratcliffe, a Republican Senator from the

Midwest with presidential ambitions, was generally thought to have been modeled on James G. Blaine of Maine, whose own presidential candidacy was only months away when the novel appeared. Ratcliffe, depending on one's point of view, is either a supreme realist or a consummate cynic. Much of the drama in the book revolves around his romance with Madeleine Lightfoot Lee, a widow who comes to Washington to learn how government really works. The book—which Adams published anonymously—was a sensational best-seller on both sides of the Atlantic, and Blaine professed to be deeply offended by the portrait. I, on the other hand, still believe that Ratcliffe was the hero of the book because he was the kind of man without illusions who made government work. Inspired, I started a new course on political fiction and biography, which included *Democracy*, Robert Penn Warren's magnificent *All the King's Men*, and selections from the first volume of Robert Caro's biography of Lyndon Johnson. I wanted my students to know how the world really worked.

I was eager to read more of Adams, but first I had to finish my new book, now tentatively entitled *Politics and War*. Dr. James Billington, the director of the Wilson Center in Washington—whose committees had consistently turned down my requests for a year in residence—offered me a month in the summer, and I used it to get going on the last part of the book, now entitled "The Second Thirty Years' War, 1914–45." By the time I returned to Pittsburgh, I was ready to start writing it. The whole book now had a very definite shape.

As I have already noted, the first section of the book—"The General Crisis of the 16th and 17th centuries, 1559–1659"—revolved around the unsuccessful attempts of monarchs to exert real national authority over their aristocrats. It was in the era of Louis XIV, I realized, that the monarchs had gotten the upper hand. Louis XIV managed to do this in France in the wake of the Fronde of the 1640s, and he had pursued relatively modest goals in his early wars. Crucially, he subsidized his fellow monarchs instead of trying to undermine them by opening up connections with their leading aristocrats. That had strengthened monarchy all over the continent and paved the way for a long period (1713–1791) of relatively small-scale wars during which Europe had prospered economically and intellectually. The Revolutionary and Napoleonic era, which I had already written up, combined monarchical ambition with new ideas about the rationalization of political life and transformed both the European map and European institutions. It also opened up the European elite somewhat to men of lesser status—led by Napoleon Bonaparte—and unleashed their ambitions. Fortunately, I argued, after 1815 the industrial revolution came along to provide young men with another outlet, allowing for another long period of peace.

After two full decades of study, I saw that two issues had dominated both the First and Second World Wars. The first was imperialism, which the great industrial powers had managed diplomatically—among themselves—until 1914. In that year, however, as my article had shown, the German government plunged the world into war to secure a greater empire, and Hitler had made even more grandiose plans after seizing power in 1933, leading to the Second World War. The British and French had become more imperial in their outlook in the interwar period as well, as I had shown in *Economic Diplomacy*. But the armed competition for empire, I showed in some detail, had led to economic disaster. The First World War had inflated the Europeans' currencies, cost them enormous sums of capital and left them burdened with heavy overseas debts. It also led to worldwide overproduction of many agricultural and industrial goods, setting the stage for the Great Depression. Hitler had concluded that autarky was the only solution and unleashed another great war to try to create it.

The second, even more tragic issue dominating European international politics was the rights of nationalities, especially the minorities within the Russian, Ottoman, Austro-Hungarian and German empires. All four of those governments relied increasingly on nationalism to strengthen their authority in the late nineteenth and early twentieth centuries, but that only made their subject nationalities more restive. The new Balkan states such as Greece and Serbia also wanted to expand further at the old empires' expense. Serbia's conflict with Austria-Hungary, of course, was one of the two triggers of the First World War. After that war broke out, both sides shamelessly bid for the support of subject populations in enemy territory with promises of postwar gains. The Germans also laid plans for the expulsion of much of their minority Polish population, while the Turks carried out genocide against their Armenian minority. The Russian, Ottoman, and Austro-Hungarian empires were destroyed by the war, and the victorious Allies helped establish a multitude of new successor states—the states I had explored in *Economic Diplomacy*. But those states inevitably contained minorities too, and the treaties they signed to assure their rights were increasingly honored in the breach in the 1920s and 1930s.

These conflicts took a horrifying turn during the Second World War. Nazi Germany, of course, aimed to create a racially homogenous empire, and to expel, enslave, or murder anyone who did not belong to the so-called Aryan race. This topic inevitably led me to the origins of the Holocaust, which I placed within the broader framework of Nazi racial policy. But the policies of the victorious powers were also drastic. After the Allies had decided to allow Poland and the USSR to annex large parts of Germany, about 12 million Germans were forcibly expelled from those territories, from a restored Czechoslovakia, and from Rumania and Yugoslavia. While the German crimes were unique, I placed them within this broader story of attempts to create homogenous national states.

The twin dreams of great empires and homogeneous national states, I wrote, also lay at the heart of the origins of totalitarianism, as Hannah Arendt had argued. And although twentieth century Europeans thought they were living in a great age of rationalism, neither dream really made much sense. Reason, as David Hume had written two centuries earlier, emerged as the slave of the passions. "Imperialism and nationalism fired the European imagination," I wrote, "not because they corresponded to reality, or even because they could easily be achieved. The secret of their appeal lies buried in the emotional development of nineteenth- and twentieth-century Western man, who has customarily proclaimed rational justifications for his particularly irrational passions. The ideas for which National

Socialism murdered millions and changed the course of European history were common European ideas, and the tragedy of National Socialism is, therefore, a European tragedy as well as a purely German one."

Politics and War was above all, I now see a work of comparative history. So was *Economic Diplomacy*, but it simply compared the policies of three major states—Germany, Britain, and France—towards a certain geographical area over a single decade. *Politics and War* compared in two different dimensions, comparing the politics and strategies of different states within each of four specific periods, and also comparing the politics of those periods to each other. While I was writing it I spent a weekend at a German history conference in Philadelphia organized by my friend Tom Childers. (Only he, I suspect, would have invited me to a conference on German history.) At one point in the discussion, one participant lamented that "none of us do comparative work, maybe because we can't afford enough research assistants." I immediately said that I did indeed do it—but I was to find that there was no real market for it. The author of *Politics and War* was also clearly qualified to teach a substantial portion of a western civilization survey, but this was the era in which such surveys were beginning to disappear from curriculums. And in any event, in contrast to the situation at Harvard in the 1940s and early 1950s, no department was making senior appointments to strengthen their undergraduate curriculum any more.

It must have been in 1988 or early 1989 that I began marketing *Politics and War*. Some efforts to find an agent or connect with a trade publisher got nowhere, but this time I struck oil at Harvard University Press. Aida Donald was again interested, and two outside readers endorsed it. Publication was scheduled for the fall of 1990.

Meanwhile, a parallel book had become a major publishing event.

Paul Kennedy was (and is) two years older than I am. Born in the north of England, he had been something of a boy wonder in British academia during the 1970s, writing several books, including *The Rise and Fall of British Naval Mastery*. We had, as we have seen, crossed paths in 1981 when he reviewed *Economic Diplomacy*, in tandem with Gerhard Weinberg's history of Hitler's foreign policy in the *TLS*. In the early 1980s, Yale had advertised a senior position in history that was pretty clearly designed for Kennedy. I had applied and received the briefest and most perfunctory of replies. He got the job. Kennedy had published a long book, *The Rise of the Anglo-German Antagonism*, dealing with the decades before the First World War, and I reviewed it for the *Journal of Modern History*. It was a very readable book and my review was very favorable. But I questioned his conclusion that "the most profound cause" of the estrangement between the two nations was economic. Indeed, the caveats I raised about his treatment of German responsibility for the war probably led to my decision to write an article on the subject myself.

Kennedy, I discovered in 1987, was also working on a general history of European war since the 16th century, which he eventually entitled *The Rise and Fall of the Great Powers*. I heard him discuss it at the Wilson Center in June 1987 and it seemed that he was taking a rather traditional approach, arguing that great powers that became over-extended and spent too much money on war inevitably declined, and posing the question of whether the US, just coming off of the Reagan era, was falling into the same trap. Kennedy had also shopped his project to trade publishers, but with more success. Donald Lamm, a leading non-fiction editor at W. W. Norton—who much later became my literary agent—had lost the rights to the book because he could not persuade his colleagues to increase their offer from $20,000 to $25,000. Both Lamm and Kennedy have dined out on this story for decades. Kennedy placed it with Random House instead.

According to legend, it was a Random House editor who suggested that Kennedy add a dimension to the book by surveying the goals, strategies, and resources of all the contemporary great powers, including the USSR, China, Japan, the United States, and the European Union. Kennedy had done so at some length in a final chapter. I was eager to review the book, and secured a copy at the AHA convention in Washington in

December 1987—the same convention, I believe, at which I met Fritz Fischer. I had once again secured the assignment from the *Journal of Modern History* and I got to work right away, probably submitting the review during January.

Kennedy based his history of European warfare from 1500 to 2000 on a simple argument: that economic strength was the key to military strength. In the major great power wars, he wrote, "victory has always gone to the side with the greatest material resources." On the other hand, he argued, nations that spent *too much* on military power would, in the long run, undermine their economies and therefore end up weaker. Looking back at the book from thirty years' distance, it occurs to me that the argument is stacked in favor of Kennedy's native Great Britain in a rather Churchillian fashion. Britain always seemed to wind up on the winning side, as Kennedy saw it, because it did not waste too much money on a standing army and used its Navy to promote trade and economic growth. It seemed to me, as I argued at some length, that Kennedy's application of this model to very different eras did not take sufficient account of historical facts. He described the period 1519–1659 as a "Hapsburg bid for mastery," folding a very long sequence of largely unrelated events into a single family's struggle for power. Continuing, he argued that the British had prevailed over Louis XIV in 1661–1713 for economic reasons, even though the best study of the issue showed that the British and French had spent about the same amount of money on those wars. I also argued that those wars ended with a new equilibrium, not a French defeat. More fundamentally, it seemed to me that the argument, by treating states as unitary actors simply trying to outdo one another in a kind of European league table, had ignored the relatively recent contributions of people like Graham Allison who had encouraged us to view policy as the outcome of institutional pressures and struggles among individuals. It also seemed to me rather unsophisticated not to ask fundamental questions about what nations in different eras were fighting for, and what their chance of achieving it was. There, I must plead guilty to one count of a reviewer's classic crime: accusing the author of writing his own book, instead of mine. But the tone of the review was polite throughout, and it paid a great deal of attention to the details of *The Rise and Fall of the Great Powers*.

It was *after* I had submitted my review that *The New Republic* did a cover story announcing that *The Rise and Fall of the Great Powers* was destined to be the book of the year because of its implications for the present and future of American foreign policy. Its appreciation focused on the last section of the book, which analyzed the economic and military strength of the United States, the European Economic Community (as it then was), the USSR, China, and Japan. Kennedy argued, with typical caution, that both the US and the USSR might, or might not, be spending too much on arms and doing too little for their economy, and predicted that the EEC, Japan, and China would someday acquire military power commensurate with their economic strength. That prediction, thirty years later, has been at most 33% correct. But as it happened, *The New Republic* and other reviews persuaded educated Americans—particularly in the business world—that they *had* to read *The Rise and Fall of the Great Powers* in order to cope intelligently with international competition in the years ahead. The book became a national and international publishing sensation, by far the most successful book written by a professional historian during the whole of my career. Meanwhile, the *Journal of Modern History* had fallen way behind in the publication of its reviews, and mine did not appear until December 1989, two full years after the publication of the book. By then it undoubtedly struck some readers as a case of sour grapes, but as I finally got a chance to tell Paul Kennedy just a few years ago, it was written before anyone had any idea of what a phenomenon the book was to become.

I was now clearer about my long-term goals. Although I knew I was contributing to Carnegie Mellon, I did not want to spend the rest of my career there. What I really wanted was to teach somewhere that I would have liked to have gone myself, a place that would have more students with whom I had more in common, and a location—either urban or rural—in which I could feel more at home. I did not expect to go back to Harvard and didn't care, and I would have been happy anywhere in the Ivy League, or at comparable universities in other parts of the country, or at any one of at least a dozen fine liberal arts colleges, or at any of a number of state universities. A favorite baseball book of mine had appeared in the early 1980s, *The Men in Blue* by Larry Gerlach. It was an oral history of the lives of about a dozen umpires from the first half of the century, and many of them told of their years in the minors, waiting to get into the big time. My case was a little different since I *had* worked in the big time, but I identified with them, especially with Emmett Ashford, the first black umpire, who languished in the minors for nearly 20 years before finally getting called up by the American League. "No matter how full the bottle of milk," Ashford's mother told him in the days before homogenizing, "there's always room for cream at the top." That was my hope and *Politics and War*, like Ashford's flamboyant style of umpiring, was designed to distinguish myself.

Appropriate jobs continued to open up, but not for me. Walter MacDougall, whose career had crossed paths with mine a couple of times already, had brought out a second book on the space race and parlayed that into a move from Berkeley (where he eventually had gotten tenure) to the University of Pennsylvania. That opened up his job at Berkeley, which was very appealing indeed. When the department advertised for a senior position, I enthusiastically replied. I was not interviewed. Instead, the job went to another Brit, Anthony Adamthwaite, who had written one book on France and the origins of the Second World War. He has stayed within his original area of specialty ever since, and brought out his last book in 1995. I remember that Swarthmore advertised a job in German history, and I wrote for that while saying that I would not come without tenure. The search chair replied that they simply could not make tenured appointments. I stared at that letter for a few minutes in my office. Evidently that was one institution that was now closed off to me forever.

A more interesting ad appeared in the late 1980s from the history department at Williams College. It called for a historian of American diplomacy, which I knew I could do and planned to write about next, and added, "senior appointment possible in exceptional circumstances." I wrote an excited letter to the search committee chair, Charles Dew, and sent him copies of my two books. As always when writing away for any job, I also included copies of my two student teaching evaluations from Harvard, while explaining that Carnegie Mellon did not write out evaluations. He replied politely that unfortunately, he thought that the college would only agree to a senior appointment "if it would advance the affirmative action goals of the institution." I called the editorial office of the AHA job bulletin to ask if such restrictions were allowed, and they replied that they were not. I wrote a rather sharp note to Dew, pointing out that he could not have told female or black candidates that they would not be considered without very grave consequences, and said that I expected to be looked at seriously. Not only did he fail to reply, but he did not return the books I had sent him months later when I asked for them. Years later two very distinguished historians of American foreign relations told me they had also applied for the job and received exactly the same response from Dew. The junior person Williams hired evidently did not work out, and by the mid-2000s, as we shall see, they had no one teaching American foreign policy at all.

Sometime in the late 1980s I also tried my hand at writing a grant proposal, the most valued project that a CMU faculty member could undertake. I applied to the United States Institute of Peace, as I remember, for a large grant to hold a conference on the Cold War entitled, "The Forty Years' Peace." Different presenters would discuss specific issues between the US and the Soviet Union and make the point that in one way or another, most of them had been resolved. Like all such grants, this one included a large request for money for university overhead. It was turned down, and I later learned that I had requested more than 50% of all the money they had available. I did not pursue the project any further. I was more successful in providing the intellectual inspiration for a grant. Jay Kadane, the statistician who had introduced me to Bayesian analysis after hearing me discuss Sacco and Vanzetti, had joined with a friend of his, David Schrum, to write a proposal for a big National Science Foundation Grant to do a probabilistic analysis of the case. They found a place for me within it. Eventually that grant came through, with significant benefit to Carnegie Mellon—and it would never have happened without me.

As I look back at 1989–90, I am rather astonished at how much I was doing. To begin with, during the summer of 1989 I actually read Henry Adams's history of the United States under Jefferson and Madison from cover to cover, making myself, I would guess, one of just a few hundred living people who had done so. The book is one of the great works of the western historical tradition, thoroughly based in archival research and equally thorough about matters domestic (the creation of Jeffersonian democracy) and foreign (the impact on the United States of the Napoleonic Wars, culminating in the War of 1812.) Adams had begun the book in Washington, after leaving Harvard College. The tragic suicide of his wife Clover, who had plunged into depression after the death of her own father, occurred in the midst of it, and like me at various periods of my life, he had buried himself in an earlier period of history. He wrote familiarly about all the major figures in the book, largely, I suspect, because he, like me, had actually known statesmen of the highest rank since his childhood. Thanks in part to his own years in London during the American Civil War, he was equally at home discussing the diplomacy and strategy of the British government, and he also wrote very perceptively about Napoleon. I was very surprised to find that no critic, as far as I know, had taken note of one of the defining features of the book. Adams had fallen in love with Thomas Jefferson as a man and as a statesman. He regarded Jefferson's attempt to substitute economic sanctions (the Embargo Act) for war with Britain as a truly tragic failure.

For Madison as President, on the other hand, Adams had almost nothing but contempt. He seemed to him unable either to set or steer a clear course amidst the greatest world war in human history and drifted into conflict without the means to contest the British successfully even in the western hemisphere. Adams' extremely sophisticated analysis of the war focused on the incapacity of the early American state, which lacked the necessary military or financial instruments to fight. Yet the ingenuity of individual Americans, he argued, had saved the nation: the metalworkers who had cast our excellent artillery and the shipwrights who had built the fast schooners that very seriously interfered with British trade around the British Isles, and were always quick enough to get away from British warships when they appeared on the horizon. Adams's great work remains, for me, one of the two best multi-volume classics of American history, ranking with Allen Nevins's *The Ordeal of the Union* on the origins of the Civil War, which I have now read twice. That book, too, I would imagine, has at this moment been read by less than 1000 living Americans. Robert Caro's great biography of Lyndon Johnson could rank in the same class, if Caro manages to finish it. I suppose I have always been too busy moving from one thing to another to commit decades to a single project.

And I was involved in another new project in the summer of 1989, well before *Politics and War* appeared in print. (I once agreed with another remarkably productive historian, Robert Dallek, that one of the secrets of a prolific historian was to get thoroughly involved in the next project before the last one has appeared in print, and I am again following my own advice as I write these words.) This one was for fun. It was about baseball.

Baseball literature, led by Bill James, was exploding during the 1980s, and I wanted to get into the act. My subject was the American League pennant race of 1948, in which the Cleveland Indians had beaten the Red Sox in a one-game playoff to decide the race, two days after the Red Sox had eliminated the Yankees from contention in Fenway Park. A great *Boston Globe* columnist, Harold Kaese, had written his farewell column in the paper about 1948 in 1973, noting that it marked the peak of interest in baseball in Boston, since the National League Braves did win the pennant. I had been fascinated by at least two other books, very different in character, which had told the story of a season from first to last. One was Jim Bouton's *Ball Four*, which had revolutionized sports writing in 1970 thanks to its frank discussion of clubhouse life and use of explicit language. The other was *The Unforgettable Season* by Gordon Fleming, which used verbatim newspaper clippings to tell the story of the 1908 National League pennant race among the New

York Giants, the Chicago Cubs, and the Pittsburgh Pirates, in which a Cubs-Giants game had to be replayed at the end of the season to decide the race because of the famous "Merkle's boner" controversy. Like Bouton and Fleming, I wanted to recreate the experience of that season, which featured an amazing cast of characters. The Indians included shortstop/manager Lou Boudreau, who knew before Opening Day that his job was on the line; Hall of Fame hurler Bob Feller, who suffered through a terrible first half; Larry Doby, the first black player in the American League; and manic, brilliant young owner Bill Veeck. The drama of the Red Sox revolved around the relationship between Ted Williams, their controversial star, and new manager Joe McCarthy, who had just taken over the team after 15 years at the helm of the Yankees. And the New Yorkers relied on Joe DiMaggio, who finished the season with a crippled heel but tallied a league-leading 39 homers and 155 runs batted in. I knew all that when I started the book, but I could not foresee what I found when I started going through the *New York Times*, the first of three newspapers in which I followed the season from beginning to end. It was a high-offense era, and the games among the three contenders were some of the most exciting I had ever encountered. In addition, until the first week in August, Connie Mack's Philadelphia Athletics were contending as well, and the lead changed nearly every day during the month of July.

Politics and War may be my most striking achievement, and *American Tragedy* is my favorite book, but nothing ever compared to the experience of researching and writing what became *Epic Season: The 1948 American League Pennant Race*. The look of the eight team standings in each day's newspaper reminded me of my childhood, and I learned the simple rhythm of the schedule in those distant days. The sound of my office phone when I was working on the book was like an alarm clock waking me from a dream, and I did many double takes to remind myself that I was back in 1989, not 1948. I also did telephone interviews with quite a few of the surviving players—although Williams, alas, never answered my letters—and drove to Cleveland to interview Bob Feller and Denny Galehouse, who had started the playoff game for the Red Sox. The original draft of the manuscript was much too detailed and much too long, and that caused trouble in the early marketing. Indeed, it was not until 1998 that the book finally saw the light of day. But it was a wonderful experience, and the response to it, as we shall see, was very gratifying.

I did not share the new project with Peter Stearns or most of my senior colleagues, although they undoubtedly heard something about it. I knew that my next academic project was going to focus on the origins of the US involvement in Vietnam, and I had begun looking at published documents about that, as well. Meanwhile, there had been some new additions to the department and some important changes in the curriculum. In 1985, I believe, we had hired Lizabeth Cohen, a freshly minted Berkeley Ph.D. who had written an impressive thesis on Chicago workers and the New Deal, and her husband, Herrick Chapman, who had written about the French aircraft industry in the 1930s. They initially had shared a job but had each been given a separate appointment after several years. They were good professional and social friends of Cathy's and mine. Joe Trotter, meanwhile, had finished a second work of social history on a different black American community and had been promoted to full professor as a result. And Peter Stearns had suddenly told the department that he wanted to bring in a new faculty member named Steve Schlossman, who had not written any books, but who had spent quite a few years researching various aspects of American public policy at the Rand Corporation. Peter presented it to me and my junior colleagues as a fait accompli, adding that Schlossman wanted to come as a full professor, "and I don't have any problem with that." I did not protest, but it seemed awfully unfair that I and my younger colleagues had to spend so many years teaching and writing just to get tenure, while an outsider whose qualifications were at best equal to our own jumped right to the top of the heap. I was however quite certain that I would be a full professor by 1991. On another front, Stearns had killed our traditional western civ equivalent, The Origins of the Modern World, and replaced it with World History. For the second time, he was putting himself in the forefront of a major academic trend.

I was rather stunned, in the spring of 1989, to receive a letter from Michael Spence, the dean of the Harvard faculty—a letter apparently addressed to virtually every alumnus of Harvard College. Spence reported that a great many senior faculty were now retiring, and that he needed contributions from us to make it possible to replace them. After some hesitation, I replied, speculating that the letter was aimed at those who had capitalized on their Harvard education financially, but explaining that I had viewed my experience there very differently. I told the story of my career as an assistant professor and sketched out what I had accomplished since, adding that I thought I had proved myself a worthy candidate for promotion. "At one time," I concluded, "I did try to contribute just about everything I had to Harvard, and I have never regretted it. The institution, however, made it clear that it didn't care about those contributions, and now I'm afraid that I can't come up with the kind of contribution your letter asked for." I received no reply.

By the spring of 1990, *Politics and War* had been accepted by Harvard Press and was scheduled to come out in the following fall. I spoke to Stearns about coming up for full professor in the next academic year. To my amazement, he was clearly uncomfortable with the idea, although he did not say why. When I mentioned that my third book was about to come out, he retorted that "it was used" as part of my tenure case, even though at that point it was only half done. I was undaunted. I had waited long enough, and I could not believe that any department would deny full professor rank to someone who had written three books—including a major multi-archival research effort, and a very large synthetic work.

It was at about this time, in the spring of 1990, that I got the telephone call that changed my life. It came from Bill Fuller, formerly of Colgate, whom I had recruited for the abortive AHA panel on the origins of the First World War back in 1983. He was now the chairman of the Strategy and Policy Department at the Naval War College in Newport.

As I was to learn, that department was nearly 20 years old. It was the brainchild of Admiral Stansfield Turner, a Rhodes Scholar and Annapolis classmate of former President Carter, who had taken over the War College in 1972, as the Vietnam War was winding down. Turner wanted to give his fellow officers a touch of the kind of education he had had at Oxford, complete with tutorials, papers, and long classic works from the western tradition. The original Strategy and Policy syllabus required the students to read a couple of entire books a week. Clausewitz's *On War* and Thucydides's *History of the Peloponnesian War* took up the first two weeks. A week included several lectures, and a three-hour seminar of about ten people, taught by a team made up of a permanent civilian faculty member and a military faculty member on assignment to the college. During the 1980s, under the leadership of the historian Al Bernstein, the department had become a bastion of neoconservatism.

Bill Fuller had other ideas. Four years younger than myself, he too had attended Harvard both as an undergraduate and a grad student. Although we had both been there for most of the 1970s, we had never met. He had heard a good deal about me from some of his fellow graduate students who had taken my lecture course, however, and he had taken the trouble to read my books. Although Bill was also a political conservative, that had nothing to do with his ambitions for the department. He had been a junior faculty member at Colgate for several years, but his wife Sarah was well-established in business in the Boston area, and the strain of commuting was too much. He then had landed a temporary position at Harvard but could not even become an assistant professor. Meanwhile, he had brought out his first book. Then he had started working at Newport, which was about 90 minutes away from his home in Westwood, Massachusetts.

Bill wanted to turn the Strategy and Policy department into the world's leading center for the study of military strategy. He himself was interested in Russian strategy, about which he was finishing a very large book, and he knew how hard it had become for anyone in diplomatic or military history to find a job anywhere. He had identified me, among others, as a target of opportunity. He had not planned on approaching me just yet, but a situation had developed very quickly. The S & P Department (as it was called) had the right to appoint two Secretary of the Navy Fellows annually to spend one year teaching at the college with a reduced load. One of Bill's candidates for 1990–1 had just backed out at the last minute, and he needed a replacement. Thus he had called me. The idea was very appealing. Because of the short notice, it was clearly impossible for me to relocate my family for the year, and Bill, working with the college leadership, managed to arrange things so that I would spend only the winter term in Newport, when I would do my teaching. I would also make a few other trips during the year to lecture. Cathy knew I could use a change and urged me to go ahead. Peter Stearns made some trouble over the situation but eventually gave in. However, I remained in residence in Pittsburgh until mid-November. I found accommodations in an apartment within the house of another faculty member, Steve Ross.

Two new jobs, both at Princeton, opened up that fall—one in the History Department and one at the Wilson School. *Politics and War* was set to appear at any moment. In August I flew to Boston, stayed with Bill, and attended the school's convocation. Sometime that fall I was invited to a conference at Princeton on nationalities problems by Arthur Waldron, a junior faculty member (and another Harvard product) who was up for tenure. Arthur told me when I arrived that he had invited me at the request of his chairman, who was interested in me for their job. I gave a talk about nationalities problems in Eastern Europe—a major subject of *Politics and War*—before, during, and now after, Communist rule. The talk was the hit of the day—but the history chair did not show up. Bill also flew me up to Newport to give my first lecture there on that hardy perennial, the outbreak of the First World War. I sought and followed, some advice on how to tailor it to the audience, paying particular attention to war plans, and it was very well received.

In early October I was still in my office in Baker Hall at CMU while my promotion case went ahead. My only teaching assignment was to advise the senior thesis of Jennifer Walter, who had taken two classes from me in the previous year. One of them was War and Revolution, and that term, for the first time, I had added an option to the paper based on *For Your Own Good* by Alice Miller. Instead of writing about one of the characters from the novels we had read, the students could also write about themselves. She had done so, describing a very turbulent childhood in very moving terms. Now she was writing something about the JFK assassination.

I sought and received, no feedback from anyone about the progress of my promotion. I was not worrying about it at all. Then, a few days before the decision was scheduled, a departmental secretary made a mistake. She put into my mailbox a note from Peter destined for the 11 full professors who would make the decision. It advised them to be sure to read a letter that had just arrived from Charlie Maier of Harvard, bearing on the case.

Two days later, there was another note from Peter in my box. "I am sorry to have to tell you," it read, "that the vote on your promotion did not go well." As I remember, the eleven full professors had to give me a vote of 1, 2, or 3 (the best) on my overall qualifications, with a 2 necessary to proceed to the next step. My total vote, he informed me, was 1.9, made up, evidently, of five votes of 3 and six votes of 1, or unsatisfactory. My five affirmative votes included from Donald Sutton, a serious Chinese scholar; my friend Dick Schoenwald; Joe Trotter, who went out of his way to express his support a couple of days later; and, I have always believed, Stearns himself. (I did not ask him flat out, but his note about Maier's letter, which was favorable, seemed to point in that direction.) The meeting had apparently been difficult. I later figured out that the six negative votes came from people whose *combined* publication output during the ten years I had been there did not match mine. It also developed that every single outside referee had recommended the promotion. I suspect the key figure in the opposition was Joel Tarr, grantsman extraordinary, who could not forgive me for wanting to be myself instead of him.

The promotion system was based upon a lie. While it was supposed to evaluate scholarship and education, the ability to secure outside funding ranked far higher than either one, especially at the full professor level. I had taken the opportunity to tell the school President, Richard Cyert—whom I knew slightly—that it did not make sense to try to insist that *every* faculty member fit the same mold. He had agreed at the time, but my department had informed me that someone so dedicated to writing and teaching was not welcome. Stearns's pathetic excuse was that promotions at Carnegie Mellon always took account only of work done since the last promotion, and that, for me, meant only half of *Politics and War*. Somehow my "colleagues" had continued to find ways to argue that most of what I did "didn't count." I took advantage of the opportunity to appeal the decision to the next level in the process, the College of Humanities and Social Sciences. In the letter I wrote the Dean I pointed out that the full professors in my department—who had disregarded the unanimous recommendation of authorities in my field—were holding us all to some different standard that had never been defined. I also said that I would never submit a request for promotion to them again. The appeal was denied.

I called Tom Childers at Penn to give him the news, and he erupted in amazement and horror. He spread the word quickly around the profession, and everyone was simply incredulous. Sam Williamson was particularly disturbed. My junior colleagues at CMU were not only disturbed, but devastated. Without exception they looked at me as the leading intellectual light of our generation within the department, and as a friend. They too all cared about scholarship and teaching, not getting grants. No one, evidently, was safe. And they knew that I was on my way at least temporarily to the War College and that the odds were that I would not return.

The Carnegie Mellon history department was throwing away a great opportunity for generational reasons. The senior faculty was made up almost entirely of members of the Silent generation, who had been unable to do any better than the Margaret Morrison Carnegie College of Home Economics back in the 1960s when the job market was booming. Most of them had published little or nothing since and only Schoenwald among them was a distinguished teacher. Now they refused to make way for far more talented and dedicated Boomer historians like Kate Lynch, Anne Rose, Andy Achenbaum, Herrick Chapman, Liz Cohen, Andrew Barnes, Mary Lindemann, and myself. And as a result, one after another, nearly all of those people—and some others as well—eventually left for greener pastures. No one there seemed to care. And after Cohen and Chapman decamped for NYU, Peter Stearns abandoned his dream of building an outstanding social history department, becoming the dean of Humanities and Social Sciences and then the provost of George Mason University.

By now, in 1990, I had spent 14 years fearing that something terrible to happen and terminate my career. My career was, in any case, alive, but oddly, now that something terrible *had* happened, I was briefly rather relieved. But that did not last. I already saw Newport as a good option, but I did not want to give up my dream of a career at an outstanding college or university.

Coincidentally, at almost the moment that the promotion was denied, Aida Donald called me from Harvard Press with remarkable news. *Politics and War* was going to be a main selection of the History Book Club, an honor which as late as 1990 was worth $15,000, which I split with the press. A few months later I used the money to buy my first grand piano. "Congratulations! That's great news!" David Fowler, one of the men who had just voted me down, told me in the history office one morning, and I replied very firmly that I was not in the mood to accept congratulations from the full professors in this department. Mary Lindemann, who was standing nearby, smiled at that.

Meanwhile I prepared for my new responsibilities.

I had to be in Newport by mid-November for the start of the winter term, and I took the train most of the way from Pittsburgh. That enabled me to read most of Clausewitz's *On War*. I had taught small pieces of it for Stanley Hoffmann at Harvard, but this was my first sustained exposure to one of the great minds of modern Europe. Clausewitz was the bible for the Strategy and Policy course because of his focus on the relationship between politics—or political goals—and war. It took me several years to become thoroughly comfortable with his basic principles, but it was worth it. Two weeks later I went to Washington for a family Thanksgiving—again taking the train at least one way—and I used that to make my way through the great Geoffrey Warner translation of Thucydides, which I had read parts of a Harvard freshman, for Hoffmann, and for the Uses of History course with May and Neustadt. Admiral Turner had put Thucydides in the curriculum in 1972 partly as an indirect means of addressing the Vietnam War. One could not, as several veterans of the college explained to me, try to talk about Vietnam in class in the early 1970s because the discussion would become much too heated. But no one, as I had already discovered, could miss the parallels between the disastrous Athenian expedition to Sicily and Vietnam.

My teaching partner was a Navy commander named Julie Kiesling, whom I shared with another SecNav fellow. Some people had apparently been concerned about how well I would fit into the War College because I was a liberal Democrat, but Julie eventually told me that it was her other teaching partner, not I, who had caused some problems with students. The course syllabus was the most extensive I had ever seen, because the course was nearly the only obligation our students had during the term. The reading totaled between 600 and 800 pages a week. The first week of the course dealt with the theory of warfare, focusing on Clausewitz and Sun Tzu. Subsequent weeks included Thucydides, the American Revolution, the wars of the French Revolution and Napoleon, Bismarck's Wars, one week on the First World War, two on the Second, a week on Korea, and a week on Vietnam. I was certainly one of the better prepared new faculty ever to show up at the War College, both because of my breadth of interests and because *Politics and War* dealt with the same fundamental issue as the S & P curriculum: how well did nations use their military to achieve the goals they had set out? As we often told our students, history suggested that at least one side in every major war had miscalculated, and often, both of them had. The military had been in a highly skeptical mood for about 15 years, ever since the end of the Vietnam War. As it happened, the preparation and execution of the Gulf War was taking place that very winter, and several of my colleagues were called down to Washington to consult about it. Since I did not yet have a security clearance, however, I was not privy to any of the discussions they had. We were all encouraged by the war's rapid conclusion and by the Bush Administration's decision to stop well short of total victory.

I was at NWC when the History Book Club announced *Politics and War* as its selection for January 1991. The idea for the book had been born thirteen years earlier in early 1978 when I had been pushing my candidacy for a job at Reed College, an outstanding liberal arts institution in Portland Oregon. By an astonishing coincidence, the review that had presumably led the club to select the book was written by Edward Segel, who belonged to the Reed history department. Every one of my books has gotten at least one review that really got it—and his was the one. It was distributed in a flyer for all club members. It began as follows.

"David Kaiser's magisterial study of politics and war is a fine counterpoint and companion volume to Paul Kennedy's *Rise and Fall of the Great Powers*. Kennedy looked at the expansion and decline of great nations from an economic-technological perspective. Kaiser argues that it is the structure of politics and of a state's values that are ultimately the sources of warfare between nations.

"Obviously such a sweeping analysis contains many points to stir discussion and argument, like Kaiser's deflation of the modern state and its pretensions, or his critiques of other historians, or his many historical characters who appear in this book to be sometimes more traditional, sometimes more innovative than in received interpretations.

"Conservative readers will be provoked by his views on the Cold War. Marxists will probably dislike the book altogether. Surely this is a good sign in both directions? I count all this a virtue and not a weakness since Kaiser's case is generally so well made and his judgment, even when arguable, is so sober and careful. Kaiser *thinks well,* and he gives the reader so much to think about—quite apart from the enormous amount of narrative material here."

"Beneath Kaiser's ·surface narrative of politics and warfare," Segel continued, "the real underlying theme of the book is the relationship between ideas, beliefs, perceptions, aspirations, on one hand, and concrete reality on the other." Kaiser, he wrote, "sets up a demanding standard of statesmanship," asking that leaders take account of reality, as well as of contemporary beliefs. More than ten years earlier, it occurs to me, I had criticized Leslie Gelb and Richard Betts's book, *The Irony of Vietnam: The System Worked*, on exactly these grounds. While Johnson's measures had reflected the consensus of informed opinion, they could not win the war. Now I had found this pattern recurring again and again, especially in eras of general war. Segel ably summarized the four sections of the book, and added his own conclusion: "This is a most interesting and (in the positive sense) weighty book. With its rejection of the Enlightenment –Revolutionary exaltation of the state and its wars, it could hardly be a more appropriate commemoration (intended or unintended) of the 200th anniversary of the appearance of Edmund Burke's *Reflections on the Revolution in France*. (At least for me that is a compliment.)"

To judge from this review, the book had done what I had wanted: to establish myself in the first rank of my profession. It was also my tribute to two centuries of historians on both sides of the Atlantic, who had helped unravel the various political, military and financial mysteries of European war. I had done exactly what I had talked about doing with Jim Wilkinson back at the Harvard history department retreat in the 1970s: I had used literally hundreds of monographs to distill a synthesis. In another great moment, my CMU colleague Mary Lindemann reported that she had spotted a man reading it in the airport. "It's wonderful," he said. I had turned a thorough investigation of historical literature into a readable account.

Yet as the winter wore on I came face to face with the very painful truth. The book was not going to have the impact on my career that I had imagined. Neither of the two Princeton departments that were looking at me asked for an interview.

Earlier, sections of the book had failed to move several other departments. Bill Fuller was delighted by my performance at the War College and offered me a permanent position, and I had a great decision to make

On the one hand, I could see there many things about the Newport environment to enjoy. Thanks to my own Army service I was not in the least troubled by its well-organized and demanding work environment. The S & P Department was full of people interested in what I was interested in, and I enjoyed several of the military faculty. The curriculum was highly stimulating, although the teaching load, from about August 10 through March 1, was far more demanding than that of any major university. But for the rest of the year we were relatively free to research and write, and many colleagues were doing just that. The salary represented at least a 50% increase from what I was making at Carnegie Mellon, where I had been given a very small raise for the next year despite the book. The War College was back in New England, and the Newport area was beautiful. I found a real estate agent and spent a Saturday looking at houses. It was clear that we could substantially upgrade our lifestyle if we moved.

In my heart, I knew I couldn't stay at Carnegie Mellon much longer. But I also knew that if I came to NWC, I would have to commit to it. My own childhood had been chaotic because we moved every few years. My sons had never gone through that. Although they were not enthusiastic about this move, I was confident—and rightly so—that they would be just as happy once we were settled. Cathy was also happy to be going back to New England. I could not expect them to uproot themselves again in the unlikely event that a dream job opened up.

And the more I thought about it, the more convinced I was that it would not. I did not as yet fully understand exactly what had made it so difficult for me to get anywhere on the job market, but I had been trying for 15 years to catch on at one of the 30 or more places I would have loved to work without result. It was clear that European diplomacy was a fading field. It was time, I decided, to stop buying lottery tickets, and in February I told Bill Fuller that I was accepting his offer. Carnegie Mellon declined to make any counteroffer to keep me there. I was only human, and the choice between an institution that wanted me and one that did not was easy to make.

Having registered my acceptance, I made two phone calls. The first went to Ernest May in Cambridge. I told him for the first time that I had been turned down for full professor at Carnegie Mellon. He too simply could not believe it. Then I told him I was going to take the job at Newport, and he congratulated me on joining "the best European history department in the world." He also thought it made more sense to teach full time for eight months and research full time for four, instead of trying to do both at once, as in most universities. I appreciated his reaction, but when I hung up, I felt awful. I called my best friend, Jim Davidson, but reached Evalinn Welling, his wife, instead. She was a dear friend as well and one of the most understanding people I have ever known. And as I told her what had happened I began to cry. I knew this was the right decision, but I had spent 15 years struggling to land a job at a university. Now I was giving it up. In subsequent years I never for one minute wished I was back at Carnegie Mellon and have never questioned that decision. I have always thought, by the way, that I would have made the same decision even if my promotion had come through. The issue was where to spend the rest of my life, and although a few academic friends never understood this—partly because they had no idea what working at CMU was like—there was really no comparison.

A great deal of teaching, writing, colleagueship and new inspiration lay ahead of me—as well as a couple of more hints of what might have been. But the death of my dreams still haunts me, even though I understand now why it was inevitable, and why it was so painful.

Therapists now recognize "love addiction" as a problem. The literature on the subject deals, obviously, with love addiction between individuals, and the problem can be found in a lot of great literature, such as Proust's *A la recherché du temps perdu*. But I have come to realize that for some people it is very easy—perhaps even easier—to fall in love with an institution, or a profession, than with a single person. These are safer targets for love addiction, for the simple reason that they do not die. They can also provide more outlets for a personality than any one individual can. These relationships can however also become dysfunctional. That is, in fact, the theme of one of my favorite novels, *From Here to Eternity*, in which Prewitt, the protagonist, is literally destroyed by his love for the US Army, the only home he has ever had. That book had a tremendous impact on me when I read it at age 15 in Senegal, but I had no idea how closely the story foreshadowed my own. John LeCarré's creation George Smiley also suffers from love addiction in both his personal and professional life and I was also very affected in 1977 when I read *Tinker, Tailor, Soldier, Spy* and experienced Smiley's double betrayal at the hands of his wife and of the traitor within the Secret Service.

Men and women who love their institutions can make truly unique contributions to them thanks to their commitment and ideals. Unfortunately for them, they have trouble compromising their ideals, and they can arouse great jealousy among their peers. All these things happened to Prewitt, to Smiley, and to myself.

I recently met someone outside academia who went through something comparable. Upton Bell, ten years older than I, grew up in the word of the NFL since his father Bert Bell was its second commissioner. He loved that world and spent the 1960s working for the Baltimore Colts. Then, in 1971—at almost the same moment that I began grad school at Harvard—he became the boy wonder general manager of the New England Patriots. He could not, however, get along with the owner, Billy Sullivan—who knew a fraction of what he did about football—and he was fired after two seasons. He never worked for an NFL team again. He described these events in his 2017 autobiography, *Present At the Creation*. We have recently become friends.

I have encountered three other such people in my non-fiction reading. All belonged to earlier generations. The first was an American League umpire, Ernie Stewart, who told his life story to Larry Gerlach in *The Men in Blue* in the late 1970s—coincidentally, right in the midst of my Harvard triumph and tragedy.

Born in Texas, Stewart had grown up in southern California during the 1920s. He was a fine athlete whose father died young. He was determined to go to college, against the wishes of his older brother, and he graduated from USC in 1935. He had washed out of minor league baseball and decided to become an umpire to stay in the game. Like so many others, he worked wherever he could in the baseball-mad US of the first half of the twentieth century. One day he shared his dreams with a scout for a major league team who had known him all his life. "In baseball," he said, "there's only one place to play, one place to manage, and one place to umpire, and that's the major leagues. Do you think I have the possibility of being a major league umpire?" "Yes, Ernie, I do," the man replied, and Stewart was on his way.

Five years later, in 1941, at age 31, he broke in with the American League. There he was mentored by Bill McGowan, universally recognized as the AL's best umpire, and who is now in the Hall of Fame. Stewart's oral history leaves no doubt that he loved umpiring the way I loved history and teaching. He had a tremendous sense of his own role and a compulsion to do the job right. And he wasn't afraid of anyone.

In 1945, former Governor and Senator Happy Chandler of Kentucky had replaced the legendary Kenesaw Mountain Landis as Commissioner. As Stewart told the story, one night at Griffith Stadium in Washington, Chandler spoke to him about improving working conditions for umpires, who had no union and few benefits in those days. At Chandler's suggestion, Stewart wrote a letter soliciting suggestions to all the umpires in the American League. One of them told the American League President, Will Harridge, about the letter. Harridge—for whom Stewart had never had much respect—was furious and immediately let Stewart know that he wanted to fire him. McGowan, Stewart's mentor, argued angrily that Stewart was the best young umpire to have come into the league in many years, one who had at least 25 years ahead of him. Stewart informed Chandler, who called a meeting with Harridge and Stewart to discuss the situation in Washington. Harridge arrived with three lawyers.

Chandler briefly pleaded Stewart's case to Harridge, who replied that Ernie "was a good umpire" but repeated that he wanted him out, and handed him a draft letter of resignation. Stewart asked Chandler what to do. "Well, son," said the Commissioner, "I guess you'll have to sign it."

"Mr. Chandler," Stewart said, "if Judge Landis was sitting in that chair where you are today, he would take that goddamn letter and tear it into bits and tell Mr. Harridge and his three lawyers to get their asses out of here. But you don't have the power that Mr. Landis had, so okay." He signed and threw the letter across the room.

There was a happy ending, Stewart explained three decades later, to the story. His wife would have left him had he remained in umpiring. He left baseball behind completely, and became a very successful small businessman. "I make more money than the President of the American League," he told Gerlach. But that I never wanted to do.

The second such man was a real-life Robert E. Lee Prewitt, David Hackworth. Born in 1930, Hackworth had joined the Merchant Marine when he was 14, and the Army about two years later, lying about his age both times. Hackworth fought in Korea, receiving a battlefield commission. When that war was over he left the Army for two years but returned as an officer in 1955 because, as he explained, civilian life was boring. Rereading his memoir, *About Face*, published in 1989, I am struck by how much Hackworth's detailed and encyclopedic memory resembles my own. Beginning in the mid-1950s, Hackworth—always outspoken and iconoclastic—rose through the ranks quite steadily. He loved the warrior ethos and his men, and he hated bureaucracy and service politics. He was utterly versed in and devoted to the best traditions, as he saw them, of the US Army. And beginning in 1965, he did three tours in Vietnam, the last in 1970–1, when he commanded a battalion of the 9th Division in the Mekong Delta. The Army was largely in disarray by that time, riddled with dissension among its Boomer troops—as I also saw in 1971 at Fort Leonard Wood—but Hackworth won the respect of his men, and they earned his.

It was at this point that Hackworth was promoted to Colonel, just one step away from General. But he was utterly disgusted by the Army's failure ever to figure out how to fight the Vietnam War properly, and with the careerism that seemed almost completely to dominate the officer corps. Several fellow officers had advised him not to go to Vietnam for a third time, on the grounds that it could do nothing for his career. Now, in 1971, with the American involvement largely wound down and the real strategic problems still unsolved, Hackworth couldn't take any more of the institution to which he had given his life. He had become friendly with several journalists, including *Washington Post* reporter Ward Just, who described him anonymously but in great detail in his book on the Army, *Military Men*. (I read that book at Fort Leonard Wood after my brother Bob sent it to me.)

On June 27, 1971—when I was still at Leonard Wood—Hackworth appeared on ABC's Sunday program, *Issues and Answers*. He began by blasting all the training for Vietnam as "totally inadequate," and talked at length about the large American casualties inflicted by friendly fire. He attacked the conventional thinking of the top leadership and criticized the "body count" measurement of success for having forced officers at every level to lie. And last but not least, he predicted, correctly, that the South Vietnamese would have great difficulty coping with a new major enemy offensive.[6] Although William Corson, a retired Marine colonel, had made similarly scathing criticisms in a 1968 book, *The Betrayal*, no serving officer had ever gone on record with comparable comments to date. Hackworth had thrown away his chance for general officer rank, and he left the Army only weeks later.

Hackworth initially moved to Australia, where he became a successful restauranteur. In the late 1980s he returned to the US, published his memoir, and became a commentator

---

6 Helped by massive US air power and an advisory presence, the South Vietnamese managed to halt a North Vietnamese offensive the next year short of victory, although a great deal of territory was lost for good. In 1975, lacking that assistance, the South Vietnamese collapsed completely.

on military affairs. I had an opportunity in the early 2000s to ask him on line if he had read *American Tragedy*. "Read your book—top!" he replied. Sadly, I never got to meet him before he died of cancer in 2005. His memoir ranks in my opinion with the greatest military literature, and I eventually managed to include a section on his Vietnam service in the War College curriculum.

The third and last example has somewhat more in common with me, and indeed, we corresponded once briefly after I reviewed one of his books. He was George F. Kennan, the great American diplomat, strategic thinker, and historian, who became famous as the architect of the containment policy beginning in 1947 when I was born.

Born in 1904, Kennan was traumatized from birth by the almost immediate death of his mother. He joined the U.S. Foreign Service soon after college and became a specialist in the Soviet Union, rising quite rapidly through the ranks. He loved history and art, but diplomacy was his calling. He served in the Moscow Embassy in the later stages of the Second World War and in 1946–7 wrote two of the foundational documents of the Cold War, the famous Long Telegram from Moscow and the "X" article, "The Sources of Soviet Conduct," in *Foreign Affairs*.

By one of history's extraordinary coincidences, Kennan in 1947–8 found himself in exactly the right place at exactly the right time. He headed the State Department's Policy Planning Staff while George C. Marshall, the wartime Chief of Staff of the Army, was Secretary of State. Marshall, as I eventually found writing a book of my own, believed in putting the smartest people he could find on his staff and trusting their judgment. During 1947–8 Marshall decided to resist Soviet expansion in Europe but to do so primarily with economic aid to Western Europe, not militarily, on the grounds that Communism posed a primarily political threat. He decided to promote a separate West German State. In Asia, Marshall repeatedly advised against intervening in the civil war in China. All of these positions came, at least in part, from Kennan.

As Kennan explained in his memoirs, his influence waned when Dean Acheson, who was more oriented towards force than diplomacy, replaced Marshall as his boss. In the early 1950s Kennan served briefly as Ambassador to the USSR, at one of the lowest points in Soviet-American relations, but then was thrown out of the country after publicly comparing the USSR to Nazi Germany. He was awaiting reassignment in Washington—still only 48 years old—when the Eisenhower Administration took over in January 1953.

As Kennan explained at length in the second volume of his extraordinary memoirs, the new Secretary of State, John Foster Dulles, had a problem. For the past five years or so, he and many other Republican leaders had been railing against the "cowardly" containment policy of the Truman Administration, and calling for a more aggressive stance of "rollback" or "liberation," most recently in the 1952 campaign. Yet it was clearly impossible to risk war to roll back the USSR in Europe, and thus, like it or not, the containment policy was not likely to change. Still Dulles had to do something to satisfy his fellow Republicans that he was on a new course. He decided to sever Kennan, the architect of containment, from the Foreign Service, using a legal provision that allowed the Secretary to forcibly retire an officer who had gone a certain number of months without a new assignment.

When Dulles told Kennan that he did not want him in the State Department any more, he suggested that Kennan go to work as an analyst for his brother Allen at the CIA. "But that," Kennan wrote years later, "I had already decided, I did not want to do. I felt that if I was not wanted where I had grown up and belonged, i.e., in the State Department, I would rather not be anywhere, and I told him so." This conversation seems to have taken place on March 14, 1953, and before Kennan left Dulles's office, the Secretary asked him to share his thoughts on the significance of the recent death of Joseph Stalin. "Pulling myself together as best I could," Kennan wrote decades later, "I said what I could say on the subject. 'That's very interesting,' he said. Then he added, reflectively: 'You know, you interest me when you talk about these matters. Very few other people do. I hope you'll come in from time to time and let us have your comments on what's going on.'" I had played variants of that scene repeatedly at Harvard, at Carnegie Mellon, and in various job talks.

The chapter on Kennan's retirement concludes with a moving account of his last day at work. He did not, like myself in 1980, have a last lecture to give, and he found himself suddenly trying to think of someone within the State Department building to whom he could say good-bye. He settled on the receptionist in the Secretary of State's office. I too almost always had very friendly relations, as we have seen, with the office staff of the institutions where I worked. Then he drove home to his beloved farm in Pennsylvania and sat on his front porch for a couple of hours. "There was plenty to think about;" he wrote later, "but someone else, I knew, would have to strike the balance, if one was ever to be struck, between justice and injustice, failure and accomplishment. I myself could not. I cannot today."

Kennan's refuge, ironically—from my point of view—was the Institute for Advanced Study at Princeton, a kind of academic heaven where he was free to do whatever he wanted. During the next forty years he began at least two multivolume works on European diplomacy but eventually abandoned both of them in midstream. In 1961–2 John F. Kennedy brought him back into the government as Ambassador to Yugoslavia—another parallel, as we shall see, to my own life. He remained a constant public presence and commentator on foreign affairs and a skeptic about the militarization of the Cold War in general and the Vietnam War in particular. During the 1980s I reviewed his book on the origins of the Franco-Russian alliance, sent him a copy of the review, and received a lovely note in return. In 2000, when *American Tragedy* appeared, I inscribed a copy and sent it to him, but he was 95 by then and I never heard that he had read it. He died at the age of 101. He never, his writings make clear, really reconciled himself to the turn his career had taken when he was 49.

I too have had many years to reflect on exactly why it was that my talents, my achievements, and above all my love for what I did, could not prevent me from being excluded from college and university life after my 43rd birthday. Great historians, I often say, do not argue with history, and I have indeed concluded that my fate was inextricably bound up with much broader intellectual trends that have transformed American higher education—and not for the better—during my adult lifetime. We shall return to these questions in later chapters. Let me merely say here that unlike Ernie Stewart, I have remained active and effective in the career I loved; that like Hackworth, I have never stopped trying to hold my own profession to the highest standards; and that unlike George F. Kennan, I have been able to start and finish a number of very large projects in subsequent years, including, now, this memoir, which I only hope can be half as interesting as his own.

VII

AT THE WAR COLLEGE

1991–99

The Strategy and Policy Department of the Naval War College remained my professional home, with one brief interruption, from 1990 until August 1, 2012. It provided an environment very different from any college or university that I have worked in, one that only certain kinds of academics could take advantage of. Partly because of my previous military service, I found it surprisingly easy to fit in. I had already discovered that both fairness and performance counted for something in the American military—just as I had discovered that they did *not* in American college and university life.

Approximately 500 military officers completed a one-year course at Newport every year. About half of them came from the Navy, the other half from the other services. The student body also included a sprinkling of civilians from the major national security bureaucracies, including the State and Defense Departments and the CIA. A few dozen foreign officers a year also came to NWC, where they not only took courses, but made several lengthy excursions around the United States as an investment in good allied relations in the future. The American officers fell into two groups, a junior class, and a senior class. The former, generally in their thirties, were usually Navy lieutenant commanders or Army, Marine and Air Force majors. The latter included Navy commanders and captains, and Army and Marine lieutenant colonels and colonels. Until

2006, when things changed radically, the S & P department taught the junior class from August until mid-November, and the senior class from mid-November (without any break) until early March. We had miscellaneous duties during the spring term but were generally free to research and write.

I had not yet learned to think in generational terms, but the composition of the student body had interesting consequences for my career. I had begun at Harvard teaching the tail end of the Boom generation (b. 1943–60),[7] and had spent ten years at CMU teaching the leading edge of Gen X. Now most of my students were once again Boomers, including a few who were older even than myself. They got younger over the next 22 years, of course, but I spent nearly my entire career teaching Boomers and Gen Xers.

Until 2006, the junior and senior classes took essentially the same course, although the junior term was two weeks shorter. Both began with a week on the theory of warfare, featuring long excerpts from Clausewitz's *On War*, and Sun Tzu's *The Art of War*. The latter text got a big boost among the public midway through my NWC career when Dr. Melfi recommended it to her patient Tony Soprano. Then, in the second week, the students were assigned Thucydides's *The Peloponnesian War* in its entirety. Subsequent weeks, which changed from time to time, included the Second Punic War between Rome and Carthage, the American Revolution (skipping just a few centuries of world history), the wars of the French Revolution and Napoleon, Bismarck's wars from 1864 through 1871, the American Civil War, the Russo-Japanese War, each of the two World Wars, the Korean War, and Vietnam. In later years, when counterinsurgency came back into vogue, we added cases on the Chinese Civil War and on Algeria to one or the other course.

The format of the courses made for a demanding schedule for faculty. Each case study began on a Thursday with two lectures. The lectures were distributed among the dozen or so senior faculty, and everyone gave between two and four a term.

---

7 I know many people are used to the dates 1946–64. The significance of this will emerge later on.

Friday was usually a free day on which the students could begin their 6–800 pages of reading. There were two more lectures on Monday. Then, each teaching team—composed of a civilian faculty member like myself, and a military moderator on a multi-year assignment to the college—gave three-hour seminars to different groups of about 10 students on Tuesday and Wednesday morning from 8:30 to 11:30, discussing the major issues of each case. That, however, was not all.

Each student wrote three 8-page papers during the term. Before doing so, he or she (less than 10% of the student body was female at the outset) had to schedule a 30-minute tutorial with the two moderators during the previous week to discuss their paper and in particular, their thesis, the argument that they intended to make. With two groups of about 10 students each, that meant that each pair of moderators had to give six— and occasionally eight—tutorials every week, taking 3–4 hours. On Monday we received, and had to read and grade, the three or four papers for the Tuesday seminar, and we had to repeat that process on Tuesday for the Wednesday seminar. We also had to agree on the grades. The week also featured a one-hour Monday meeting of the faculty, called a Bootstrap, in which one designated faculty member would present his ideas on how to teach this particular unit. During my 21-year career at NWC I must have given between 1000 and 2000 tutorials and read the same number of papers. Because of lectures and seminars, we literally had to be in our offices by 0800, as we put it, four days a week. But because Cathy and Dan and Tom and I had settled in Jamestown, the small island on the other side of the Newport Bridge that I could see outside my office window, it took me only ten minutes to drive to work. I had to give up bicycle commuting because bikes are banned from the Newport Bridge, but our island was a biker's paradise.

This teaching load, obviously, was incomparably greater than that faced at Harvard, Carnegie Mellon, or any other leading civilian college or university that I know of. In addition, civilian faculty taught, as it were, in full view, since we all had military colleagues in our offices and were teaching the same course, and professors had to take the job very seriously.

Several gifted people who could not did not catch on in the department and had to leave. But I did not mind the routine, and I realized very quickly that the college offered me real scope for my talents. The S & P course required faculty and students to know a great deal about a huge range of history—and to see common threads uniting, for instance, the Napoleonic Wars and the Second World War, or the Sicilian Expedition and the Vietnam War. It was a course for big thinkers who knew a lot about a lot of different subjects, and that was the kind of person that I was. It did not take me long to earn recognition as a key member of the team. Teaching within the team also carried with it certain frustrations. I gradually developed my own ideas about what books should be read and what lectures should be given, but inevitably, as only one faculty member, my influence had to be limited, But I managed to accept that as well, for as long as I felt that I had been given my share of responsibility.

And I was not alone. The great joy of the job was the other faculty, both civilian and military, with whom I got to work.

Bill Fuller, the determined S & P chairman who had brought me to Newport, had assembled an extraordinary group of faculty members. The department had already included Steve Ross, who had come to Newport from the University of Texas in the 1980s, and who was an authority on two completely different subjects, the wars of the French Revolution and Napoleon, and American war plans, about which he was producing a series of books George Baer—who like Ross was a decade older than I was—had left tenure at the University of California at Santa Cruz to come to Newport. He was another Harvard Ph.D. and May student who had written at least two books on the diplomacy of the 1930s, and was now finishing his masterpiece, *100 Years of Seapower*, a history of the US Navy since 1898. Bill had also enticed Michael Handel, an Israeli-American political scientist who had studied with Stanley Hoffmann at Harvard, from the Army War College at Carlisle, PA. A short, squat dynamo who was never at a loss for words, Michael had written many books on Clausewitz and on the problems of intelligence. After growing up in Israel and earning his doctorate at Harvard, he had returned to Israel with an American wife and several children in the 1980s, but eventually left because of the rightward turn of Israeli politics. Michael was interested in nearly everything, and Clausewitz, whom I was beginning to explore in detail, became a bond between us.

Bill also hired Arthur Waldron, an excellent historian of modern China, who had just been turned down for tenure at Princeton despite impressive publishing credentials. Like Michael, Arthur had a somewhat hard-edged personality, but I never had any trouble getting along with either of them. Arthur was the only colleague I had at the college who managed to move back into civilian academia, eventually becoming a tenured professor at the University of Pennsylvania. Another outstanding scholar, Doug Porch, came to us from the Citadel in 1992. Doug had already written several books on aspects of French imperialism and he has remained prolific all his life, most recently writing a brilliant history of the theory and practice of counterinsurgency. He became a cycling partner of mine and remains a dear friend. Unfortunately Doug did not find the Newport schedule congenial, and after a couple of years, he moved to the Naval Postgraduate School in Monterrey, California.

The department acquired—or rather, reacquired—another remarkable faculty member in 1993. Alberto Coll, then about 40, was a Cuban-American refugee from Castro and a classic immigrant success story. He had graduated from Princeton and earned both a Ph.D. in political science and a law degree, and he had taught at NWC during the 1980s. A conservative Republican, he had become a Deputy Assistant Secretary of Defense under George H. W. Bush. When Bill Clinton defeated Bush in 1992, he arranged to return to the S & P department. Several people anticipated some friction between Alberto and myself because he was obviously a staunch Republican while I was the most vocal (although far from the only) Democrat in the department. They could not have been more wrong. Alberto's life and career—including his educational performance and his meteoric rise in Washington—could not help but remind me of my own father's. But Alberto was also a genuine intellectual who had chosen to return to the intense teaching environment of the War College, rather than to join the Heritage Foundation or a major Republican law firm, as he surely could have. We got along very well from the beginning and eventually became, and remain, close friends. And in the 2000s, I was both astonished and gratified to see Alberto, deeply disturbed even before 9/11 by the tenor of the George W. Bush Administration, move rapidly leftward until by 2004 he had become a Democrat. Today he teaches law at DePaul University in Chicago.

Bill Fuller constantly advocated for scholarship, as well as teaching, in his dealings with the administration. The job of chairman was extremely difficult for him, however, because he lived in Westwood, Massachusetts, giving him a commute of more than an hour every day, and forcing him to rent a small place in Newport during the term. He stepped down as chair only a year after I arrived, and George Baer replaced him. This was something of a shock initially, but George turned out to be a wonderful boss as well as a dear friend. The department contained a number of headstrong members who felt things would go much better if they were in charge of everything, and he balanced them carefully against one another. He also handled a great many petty demands on our time from the Administration without even letting us know about them, which was very wise. The Navy was always pressing us, through the Admirals who ran the school for several years at a time, to tailor the course more narrowly to reflect the strategic flavor of the month or the Navy's view of what conflicts were likely to occur. Many (though not all) high-ranking officers could not quite grasp the distinction between *training*, which taught officers how to perform a specific task the way it needed to be performed, and *education*, which prepared men and women more generally for the intellectual and philosophical challenges of life. The chairman had to convince his bosses that we were doing enough of the former while keeping our own focus on the latter, and that is what George managed to do.

Busy as we were, the S & P faculty often found time to lunch together in those years, rather like the young faculty at

CMU in the early 1980s. I remember lunching à deux with Steve Ross, who could be rather crotchety, during George's first year in office. When he began complaining about George's leadership style, I replied that I didn't like to complain about any chairman because I knew he was doing a job that I did not want. We moved on to other things. A couple of weeks later, in a larger lunch party, Steve paid me a very nice compliment. "When you go to lunch with Kaiser," he said, "you don't go for gossip. You talk substance."

A great many people tended to assume that the War College glorified war. Nothing could have been further from the truth, especially in S & P. Our course dealt with the use of force to achieve national political goals, and the heroes of the course who had managed to do so wisely, including George Washington, Bismarck, and Franklin Roosevelt, were few and far between. The Vietnam War had affected the US military far more deeply than it had affected academic foreign policy specialists, most of whom remained optimistic about the use of force. The post-Vietnam military—symbolized by Colin Powell, the Chairman of the Joint Chiefs at the moment I arrived in Newport—was determined above all only to fight wars that could be won quickly and relatively cheaply. The Bush Administration's handling of the first Gulf War, for which the President carefully assembled a huge coalition, slowly built public support, deployed more than adequate force, and contented himself with the limited objective of freeing Kuwait, was a masterpiece of policy and strategy. I emphasized again and again with my students that their best hope of changing the world for the better was to speak very clearly to civilian leadership regarding exactly what military force could, and could not, accomplish. The course included a number of very dramatic examples of civilians or military leaders warning their nations about potentially disastrous courses of action, from Nicias telling the Athenians not to undertake the Sicilian expedition to George Ball's 1964 warning not to undertake the Vietnam War. I used that analogy to great effect in a lecture on Vietnam. We felt we were contributing to the nation's wellbeing by promoting sound strategic thinking, and we may have done so—but only marginally. For that, the Navy was much to blame.

While the NWC (as it is customarily known) rightly enjoyed the reputation of the best of ten or so War Colleges maintained by the various military services, its relationship to the Navy had become, and remains, a bit paradoxical. As recently as the interwar period, when the Navy bore the main responsibility for the defense of the United States, an assignment to Newport as a faculty member had been a much-coveted move for ambitious officers. I discovered researching the origins of the Second World War that many of the senior admirals in 1940–1 had taught at Newport, and one of them, Admiral Nimitz, had famously remarked that almost everything that happened in the Pacific War had been anticipated and discussed much earlier at the War College. The experience of the Second World War, however, evidently convinced the Navy that nothing remained to be learned about warfare, and in the next 20 years it became fixated on carving out its role in the new nuclear world. Admiral Stansfield Turner, who started S & P in the wake of Vietnam, understood the need for sophisticated strategic thinking, but most of the Navy brass did not. The law required officers to have certain military educational qualifications to proceed to higher rank, but the Navy tried to give them those qualifications in the easiest possible way—and developed alternatives to studying at Newport or one of the other War Colleges. Fast track officers, they believed, belonged at sea, and many of those destined for high command never made it to Newport. And sadly, for most of the Navy Commanders and Captains who joined the S & P faculty for three years or more, that billet was their last before retirement. After three years in the classroom with us, they surely ranked among the most sophisticated strategic thinkers not only in the Navy, but in the world—but the nation almost never took advantage of that expertise. I am glad to report that several of our Army faculty did become general officers, but I am not aware of any naval officer I taught with who earned a star.

I made, and still have, some deep friendships with my civilian colleagues, but as I look back on my years at Newport, my relations with my military moderators stand out as the most enjoyable part of the job. Their academic backgrounds and historical knowledge varied widely, but they were all intelligent men and women who took a very conscientious approach to the job. Some of my civilian colleagues ran their whole three-hour seminars themselves, but I insisted that my co-moderators take responsibility for up to half the time in class. Every week I had a list of about six topics to discuss, and they took three of them. The first rule of team teaching, in my opinion, is not to get in each other's way, and thus I generally kept silent while they were learning the discussion. I wanted the students to feel that the military partner was fully equal, partly in order to make clear to the students that they were expected to really master the material. My co-moderators included Julie Kiesling, Jim Ponzo, Daryl King, Lois Schoonover, Dan Withers, Dean Brown, Ron Oard, Jeff Gordon, Pete Janotta, Kyle Barrett, Bob Flynn, and Rob Krivacs of the Navy; Marines Dan Phipps, Bob Larkin, Neil Hartenstein, and John Reardon; Kevin Darnell and Scott Jarvis of the Air Force; and Gary Tochet and Jon Scott Logel of the Army. There was only one of them whom I did not personally like, and he did a fine job in the seminar. They all had the kind of versatile, practical intelligence that a military career requires, and some of them were genuine intellectuals as well. Military men and women have a lot of time on their hands during their careers, and they include a lot of voracious readers and film buffs. Dan Withers, a Navy commander who for unknown reasons never rose as high as his talents warranted, deserves special mention. He loved teaching S & P, and he shared two terrific insights with me that became part of my teaching and lectures. The whole NWC experience confirmed my firm belief that the tiny number of genuine intellectuals among us are scattered quite randomly among the population.

I had been leading discussions for a long time, but my technique improved now that I had to focus on it. The majority of teachers, I believe, ask questions as tests, looking for particular answers. That turns class into a guessing game, such as I had experienced as a freshman in Hum 6, and isn't much fun for anyone. I made it a rule for myself never to ask a question that had only one answer, and when I found myself doing so, I would shift gears in mid-sentence and simply say what I had to say. It was gratifying and reassuring when students came up with an answer I agreed with, but the most fun moments occurred when a student came up with something I had never thought of. I always perked up and raised my voice a little when that happened, and that, ironically, tended to frighten them into thinking that they had done something wrong. I assured them that the opposite was true. I knew what I thought, and it was boring to hear them regurgitate it. It was more fun to learn what they thought. And it was most gratifying to let them find the right answer themselves.

In book 1 of Thucydides' *The Peloponnesian War*, both the Spartan and Athenian leaders, Archidamus and Pericles, give what we called a "net assessment," analyzing how the war was likely to go. Archidamus prophetically told the Spartans that the war was likely to be a very long one because there was no easy way to defeat the Athenians, while Pericles was more optimistic about his city's chances. One paper topic, which I always assigned, asked the student which of them had done a better job. I remember a quiet Marine, Mark Begin, who came into the office for his tutorial arguing that Pericles had done better. When I told one of my most brilliant colleagues about this, he exclaimed, "I hope you talked him out of that!", because we all generally felt that Archidamus had done better. But I hadn't, because I didn't believe in telling my students what to think. And two days later, Mark returned to our office to announce that he had changed his mind. The whole point of the course, I often repeated, was to teach the students to write strategic appreciations later in their careers, where there would be no professor to tell them what to think or give a grade.

Another hardly perennial among the paper topics asked students to analyze the dispute between Truman and MacArthur, with particular emphasis on who was responsible for the disastrous decision to march to the Yalu, leaving the UN troops vulnerable to Chinese intervention. One year I had two fine students doing that paper in different seminars. One put most of the blame on Truman; the other put most of the blame on

MacArthur. Together they convinced me, at the very least, that either one of them might have avoided the catastrophe by doing his job better, and my co-moderator and I awarded them each an A.

I really enjoyed being back in the lecture hall, even if for only three or four hours a term. During my first decade, my topics included the origins of the Vietnam War, Franklin Roosevelt and the Second World War, and a rather creative lecture, if I do say so myself, applying Clausewitz's concept of the trinity of war to the First World War, which was eventually published.[8] Many of my colleagues also gave excellent lectures. But the students, although they gave us good ratings, never got nearly as much out of them as they should have. They regarded them as "briefs," and almost none of them brought a notebook to class or took notes. Their level of effort varied a great deal. Some of them, especially in the junior course, took the whole experience very seriously and made a real effort to do all the reading and contribute every week in class. Others sized up the situation and figured out exactly how little they could get away with doing, and behaved accordingly. These problems got worse after 9/11, when the administration made a number of important changes in the program.

The S & P curriculum was demanding and fascinating. It took me several years to really understand the course and develop my own ideas about the key issues in the various cases and how to connect them up during the course of the term. But I did not want to confine myself to studying the origins and course of wars. The NWC also included an electives program, courses that met once a week, on Wednesday or Thursday afternoon, for three hours. They required relatively little written work, and were graded pass-fail. And in those days it *was* a genuine electives program whose director would approve literally anything that a professor wanted to explore. I resurrected a shorter version of War and Revolution, my favorite CMU course, and exposed some NWC students to Pasternak, Solzhenitsyn, and

---

8 "Clausewitz and the First World War," *Infinity Journal, Special Edition, Clausewitz and Contemporary Conflict*, February 2012, pp. 4–7.

Alice Miller. The enrollments were initially very small, but I eventually increased them simply by writing a sexier course description. I always taught the elective on Wednesday afternoon. That meant that Wednesdays featured two three-hour seminars, with just an hour and a half in between, but it meant that my teaching week was over at 11:30 on Thursday, which I preferred.

Writing these pages about the environment of which I became a part, I feel sorry for some of my academic acquaintances who could never understand why I left CMU for the War College. In addition to being wanted—always an important consideration—I took part in a common intellectual enterprise to which I could make a critical contribution. I was surrounded by men and women interested in the same set of problems, and we fed one another generously. At CMU I had worked almost entirely on my own. I was also living on the beautiful New England coast, instead of in a rust belt city packed onto a series of hillsides, and I earned much more money. I missed my undergraduates, but the overall balance sheet was overwhelmingly in the black, and not for one minute did I ever regret the decision. Meanwhile, I was launched on another big book.

The Vietnam War remained the key event of my own life as of the early 1990s, as well as the event that had made S & P and the War College what it was, thanks to Stansfield Turner. Trained to understand the origins of wars, I had decided after finishing *Politics and War* to return to American history and try to unravel this great mystery when sources began to become available. By the early 1990s the volumes from the State Department's *Foreign Relations of the United States* on the Kennedy Administration and Vietnam and other important topics were appearing, and the early Johnson Administration ones were expected within a few years. Additional material was available at the Kennedy and Johnson presidential libraries. As an added bonus, my security clearance enabled me to examine classified materials in certain government archives, particularly at the National Defense University in Washington, and I made Freedom of Information requests for some of the things I saw, most of which were eventually successful.

I had learned writing *Economic Diplomacy* that one had to be willing to go back in time beyond the period one planned to focus on to understand where issues had come from. My investigations into the Eisenhower Administration had stunning results. Eisenhower's reputation during the 1970s and 1980s had improved markedly among historians for the simple reason that, in contrast to his successors, he had ended the Korean War quite rapidly[9] and had not gotten the United States into any similar conflicts during the next eight years. Yet what I found undermined that cheerful picture. To begin with, after failing to intervene to help the French in 1954, the well-organized Eisenhower Administration had decided formally that it *would* intervene, alone if necessary, to halt Communist aggression against a whole host of nations, including Laos and South Vietnam. Secondly, a long series of top-level policy papers had stated that the US would use tactical nuclear weapons in such contingencies. In fact, the services under Eisenhower had been configured so as to make it impossible to undertake almost any major operation without using nuclear weapons. And thirdly, in 1959–60, a political crisis in Laos had erupted because of misguided US attempts to install and maintain a pro-western government instead of a neutral one. By late 1960 that crisis had turned into a civil war, and the Eisenhower Administration was on the verge of implementing its plans and intervening in that war at the moment that it left office. John F. Kennedy immediately faced recommendations to put US troops in Laos, complete with plans to use nuclear weapons if they found themselves surrounded by superior Communist Chinese or North Vietnamese forces.

And as I read through the 1961 *Foreign Relations* volumes on both Vietnam and Laos, a new story of JFK and Vietnam emerged. Since at least 1965 many had blamed Kennedy for the war because at the end of 1961 he had agreed to the dispatch of several thousand American troops to South Vietnam,

---

9 Although *not*, as an excellent article by Roger Dingman showed in the 1990s, by threatening the use of atomic weapons, as he and John Foster Dulles had long claimed. Dingman, "Atomic Diplomacy During the Korean War," *International Security* vol. 13 no. 3, pp. 50–91.

thereby deepening our involvement. What I found, however, was that he had agreed to that only after repeatedly rejecting proposals to undertake full-scale military interventions in Laos, in South Vietnam, or in both. Instead, in Laos, he had changed the fundamental US policy from supporting weak pro-western forces to backing a new neutral government. The need for such a government was, in fact, the only thing he and Khrushchev agreed upon in their famous meeting in Vienna in June 1961. Kennedy's entire national security team, including Secretary of State Dean Rusk, Secretary of Defense Robert McNamara, and National Security Adviser McGeorge Bundy, had supported intervention, but he had overruled them all. And in November 1961, at the same moment that he had rejected a multi-division commitment to South Vietnam but agreed to dispatch a few thousand support troops and advisers, he had reshuffled his team, moving Walt Rostow, the foremost proponent of armed intervention, out of the White House, and putting my father's old boss Averell Harriman in charge of Southeast Asia as Assistant Secretary of State for the Far East.

I read the available *Foreign Relations* volumes on other topics as well, including Germany and Berlin. Kennedy's rejection of war in Southeast Asia was part of a broader attempt to move away from the endless confrontations of the Cold War. He had also wanted in 1961 to make some dramatic new proposals on Berlin and Germany, but had received no help from Khrushchev in moving toward détente and had bowed to his advisers' caution on that point. He also was making clear to numerous third world leaders that his Administration, unlike Eisenhower's, sympathized with attempts to remain neutral between Washington and Moscow. The exception, it was already clear, was Cuba, where he was determined to replace the Castro government.

It also became clear that the Kennedy Administration's problems with South Vietnamese President Ngo Dinh Diem were nothing new. Diem from virtually the moment that he took power with US support in 1954 had aroused many doubts among Americans on the scene that he could ever lead South Vietnam effectively. Late in the Eisenhower Administration,

Ambassador Elbridge Durbrow had demanded that Diem send his brother and Interior Minister, Ngo Dinh Nhu, out of the country. Diem had refused, just as he would refuse the same suggestion from the Kennedy Administration in the late summer of 1963. The steady deterioration of Diem's support in South Vietnam emerged clearly from the *FRUS* volumes.

In 1993, I believe, I was invited to the second in a series of conferences on various aspects of the Vietnam War at the LBJ Library in Austin. It was by far the most exciting and professional conference that I had ever attended, featuring contributions from historians Douglas Pike—the world's leading authority on the North Vietnamese and Viet Cong—Lloyd Gardner of Rutgers, Larry Berman, who was writing a trilogy on Vietnam from 1965 through 1973, and William Conrad Gibbons. Bill Gibbons was in the midst of an extraordinary project. A Washington veteran and one-time Senate staffer, he had a lifetime contract with the Senate Foreign Relations Committee to write a definitive history of the US and Vietnam. While it was entitled "Executive-Legislative Relationships" and spent a lot of time on the role of Congress, it also gave a remarkably thorough account of policymaking in Washington. Bill was a wonderful Virginia gentleman with an encyclopedic knowledge of the archives. Although we ultimately disagreed on JFK's intentions in Vietnam, we became dear friends, and he thoroughly approved of what I wrote about the Johnson Administration. Bill eventually brought out four volumes of his study, bringing the story up to the eve of the Tet Offensive in 1968. Unfortunately, a long and debilitating illness did not allow him to publish any more before his death in 2015.

In 1994, the LBJ Library provided research support that enabled me to spend three weeks in Austin researching key episodes in the Johnson Administration's approach to Vietnam in 1964–5. This was the longest research trip I had been on since graduate school and those three weeks were among the most intense of my life. Technology had gone forward since my months at the PRO in London in 1974, and I was now taking notes on my first laptop computer. The boxes of documents we were working on sat on a cart that was locked up at night, and the librarians allowed us to leave our computer on the cart every night as well, saving a lot of trouble. I had become a serious bicyclist after a minor knee operation in 1991, and I brought my bike to Austin and used it to get to and from my very modest motel, as well as to go on some longer rides in the countryside. I spent my evenings reading French novels in coffeehouses, and enjoyed several conversations with my contemporary Jamie Galbraith—another Kennedy Ambassador's son—and also with Walt Rostow. Rostow and my father had known each other at Oxford, and he and his wife Elspeth were unfailingly courteous even though it was quite obvious that he would never agree with what I had to say about LBJ and Vietnam.

My key sources included very extensive files on the work of a small committee that Johnson had established the week after his election in 1964 to plan the next steps in Vietnam. Its key players were two subcabinet officials, William Bundy from State and John McNaughton from Defense, and it became clear as I read their lengthy drafts that both of them were trying to steer the Administration away from all-out intervention in the conflict and towards a scaling back of US objectives. Yet they were destined to be overruled by their superiors, especially Dean Rusk, who insisted that the US could not be satisfied with trying and failing.

Months and years of painstaking research—and another critical FOIA request—led me to one of the book's most important conclusions. Several books had already portrayed President Johnson has having decided on the war in stages between late 1964 and the middle of 1965, first choosing to bomb North Vietnam, then sending in some Marines at Da Nang, and only months later deciding upon a major troop commitment. Gradually I began to see that there had really been only one decision, in early December 1964, from which all else followed. The document that Johnson approved at that time—the product of the planning process headed by William Bundy—foresaw the beginning of a sustained bombing campaign within the near future, accompanied by "appropriate U.S. deployments to handle any contingency." That phrase finally caught my eye after several readings. A footnote to the document in *FRUS* mentioned that it was accompanied by unpublished appendices, which I FOIAed from the LBJ library. When they arrived, they included a massive schedule of planned deployments to South Vietnam and Thailand of both ground troops and air units, beginning with the landing of the Marines at Da Nang on D + 3, that is, three days after sustained bombing began. (As it turned out, the ground units destined for Thailand went to Vietnam instead.) Historians had also been fooled because Johnson refused to say, on paper at least, exactly when he had authorized the sustained bombing of North Vietnam to begin. But it did begin on March 2, and the Marine deployments began on March 8, just a couple of days behind schedule. Westmoreland's subsequent troop requests all came right out of the December timetable. And I also discovered that the idea that the United States might have won the war by deploying troops more quickly—one dearly beloved by many military men—took no account of the facts. South Vietnam simply did not have the logistical base to absorb troops more quickly than they in fact arrived. The American buildup had proceeded at maximum pace until at least mid-1967.

I researched the book in other ways. Just as I had read the London *Economist* for the entire decade of the 1930s to begin my research on *Economic Diplomacy*, I wound up going through the front and opinion pages of the *New York Times* for the whole of 1961–65. These exercises not only provided me with useful specific information but also embedded me in the broader issues, thoughts, and feelings of the time. And all my research on this project was extraordinarily intense because I could so often remember exactly where I had been and what I had been doing at the time of the events I was reading about. It was quite a shock to discover that General Westmoreland had sent his cable requesting 44 infantry battalions to fight the war—the irrevocable step towards the larger conflict—on June 7, 1965, which happened to be my eighteenth birthday. I was particularly interested to figure out where I had been on July 28, 1965, the day that President Johnson had announced the new troop deployments. I knew I had started a cross-country car trip with another family on July 18, and I remembered the details of the trip well enough to determine with some certainty that I had been in Zion National Park that morning, climbing to the top of Angel's Landing. I planned to put that into the book.

I was ready to begin writing what became *American Tragedy: Kennedy, Johnson and the Origins of the Vietnam War* by late 1995. Meanwhile, I had been paying some attention to what had been happening in the historical profession, and I had discovered a new outlet for professional activity.

During my time at Carnegie Mellon in the 1980s, and even earlier at Harvard, I had taken note of the gradual eclipse of political and diplomatic history and the new prominence of social history, to which Peter Stearns and the Carnegie Mellon department had been so devoted. Gordon Craig, from my parents' generation (and, coincidentally, a long-standing friend of my father's) had warned about the decline of diplomatic history in particular in his presidential address to the American Historical Association in 1982. The presidency of the AHA in those days was reserved for distinguished historians nearing retirement, and not until 1987 was a member of the Silent generation (b. 1925–42) elected to break the monopoly of the GI generation (b. 1904–24), whose representatives were quite traditional in approach and interests. Thus, William McNeil in 1985 reaffirmed the idea of scientific history while recognizing that the discipline's conclusions would always be subject to change, and Carl Degler in 1986 called for an overarching framework for the study of US history. The first President from the Silent Generation, Natalie Zemon Davis, took a somewhat more theoretical approach to the history of the historical profession, looking for "two bodies" of history in the early modern period. In 1993, another Silent generation historian, Louise Tilly, was the first to notice what had been going on around us for some time, when she referred to a new kind of social historian, one who had "rejected the very possibility of explanation and adopted a radical skepticism toward any reliable knowledge of the past." By that time I was at the War College, and my eyes were opening thanks to an extraordinary contemporary of mine.

Bill James, who had introduced the world to "sabermetrics"—new forms of the statistical analysis of baseball—in the early 1980s, had been the first member of my own generation to substantially expand my intellectual horizons and inspire me to do something new. Camille Paglia was the second. She was an exact contemporary, born to an Italian-American family in upstate New York in 1947. She evidently skipped a year of primary school and graduated from SUNY Binghamton in 1968, and earned her Ph.D. in six years at Yale, where she was fortunate to fall into the orbit of a truly big thinker, Harold Bloom. By then she was already teaching at Bennington College, but she was evidently turned down for tenure sometime in the late 1970s. For the next five years or so she worked only at part-time academic jobs. Then, in 1984, she found a solution parallel to the one I adopted in 1991: teaching at the University of the Arts, a Philadelphia art school. It is not coincidental that Camille Paglia and David Kaiser, two of the outstanding scholars of the Boom generation, had to spend most of their careers teaching some form of the humanities at trade schools.

Paglia had struggled for years looking for a publisher for her dissertation. It had finally appeared in 1990 under the title, *Sexual Personae: Art and Decadence from Nefertiti to Emily Dickinson.* "Paglia," wrote one reviewer, "makes more outrageous claims in her first 20 pages than most academics dare in a lifetime"—and that was true. Fully committed to the intellectual principles of western civilization—the commitment that has made both of us outcasts in academia—she nonetheless saw that civilization as endlessly at war with the uncontrollable, destructive elements of nature in general and human nature in particular. Adopting a view that feminist academics were already branding as hopelessly masculine, she assigned women and their bodies to a special place in nature, and did not shrink from the inevitably violent aspects of sex, no matter why it was undertaken. She believed unashamedly in both pornography and prostitution. She used the theme of androgyny—one with great personal resonance for her—to explore these issues through the ages. Another theme was decadence, which, she had realized, characterized our own age. Little did she know how far it might go.

The energy and eclecticism of *Sexual Personae* fascinated me, but I learned far more from some of the criticism she published in two collections during the first half of the 1990s, *Sex, Art and American Culture* (1992), and *Vamps and Tramps* (1994). The centerpiece of the former was a very long review essay on two recent postmodern books on ancient Greece, *One Hundred Years of Homosexuality* by David M. Halperin, and *The Constraints of Desire* by John J. Winkler, who had recently died of AIDS. Reading a stream of gushing blurbs on the back of Halperin's book, Paglia asked herself, "What profession am I in? What are its values?" That question was also troubling me more and more, now that I was at a safe distance from its mainstream. Then, one by one, Paglia identified huge problems within these works that were spreading through both literary criticism and now, history. Rereading this essay 25 years later I am struck by how many of the things that outraged Paglia—and myself— have become so utterly commonplace today that no one else would bother even to mention them.

The first and perhaps biggest problem was the idea that a true intellectual revolution had taken place during the previous 15 or 20 years, largely thanks to the French author Michel Foucault. "The most outrageous aspect of *One Hundred Years* is its contemporary parochialism," she wrote, "its strident hypothesis . . . that the entire foundation of classical learning, notably in classical anthropology, is now irrelevant." "The elevation of Foucault to guru status by American and British academics," she wrote on the next page, "is a tale that belongs to the history of cults." Halperin, she saw, lived in a closed intellectual universe of like-minded contemporaries, most of whom were ignorant of much of the scholarship and many of the facts of their subjects. Under Foucault's influence, all relations among humans were reduced to power relations, which to Paglia, with her classical reverence for sex of all kinds, seemed utterly absurd.

Paglia mercilessly criticized Halperin and Winkler for tactics that became commonplace during the 1990s and later. Both set up battalions of straw men, scholars from the past whose benighted opinions, in fact, bore little or no relation to the serious work that had actually been done on their topics. Both adopted the French fashion that reality lies only in language, which in turn is an instrument of power, not an attempt to document reality. In order to make sources fit their arguments, both of them had to argue that sources actually meant the opposite of what they appeared to say. "Contemporary political wish lists must not be projected backward to distort the historical record," she wrote at one point—alas, much too late. And Paglia pled for a return to the German tradition of the 19th century that held that only the broadest possible knowledge of history, art, and civilization could yield insights of lasting value. That was the ideal to which she, and I, had devoted our lives. "By your books, ye shall know them," she wrote; "A scholar's real audience is not yet born."

Paglia also specifically came out against the social and political trends which were destined to destroy academia and infect liberal politics over the next 25 years. "A feeling of respect for the past," she wrote, "is the great gift we can bequeath to our students trapped in the busy, bright, brazen present"—and this was decades before smartphones. "Individual authors or works may go in and out of favor (both Shakespeare and Bach had to be revived by Romanticism), but the overall line of Western culture will never change. *Every woman, black or Oriental raised and writing in English is a product of that main line.*" [emphasis added.] While she wanted to preserve non-western traditions, she left no doubt that the future of the world belonged to western civilization: "Modernization means Westernization. The modern technological world is the product of the Greco-Roman line of mathematics, science, and analytic thought." And facts were facts: if they weren't, bridges would not stand up straight, and cars would not move. Western civilization had provided islands of stability and freedom within the vast sea of human misery and cruelty—the sea to which much of the world now, 25 years later, is now returning.

Although Paglia never said this in so many words, she was really preaching the extraordinary love that the best of the western tradition can inspire. The greatest sin of the academic establishment of her generation and mine has been to reduce those achievements to mere instruments of straight white male oppression which deserve our contempt. Hers was the same love I had felt for great works of history from Thucydides to Henry Adams, Albertini, Allen Nevins and the rest, and for the enterprise of working through archives and fashioning their raw material into works of art. And that remains the aspect of my own work that most academics have utterly failed even to acknowledge, much less to appreciate, as the years have passed.

Dazzled by her Orwellian polemical virtuosity and struck by the similarities between us, I immediately wrote Paglia a letter at her school. She was now a celebrity, and I received a form note from her chairman informing me that unsolicited manuscripts and correspondence were "routinely discarded by the staff." This was the first of several unsuccessful attempts to contact her, although we were finally introduced in the spring of 2008, I believe, by a mutual friend, the journalist and broadcaster Christopher Lydon. I got her email address then and wrote her but heard nothing back. But she opened my eyes. Unlike her, I remained first and foremost a scholar, while she became an international celebrity. Sadly, I have been truer to that vocation than she. *Sexual Personae* concluded in the late 19th century, and a promised second volume never appeared. But I shall always regard her as a kindred spirit.

My first chance to enter the lists in this critical battle came at almost the same moment, in October 1992, when *Perspectives*, the newsletter of the American Historical Association (AHA), republished an article by Joan Wallach Scott, a feminist historian from Princeton, entitled, "The New University: Beyond Political Correctness." Scott attacked several recent critics of trends in academia—including Camille Paglia—and laid down what amounted to certain revealed truths of her own. Scott referred repeatedly to the "production of knowledge" as a key function of a university—an odd locution to those like myself who believed that knowledge had to be discovered, rather than "produced." Scott stated her position most clearly in the following paragraph:

"Contests about knowledge are now understood to be political, not only because they are contests, but because they are explicitly about the interests of groups (rather than the opinions of individuals) in the substance and form of knowledge.

For example, African-Americans object to the treatment in textbooks of their history only under the rubric of slavery and the Civil War, arguing that this makes only a brief chapter of their experience visible. Women suggest that the focus on politics and war as major historical events diminishes the activities and contributions of the majority of the population. Both groups argue that the interests of white males are advanced when their lives are taken as historically typical and, therefore, more significant than others. The introduction of questions of group interest and power into the knowledge debates has 'politicized' them in new ways. But while this politicization is sometimes extreme and tendentious, the explicit discussion of interest is inevitable, and—at the risk of making a virtue of necessity—a good thing."[10]

Now I had spent my career writing about "politics and war," most recently in an entire book of that name—but not because I believed the lives of the white males I researched to be "historically typical," either of other white males or of humanity as a whole. Nor had I been trying to slight the lives of women or nonwhites (the expression "people of color", an attempt to make whites invisible, had evidently not yet come into vogue.) I had written about them because of their unique power to affect the lives of all of us, very critically analyzing their exercise of that power, and the impact that it had upon the average citizenry of the world. And it seems to me now more than ever that the argument that the lives of kings, prime ministers and presidents should not be "privileged" by historians at the expense of more ordinary men and women is a luxury indulged by people who have been lucky enough to spend their lives in the extraordinarily stable world of the late 20th and early 21st century, and who utterly take for granted the political achievements of their parents' and grandparents' generations, which created it. Nor do I believe that it is simply a coincidence that after at least three decades of downgrading political and diplomatic history at our elite institutions, our

---

10   https://www.historians.org/publications-and-directories/perspectives-on-history/october-1992/the-new-university-beyond-political-correctness

current elite seems utterly unable to cope with the fourth great crisis of American political history, or halt a worldwide movement towards greater anarchy.

Six months later, another historian, Jerry Muller of Catholic University, replied to Scott, explicitly denying that historians could not write effectively and accurately about other demographic groups, and branding Scott's statement that "intellectual life is merely the will to power of particular groups" as profoundly anti-intellectual. He also noted that of nineteen candidates then nominated for AHA offices, five worked in class and labor issues, ten in women's or gender history issues, and seven in racial issues, while none worked in economic history, international relations, military history, or history of science. In a very brief reply, Scott dismissed Muller and cited Camille Paglia, of all people, as a true example of "anti-intellectualism." Seeing the battle lines marked and knowing where I stood, I called *Perspectives* to ask if they would be interested in further comments on the controversy. The editor said he would welcome them, and I wrote a brief letter quoting from Scott's book, *Gender and the Politics of History*. She had written that knowledge "produced by cultures and societies" is "not absolute or true, but always relative"; that one must question "the notions that history can faithfully document lived reality" and that "archives are repositories of facts"; and that her motive in using Foucault's theory in history was "avowedly political: to point out and change inequalities between women and men." "The quotations," I wrote, "amount to a declaration of disinterest in the past as such."

Two issues later, *Perspectives* printed a letter by Professor Mary Elizabeth Perry of Occidental College and UCLA arguing that Jerry Muller's piece "demonstrates the intellectual bankruptcy of those who sneer at 'political correctness '. . . . In contrast to Scott's thoughtful essay, Muller's outburst utterly fails to contribute to the discussion." My letter, however, did not appear. I called the editor who had encouraged me to write it and asked for an explanation. "We received a number of letters," he replied. "I wanted to publish them all, but my colleagues here didn't want to publish any of them. Professor

Perry, however, is a member of the AHA Council, and she made strong representations to get her letter published, and it was." A further appeal from me to the chair of the AHA Council, Louise Tilly, was referred to the research division, which replied months later that since both opposing positions had been stated, there was no need to publish anything more. Some historians, clearly, were now more equal than others.

I discovered a related trend sometime in 1992 or so, when I called the *American Historical Review* to inquire when a review of *Politics and War* might appear. "We listed that book," an editor told me, indicating that the journal had listed it as a book received but had declined to review a tome analyzing four centuries of European history and published by one of the nation's most distinguished university presses. I called Aida Donald, my editor, and drafted a note for the AHR asking them to reconsider. They did and assigned the book to a professor at a small Texas university, who wrote a mediocre review. That turned out to be the last book I wrote that was ever reviewed by my profession's leading journal, whose editors were consciously trying to avoid books about well-known topics in the history of the North Atlantic world.

Then, in 1994, the new history found its way into my own field, in a long symposium in an issue of *Diplomatic History*, the journal of the Society of Historians of American Foreign Relations. It included articles by two historians, Lisa McEnaney and Emily Rosenberg, applying what they called a "cultural studies" approach to two relatively recent periods in American history: the eve of the Second World War, and the Cold War during the 1950s. It immediately occurred to me that these articles paralleled the books by David Halperin and John Winkler that Paglia had excoriated in "Junk Bonds and Corporate Raiders," and I decided to write a parallel piece. As it turned out, it was never published, but I certainly learned a great deal doing it.

Emily Rosenberg tried to explain to her readers what cultural studies were. "Cultural studies," she wrote, "is [sic] concerned with rethinking categories of knowledge and examining forms of power. In the spirit of cultural studies, this essay explicitly works across, or in defiance of, the supposed divisions of 'private' (gender roles) and 'public' (international politics), of mass culture and elite decision making, of material domains and symbolic orders, of 'realism' and 'idealism.' The boundaries of such conventional binaries may be bridged by the concept of 'discourse,' which deals with interrelationships between the construction of institutions that embody power and the symbolic codes that constitute 'truth' or 'naturalness.' Discursive analysis can highlight connections between seemingly unrelated categories of experience, in this case, international affairs and domestic relationships."[11] Reading those words 23 years later, I am quite sure that educated lay people would find them just as difficult now as they would have in 1994. Yet the ideas behind them have found their way into our politics and culture and have become elements of mainstream left-wing thought.

What McEnaney and Rosenberg were arguing, in fact, was that both institutions and language reflected a single system of power, which specifically favored white males over women and nonwhites. What I emphasized in my critique was that they really used comments about gender and the family as *metaphors* for larger systems of power, including the national security state that developed after the Cold War. That technique, it seemed to me, was really quite unrelated to attempts to use primary sources to explain what happened in the past. But that was not all. Like Paglia with Winkler and Halperin, I found again and again that the authors really provided little or no data for their assertions. McEnaney focused on a women's isolationist group, the America First Movement (not to be confused with the much more famous America First Committee.) "Patriotism and isolationism, America-First style," she wrote, "was *fundamentally* [emphasis added] a defense of the nuclear family structure and the conventional gender roles that made this movement's vision of social and sexual purity possible and sustainable. American First, therefore, infused the traditional political and diplomatic meanings of isolationism with

---

11 Emily S. Rosenberg, "'Foreign Affairs' After World War II," *Diplomatic* History (winter 1994), pp. 59–60,

a social meaning." But McEnaney, incredibly, did not offer a single quote to substantiate this position. Grasping at straws, she discussed similarities between the America First Movement and Gerald L. K. Smith's Christian Anti-Communist Crusade, and argued that his newspaper was full of rhetoric specifying "appropriate gender roles." But the only quote she gave from him simply asked God to "give us men! A time like this demands strong minds. . . . Men who have honor, men who will not lie; [men] who can stand before a demagogue," by which he meant Franklin Roosevelt. Nor, of course, was there the slightest evidence that women or women's groups *favoring* intervention in the war, of which there were some, had different views of proper family structure than the isolationists.

Rosenberg's argument was even more tenuous. She focused on two postwar movies, *A Foreign Affair*, starring Jean Arthur and Marlene Dietrich, and *The Man in the Grey Flannel Suit* with Gregory Peck and Jennifer Jones. In the first, Arthur, a single Congresswoman from Iowa, wins an American officer away from the wicked German cabaret singer Marlene Dietrich. In the second, Peck, a New York executive living in Connecticut, has to confess to his wife that a wartime affair with an Italian resulted in a child. Rosenberg's broader point read as follows: "The key issue in the overlapping discourses related to international and domestic orders was that of male/ American 'responsibility.' On the international level, 'exercising responsibility' and 'taking charge' comprised the discourses that constructed the National Security Act and CIA, the Marshall Plan and NATO. . . . The movie illuminates, *perhaps better than policy documents themselves*, the ideology of male responsibility that helped shape and institutionalize these programs.[Emphasis added.]" But of course, the key issue in those programs was one of *national* responsibility, not *male* responsibility, and the debate about them simply related to whether the nation should undertake the commitments they embodied. Of course, political responsibility in those days was mostly (although not exclusively) exercised by men, but that obviously does not mean that they exercised it according to their ideas of what *men*, as opposed to *women*, should do.

Indeed, as I had found in my first term in grad school, every major decision in that era ignited fierce debates *between* men.

Of the six historians asked to comment, five gave the two articles uncritical praise while extending the same methodology to other topics. They too often did violence to their sources and misstated basic facts. The last, Bruce Kuklick, with whom I was well acquainted, had originally been enlisted as a referee for the articles but his recommendation against publication had been ignored. Quoting the same passage I used above from Rosenberg about "taking charge," he described it as "intellectual junk," the equivalent of eating at McDonald's.

Only eight years had passed since Theodore Draper's revealing articles about the new school of historians of American Communism, but this symposium and the contributors' footnotes showed that the transformation it foreshadowed had gone a very long way. Borrowing from French theorists led by Michel Foucault, the contributors were arguing essentially that all history revolved around one issue: the use of discourse to enshrine white male hegemony over other groups. They had lost interest in the past as such. Like Paglia, I asked myself what profession I was now in. I sent my article to the *New York Review of Books*, where the editor, Barbara Epstein, said that it was "preaching to the converted" in her office but declined it. I also sent it to my old friend Stanley Hoffmann, who strongly advised against publishing it because it would make me too many enemies. "Well," I replied, "they can't do anything to me here, and I'm not going anywhere else." But I gave up getting it into print

I have mentioned that Louise Tilly had made the first allusion to the new type of history—which in my opinion was never history at all—in an AHA Presidential address in 1993. But in the next year, 1994—the same year as the symposium— Professor Thomas Holt of the University of Chicago took things to the next level in his presidential address on language and the black American experience. Holt had been born in November 1942, absolutely at the end of the Silent generation. He took a specifically postmodern approach, beginning with the statement about race. "It is important to note that theirs [W. E. B.

Du Bois's and Franz Fanon's] is, in fact, a *discovery* of race, for their 'race' inheres neither in biology nor in culture but must be summoned to consciousness by their encounters in social space and historical time." His talk tried to show how various everyday customs and rituals, including minstrelsy, embodied a broader ideology of racial superiority. Like Draper's historians of American Communism, he specifically related the topic of his talk to his own personal experience. He wound up by standing "political correctness" on its head, arguing that it was the tool of capitalist and racial privilege. The problem, he said, was to help black scholars and Americans trying to create new selves in defiance of the power structure, partly by redefining the history around them. He received a standing ovation.

The idea behind the Communist studies of the early 1980s—that one's personal experience gave one unique insights into the problems of one's own group and insulated one from criticism from outsiders—was now firmly established among many female and black historians—although by no means all. More than twenty years later, that idea dominates not only history—whose influence among students has shrunk drastically during that period—but campus life. It is behind the numerous campus controversies over slavery, micro-aggressions, and sexual assault. We shall return to its impact as we near the end of our story.

At the same moment—in 1994 or 1995—I discovered another very satisfying professional outlet, the H-Diplo email list. Originally organized, I believe, by John Lewis Gaddis when he was at Miami University in Ohio, it was open to anyone who wanted to sign up, and by 1995 it was the site of very lively discussions of all sorts of topics in diplomatic history. Reviewing its archives, I find myself participating at length in controversies about the decision to drop the A-bomb (provoked by the 50th anniversary in 1995), intelligence and Pearl Harbor, and various aspects of the Vietnam War. One extraordinary moment took place after the Venona revelations about Soviet spying in the United States, when Morton Sobell, who had spent decades in prison after his conviction for participating in Julius Rosenberg's industrial spy ring, joined the list to question the Venona findings about Rosenberg and to repeat his claim of innocence. When I asked him on the list to explain exactly what he meant by claiming innocence—did he mean that he had not given away atomic secrets, or that he had not spied at all?—he violently attacked me in return for "cross-examining" him. More than ten years later, in 2008, Sobell acknowledged that he had in fact been a spy. Several other historians—nearly all of them my age or older—also thoroughly enjoyed H-Diplo, perhaps because those who still held positions in diplomatic history—especially European diplomatic history—were now almost completely isolated within their own departments. I am sure that H-Diplo made me better known, more admired, and also, among some, more disliked than all the books I had written put together. Later it too became the site of some very lively discussions of post-modernist approaches to diplomatic history.

Another dissenting forum had opened up in the late 1980s. The National Association of Scholars aimed to defend traditional approaches in the humanities, and I joined in the early 1990s. It was not in any sense a political organization, but included scholars ranging from conservatives like Paul Hollander to the Marxist historian Eugene Genovese, all of whom were concerned by the rise of postmodernism. The association formed chapters at many major universities. At Duke, the postmodernist Stanley Fish, then chairman of the English Department, attacked it as "racist, sexist, and homo-phobic," and wrote a letter to the Administration arguing that its members should be banned from committees on the curriculum and on tenure. Later, Fish said he had not meant this seriously. Looking through my archive of articles from its quarterly journal, *Academic Questions*, I am impressed by their intellectual caliber and the prescience with which they identified the coming trends in academia. They included some very trenchant attacks on some of the new leading lights of academia, including one by John Ellis on my one-time teacher Frederic Jameson; a very carefully argued critique of the phi-losopher Martha Nussbaum by John Finnis; and a remarkable piece by Paul A. Cantor on Stephen Greenblatt and his "new historicism" in literary criticism.[12] But the association was unable to do much more than to provide like-minded scholars around the country with the feeling that they were not alone, and most of the contributors came from the older generation, foreshadowing its eventual decline.

The mid-1990s were busy years for me on many fronts. I had started bicycling around Rhode Island's country roads in 1991, after some minor knee surgery, and had rapidly become addicted. In 1993 an Air Force lieutenant colonel named Tom Ehrhard published a four-day-a-week training program in *Bicycling* magazine, and I eagerly embarked upon it. I also managed to make contact with Ehrhard, who turned out to have academic ambitions himself, and eventually earned a Ph.D. in Political Science from Johns Hopkins. At the end of 1994, I rode my first two centuries or 100-mile bike rides. In the summer of 1995, the family took my older son Dan on a series of college visits around the east coast, which inevitably stirred some powerful feelings in my breast. As in Pittsburgh, I was very active as a coach in the town soccer program, although I never went back to refereeing.

Sometime in 1995, I experienced one of the great intellectual turning points of my life. In the previous year, I had attended my 25th reunion at Harvard. Three different members of my freshman economics 1 section came up to me to say how well they remembered me from that class, and I was amused that none of them had even realized that the class had also included Al Gore, who attended the reunion as Vice President of the United States. At one event, I struck up a conversation with a classmate named Bill Strauss, who held a law degree and an MA from the JFK School of government but now made his living as the producer of the Capitol Steps comedy troupe. As he explained in his write-up for our 25th reunion book, he had originally put the group together for a dramatic production at Christmas time while working as a Senate staffer. "We had planned on a nativity play," he wrote,

---

12 These appeared respectively in the issues of spring 1994, Fall 1994, and Fall 1993.

"but we couldn't find three wise men and a virgin in all of Congress." Strauss was the co-author of an excellent 1980s book on the draft and the Vietnam War, *Chance and Circumstance*, which I had used in a course at Carnegie Mellon. Just three years earlier, in 1991, he and Neil Howe had published *Generations, The History of America's Future*, which I had noticed sitting on the new book shelf of the War College Library but had never picked up. In a brief conversation, Bill shared some of his generational insights about the history of the last 30 years or so. At some point during the next year, I picked *Generations* off the shelf and started reading. For most of that week, I was so excited that I had great difficulty sleeping at all.

Strauss and Howe, I quickly realized, had rediscovered America. Both were amateur historians (although Howe, who now worked for the Concord Coalition, had spent a number of years as a history grad student.) But they were widely read, quick to make connections, and mercifully free of the intellectual and professional inhibitions that would have prevented any contemporary professional historian—including myself—from even undertaking, much less completing, their book. (*Politics and War* had similarly involved a great deal of research on many different topics, and my research had been more thorough than theirs, but I had not come up with comparably creative insights. Thankfully I was neither jealous nor intimidated when confronted with two contemporaries who had done something that I never could have.) They had discovered two patterns in American history, a generational pattern, and a sequence of eras which they later called "turnings." And their book had tremendous implications both for the past and the future.

Beginning with the Pilgrims who settled Massachusetts, Strauss and Howe had identified 18 different American generations, including one—the Millennial generation—whose members were no more than 9 years old when the book came out. But they sorted those generations into a recurring pattern of 4 archetypes, called Prophets, Nomads, Heroes, and Artists.[13] And critically, they related the generational sequence to a recurring sequence of roughly twenty-year eras of American history: a High, an Awakening, an Unraveling, and a Crisis. The last High, which they (and I) had lived through as children, lasted from 1946 through 1964. The Awakening had lasted from 1965 through 1984, and the Unraveling was in full swing when the book came out.

The last crisis had lasted from 1929 through 1945, including the Great Depression and the Second World War. That was the third periodic crisis since the foundation of the Republic, after the American Revolution and the Constitution (1774–1794) and the Civil War (about 1860–68). The whole four-stroke cycle consistently lasted about 80 years. Doing the math, the authors predicted that another great crisis would begin sometime in the first 10–15 years of the 21st century. That was the main theme of their next book, *The Fourth Turning*, which appeared in 1997. And now, of course, twenty years later, that prediction has beyond the shadow of a doubt come true.

The generations living in 1995 (when I first read the book) provided superb examples of the archetypes they defined. Tom Brokaw had not yet discovered the "greatest generation' when *Generations* appeared, and Strauss and Howe called our parents the GI generation, born from around 1904 through 1924.[14] They had been raised to obey rules and sacrifice for the group (the theme of a great deal of juvenile fiction about sports, written by GIs, which I had read as a kid.) They had made it through the Depression and the world war, albeit with the help of substantial daily doses of nicotine and alcohol, and they

---

13 Originally, in *Generations*, the archetypes are named Idealists, Reactives, Civics, and Adaptives. They changed the names to the ones I have used in the text in *The Fourth Turning*, which appeared in 1997, and I am using them for convenience.

14 That is not what *Generations* says: it dates the GI generation as born from 1901 through 1924. The latter date has held up very well, because it represents the latest birth year for most young men who found their way *to combat* during the Second World War. The earlier date, I thought immediately, had been set a few years too early and I have consistent argued for 1904–24 ever since.

had given birth to large families after the war. And the federal government had looked after them very well at literally every stage of their lives, beginning with the New Deal programs of the 1930s through the GI bill, generous mortgages, a family-friendly tax code, Medicare in 1966 when their parents had all retired, and generous Social Security benefits when they started retiring in the early 1970s. They had performed brilliantly in science and economics, but much less well in literature and the arts. They believed in and had created a mass-produced, uniform society. All this was characteristic of Hero generations.

The next generation, the Silent generation (born 1925–42) included many of the teachers who had the most influence on me, including Ernest May and Sam Williamson, and most of the senior faculty at Carnegie Mellon. Silents were children of crisis who grew up sensitive to their parents' emotional needs. They had observed the strict codes of the GIs as young adults during the High (1946–64), but began focusing on smoothing out the rough edges of their society, making it more inclusive (see King, Martin Luther, Jr., and Steinem, Gloria), and using a mix of empathy and mathematical analysis to improve it. Silent academics had been the pioneers of postmodernism and political correctness on campus, as we have seen, and were in charge of most American colleges and universities by the mid-1990s. They belonged to what Strauss and Howe called the Artist archetype, and could be expected to maintain some commitment to postwar institutions for as long as they lived. But already, by the mid-1990s, they were being driven out of Washington by the next-younger generation, which had no commitment to those values at all.

The Boom generation had hitherto been defined demographically to include all those born from 1946 through 1964, but Strauss and Howe, in a typical flash of brilliance, defined it experientially instead. To them, Boomers were born from 1943 through 1960, and thus included all Americans who had no memory whatever of Franklin Roosevelt on the one hand, and at least some memory of John F. Kennedy on the other. Boomers belonged to the Prophet archetype, whose mission was to redefine society's values. They had seized upon that mission eagerly in the late 1960s. Bill Strauss, to whom I became very close, eventually persuaded me that the Vietnam War, while important, had not fundamentally changed the course of history in this respect. It made it much easier for our generation to repudiate all our parents' works, but if it hadn't been Vietnam, Bill said, "it would have been something else," and now, decades later, I'm inclined to agree with him. What distinguished Boomers of all types by the mid-1990s was frightening self-assurance and the belief that whatever they wanted must be the best thing not only for themselves but for everyone else. And I immediately realized that my contemporaries had never shown much respect for institutions, rules, or established procedures.

The oldest members of what Strauss and Howe originally called the Thirteenth Generation were 30 when *Generations* came out, but by the time of *The Fourth Turning* they had a new name: Generation X. They were a Nomad generation, whose childhood coincided with the turbulent Awakening. That had hit many of them very hard when their parents—initially members of the Silent generation—had divorced in large numbers, leaving them angry, independent, and deeply distrustful of institutions. It was not clear in 1991 that, having been very loosely parented themselves, they would become "helicopter parents" 15 or 20 years later. Their first political hero—as I had noticed at NWC—was Ronald Reagan, and while they were generally liberal on social issues, they were more conservative on economic ones. They would be middle managers during the coming crisis.

Strauss and Howe had enormous hopes for the Millennial generation, who had been born beginning in 1982. They noticed a national surge in interest in infants at that point, marked by the rescue of Baby Jessica and the spread of Baby on Board stickers. The Millennials were already facing "zero tolerance" policies in schools, where some were even wearing uniforms. Strauss and Howe expected a Boomer equivalent of Lincoln or FDR to rally them in the great crisis of the 2000s to come and expected that crisis to restore civic virtues in the US. I was excited by that prospect.

My brain, I have come to understand, works rather like an Excel spreadsheet, but one with at least three or four dimensions, instead of just two. I instinctively check any new data point against others in the same row, column, or, if you will, tower. And while Strauss and Howe might well have gone a bit too far out on certain limbs, jumped to some minor conclusions, and missed the right generational boundary a few times, I had only relatively minor objections because so much of what they had to say checked out. My own conflicts with my parents suddenly became clear to me, as did my relations with historians and students from various different generations. I now understand the beauty of my relationships with my Harvard students in the late 1970s: I was from the beginning of the Boom, they came from the end. My move to Carnegie Mellon coincided with a generational shift in the undergraduate population. My wife Cathy and I were increasingly having difficulties because, Boomers that we were, neither could admit that what the other person wanted was important. And my sons, born on two sides of a generational boundary, fit their defined archetypes very well—Dan was a free spirit and an expert on doing just what was necessary to succeed, while Tom was much more of a straight arrow who was always looking for new ways to achieve. I did see, however, that I did not fit the Boomer archetype all that well. I had begun life as more of an Artist—like a member of the older Silent generation—although I had developed my own ideas about politics in the late 1960s. But then, the turmoil in my career had turned me into more of a Nomad, literally and figuratively, and I knew how intellectually isolated I was. My interest in Strauss and Howe increased that isolation. Many of my NWC colleagues thought I had gone crazy, although some accepted key aspects of the theory.

That was not all. Given my background, I immediately started looking for the generations and turnings cycles in other countries, too. Western Europe, I realized, was clearly on roughly the same cycle as the US, and so was East Asia. The 1860s and the 1940s had been watershed moments for Britain, France, Germany, China and Japan, as well as for the United States. Russia and Eastern Europe, on the other hand, were about 15 years ahead of the North Atlantic world, and the Crisis of the Russian revolution had already been followed just a little less than 80 years later by the collapse of Communism. I also began to understand my kinship with members of earlier Prophet generations. Historians Charles A. Beard and W. E. B. Du Bois belonged to the post-civil war Missionary generation and viewed history from Olympian heights, as I had already tried to do. The theory also opened up new views of one of my favorite art forms, the movies. The last five or six generational archetypes jumped off the screen when one knew what to look for. I had seen *The Treasure of the Sierra Madre* for the first of many times in the middle of my freshman year at Harvard, and the film in general, and the old prospector Howard—played by Walter Huston—had blown me away. Now I knew why. Howard (from the Missionary generation) was the first Prophet at the height of his powers that I had ever really seen. He never stopped both thinking and acting.

During the year after reading *Generations*, I talked occasionally with Bill Strauss, and he told me about the impending publication of *The Fourth Turning*. I had begun reviewing non-fiction books for the *Boston Globe* not long before, and I secured the assignment to review this one. It was perhaps the only fully appreciative and understanding review that any of their books every got. "As a Baby Boomer like the authors, born in 1947," I concluded, "I put down *The Fourth Turning* with a mixture of terror and excitement. Despite the turbulence of the last thirty years, most of us born during the High have lived relatively comfortable and rewarding lives, free of serious economic or physical threats to our well-being. It requires a big leap to believe that all this could change. Yet at the same time, my pulse quickens as I think that the next two decades could see the kinds of apocalyptic events in whose shadow I was born, and about which I have read all my life; that somewhere in my generation may yet lurk a Lincoln or a Franklin Roosevelt who will lead the nation through the crisis; and that if I live to be 100—as hundreds of thousands of my contemporaries are expected to do—I might even get a glimpse of the new Awakening. Strauss and Howe have taken a gamble.

If the United States calmly makes it to 2015, their work will end up in the ash-can of history, but if they are right they will take their place among the great American prophets. And they have given themselves and their contemporaries plenty of time to find out." As it turns out, their prediction of a crisis has come true—but the outcome has not at all been what they had hoped for.

I was now in the midst of writing *American Tragedy*, and it became, among other things, a generational analysis, focusing on the GIs who had led us into that calamity and the younger officials from the Silent generation who had almost immediately begun to question it. After *The Fourth Turning* came out, Strauss and Howe put up an online forum where a number of acolytes from around the country gathered and began, literally, developing new science, day after day. That forum, unfortunately, degenerated into a series of flame wars during the Bush II administration—paralleling developments in the country at large—but it has been supplanted by a closed Facebook page. Both have been a major focus of my intellectual activity for the last 20 years, and their leading members, including Boomer Lis Libengood (a Texan), Xers Deanna Beppu (a Hawaiian), Matthew Elmslie (a Canadian), Ryen William Thomas (a South Carolinian), James McClatchey (a Georgian), and Amy Bell (another Texan), and Millennials Chas Donald (from Pennsylvania), Cole and Darius Young (Marylanders) and many more, have become friends for life—including many whom I have never met face to face. They are among the amateurs who are keeping the western intellectual tradition alive.

In 1999, I believe, I attempted to bring Strauss and Howe to the attention of my profession by submitting a panel on their ideas to the program committee of the American Historical Association Convention for that year. Both Bill and Neil agreed to participate, and in addition to myself, I recruited David Krein, a fine historian of Victorian Britain who had found statistical evidence for Strauss and Howe's theories in an analysis of the British House of Commons, and my old friend Anne Rose to serve as commentator. The panelists had written 13 books among them, but the program committee responded with a rejection form letter, informing us that it had to try to secure the proper balance among various topics. That, for me, was the last straw, and I allowed my membership in the AHA to lapse. I also published an article in *Academic Questions* in 2000, "My War with the AHA," detailing all my interactions with that august body, and predicting that it was destined to wither and die because the kind of history that it now offered had nothing to offer to the general public.[15]

I became very close not only to Bill Strauss, but also to his whole family—his wife Janie, a long-time member of the school board in Fairfax County, Virginia, and his four kids, two on each side of the Xer-Millennial divide. I stayed at their house for many weeks of research trips on my next two books. Bill and Neil joined Bill James and Camille Paglia as the members of my own generation who had truly expanded my intellectual horizons. That list has not gotten any longer in the last twenty years.

At about the time that *The Fourth Turning* appeared, I finally managed to find a publisher for *Epic Season: The 1948 American League Pennant Race*. Although quite a few baseball books were appearing in the 1990s, no major publisher would ever touch it. Eventually, I sounded out my Harvard classmate Bruce Wilcox at the University of Massachusetts Press, who had published *Postmortem* back in 1985. He, fortunately, had an editor working for him named Clark Dougan, who was a baseball freak and a Cleveland Indians fan, and they took it on. It appeared in the spring of 1998, and to my amazement, it drew a rave review from Ron Fimrite of *Sports Illustrated*. I have received many compliments on it from fellow researchers at meetings of the Society for American Baseball Research. By that time, *American Tragedy* was finished as well, and the marketing of it was underway.

Some years earlier, a War College colleague had put me in touch with his New York agent, and I had signed on with him as well. He agreed that *American Tragedy* was a worthy book for a trade publisher, but he insisted that since I had never written

---

15 David Kaiser, "My War with the AHA," *Academic Questions*, spring 2000, pp. 70–77.

a trade book before, he could not start marketing it until it was finished. I realize now that that was a dreadful mistake. A book proposal functions like a Rorschach blot, enabling the editor to see whatever he or she likes in the book; a full ms. is what it is. When the time came to send it around, no trade editor was willing to bite, and in the end, he sold it to the Harvard University Press, which had published *Politics and War*. Realizing that the agent had done nothing for me that I could not have done for myself, I terminated our relationship shortly thereafter.

By this time I was in the midst of a personal crisis as well. Cathy and I had been drifting apart for a long time. I have no wish to belabor the details of the trouble that had arisen with the woman who had been such a big part of the happiest period of my life and with whom I had raised our two children (the younger of whom, Tom, was now 16.) But in early 1998 divorce proceedings began. The process went relatively smoothly and was complete by the end of that year. Neither of our sons showed any serious ill effects, and my own relationship with them became at least as strong as ever. Even though the decision was clearly for the best, it was traumatic and took some time to recover from.

As the winter term of 1997–8 wound down at the War College, I decided to try to distract myself from my personal life with a new elective course. The electives program was still very informally run in those days, and I had no trouble getting it approved on the spot. Entitled *Generations in Film*, it was based upon Strauss and Howe. The students—a mix of Boomers and Xers at that point—read *Generations* (later replaced by *The Fourth Turning*). Then we watched one movie a week in class (the classes lasted three hours), and they were assigned one for homework. Discussions focused on generational archetypes.

The GI generation was still very much alive in 1998, and the course began with two films about their youth, *They Made Me a Criminal* starring John Garfield (b. 1913) and *Boystown*. It then moved into the war, for which my favorite film was, and remains, *Mr. Roberts*. The early postwar period was covered by *The Best Years of Our Lives*, which was too long to use in class, and a wonderful unknown film provided by American Movie

Classics, *An Apartment for Peggy*. Set at a college in 1947, the film featured a GI (William Holden) studying to be a teacher, his bubbly Silent wife (Jeanne Crain), and their landlord, a retired, Missionary professor of philosophy (Edmund Gwenn, who in the same year starred in *Miracle on 34th Street*.) All played their generational parts to perfection.

For the 1950s I picked *Twelve Angry Men* to show midlife GIs at their best, and *The Apartment* to show them at their worst. *The Apartment* also introduced the young adult Silent generation in the persons of Jack Lemmon and Shirley McLaine, who let the GIs walk all over them for most of the film. The best films about the Awakening were *One Flew Over the Cuckoo's Nest*, which captured the stifling aspects of the High and the liberating feel of the Awakening perfectly, and *Getting Straight*, an astonishingly true to life campus drama of the late 1960s featuring Eliot Gould and Candace Bergen. It was a remarkable foil to *An Apartment for Peggy*. And then came the film that seemed to have been made for the course: *Same Time, Next Year*, with Alan Alda and Ellen Burstyn as two Silents meeting for a weekend affair every year from 1951 to 1977, and showing the changes their generation had lived through.

The filmmaker Oliver Stone has always understood generational issues, and *Platoon* and *Born on the Fourth of July* captured the impact of Vietnam on his, and my generation. *Wall Street* beautifully captured the transition to the Unraveling and featured Charlie Sheen as the first adult Gen Xer in the course, and Michael Douglas's Gordon Gecko as the first portrait of a Boomer in power. And then came one of my favorite films of all time, Sidney Lumet's *Running on Empty*, about two Boomer parents and their Xer kids who had spent 16 years on the run from the FBI after bombing a campus building to protest the Vietnam War. It never failed to have a powerful effect. With the next great crisis looming at some point in the future, I liked to conclude the class with *The Treasure of the Sierra Madre*. Its three prospectors—the Missionary Walter Huston, the Lost Humphrey Bogart, and the GI Tim Holt—represented their generations perfectly, and they were parallel to the Boomers, Gen Xers and Millennials who were about to take center stage.

(Millennials did not enter my War College classes until about 2012.)

The atmosphere in the first class was electric, because we knew we were doing something entirely new. I always gave the students the option of writing a generational analysis of their own life for the final paper, and it was always the most popular option. They also did at least one book report, choosing the book from a long list. I was thrilled to be doing this, and suddenly had a new dream: to bring that class to a group of Millennials at a college or university.

That class also came to my rescue at another key moment that spring. Aida Donald was now my editor at Harvard Press, as she had been for *Politics and War*. While she had a reputation for being difficult to deal with, I had had no problems with her—until now. The draft of *American Tragedy* included a five-page epilogue that I had thought about for many years. Entitled "Tragedy and History," it began placing myself at the top of Angel's Landing in Zion National Park on July 28, 1965, the day that Lyndon Johnson made it clear that the United States was in the war to stay. I tried to convey my joy of being alive and a young American at that moment—a moment of triumph for my country in general and my parents' generation in particular, a triumph they were about to throw away in a war that would destroy their world and mine. I used some specifically Greek imagery, and I also compared the book I had just finished to Thucydides's *The Peloponnesian War*, Albertini's *Origins of the War of 1914*, and Fritz Fischer's *Germany's Aims in the First World War*, other books by historians critical of their own nation's greatest mistakes. I had never put more feeling into anything written for publication.

Mrs. Donald immediately made clear that she did not like it. I replied that I would be very reluctant to see it taken out. Then I went down to the office of my department chair and dear friend George Baer and gave the five pages to him. He told me a little while later they had brought tears to his eyes. That very week, I had one of my students in Generations in Film read it to the rest, and the reaction was very favorable. That did it—nothing would make me give them up now. The argument between Aida Donald and myself grew more and more bitter as the publication date neared. I prevailed, although I had to drop some of the key language from the text—but she and I literally never spoke again. Oddly, not a single reviewer ever referred either positively or negatively to those pages, but many readers have. "David Kaiser," a blogger whom I did not know wrote in 2006,"is the author of *American Tragedy: Kennedy, Johnson, and the Origins of the Vietnam War*, a book that details the foibles, obsessions, decision-making and delusion of our leaders and generals. The book's poignant epilogue always makes me weep." That was all the reward I ever needed.

Years later, I acquired a book by Peter Bogdanovich, *Who the Devil Made It?*, composed of his interviews with great filmmakers. I was particularly struck by his talk with Otto Preminger, who had broken in as a director with the film noir *Laura* and proceeded to make a long series of exceptional movies, including *The Man with the Golden Arm, Anatomy of a Murder*, and *Exodus*. What came out in Preminger's account of film after film was his willingness to do anything and endure any humiliation in order to make the film come out as he had planned. That was me, and I am convinced that any great author or artist needs that determination, wherever it comes from. Orwell showed the same quality when the Book of the Month Club initially refused to accept *1984* unless he would drop two substantial portions of the text, and was rewarded when they caved in and took it anyway when he refused to agree.

It was not until early 2000 that *American Tragedy* finally appeared. That was the beginning of another key period in my life, marked by new joy in my personal life, another big project revolving around a great drama of my youth, and new but ultimately tragic twists in my difficult relationship with my chosen profession and the institution that had made me what I am. And at the same time, the great crisis that Strauss and Howe had predicted got underway.

VII

IN A NEW CENTURY

2000–2006

I n early 1998. I was invited by Akira Iriye of Harvard to a 70th birthday celebration for my adviser Ernest May late in that year. Iriye had been a Ph.D. student of May's himself in the early 1960s, and I had read his first book, *After Imperialism*, in May's course in the spring of 1967. He had returned to Harvard with tenure after I left. Iriye also invited me to contribute an essay to a collection that was going to be published to commemorate the event, what the Germans call a *Festschrift*. I decided to take a generational approach, and as soon as I began looking at May's career from that angle, I found very striking results.

"Ernest May," I began, "born in 1928, belongs to the Silent Generation, a designation which will not, I suspect, strike those who know him as anomalous." May's taciturnity was legendary. "The Silent," Strauss and Howe had written, "have spent a lifetime plumbing inner wellsprings older G.I.s seldom felt while maintaining a sense of social obligation Boomers haven't shared . . . Lacking an independent voice, they have adopted the moral relativism of the skilled arbitrator, mediating arguments between others."[16] "These characteristics," I suggested, "have distinguished much of Ernest May's work, both as a historian and an administrator. The May Group in the 1960s

---

16 *Generations*, p. 282.

specifically investigated the role of bureaucracy and process in the formation of foreign policy, with results that have exerted enormous influence upon historians and political scientists ever since. May's work with transition teams at the Institute of Politics has tried to smooth the process of replacing one presidential administration with another. The Uses of History course has tried to introduce a new element into the formation of policy, in an effort to make it more rational." That, however, was only the beginning.

The Silent generation belongs to the Artist archetype. Artist generations are children during the periodic great crises that redefine societies and states, and the Silents were children during the Great Depression and the Second World War. May was probably the first Silent to be tenured at Harvard. Their parallel generations in American national history were the Compromise generation, including Henry Clay and Daniel Webster, who had been born during the period of the revolution and the Constitution, and the Progressive generation, children during the Civil War. What was astonishing was that nearly all May's research had dealt with the Progressives and the Compromisers, that is, with generations from the Artist archetype. His first book, *The World War and American Isolation, 1914–17*, focused on Woodrow Wilson and a parallel German figure, the Chancellor Bethmann Hollweg, who had been children during the Civil War and the founding of the German empire, respectively. His second book, *Imperial Democracy*, focused on the first President of the Progressive generation, William McKinley. And both of those books emphasized the great care their subjects took in reaching decisions, in seeking out all points of view, and in trying to please the maximum number of people possible. In the mid-1970s—just as his own Silent generation was apparently ready to take power from the GIs in Washington—May had published *The Making of the Monroe Doctrine*, which specifically contrasted President Monroe, the last President from the Republican generation of Hamilton, Jefferson and Madison, with the younger Compromisers—Andrew Jackson, William Crawford, John Quincy

Adams and Henry Clay—who were trying to succeed him. May, in short, had obviously been unconsciously drawn to his own archetype. Iriye was sufficiently intrigued by this analysis to make me one of the featured speakers at the event, where my talk made an obvious hit. He also told me that he was using *Politics and War* in a graduate course. Sam Williamson, now the President of the University of the South, also attended and a good time was had by all.

Some years later, I managed to arrange my projected panel on generational theory after all, not at the AHA, which had rejected it, but at the convention of the new Historical Society, which some intrepid scholars had tried to found as a counterweight. Bill Strauss could not attend for medical reasons, and David Krein, who had applied the theory to Victorian Britain, had to mail in his excellent contribution because he could not leave his sick wife. But Neil Howe came, and my old friend Anne Rose chaired the panel. My own paper, "The Great Atlantic Crises, 1774–1962," discussed how the theory and the crises it identified tracked events in Britain, France, and Germany, as well as in the United States. The historian Bruce Kuklick, who was present, offered to get it published in the journal *The Monist*, which was writing a special issue on international order, and it was. It occurred to me that the article could be the foundation for an excellent college course, but I had nowhere to give it.

Meanwhile, things continued as usual at the War College, where my colleagues were very supportive in my time of personal trouble. My teaching partner in 1999–2000 was a Marine colonel named Neil Hartenstein, who, like nearly every partner I ever had, found his own ways to contribute to the students' education. Our students included an Air Force lieutenant colonel named Kevin Darnell, who drew one of the first papers, the analysis of the Sicilian expedition undertaken by the Athenians in the Peloponnesian War.

Kevin Darnell

To set the context for my first meeting with David Kaiser, I feel I must recall some of the history that led me to the Naval War College in Newport, Rhode Island.

I was a United States Air Force squadron commander in Panama in the late 1990s. Like most officers in my position, a lieutenant colonel reaching the end of a successful command tour, I was hopeful—not certain—of getting an appointment to attend a War College in residence next. Not all officers are granted the opportunity to spend a year dedicated to studying their profession, and it was well known that making the next promotion to full colonel practically required it. So when the day came to submit my "wish list" of next assignments for my boss's consideration, the importance of a school assignment was already planted in my thoughts. Several years earlier, as a new major, I had attended the Air Command and Staff College at Maxwell Air Force Base in Montgomery, Alabama. Colonel John Warden was Commandant at ACSC. Colonel Warden is famous in certain circles for having crafted the air campaign against Iraq in 1991 that made the ground invasion as close to a walkover as has been seen in the modern history of combat. As we approached the second half of the school year, Colonel Warden announced that he was setting up an alternative curriculum for a select number of students. He wanted to have officers read whole books, not only snippets or the opinion pieces that characterized the core program of instruction. He then wanted us to critically analyze the lessons drawn from the texts and as often as possible, discuss the ideas with recognized experts or the authors themselves. It was in this setting that I was first introduced to General Clausewitz's classic, *On War*.

I do not remember where I first learned of the Naval War College, but by 1998 I knew that it was thought of as the most intellectually demanding, toughest school among the armed forces' various senior service school programs. My academic performance at ACSC was solid, but not extraordinary. I expected more of the same at Newport. I could have chosen the perceived "gentlemen's" courses of the Army or Air Force, but something instilled by Colonel Warden's reading-intensive curriculum led me to take my chances with the Naval War College.

And so I selected to go to the Naval War College as my first choice, and got it. With hardly a chance to catch my breath from the process of repatriating from Panama, my family and I crossed the Pell Bridge to Aquidneck Island in August of 1999. We arrived to an idyllic scene of sailing boats and yachts in the harbor, and the War College prominently placed on Coasters Harbor Island.

My hopes and fears were both about to be fulfilled in ample supply. The introduction to the Naval War College stressed the methodology that I had become familiar with in Maxwell—reading, reading, and more reading. We were told that 600 pages a week would be common, a scary proposition for all but the most committed bookworms. And for my first foray into the Navy curriculum, I would be starting with Strategy and Policy—the beast of the school, with the most illustrious professors and the hardest grading standards in what was already the toughest War College program in the country, if not the world.

As with many propitious things in life, chance led me to David as my first professor in Newport. Unlike any other military school I had experienced, my seminar classmates, about 12 of us, sat in our newly purchased civilian business clothes and faced David and his teaching partner, a Marine colonel named Neil Hartenstein. I was used to being in uniform for every military training event, and here we were in our new coats and ties (I assume the women already had a closet of suitable clothing; I was probably wrong) facing off with a senior Marine officer and a Harvard Ph.D. It already looked like I was in trouble, academically and professionally.

And so the S&P program began. Truthfully, most of it is a blur. S&P assigned "short" 8-page papers to students on a rotating basis, a chance to exercise our developing ability to apply critical analysis to the subject. David had said in our introductory seminar that it was all right to apply some creativity to our papers, even to the point of role-playing a part in the history.

The first week of papers was on Thucydides's *The History of the Peloponnesian War* and, for better or worse, one landed on me. I had a paper to write. I fell in love with this history that I realized I knew nothing about. The department lecturers were amazing in providing an overview of the major actions and players, and the book was mesmerizing. As I sat in my little closet of a study in my Navy family quarters, I stared at a blank screen and wondered how I could possibly answer my assigned essay question: Was the Sicilian Campaign a bad idea, or a good idea badly executed? Such a seemingly simple question only sent chills up my spine. Only a devilish Ivy League-educated mind could have come up with something this impossible to answer.

I worked throughout the weekend, so my paper would meet the Monday morning deadline. I took David's challenge and wrote it in the first person as an unknown Athenian strategist and participant at Sicily who decried the various errors made both in policy and strategy that led to the campaign's failure. Though it took me an inordinate amount of time to write the paper, most of that was in editing. I flew through the first draft, the thoughts flowing almost effortlessly as the speaker talked through the major problems he had experienced under poor civil and military leadership. The essay wrote itself, and I saw that this was only possible because of two things: having actually read the book, and experiencing what it was like to have really serious-minded experts lecture on the subject.

Student papers were distributed before class and were the main topic of discussion in seminar. Like practically every student, I was focused on my grade as much as on the feedback from the professors. I would soon learn to reverse my concerns. The Naval War College was a program that rewarded those who took criticism well and incorporated it into the next assignment. If you realized this early on, then the true value of the program became apparent later—it changed my entire view of what constitutes evidence and persuasive argument. With David as my teacher, I could have spent the whole year in S&P and never grown tired. He challenged every assumption made by any of us, and thus taught us that assumptions are only valid if they can be defended by evidence and compelling analysis. I wrote two more papers during the S&P phase of the curriculum, and they remain clear in my memory. I was taught that to really understand something, you have to not only study it—you have to write about it.

~

American Tragedy appeared early in 2000. I dedicated it to several dozen Americans, broken down by generation from the Lost generation through the Boom, who had in my judgement behaved heroically during that conflict—politicians, judges, activists of various kinds, bureaucrats and military men who had spoken out against the war or the ways in which it was being fought. They included several veterans who had become activists, and Oliver Stone, a wounded veteran himself who had become the cinematic chronicler of the war. I was very proud that the book was also blurbed very enthusiastically by members of four different generations: John Kenneth Galbraith and Arthur Schlesinger from the GIs, Silents Robert Dallek and Ernest May, Boomer Alan Brinkley, and unrelated Gen Xer Douglas Brinkley. Harvard University Press evidently did an excellent job of promoting it, and it was very widely reviewed. Kai Bird in the *Washington Post* and Stanley Cutler in the *Chicago Tribune* were very appreciative; two others were less so. This was the first of my books to be reviewed in the Sunday *New York Times*, but the reviewer turned out to be a young scholar who had given an unsuccessful job talk to my department at NWC. I must have been away on a leave or research trip because I am sure I did not hear it, but his review was patronizing in the extreme. At *Harper's*, Lewis Lapham, the editor—whom I had never met—had evidently been alerted to the book by John Kenneth Galbraith. Lapham assigned the book to James William Gibson, a Boomer sociologist—not a historian—and author of *The Perfect War: Technowar in Vietnam*. In a very long review, Gibson dismissed my analysis and the whole idea that the identity of the President might have made a difference as to whether we would have gone to war or not. I comforted myself with the old adage that there is no such thing as bad publicity. In the end, if I am not mistaken, *American Tragedy* sold more than 20,000 hardcover copies. I also received a wonderful letter from retired CBS correspondent Robert Pierpoint, which began, "Your book, *American Tragedy*, is a masterpiece," and went on to describe his own dealings with Lyndon Johnson. I had mentioned that Johnson had a habit of accusing pesky critics of Communism in difficult moments, and he reported that he had been the target of such an accusation himself. The book was also the subject of a lengthy forum on H-Diplo. Of the numerous academic reviews it received, not one really attempted to actually describe the book I had written. Its historical and artistic ambition went well beyond current professional horizons.

My personal life was reviving in 2000 as well, and I had had two short relationships with new women. The second was an investment banker who had placed an ad in the *New York Review of Books*, but although we managed to stay away from politics and did some skiing and biking together, things were not destined to last. Then came one of the most extraordinary strokes of luck that I had ever experienced.

My other main source of personal ads was the Providence edition of the *Boston Phoenix*, the alternative paper that I had read religiously in my youth when it began appearing the late 1960s. Men and women who placed ads in it now recorded phone messages, of which I had listened to a great many. I had met a few people that way, but without result. On July 14, 2000, I had just returned from a conference on Thucydides in Jackson Hole, Wyoming, led by my dear friend and colleague Alberto Coll and sponsored by the Liberty Fund, which had several connections to the War College. I checked the ads again and noticed one from a woman in Boston looking for a man of at least 40. I immediately dialed the site's 900 number to listen to her message. It was brief, charming, and mentioned that she was looking for a kind of "mentor relationship." I have always been very sensitive to voices. Although I have had a dreadful memory for faces all my life—probably my biggest flaw as a teacher—I have a remarkable knack for recognizing actors in film and television, and I realized a long time ago that it was their voices that enabled me to do it. This woman's voice was lovely. I left a return message for her at once. Within 24 hours we had exchanged pictures, and the omens were looking more favorable than ever. She was petite and curvy, a type that had always attracted me, but which I had never actively sought out. I agreed to come to Boston that Sunday to meet, and we first saw each other beneath the Charles Street T station, just a couple of blocks from Charles River Park, where she was living.

Patti Cassidy was even more striking in person than in her pictures. I had assumed from her ad that she was probably in her forties, but it turned out that she had turned 53—my age—seven months before I had. She was very interested in film, as I was, and had made documentaries and written plays of her own. But what was most striking was her attitude towards Boston and towards life. She had grown up in the Albany, New York area, making us neighbors without knowing it in the late 1950s, but had moved to Arizona with her husband in the early 1970s. Eventually, they had homesteaded on a ranch. In the meantime, she had worked as a clerk in various emergency rooms. She had been divorced in 1993 and had spent the next six years in Tucson, working in ERs, writing plays, and actively socializing. But she had long dreamed of coming to Boston, where she had spent a year living on Beacon Hill in 1968–9. Just about six months earlier, late in 1999, she had done so. Now she had a high-rise studio apartment and a job at Mass General, and she was obviously in love with her new life. Partly, perhaps, because she had never had children, she had a very youthful attitude, and it occurred to me in the middle of our first afternoon that she was reminding me of myself at age 23, when I had returned to Cambridge after my year in exile in 1970. Things moved very quickly between us. Generations, inevitably, came up early in our acquaintance, and she was fascinated by this new way of looking at things. She was in fact far more of a Boomer than I was. Within a year, I managed to persuade her to move to Rhode Island and live with me. She initially sublet her apartment, and she cried when she cleaned it out about a year later. I felt terrible because I wanted to be back in Boston as much as she did, but could not manage it. Eventually, however, we did. We have been very happy together ever since.

In June 2001, the commencement speaker at the Naval War College was former President George H. W. Bush. In his address, he gave a brilliant analysis of the 1991 Gulf War, focusing on the many reasons why it would have been a terrible mistake for the United States to have gone to Baghdad and overthrown Saddam Hussein. At about the same time, my colleagues and I suffered a terrible blow when Michael Handel, our resident authority on Clausewitz, died of pancreatic cancer. Michael, whose work and family were his only interests, spent his last few months planning a conference in his honor, complete with a book of readings. On my last visit to his house, he suggested that I do something we had talked about a number of times—an analysis of strategy in sports and in war. The next morning, my phone rang about 9:00 AM. "Kaiser!" said the familiar Hebrew-accented voice. "You kept me up half the night thinking about your paper!" He proceeded to read me a list of ten possible topics for me to discuss. Michael was determined to die as he had lived intellectually engaged, and he did. When the news of his illness had first been revealed, I had also gone into Chairman George Baer's office and volunteered to take over the introductory lecture on Clausewitz. I did, and it became one of my proudest achievements at the college.

In the late summer of 2001, I began teaching Strategy and Policy again. My teaching partner was Kevin Darnell, who had been my student in the course only 18 months earlier and who had now joined our faculty. On the morning of the 11th of September at 8:30 AM we began our three-hour seminar on the Napoleonic Wars. These were still the days before wifi or smartphones, and we passed the next 90 minutes without a clue as to what was happening in New York and elsewhere. When we broke at 10:00 for coffee, we heard the news and realized class would not resume. Trained to react to crises, the military personnel shut down completely emotionally. Glued to one of our few television monitors, I saw the almost simultaneous collapse of the two twin towers and heard that the Pentagon had been hit. By noon we had been sent home.

The War College, as it turned out, would never be the same again. All the departments immediately came under pressure to make the curriculum more relevant to terrorism and, after the invasions of Afghanistan and then Iraq, counterinsurgency. Sadly, in an attempt to assert more control over the departments, the administration removed the sitting department chairs, including George Baer. His successors did not match the standard he and Bill Fuller had set. The war in Iraq left the Democrats on the faculty feeling a good deal more isolated, and we began to have a lot of hushed conversations in hallway corners. And over the next few years, the loss of Michael Handel was followed by the departures of Arthur Waldron (who landed a fine job at the University of Pennsylvania), Alberto Coll (who initially moved to another part of the college and later became a law professor), George Baer (who moved to California), and eventually, Bill Fuller, who retired early. They were irreplaceable, and although we added some fine new faculty as the years went by, the department never regained its previous stature. Dex Wilson, fresh from Harvard, became our resident authority on Sun Tzu (and has now recorded a whole strategy course for The Great Courses), and Sally Paine has emerged as a remarkable scholar of Far Eastern war. They were both historians, but diplomatic history had become so unfashionable that most new hires, as the new century wore on, were political scientists, who had a habit of substituting concepts from their own discipline for the ones we had developed in Newport.

In that same month of September 2001, I received a phone call that seemed likely to transform my life. Bill Kirby of the history department at Harvard called to ask if I would be a candidate for one of two senior positions in diplomatic history that the department wanted to fill that year. "Does this mean that Ernest is retiring?" I asked. "He. . might be," he said. (In fact, May moved all his teaching out of the history department and into the JFK School shortly thereafter.) Kirby did not ask me to write a letter, submit a C.V., or solicit recommendations.

I had evidently made a very good impression on him at May's 70th birthday event. I thought about sending him my CUE guide teaching reviews from 1978 and 1979, but as my old student Matthew Diller put it, "since they didn't care about not having your teaching for the last 20 years they aren't likely to care much about it now," and I didn't. An interview was scheduled for about a month later. I called Patti, who was ecstatic. I also opened one of my favorite works, the diaries of Harold Nicolson, who surveyed his own life at a critical moment. "Success," he wrote, "should come late in life, to make up for the loss of youth." He had been 54 when he wrote those words in 1941, and I was 54 in 2001.

The Harvard history department now included my former Carnegie Mellon colleague Lizabeth Cohen. Although she would always have described herself as a social rather than a political historian, they had hired her to fill a gap in twentieth-century US political history. I immediately wrote her a note mentioning that I would be coming, and she replied mentioning that she had spent quite a bit of time with *American Tragedy* in preparation for a lecture on Vietnam. "Quite a research job, David!" she wrote. My biggest question was now what to discuss in my job talk. I was already quite certain that my next book would take advantage of a huge release of documents to investigate the Kennedy assassination, but any mention of that third rail topic would doom my candidacy on the spot. Thus I decided to give more of a hint of what I might be able to contribute in the classroom. I wrote a talk analyzing the Cold War as a struggle fought on three fronts. The first was the strategic nuclear front, the actual threatened war between the US and the USSR. The second was the frontier between the spheres of influence they had established in Europe and Northeast Asia at the end of the Second World War, and the third was in the third world. I wrote Liz Cohen again on the eve of my visit to Cambridge to try to make sure she would be there. Liz was frantically trying to finish her long-awaited *second* book. Her first had sufficed to get her hired not only at Carnegie Mellon, but at NYU and then at Harvard as well. She was one of many academics who made a great career out of a well-received first book and the promise of another that takes decades—and, occasionally, forever—to appear.

The only faculty members I met with before my talk were Kirby, the search committee chair, and David Blackbourn, the chairman—a Brit who had finally landed the job in German history that had been vacant for so long. He had now abandoned political history and was writing something on the environment in 19th century Germany. May was part of the search committee, as was Akira Iriye, his one-time student, who was also near retirement. Charlie Maier, whom I had known when he was an assistant professor, and I was a grad student, was as well. He had been brought back to Harvard in 1980, seven years after his failure to get tenure. In his 1979 job talk, he had discussed the sequel to his first book on the "stabilization" of Western Europe after the First World War, which would do the same for the aftermath of the Second World War. That book had never been written. The committee also included John Coatsworth, an historian of Latin America; my old friend Steve Thernstrom, whose conservative politics had increasingly isolated him within the department; and James Kloppenberg, an intellectual historian who had recently published a far-reaching book on progressive thought in the late 19th-century US and Western Europe.

My talk, in the history department library, seemed to go very well. Charlie Maier seemed rather taken aback by my novel approach to the Cold War and tried to critique it theoretically, as he was often wont to do. But Liz Cohen, who did show up, betrayed our friendship, asking me bluntly to justify myself in the context of a profession that had "changed' so much—in other words, to defend myself for doing an obsolete kind of history. I attempted to do so, but I wish now I had said what I thought: that I assumed that the search showed that some of her colleagues shared my own fear that it might change too much. She was not appeased.

The committee and I then repaired to a very pleasant dinner. May pronounced *American Tragedy* a "terrific book," and asked me why I hadn't included any generational analysis in my talk. I did not reply honestly that I had not wanted to doom my chances of getting the job. Akira Iriye referred warmly to *Politics and War*. I asked Coatsworth some questions about Latin America. Then Kirby made a point of walking me back to the hotel where Patti was waiting for me, the one built on the site of the old Gulf station at the corner of Harvard Yard, right across the street from Pennypacker Hall where I had lived as a freshman 36 years earlier. He told me he thought my talk had gone very well and seemed quite excited by the possibility of having me back. "I thought about sending you my CUE guide reports," I said. "I read them when I was chairman!" he exclaimed. "I couldn't believe it. How could we have let all this talent get away?" It really seemed likely that the impossible was going to happen.

Unfortunately, as so often seems to happen in academia, a new element had been introduced into the situation.

Harvard had a new President that fall, the economist Larry Summers. Summers, fresh from a stint as Bill Clinton's Treasury Secretary and later to be a senior adviser to Barack Obama, was destined for a relatively brief and stormy career as Harvard's first Boomer President, marked by a confrontation with Cornel West that led to his departure for Princeton, numerous changes of personnel at the university's highest levels, and some controversial remarks about women in science. But another catastrophic mistake kicked off his tenure. On January 14, 2002, the Harvard Crimson, following up a story in the *Wall Street Journal*, reported that Summers had personally stopped the hiring of two tenured professors, political scientist Istvan Hunt of Cambridge University and music professor Karol Berger of Stanford, on the grounds that they were too old. They were both 54—like me. Toeing the line, Dean of the Faculty Jeremy Knowles emailed the Crimson that he agreed with Summers that "adjectives like 'exciting, promising, and brilliant,' tend to be more persuasive than adjectives like 'distinguished, and eminent'" when describing candidates. Age discrimination was, of course, illegal, and another university spokesman said that he didn't believe Summers was "explicitly implying age" when he told the *Wall Street Journal* that he was focusing "on what portion of a person's work lies in the future." Once again, it seemed, I was fighting something that had nothing to do with me personally and was utterly beyond my control.

It took the history department a couple of more months to make its selections. The first was indeed a contemporary of mine—actually a few years older—an historian of the Soviet Union named Norman Naimark, who taught at Stanford. Several well-informed people found the choice rather odd because Naimark's relationship with Stanford was comparable to mine with Harvard—he had earned his B.A. there and by all accounts was most unlikely to leave northern California. The second choice was indeed much younger. He was the Brit Niall Ferguson, only 37, who taught at Oxford, where he had earned his Ph.D. only 12 years earlier. Ferguson was then the author of three books: a study of the German hyperinflation in the 1920s; a biography of the Rothschild family running to more than 1000 pages; and most recently, *The Pity of War*, an idiosyncratic study of the First World War.

The reader will recall that I had been studying, teaching, writing about, and lecturing about the origins of the First World War in great detail since the fall of 1967, when I took Sam Williamson's undergraduate seminar on the topic. Ferguson's book was organized thematically, and he had relied on a platoon of research assistants. The argument of the book reminded me of Peter Stearns's informal definition of traditional historical methodology: find out what others have written about a topic, and write the opposite. That Germany was primarily responsible for the outbreak of world war in 1914 had been solidly established by Albertini, by Fritz Fischer, and in a small way by myself, but Ferguson now denied it. He blamed, not the French and the Russians—a common argument in the 1920s and 1930s—but rather his own British nation, whom he claimed had sent mixed signals. He claimed, in the face of the evidence to the contrary, that the Germans had only the most limited war aims against France, Belgium, and Russia. And, as a result, he argued, the British had done themselves and the world a terrible disservice by entering the war in 1914 at all, instead of allowing Germany to win it and create something like the EU 80 years earlier! Among the older historians who were not impressed was Paul Kennedy, who wrote the angriest prose I had ever seen come from his pen in response. Ferguson certainly had a different historical technique than I did. After his research assistants finished their labors, he wrote *The Pity of War* in just five months.

And like Tony Judt, Jeff Eley, David Blackbourn, and so many other British historians, Ferguson now dreamed of leaving the low British academic salaries and heavy teaching loads behind and finding an easier position in the New World. A *New Yorker* profile had helped make him the flavor of the month, and he had received one offer from the University of Pennsylvania and accepted one from NYU. Yet Harvard now wanted him and was not to be denied. My contacts at Harvard—including Kirby, whom I spoke to in May 2002—recognized that neither Naimark nor Ferguson was going to be easy to recruit. Kirby added that I had been a favorite—perhaps *the* favorite—of the outside referees whom Harvard had asked to rate the various candidates. That, very likely, owed a great deal to all the words I had written on H-Diplo, as well as for my books and articles, and I still appreciate it very much. But it had not swayed Kirby and his colleagues.

I was now in exactly the same position I had been in in 1978, waiting for other historians to make a decision in the hope that I might be selected if they said no. I wished that I had insisted on a quick yes or no decision back when I had first been approached in the previous fall, but I could not give up the possibility that I might once again be chosen. Kirby, meanwhile, became the Provost, I believe, taking him out of the departmental picture. (He could not get along with Summers and did not last long.) In the fall of 2002 I wrote Akira Iriye, who was finishing his Harvard career as chairman, making clear that I wanted to be dropped if they re-opened the search. He replied that the department was awaiting the responses of its preferred candidates. Meanwhile, my ptsd symptoms from 1977–80 had returned, led by insomnia. I began taking Xanax to sleep at night, and it was not for more than a decade that I managed to break that habit. (I never took any during the day.)

The courtship of Ferguson played out in public over the next year or more, and he finally agreed to come to Harvard. About Naimark I heard nothing—and I heard nothing from Iriye or anyone else either. Finally, in early 2004—nearly two and half years since Kirby had first contacted me—I wrote Iriye and Kirby at length, withdrawing my candidacy. An embarrassed Iriye immediately replied explaining that the search had been completed some time ago and apologizing for not letting me know. Naimark had indeed turned them down and remained at Stanford—and they had hired a freshly minted Ph.D., Erez Manela, at the junior level. Summers' prejudice against older faculty had obviously carried great weight.

This, I knew, had probably been my last chance to get back into university life. During that same period, Cornell had advertised for a senior Americanist to replace the eminent Walter LaFeber, a cold war historian. While I was not especially excited over the possibility of spending the rest of my life in Ithaca, New York, I put my hat into the ring. Another candidate was Fred Logevall, a Yale Ph.D. whose own book on the origins of the Vietnam War, *Choosing War*, had come out at virtually the same moment as *American Tragedy*. There were two differences that I could see between Logevall and myself. First, *Choosing War* was much more limited in scope than *American Tragedy* and did not cover the period of the Kennedy Administration. Second, while *Choosing War* was his only book, I had written four others. I was eliminated in the first round of the search without an interview, and Logevall got the job. My books on Europe were obviously a liability, not an asset.

Ferguson, like his idol Henry Kissinger—the subject of a biography of which he has now finished the first volume—parlayed his Harvard professorship into greater fame, fortune, and power. He wrote several essay-style books in the 2000s urging his adopted country to play the role of an imperial power with gusto, and loudly supported the war in Iraq. He made large sums of money sharing his economic and political expertise with hedge funds. During the 2012 election, he emerged as a bitter opponent of Barack Obama, whom he denounced in language similar to Mitt Romney's, and an enthusiastic acolyte of

Paul Ryan. He is in short very much at home in our new Gilded Age—but he is no longer at home at Harvard. Following in the footsteps of other Brits, he decamped a few years ago for even greener pastures at Stanford.

A year or two after Ferguson was appointed, Ernest May told a mutual friend, someone, I trust completely, that he—May—had lobbied President Larry Summers hard to give Ferguson whatever he wanted. "He will be the Henry Louis Gates of the History Department," May said. He presumably was referring to Gates's entrepreneurial abilities, much on display in his role as director of the Du Bois Institute at Harvard. I believe that in the end, I was the most accomplished Ph.D. student May had ever had, and I wish the nice things he said about several of my books had counted more for him when the chips were down. But as I already knew, he had a habit of going with the flow, and he was not about to challenge Summers's opposition to hiring older faculty. Ironically, a few years later, in 2004, I was having my 35th reunion while my old student Jonathan Alter, now a very well-known journalist, was having his 25th. A Crimson reporter did a long feature about Alter and interviewed Summers. "I've known Alter for a long time, and we talked on and off when I was in Washington," Summers remembered, "but I was first bowled over by him when he was writing his under- graduate thesis on Vietnam . . . a lot of people write theses about Vietnam, but most people who are college seniors don't have the sophistication to interview the best and the brightest political figures like McNamara and 290 other people. That just left me enormously impressed." He didn't know or care who had advised that thesis.

Erez Manela, meanwhile, published his first book, on the impact of Wilson and his fourteen points in four Third World countries—and was granted tenure by the History Department in 2009 on the basis of it. "His work is very important because he is part of a very small group of historians who are moving the traditional field of diplomatic history, which for a long time had been concerned with the foreign policies of the larg- est, often western nations, to a more international history," said Lizabeth Cohen, who was now the department chair. Manela's second book, on the eradication of smallpox during the 1970s, has not yet appeared.

Had I been hired, I might still be giving Generations in Film as a freshman seminar, and perhaps a two-semester lecture course on the four great Atlantic Crises of 1774–1803, 1860–1875, 1929–1945, and 2001–?. A subsequent episode in my career confirmed that they would have been very popular and had real impact. That possibility, however, was not one that anyone at Harvard cared about. There cannot be more than a handful of institutions of higher education left in the whole United States in which administrators are thinking seriously about the education their students are receiving.[17]

Ironically, by the time I finally found out that I would not be returning to Harvard, my relationship with it had entered yet another phase, involving my dear friend and classmate Bill Strauss. In 1999, when I was slowly recovering from my divorce, I was stunned when Bill told me that he had been diagnosed with pancreatic cancer, the same disease that had taken the life of another dear friend, Bill Young, 20 years earlier. Bill Strauss had however been diagnosed very early, and the cancer was completely removed from his pancreas by a new procedure, the Whipple operation, at Johns Hopkins. He initially made a complete recovery. Unfortunately, however, it turned out the cancer had already spread to his liver—albeit very slowly—and he underwent a chemotherapy regimen a couple of years later. In 2004 he had to go through it again, and it looked for some time as if this round of chemotherapy would kill him. Yet he did recover then and remained active until the same cycle was repeated, with fatal results, in 2007.[18]

It must have been in 2003 that Bill called me to discuss something he had just heard. Two managers of the Harvard

---

17 This situation now seems to be changing—but not for the better. Increasingly I am hearing the Diversity Offices in various schools are questioning faculty about the content of their courses to try to bring them in line with prevailing values.

18 As it happened, Bill had exactly the same cancer as Steve Jobs, and seems to have lived with it exactly as long as Jobs did, even though Jobs had a liver transplant, which Bill's doctors had advised him against.

Endowment, then led by Jack Meyer, were going to receive bonuses of more than $10 million—in one case, of $17.5 million. Bill—who like me had college-age children—was well aware of the steady increases in tuition at Harvard and elsewhere. He was a social conservative but an economic liberal, and he was simply appalled that anyone could receive compensation of that order of magnitude from a university. So was I. Bill was also influenced, I think, by something else that had just happened to him. One of the first graduates of the JFK School of Government, Bill had been asked to serve on a senior advisory board—provided that he could make a contribution of, I believe, $25,000. He explained his medical situation to the manager who had invited him, and they agreed to waive this customary requirement. But after one year—perhaps because he was still alive?—they insisted, and he dropped off the board. But it was principle, not the snub, that motivated him, and me.

Looking into the situation, we discovered that Meyer and his co-workers had turned the endowment into a hedge fund. I recruited about half a dozen classmates to sign a letter to President Summers protesting this level of compensation, asking that some of the money be diverted to tuition relief, and instituting a rule that no employee of the university make more money than the University President, who at that time earned less than $1 million a year. We publicized our views and our letter in the press, where it created something of a sensation. I and other classmates were quoted repeatedly in major newspapers. I received a letter from a retired university fund manager praising our stand. He argued that paying managers based on the amount of money they managed was as nonsensical as paying a train engineer based on the number of cars in his train. He also criticized the system of benchmarks that allowed the managers to earn huge sums whether the endowment had grown much or not, and said that his dog could have beaten one of the benchmarks during the year that has just passed. But we were consistently criticized by financial journalists, including Michael Lewis, the author of *Liar's Poker, Moneyball,* and, much later, *The Big Short.*

I and my classmates have continued this campaign intermittently from that day to this, commenting every couple of years on the compensation that Harvard has to report on form 990s (the non-profit's equivalent of a tax return) and on the performance of the Endowment. We addressed at least half a dozen letters to President Summers and his successor Drew Faust, but neither one of them ever signed a return letter, perhaps because none of us had made large cash contributions to the university. (The group included academics, an entertainer (Bill), a journalist, two litigating attorneys, and a clergyman, among others.) When Summers addressed our class at our 2004 reunion, he called us "deeply misguided" but took a direct question from one of us. At subsequent reunions President Faust has taken only written questions. In the wake of our first letters, Jack Meyer and some of his colleagues left Harvard Management, formed hedge funds of their own, and managed portions of the endowment privately, meaning that the university no longer had to report their compensation. The compensation of the top managers fell to below $10 million.

By 2006 or so I was beginning to wonder if the managers were really earning their money, because I noticed that the amount of money that the endowment was contributing to the running of the University did not seem to be increasing as fast as the endowment's value. But then, a year later, the financial crisis began, and by 2009 the fund managers were exposed, along with the rest of the masters of the universe on Wall Street, for having invested in various bubbles. The university lost about 1/3 of the endowment almost overnight, with devastating consequences for its operations, including widespread layoffs among staff. But the compensation for the managers suffered only one relatively modest one-year decline, and its upward climb resumed, despite our protests. In 2016, after several years of essentially flat returns (but increasing compensation), new leadership decided to farm out all the management of the endowment to private firms. That means that the compensation of the managers will no longer be publicly available for inspection, but the Harvard endowment, conceived as a means of promoting the best of American higher education, will continue to create more of the enormous fortunes that are one of the hallmarks of our age.

Early in 2018, Harvard chose a new President, Lawrence Bacow, and my classmates and I wrote another letter. Changes in the tax law now figured to cost Harvard about $40 million a year, and we showed how the institution could find that money simply by putting half the endowment in index funds, following the suggestion of Warren Buffett. We received an immediate polite and appreciative response from Bacow. I suppose that some readers may now wonder whether my participation in the campaign owed anything to the way Harvard had treated me. It did not. I would have been delighted to have signed the same letters as a full member of the Harvard faculty, and to raise the same issues in faculty meetings in University Hall.

I was now, of course, out of university life. One son, Dan, had graduated from Pomona College in 2001, and my second son Tom had entered George Washington University in 2000. The college visits I made with them were quite painful for me because I was walking on the grounds of institutions that no longer had any place for me. But I was deeply disturbed not only what was happening intellectually to the humanities but by the enormous cost of higher education. Bill and I computed that students were now paying almost three times as much as we did annually, even after adjusting for inflation. Not one of the signatories of our letters had graduated in 1969 with any significant debt, leaving us free to pursue any career we wanted. We did, perhaps, help convince Harvard to offer more financial aid, but all leading universities are both more expensive and more oriented around their earning power than they were half a century ago. That, in my opinion, is a disaster for the nation, and I am glad at least to have spoken out against it and to have persuaded some classmates to do the same.

In the meantime, I had embarked on another huge research project.

American Tragedy had concluded that the United States had fought the Vietnam War because of the death of John F. Kennedy. I see now that it was natural enough that I immediately decided to find out exactly why he had died. I had wanted to investigate the assassination thoroughly for a long time, and now, an astonishing new opportunity had opened up. Interest in the assassination had mushroomed again in 1991, shortly after my move to Rhode Island, when Oliver Stone released his movie, *JFK*. While I deeply regretted that Stone had not consulted better authorities before writing his film—such as myself—the consequences of what he had done were astonishing. The Congress passed a law authorizing the fullest possible release of all government records relating to the assassination. The act created a board to review the records, and the key figure on the board turned out to be Anna Nelson, an excellent historian at American University whom I already knew. Under her leadership, the board adopted a very broad definition of an assassination-related record. What resulted was not only the release of all the FBI's files relating to their investigation of the case but hundreds of thousands of pages of FBI documents on organized crime figures and incomparably the largest release of CIA documents that has ever been made. These were now sitting in a special collection of the National Archives building in College Park, Maryland, and I was determined to get my hands on them. I had been very interested in the evidence for the involvement of organized crime since writing my piece for the *Washington Post* in 1983 when I had had long talks with G. Robert Blakey. Since then, a good deal more evidence had emerged to support it. In 1997, I had published a review article in the journal Intelligence and National Security that included one critical new finding. A good deal of information had come to light in the mid-1970s about the CIA's and other repeated attempts to assassinate Fidel Castro. About two months before the assassination of JFK, Lee Harvey Oswald had gone to Mexico City and tried unsuccessfully to get a visa to travel to Havana. I had become convinced that he had done so in order to try to assassinate Castro, although I did not argue that he did so on behalf of the CIA.

I do not recall exactly how I made contact with Paul Hoch, a Berkeley librarian who was one of the best-known amateur researchers on the case, but I became a member of an email list of researchers that he maintained. That list should have made clear to me what kind of reception I could expect for the eventual book I might write, but it was not until after the book appeared that I fully grasped what the situation was. With almost the sole exception of Bob Blakey, the major students of the case fell into one of two camps. Both, I eventually realized, were actually faith-based approaches, operating from opposite premises. But what held each church together, I realized, was not simply a conclusion, but a relatively straightforward methodology.

On one side, the Church of the Lone Assassin took the view of the Warren Commission that both Lee Harvey Oswald and Jack Ruby were lone nuts with no broader connections. In public its most visible representative by around 2000 was Gerald Posner, who had written *Case Closed* as a response to Oliver Stone in the early 1990s and watched it soar to the top of the best-seller lists. Because members of this church rejected any conspiracy, they reflexively argued that any evidence of conspiracy—or of official cover-up—must be false. Now it is always possible to find some reason to disbelieve *any* piece of evidence. That, indeed, is how trial lawyers make their living. Posner, as it happened, was a journalist, and he used a journalistic technique to discredit any troublesome piece of evidence: he found someone else who didn't believe it, and quoted him. Others, better versed in the case, could usually find some anomaly in a witness's testimony or some negative piece of information about that witness to serve as their excuse for disregarding him. And confronted with evidence of official wrongdoing, members of the Church of the Lone Assassin generally argued that they were the doings of "clueless bureaucrats," or that the evidence of wrongdoing had been wrongly recorded, or that it wasn't really wrongdoing at all.

On the other side stood the Church of Grand Conspiracy, whose most famous acolyte was now Oliver Stone. They believed not simply in a conspiracy, but in a massive conspiracy involving various agencies of the US government, led by the CIA. They tended to believe that Oswald was completely innocent and that firearms and autopsy evidence had been fabricated to prove his guilt. Hardly any of them, however, were willing to be specific about the identity of the conspirators, much less about who had actually done the shooting. They too had their own methodology. Any discrepancy in the evidence, any contradictory testimony, or any controversial finding (such as the single bullet theory), they interpreted as evidence both of a conspiracy and a cover-up. Since such anomalies were bound to occur constantly in such a complex case, they would never run out of grist for their mill.

Now as I knew very well by the time I began systematic research, the House Assassinations Committee in 1977–8 had very carefully looked into the evidence for Oswald's guilt, including the firearms evidence tying the bullets to his rifle and the physics of the single-bullet theory, and found it all to be sound. That had only persuaded the Church of the Grand Conspiracy that Blakey and his staff had been conspirators after the fact. (Meanwhile, authors like Posner freely quoted Blakey and the Committee report to defend the single bullet theory, while ignoring or rejecting his firm belief that an organized crime conspiracy was behind Oswald.) Thus I began work convinced that Oswald had fired the fatal shots, and I discovered nothing to change my mind. But I also had some idea of how much evidence there was that leaders of organized crime had planned the assassination as a means of stopping Attorney General Robert Kennedy's determined attempt to put them all in jail. What I did not know was how specific I would be able to be in identifying key conspirators, and in fitting Oswald's activities into several larger patterns.

The necessary research effort was a daunting one. On the one hand, a great deal of material, including all the public testimony and all the reports of the House Committee, was now available online, as were many of the findings of the Senate Select Committee on Intelligence from 1975–6. But the FBI and CIA files were in College Park, where I could spend only about a month a year. On my first trip, I went right to the main FBI file on Oswald and started going through it. Meanwhile, I made a critical research breakthrough that enabled me, I am sure, to write a far more thorough and complete book than I could have even 10 years earlier. It is a breakthrough that other researchers would do well to use as well.

In the 1970s, researching the microfilmed German archives for *Economic Diplomacy and the Origins of the Second World War*, I had used notecards, putting a brief heading at the top of each one to indicate what it was about, and putting the date prominently at the top. That allowed me to sort the cards by topic and by date before writing up the material. Now, I realized, Microsoft Excel could enable me to do the same thing. I designed a research spreadsheet, more or less on the fly, and have modified the design only slightly ever since. Each row was dedicated to a specific document, such as an FBI report. The first few cells in the row—columns A–C—identified the document, gave the file from which it came (an entry which could be copied on down the appropriate column for as long as the file lasted), and gave its date. An additional column—absolutely crucial for this project—gave the date *of the incident which the document discussed*, as opposed to the date that it was written. Then came cells for headings and subheadings, such as Oswald—Mexico, or Oswald—New Orleans, or Assassination—eyewitness, and so forth. And then came a cell for the summary of the information in the document—and one could put literally as much as one wanted into one cell. All this was absolutely essential for the FBI files because documents going into the main Oswald file were simply added to it based on the order in which they were received in Washington, and 15 unrelated documents might separate two reports on the same subject. When the research was complete, I could simply sort the rows by heading, subhead, and date of incident, and the documentation for a whole piece of the book would be perfectly organized.

That was not all, Excel was, of course, searchable, and it took only seconds to find if a certain Cuban exile or Mafioso referenced in a new document had already shown up elsewhere. And when the time came to write the book, I discovered that Excel could actually create whole footnotes by concatenating the cells that dated the document and identified the file from which it came. It has been my misfortune to spend my life doing serious historical research and writing during decades when such research was falling out of fashion both inside and outside academia. But it has been my good fortune to be able to take advantage both of the availability of online research materials, and of software like Excel. New technology, in my opinion, has made the processes of historical research and writing far more efficient, and I have taken full advantage of what they had to offer. Several times in the 21st century I offered to explain this technique in a presentation before a university history department, but no one ever took me up on it.

The spreadsheets also made it much easier to use research assistants, and I could not do without them for this book. Help came my way from Art Eckstein, an ancient historian at the University of Maryland whom George Baer had brought to Newport to give guest lectures on several occasions. The archives were very near the campus, and he provided me with excellent history undergraduates who worked for work-study rates. They very easily learned how to enter data in the spreadsheet. As it turned out, I used them almost exclusively to go through FBI files. It did not take me long to fall in love with J. Edgar Hoover's FBI. Whatever the politics and specific goals of the director and his men, they understood research and knew how to write it up. When they wanted to find out about someone or something, what they did not find out what was not worth knowing. The CIA, however, worked very differently. Their documents were written in very cryptic language, filled with code names known as cryptonyms. In addition, many of their documents were also designed to conceal, rather than record, information. I spent most of my time at College Park reading those myself.

My favorite research assistant was my own son Tom, who had started college at George Washington in 2000 (and who reached the College Park archives in a handy shuttle bus from the downtown branch.) He, like his father, had been interested in history since childhood, and he must have been about 8 when he first learned the presidents in their order. When I came home from work while my sons were growing up, his brother Dan would always ask me how my day was, and he meant it. Tom would never waste any time on that—he would start right on the most interesting thing that had come up in school that day. He had started out at GW in political science but found it rather scanty on facts and switched to history.

"Don't worry, Dad"—he said—"I'm not going to write it, I'm going to make it." But he had been interested in the case since *JFK* came out when he was 10, and he eagerly jumped in and wrote up some of the most important documents on one of the most critical episodes in the case, known as the Odio incident.

Inside the large reading room, the few JFK researchers were easily identifiable by a special tag on their boxes of documents sitting on their individual carts. One day in the archive that enabled me to make contact with the remarkable Malcolm Blount. Malcolm, who ran a British mental health clinic, had become interested in the JFK case after Oliver Stone's movie came out. (He got the joke when I asked him if his clinic had a wing for JFK fanatics.) He had no plans to write anything about the case, but he spent all his vacation time in College Park, trying to read literally every one of the millions of pages in the collection. I continually shared new veins of evidence with him, and he usually could identify some obscure file where I would find more on the same subject. Not once did one of his leads fail to pan out. I have come to know at least two other such researchers well, men who have no writing ambitions but simply enjoy retreating into the early 1960s in their spare time. They have contributed very important data to the case.

The Road to Dallas remains in print and available, and it tells a series of complex, interconnected stories involving the FBI, the Justice Department, and the Mob; Castro's revolution and the CIA's and the Kennedy Administration's attempts to overthrow it; a network of anti-Castro organizations, many of them tied to the CIA, the mob, or both; Jack Ruby's life within organized crime enterprises; and Oswald's activities after returning to the US from the USSR in 1962. It also remains the most thorough account of Eisenhower and Kennedy Administration policy towards Cuba and the CIA's many attempts to assassinate Castro. It included a large and fascinating cast of characters, and I eventually wrote a treatment on how it might become a TV miniseries, but could not, alas, arouse any interest. I shall share only two critical findings here.

In the spring of 1963, about a year after returning to the US, Lee Oswald moved with his wife and child from the Dallas-Fort Worth area to his hometown of New Orleans. While there, he established a phantom chapter of the pro-Castro Fair Play for Cuba Committee, a Communist front organization. Although the New York headquarters of the committee immediately recognized Oswald as nothing but trouble and stopped answering his letters, he handed out the organization's leaflets around New Orleans, was arrested as a result of a street fight with some anti-Castro Cubans, and then participated in a local radio debate on Cuba. During that debate, a local right-wing activist exposed him as a former defector to the Soviet Union. There were never any other members of Oswald's chapter.

On November 23, 1963, I was the first to discover, an FBI assistant director wrote Hoover a memo on the bureau and the FPCC, whose connection to Oswald was already in the news. It explained that the FBI had been carrying on a COINTELPRO operation to disrupt the FPCC for several years, including attempts to discredit it in the press. Hoover's office prepared a new version of the memo to submit to the Attorney General, but omitted any mention of the COINTELPRO campaign.

The plot thickened when I read the 1976 Church Committee report on COINTELPRO. It did *not* list the FPCC as one of its targets, although I later found that the staff knew that it was. But it explained that COINTELPRO operations had often been subcontracted to private right-wing groups (such as the American Legion) and that on at least one occasion in the South, a fake chapter of a left-wing group had been formed to discredit it. I concluded that Oswald had been participating in a two-part COINTELPRO effort in New Orleans. His leafleting was designed to identify as yet unknown pro-Castro elements in the city (and apparently failed completely to do so), while the radio interview was staged (with some help from the House Un-American Activities Committee) to discredit both Oswald and the organization that he supposedly represented. Later in the same month of September 1963, Oswald went to Mexico City and tried unsuccessfully to use his *bona fides* as a pro-Castro activist to get a visa to Havana. He failed because officials at the Cuban consulate saw no reason to trust him.

But my biggest finding directly connected the mob, and particularly Santo Trafficante, at one time a major mob boss both in Tampa and in Havana, to Oswald and the assassination. John Martino was a Trafficante associate who had worked in Havana casinos before 1959. After Castro's takeover that year, he had been arrested in Havana while trying to smuggle out money and sentenced to a long prison term. In ill health, he had been released in mid-1962, returned to the US, and begun working as an anti-Castro activist in the Miami area. He had also made connections within the extreme right, which provided him with a ghostwriter, Nathan Weyl, for his book, *I Was Castro's Prisoner*, which appeared in 1963.

In June of 1963, I discovered, Martino was involved in an extraordinary operation, the Bayo-Pawley raid, named after Eddie Bayo, a Cuban exile, and William Pawley, a transit magnate and anti-Castro activist, who had also turned out to be the first person, apparently, who suggested to President Eisenhower that Castro ought to be assassinated. I found an extraordinary CIA file on the raid at College Park. Martino had secured help for the raid from the Agency, claiming that a team of Cuban exiles would land in Cuba and bring out three Soviet missile technicians who, he said, had remained there after the end of the missile crisis in October 1962. Martino also secured the cooperation of the Senate Internal Security Subcommittee, which wanted to hold hearings in which the Soviet defectors would discredit the Kennedy Administration. But in fact, there were no Soviet technicians. The plot was yet another attempt to put an assassination team into Cuba to deal with Castro, using explosives that Martino had provided. Another witness, a mercenary named Loran Hall—who had been involved in planning the raid—testified to a meeting between Martino and mob bosses Sam Giancana and Trafficante about the raid. And Hall, I also found, had met a Cuban exile named Silvia Odio in Dallas in the company of Lee Harvey Oswald in early October 1963, and had talked about the possibility of Oswald's assassinating either Castro or JFK.

It turned out that evidence of Martino's complicity in the assassination of the President was buried in the files of the House Assassinations Committee. Martino had died in 1975, but two years later a business partner of his had anonymously contacted the committee's staff to explain that Martino had told him that he had put the assassination plot together. He had said the same thing to a newspaper reporter named Cummings, whom I was able to interview. But then, in the midst of my research, another bombshell dropped.

Martino had a son, Edward, who was one year older than I was and who had become a clinical psychologist. He had made contact with another researcher, Larry Hancock, who holds an annual conference in Dallas. In 2006, when I had begun writing the book, Ed posted his own account of the events of 1959–63 on Hancock's website. He told how, several weeks before the Kennedy assassination, his family of news junkies had been watching a nightly news broadcast when the announcer referred to JFK's forthcoming trip to Dallas. (The occasion was almost surely Adlai Stevenson's earlier visit to Dallas when he was set upon physically by right-wing activists.) "If he goes to Dallas," Ed's father had remarked, "they are going to kill him." On the morning of November 22, Martino told his son to stay home from school and keep the radio on. As soon as the news came in from Dallas, Martino began working the phones, calling his media contacts to try to link Oswald to Cuba and Castro.

The final House Committee report argued that Kennedy was probably assassinated by a conspiracy involving organized crime, but did not mention Martino. I thought for a long time about how I, a lone historian, could have gotten more out of their material than they did. The biggest reason, in all likelihood, was time. I spent about seven years researching and writing *The Road to Dallas*, and I had everything they had found available when I started. The committee sat for only two years and wasted its first few months over personality conflicts. And as Graham Allison would have appreciated, interpersonal factors also played a role. The investigator who discovered Martino was a journalist, Gaeton Fonzi, who, as his own memoir shows, became obsessed with the idea that CIA personnel had become involved in the assassination. And he clearly did not work well with Blakey, who had begun to focus on the organized crime angle. The critical material that the committee uncovered about Martino—and also about Loran Hall—fell through the cracks.

I now had a new library agent, the former Norton editor Don Lamm. He made every attempt to market the assassination book to trade publishers—but without result. The question they all asked, undoubtedly, was one that I had heard many times before and would hear again: "How is it different from all the other books on this?" The answer, in fact, was that it would be different because David Kaiser was writing it, and anyone who had read any of my books would know what that meant. Thus, in the end, it was back into the University press market. Aida Donald had retired from Harvard Press, but a new editor, Kathleen McDermott, was enthusiastic. So was another young editor at Yale named Lara Heimert—whom I did not yet know. We sold the book to Harvard, but thanks to Yale, the advance remains the largest that I have ever received.

In the fall of 2004, in the midst of George W. Bush's re-election campaign, I found yet another outlet for self-expression, my blog, historyunfolding.com. I began posting once every couple of weeks, using both historical knowledge and the theory of generations and turnings to comment on current events. Checking the archive, I find that it took until 2006 for me to start posting weekly. The blog initially had about 40 readers a week but grew quite quickly. One of the first posts, "George W. Bush, Man of the Sixties," illustrated the non-partisan aspects of generational theory. Bush loved to say how the spirt of the nation had changed from "If it feels good, do it" to "Let's roll," but I argued that if anyone ever exemplified the first (Boomer) motto, it was George W. Bush. Neither invading Iraq nor cutting taxes made any sense, but they felt good to him—and he did them. The blog has continued to grow and grow, and now attracts 4–500 readers a day, or about 3000 a week. Early in 2018, it received its millionth visit. It reminds me of Orwell's wartime weekly *As I Please* columns, although it is often much longer. Like him, I can be reading the paper in the morning, get an idea, and have it out in the world forever within about an hour.

In 2005–6 I began writing *The Road to Dallas* while still teaching at the War College. The school was in the midst of a tremendous upheaval. The Pentagon had given responsibility for graduate military education to a special office, and that office had written guidelines for what different levels of military education should accomplish. The objectives had nothing to do with course content: they were designed to create officers in the image their authors had in mind. Thus, some objectives specified that students should emerge

- "Aware of maritime, joint, interagency, and multinational operations and their strategic effects
- Skilled in applying sea power to achieve operational and strategic effects across a wide range of conflicts
- Capable of integrating operational capabilities with other instruments of national power to achieve enduring strategic effects
- Understand challenges in accomplishing interagency and multinational Coordination."

In addition, we were ordered for the first time to write very different syllabuses for the junior and senior courses.

I, as usual, was too busy teaching, researching and writing to push for a critical role in this process, although I certainly expected to do my fair share of the work. Everyone had to explain how the particular cases they wrote met some of the learning objectives laid down by the Pentagon. But other colleagues saw this as an opportunity to reshape the syllabus. They did not improve it. Every case (except the ones I wrote) began with a single-spaced introduction of several entire pages explaining exactly what the case was supposed to do. This essentially invited the students not to do any of the work, since it told them what we expected them to learn. And instead of a reading list for an outstanding undergraduate course such as we had traditionally had, the readings for many cases (mine again excepted) looked more like lists designed to prepare students for graduate general exams. Many cases included 15–20 different readings, most of them short, so that students could touch various bases, rather than get deeply involved in two or three fine books. Last but hardly least, new departmental leadership decided to reduce workloads drastically for both senior faculty and students. Instead of three papers per term, students would henceforth write only two, cutting the grading load by 33%. I had had a number of students who only "got it" on the third paper, and I was very much opposed to this, but there was nothing I could do. In any case, something else had distracted me.

Sometime in early December 2005, I received an email from Professor James McAllister of Williams College, whom I did not know. McAllister was an historically oriented political scientist, who had written a book about American policy towards West Germany in the late 1940s and was now working on a new one about Vietnam. He had come to know me on H-Diplo. He taught American foreign policy, and he had become frustrated because the Williams College history department was no longer teaching any American foreign policy at all. In response, he had found a donor who gave the money to create a Stanley Kaplan professorship (named after a Second World War American casualty, not after the master of test preparation.) This rotating chair would bring one historian of American foreign policy to the college every year to teach two courses on the subject. He wanted me to be the first incumbent. I eagerly accepted.

James and I had to work out what I would teach. I was desperate to try out Generations in Film on a group of bright Millennial undergraduates, but he ruled that out as one of my two projected courses because it wasn't focused on American foreign policy. For those, I decided to begin by expanding on some of the units in the NWC curriculum, and teach a larger course called Wilson, Roosevelt, and the Two World Wars. In the spring I planned an undergraduate seminar on Vietnam. But I discovered that I might teach Generations in Film in January, when students took one winter study course, and that was what I planned to do. Realizing that this was going to be a memorable year, I began keeping a journal for only the second time in my life.

The spring of 2006 turned out to be busy in other ways. My younger son had announced that he was getting married in Jamestown to a fellow teacher he had met while in Mississippi for Teach for America. That experience had convinced him to give up his plans to go to law school, and he was now going to work for a charter school in Brooklyn. (As it turned out, he became principal of that school within just a few years and is now one of the leading executives in Achievement First, the outfit that ran it and now has charter schools in three states.) And given that Patti was giving up the part-time job as an ER clerk that she had held for years to go to Williamstown—and her insurance—we decided to get married as well. My old friend Jim Davidson, now a clergyman, performed the ceremony in the Boston Public Garden on May 7, 2006. We have lived happily ever after.

It took some time, but eventually, we found a War College student and his family to rent our Jamestown house. We also found a nice home in Williamstown, owned by a retired faculty member and complete with a grand piano, to live in there. The college granted me a year of unpaid leave. James had me up to Williamstown—located at the far northwest corner of Massachusetts, just a few miles from both the Vermont and New York borders—to give a talk comparing Iraq and Vietnam that spring. Two seniors approached me afterwards, commented that there was no one like me in the history department now, and said that they would be sorry to miss me the following year. In August 2006 we packed up and drove our cars to Williamstown. For the second time in a career, I would be teaching in a college that I would have been glad to attend myself. My dream had come true.

IX

BACK AT HOME

2006–7

Williamstown was tiny and remote. More than 40 years earlier, a Philadelphia family whom I knew very well had driven into it with their oldest son, a convinced urbanite, during his college tour. "Don't even stop!" he had exclaimed, and they didn't. But I didn't really care. The setting was spectacular—the college nestled at the foot of Mt. Greylock, the highest peak in Massachusetts, in a valley surrounded by mountains and bisected by the Appalachian Trail. Local biking opportunities abounded. I immediately felt right at home.

I also felt right at home at Williams. My office—whose regular occupant was on leave for the year—sat in the kind of frame house one finds all around Harvard, just five minutes away from the local coffee house where I dropped in every afternoon. The biking was demanding but beautiful. In addition, I now had an alternative way to do aerobic workouts: hiking up and down the surrounding mountains on the Appalachian Trail. By the end of the year, I was in the best shape that I had been in for ten years. The library, while well below major university standards, was far superior to the War College, and the available online databases were very useful. And when winter came, I found myself only one hour away from Stratton Mountain, where I had skied many times in the 1960s and 1970s. This was the only time in my whole life that I could simply go skiing for a day.

The students were engaged, steady, and generally high achievers—although not necessarily on the intellectual front. Athletics played a huge role in student life, and the men's and women's varsity teams tended to be very competitive at the Division II level that the school played at. Smartphones had not yet taken over the world in 2006–7, and I never had to worry about students looking at them during class. I had of course been intimately involved with my own sons and many of their friends and always felt at ease with them, but I couldn't be sure what would happen now.

I prepared very carefully for the first class, printing out large pictures of the roughly 20 students and studying them carefully to get everyone's name into my head. Names and faces have been a problem for me all my life, but this time I was determined to solve it. The reading combined books by my old adviser May, who had written his dissertation on US entry into the First World War; by Charles Beard on FDR's diplomacy during the 1930s; and Robert Sherwood's classic, *Roosevelt and Hopkins*, on the Second World War itself. It also included collections of documents that I put together and had xeroxed for the students, including diplomatic papers, excerpts from Wilson's and FDR's speeches, and accounts of some meetings of national leaders at Versailles and later during the Second World War. Thanks to the web, all this was much quicker and easier than it had been at Harvard or Carnegie Mellon. My classroom, in an older building, had a media station near the front where I planned to spend most of my time at the computer, and I put together a few PowerPoint slides for each class.

To understand the First World War one has to begin with Europe, and I spent the first two classes there. The first reading for the first class was a talk a very young W. E. B. Du Bois had given upon his return from studying in Europe in the 1890s, comparing the major European nations. Like many Americans, he had admired the discipline, scholarship, and honest, clean government he found in Germany. Then I did a quick review of US politics in the Progressive Era, using the wonderful maps from Wikipedia to look at several successive presidential elections. The 2004 map also enabled me to show how the areas of

Republican and Democratic strength had completely reversed themselves during the last century.

In the second class, I returned to one of my favorite lectures on the origins of the First World War, blaming Serbia, Austria-Hungary, and Germany just as in the old days. This time, however, I had also made a slide of the last page of the table of contents of volume III of Albertini's great work. I zoomed in on the subheads of the very last chapter, describing the decisions by various minor powers, including the Scandinavian countries; the Netherlands; Switzerland; Spain and Portugal; and then, at the very bottom, "the United States and Wilson's last effort to save peace," which had gone nowhere. That allowed me to conclude with Albertini's magnificent last words once again:

> "It must be remembered that relations between the United States and the European powers were not what they later became, and the President did not yet enjoy the prestige which he was to acquire. Wilson's appeal came too late to influence the course of events, and was made when the European powers, flung into the maelstrom of war, and wholly dominated by the will to fight and to win, had no idea of the length of the struggle, the destruction of life and property it was to cause, or the train of evil consequences it was to bring in its wake. European diplomacy, which in the course of the July Crisis had so often demonstrated its ineptitude, was henceforth silent. It was now the turn of the big guns to speak."

Things took a most unexpected turn for me in the next week when I went to the hospital in North Adams for some minor surgery. More than 20 years earlier, in Pittsburgh, a surgeon had moved a few small nodules from under my skin in the groin area, and a pathologist had pronounced them harmless. The procedure had however left an odd scar there from that day forward, to which no one had ever paid any attention. During the hectic summer before our move, I had noticed that the skin around it was swelling, and I saw a doctor and a surgeon in Williamstown who thought I had a cyst. I was preparing for two bike rides—I was in very good shape at that point—and they assured me I would be fine in a few days. It didn't turn out that way.

As I watched, awake, the surgeon removed a rather large growth from the incision, and said that he had to run it down to pathology. It obviously was not a cyst. When he returned, he announced, "the pathologist thinks it's a lymphoma"—the first in a series of terrible medical measures I encountered in the next couple of weeks. I stopped by the drugstore to fill a painkiller prescription, went home, and told Patti. Then, just a couple of hours later, the surgeon called to say that it was *not* a lymphoma, but some kind of malignant fibrous tumor. All this happened on Friday (my class met Tuesday and Thursday), and it was not until Monday that he called with a firm diagnosis. The lab said I had dermatofibrosarcoma protruberans, a rare skin tumor. Uncle Google reassured Patti and me that it rarely metastasized. Catherine Ross, Jon Rieder's wife, turned out to have a niece who was a doctor at the Dana Farber cancer institute, and she helped me get an appointment about ten days in the future. Meanwhile, my local doctor got me an appointment with a local oncologist.

I said nothing in class about this the next week. Indeed, I was a little concerned with how things were going, because, as often happens, two students were answering almost all my questions. One was a freshman taking Air Force ROTC at another campus, and the other was a junior named Roy Garcia, who had been a war and diplomacy nerd for most of his life. (He later told me that he had read William L. Shirer's *Rise and Fall of the Third Reich* when he was in middle school.) While teachers can easily start to rely on such students, they tend to drive the rest of the class a little crazy, and I announced that I would no longer call on either of them until I had called on someone else first. That worked.

The local oncologist now made a terrible mistake and ordered me a CT-scan. When the results came in a couple of days later—about a week before my Dana Farber appointment—he called to say that I had a two-centimeter spot on my liver and some microscopic spots in my lungs. Suddenly it seemed not merely possible, but quite likely, that I was terminally ill. I was keeping the news pretty closely held but shared it with some close friends and, of course, my sons. That week was educational. I was much less frightened of dying than I might have thought, and very keenly aware that I had gotten far more out of life than most people. I knew my books would survive me. Like Oliver Wendell Holmes, Jr., lying in a field hospital after his first wound during the Civil War, I spent about a half a minute wondering if I should get religion but gave up the idea as hopelessly hypocritical. I was afraid of wasting away, but my biggest fear was that I would die without finishing *The Road to Dallas*. I thought that my son Tom, who had helped research it, might be able to do that, with suitable guidance, if necessary, but I didn't ask him yet. Later, when the crisis was passed, he assured me that he would have. I taught two more classes that week. It was not easy teaching while knowing that I might have a fatal illness, but I managed it and said essentially nothing to the class about what had happened. In late 2016, a *Jeopardy* contestant named Cindy Stowell won six matches while she was terminally ill with cancer, and died before the shows aired. Watching her play, I could pick out the moments when she suddenly remembered that she had only a short time to live, because I had felt the same chill standing in front of my class during those two weeks.

When we arrived at Dana Farber, I went in to see the doctor alone. I was prepared for the worst and told her that I was a patient who wanted to know. But she replied that she and a surgeon had been studying the pathology on my tumor all morning—and they were convinced that it would *not* metastasize. She did not know about the CT-scan results, but I had brought them with me on a CD. "The things in your lungs don't impress me," she said, but I did have to have a liver ultrasound. I had a benign hemangioma, a common condition that I have apparently continued to live with from that day to this. The surgery was scheduled for about ten days later, and it was fully successful. I walked around with a drain sticking out of my abdomen for about another week, and within a month after that, I had resumed full activity.

For some years thereafter I had regular follow-ups at Dana Farber, and eventually, when pressed, the nurse practitioner confirmed to me that dermatofibrosarcoma protruberans should not really be called cancer at all. While it can be very locally aggressive, growing to a huge size, and cause serious secondary problems if one has it in a sensitive area, it never metastasizes, and she told me they had recently removed a large tumor from an elderly woman who had walked around with it for 40 years. The local oncologist's decision to order the CT-scan had been financially and medically inexcusable, but it was typical of the worst of American medical care. I was very proud that I missed only one class because of the surgery, and the term resumed.

By the time of the last class before the midterm, in mid-October, discussions were going very well. On that day we discussed the US failure to ratify the Versailles Treaty, and I suggested that Wilson had made a critical mistake when he began demonizing the German government when the US entered the war, making the "peace without victory" which he had already called for impossible. In one of my better classroom moments, I asked whether any leader had ever fought a war without demonizing the enemy—and answered my own question, yes. With the classroom computer logged on to the web, I pulled Lincoln's second inaugural from 1864 up and put it on the screen at the head of the class. When the war began, Lincoln said, "Each looked for an easier triumph, and a result less fundamental and astounding. Both read the same Bible and pray to the same God, and each invokes His aid against the other. It may seem strange that any men should dare to ask a just God's assistance in wringing their bread from the sweat of other men's faces, but let us judge not, that we be not judged. The prayers of both could not be answered. That of neither has been answered fully. The Almighty has His own purposes."

A shy student came to ask some questions the day before the midterm, and I asked her how she thought the class was going. She replied that it was her favorite one. The midterms were solid if not spectacular. One optional question asked why Wilson was unable to achieve the "peace without victory" that he wanted, and no one was creative or courageous enough to suggest that it was because he decided to enter the war. The real breakthrough in the class happened in late October, and here I'll quote from how I described it at the time.

"This class was designed to cover the impact of the Depression in the US and Germany, by looking at election stats, economic stats, and two speeches from March 1933, FDR's inaugural and a speech of Hitler's stressing national purification and international peace. I had prepared one of my better slide shows for it, but found to my horror when I arrived that I had forgotten to save it onto the college drive and thus couldn't pull it up in the classroom Fortunately Jeff Castiglione, a Marine Corps ROTC student, had his truck available, and drove me the half mile or so to my office. We were less than 10 minutes late getting started.

"The breakthrough came when we got to FDR's inaugural, and I asked for reactions to it. Dave Turner's hand immediately went up. He explained that he had actually listened to the speech on the night before, allowing me to point out how much audio there was now available on the web. He said Roosevelt's timing made the speech far more effective than the simple printed word. 'Have you ever heard as effective a speech from any living person?' I asked. 'No,' he replied bluntly. 'That was easy,' I said. He also acknowledged, when I brought it up, Roosevelt's enthusiasm—he was looking forward to coping with things.

"I then ran down about half a dozen pieces of New Deal legislation, contrasting those acts that had attempted to deal with the emergency with those like the SEC, the Wagner Act, and Social Security that had laid the foundation for modern America. I talked about how regulatory structures were breaking down now that no one actually remembered the depression and the crash. I showed them a *Chicago Tribune* editorial from the day before the 1936 election claiming that our way of life was at stake. It reminded them of current partisanship, but we agreed, interestingly enough, that things were not so bad now, at least not yet.

"When we got to Hitler, they immediately noticed that he appealed to the 14 points and mentioned Germany's betrayal. I explained that that was really a debating point, and Hitler was a very clever debater. Then I talked some about Germany's economic recovery and its limitations, going back to the material in my first book. I had to point out how heavily Hitler's speech emphasized purifying the national community.

"This is going to be great from here on, I think." And it was.

Over the next few weeks, we used one of the databases to look at lots of polling data about attitudes towards the war, while I thought about FDR's strategy. I was in the last chapters of *The Road to Dallas* now, but I had thought thirty years earlier about writing something on the US entry into the Second World War. Now I was beginning to understand that Roosevelt in 1940 had seriously been simply trying to defend the Western Hemisphere, but that after the German attack on the USSR in June 1941, he began thinking in terms of an all-out war that the US would win with its productive capacity. Starting in 2009 or so this became the theme of another book, *No End Save Victory*. I also did a great class on the war at home, featuring excerpts from a VHS copy of *The Life and Times of Rosie the Riveter* and excerpts from Studs Terkel's *The Good War*, including the reminiscences of two black soldiers.

The final was really based on the themes of the S & P course in Newport. Here it is.

I. (66.7%)

It is generally agreed that Roosevelt was more successful as a war leader than Wilson; the question that the course has tried to answer, is why.

Here, in no particular order, is a list important elements of Wilson and Roosevelt's war leadership.

1. Their perception and communication of the threats
   the United States faced.

2. Their prewar diplomacy.

3. Their success as domestic politicians and political leaders

4. Their influence upon the strategic conduct of the wars they engaged in.

5. Their ability to prepare the United States economically and materially for war.

6. Their wartime diplomacy with their allies.

7. Their good or bad luck.

8. Their conception, and communication, of American war aims.

Your job is to select *three* of these elements as the *most important* in making the difference between Wilson's failure and Roosevelt's success, and to explain why they were critical. In the event that you believe some other factor not listed above was at least as important as one of these eight, you are welcome to include it as one of your three key elements. (Be careful, though, that you are not simply restating one of these eight in different words.)

II. (33.3%)

1. In light of his own objectives, did Wilson make a mistake to enter the First World War at all?

2. In light of the long-term outcome, should the United States have made a greater effort to avoid war in the Pacific in 1941–5 and fought only in the Atlantic?

3. Some Americans are still criticizing President Roosevelt for allowing Eastern Europe to fall into Soviet hands. Do you believe that criticism is justified?

4. What possible alternative courses of action do you think Roosevelt considered between September 1939 and December 1941, and when do you think he definitely decided to get into the war as soon as he could?

Returning to the Harvard tradition in which I had been raised, I weighted the final very heavily in determining the course grade. It gave them a chance really to show how much they had learned, and if they took it, they deserved an appropriate reward. Many did not appreciate the grading structure, but the high quality of the exams showed that it had worked. After returning them all, I got to see their course critiques, which they had turned in a few weeks earlier. A few were mediocre. Most were not.

"I really enjoyed the way you integrated different technology to our class on a daily basis. Videos, audio clips of old speeches, typing "notes" instead of using blackboard and especially the *maps*. These were extremely helpful and informative. Readings were good for the most part, and class discussions were lively. My biggest complaint for the class is the way you structured the grading/evaluations. Very heavily weighted on the end of the semester without sufficient feedback. Also, not having a class participation segment of the grade in a discussion section seemed strange to me."

"Class was okay. Too many stupid students." (I had *no* idea who that was.)

"Prof. Kaiser,

I have absolutely loved this class. I think it really might be my favorite class I have taken at Williams. The subject is really interesting, and I actually enjoyed reading the documents provided because they sort of brought to life the subjects we were discussing. Reading actual minutes from meetings and actual telegrams made reading secondary sources about them much more interesting. Also, I thought the discussions and questions you posed were very helpful and effective. The only negative comment I have was the extremely large amount of reading. I don't mean to complain and don't have a problem with a lot of work, just sometimes it was fairly daunting. The reading was always extremely interesting, though, so I suppose it works out. Overall, the class was great!"

"This has by far been one of the best classes I have taken at my four years in Williams. The subject material was exceptionally interesting, the readings were engaging, and lectures were always thought-provoking. I particularly enjoyed the group presentations!" That one was signed.

"I enjoyed this class immensely. I thought the discussions were great, as were the lectures. It was nice to get some information and insight into two huge events in history, and two of the most influential figures in American history. I've always been confused about what occurred in the First World War, and now I feel much more knowledgeable about both world wars. Thanks."

"Professor Kaiser,

Your knowledge of the material and how you choose to convey it to the class is truly exceptional. Reading primary documents and looking at newspaper headlines and polls made for an interesting and effective way of looking at History. It has been a pleasure being in your class, and I look forward to (hopefully) taking your Vietnam class in the spring." (signed.)

I sent them all an email complimenting them on the finals and defending the structure of the grading, and concluding with a list of suggested reading. I had done it. Several weeks later, I told an old friend that I had gone to Williams hoping to prove that I hadn't simply dreamed everything that had happened years earlier at Harvard. And as I said that, I began to cry.

The evaluations suggested that my real strategy for the year might conceivably work. I had hoped, of course, to make enough of an impression to stay at Williams and finish my career there. Before I arrived, James McAllister had asked me on behalf of the History department chair, Regina Kunzel, whether I wanted to act as a full member of her department during my stay. I had said that I did, attended department meetings, and even gave an evening presentation to the department on generations and turnings. The demographics of the department were clear. Most of the younger members were female, and none of them taught political history of any kind. The most popular professors were older ones teaching traditional topics, led by Charles Dew, the Civil War historian who, two decades earlier, had written me that I could not be a candidate for a senior position in his department because I was white and male. (I met him a few times in 2006–7 but never mentioned that.)

One of the heavy hitters in the department was Chris Waters, an historian of Britain who started grad school at Harvard when I was an assistant professor. He heavily promoted a talk midway through the term by a young historian from Britain. The topic, drawn from a recent, prize-winning book, was about sexuality and gender in a major European capital during the interwar period, but it focused specifically on an item of women's cosmetics, a powder puff. Essentially it described how the police had used lipstick as evidence of men seeking homosexual partners (which, the presenter acknowledged, it probably was.) But like most postmodern work, the facts were almost incidental to the riffs going on about coded bodies, transgressive sexual behaviors, hegemonic structures, and anxieties within the power structure. Meanwhile, the presenter also took bows to the commodification of beauty (through cosmetics), the importance of industrial processes, etc. One of my best students attended as well, and I took an opportunity to ask him about the talk a few days later. He himself had traditional interests, but he said that about 90% of the history at Williams was of that type. The courses that were not were taught by older faculty, and political history was clearly likely to disappear within another ten years or so. It seemed to me that I could contribute a great deal more if given the chance.

The term had been an exhausting one, and during the Christmas vacation I often asked myself *why* I had given up a month off and a good deal of skiing to do Generations in Film during January. I also immediately encountered some pushback when the class met and I announced that we would be meeting almost every day—the only way to see enough films. But it didn't take the class long to get going and for these Millennials to get the idea that they represented the same Hero archetype as the GIs with which we began the course.

Ali Tozier

Williams chose me. I grew up in Maine attending a small high school where I often felt uninspired by my peers. I have a distinct memory of being frustrated looking around at my classmates after the teacher asked a question: none of them seemed interested. I, on the other hand, had my hand ready to go up, but I was conscious of the fact that I had just answered the last three questions. Why weren't they participating? Class would be so much more fun if more people were engaged, I remember thinking. I have to get out of this state and go find others with a similar passion for learning.

Williams was my dream college, the perfect fit for a young, wide-eyed girl like me. However, I didn't realize it at first. The swimming coach called to recruit me to the school the summer before my senior year of H.S., convincing me to attend a recruit weekend in the fall. It has been about 12 years since that recruiting weekend, and scenes from it still play vividly in my mind. I was astounded by the caliber of people I spoke with, the joy, and—yes—the passion that I felt all around me. The place filled up my soul and freed my spirit to take root and shape the person I would be for the rest of my years. So, that's how I got to Williams.

I thought I might want to be a lawyer because that is what many had predicted for me. At college, though, I let my creativity flourish and began to doubt if the path of an attorney was in line with my true gifts. I became interested in the question of how I could best give back to the world, and I started to gravitate towards the idea of becoming a filmmaker. In the fall of my sophomore year, in 2006, I had to choose a winter study class, which meant a class that I would take exclusively in the month of January. Looking through all my options, I saw something listed about being a lawyer. I decided to take that because, I realized, I knew nothing about what it meant to be a lawyer. Maybe this class would help me decide if those predictions of others were onto something.

I remember walking into the first class of being a lawyer. I was a little late, and the room was filled. Eyes turned to me, and

I self-consciously hurried to the one seat that was still unoccupied near the front of the room. Putting my stuff down and looking up, I saw three white, somewhat overweight, "distinguished" (read: old) men standing at the front of the room, looking incredibly pleased with themselves. To this day, I remember how their posture and "smug" energy turned me off right away, within 30 seconds even. Then they started talking. I have no idea what they said. I have an image of me looking sideways at them, out of curiosity, thinking something along the lines of, "Seriously?"

I didn't care about what they were talking about because I was just reacting to how they were talking. The ego in the room was suffocating. It was like a cloud that just kept getting bigger and bigger, and almost like I could see it about to swallow me. I remember having a moment of panic, about to be swallowed, trapped. Then, in the split of a second, I thought to myself, "NOPE," and I grabbed my things and bolted out of that classroom. All the same, eyes are watching me again, I'm sure. I won't know for sure because I never looked back. I ran to the registrar's office. I told her please, there had been a horrible mistake. I needed another class. Was it too late?

She let me choose another class and passed me a list of what was still available. I scrolled down quickly, saw "Generations and Turnings in Film," and pointed, still out of breath, that one please. That's how I got to David Kaiser's class.

There are not many classes from Williams I remember as clearly as David Kaiser's. From his first class, I immediately noticed the passion he had for what he was talking about, and his gratitude to be able to share. That in turned sparked my own curiosity. I wanted to understand: why did he love this so much? Maybe I would, too...

We began to learn about the theory of generations impacting each other and presenting a pattern of 4. We analyzed this concept by looking into films representative of different generations. We recognized the qualities each generation expressed and considered how it played into the theory we were reading in the course's book. Fascinatingly, we also took this loose blueprint pattern and placed it over history, seeing how significant events in history fell in line with a pattern brought out by the underlying structure of 4 generations repeating themselves. Once I saw this, and it made sense, I was hooked. I loved understanding how everything was connected; I loved feeling as though more made sense about the world than had previously, before I rushed into David Kaiser's classroom.

I was also able to take this newfound understanding and apply it to my own personal history. Seeing these patterns uncovered helped me make sense of so much: from how my grandparents acted and why all the way to the reasons behind my own actions in my own childhood. Understanding it all gave me immense comfort. It made me want to learn more about patterns and how much is influencing us that we aren't even aware of…

After college, I became interested in learning Myers Briggs, as well as other teachings about personalities and qualities that people have studied. Once I learned more, I felt my whole world open up. I became more understanding and more flexible in navigating the world around me. Knowledge is power. I have often thought about David Kaiser's class and the profound impact it had. I also know that my learning about his teaching is not finished, and I will continue to study the world around me for years to come.

～

There were two critical moments during the course—critical for me, as well as for them. The first came when we watched *Twelve Angry Men*, one of my two favorite films to show midlife GIs at their best. The leading example, of course, is Henry Fonda, who slowly swings all the jurors around with his calm patient, low-key reasoning, and brings the same qualities out in almost all of them. I asked the class to list virtues, as shown by the movie. They mentioned civic duty, open-mindedness, rationality, a willingness to listen, respect for others, and responsibility. Then we turned to vices, exemplified in the movie by Jack Warden, Ed Begley, and Lee J. Cobb. They listed excitability, self-righteousness, racism, and prejudice, giving way to one's feelings, and being confrontational. "I'm getting very depressed here," I said, in the middle of drawing up that list, because I realized it was practically a perfect description of my own Boom generation. We built on that about a week later when we got to *Wall Street* and met Gordon Gecko.

The second key moment came when we watched what will always be the great movie about the childhood of Generation X, *The Bad News Bears*. We did the virtues/vices exercise again, and this time the virtues were individual ones: self-reliance, independence, and a lack of illusions. But to my great surprise, several cited anger as a vice, especially as represented by Tanner, the kid who is always willing to fight at the drop of a hat, who is always a favorite of Boomers and Silents. And as we talked some more, it became clear that they were terrified by the anger shown by these Xer kids, and shocked by the way they talked to the adults. One of the best students remarked that as a kid she could never believe her parents might be wrong—if she couldn't have something she wanted she assumed it must be her own fault. And a light went on for me. "You guys seem to have had a deal with your parents that you understood how you should act and what you should do, and you did it, and you got rewarded," I said. And most of them immediately nodded. I wonder how they would see this issue a dozen years later.

I began the last class by thanking Bill Strauss and Neil Howe, by saying that as far as I knew I was the only professional historian in the country actually teaching the theory, and mentioning the appeal of the idea of crisis and the generational constellation that goes with it to the collective unconscious. One can find the same pattern in the Bible, the Iliad, in Star Wars, the Arthurian legend, the Ring cycle, and in Harry Potter. Then we watched *The Treasure of the Sierra Madre*, whose generational constellation mirrors what we were already facing then, with Walter Huston, Bogart and Tim Holt playing the roles that now fell to Boomers, Xers, and Millennials like themselves. When I asked for their comments several indicated that they were glad to be able to place themselves in a broader historical scheme. I concluded with two reflections in elderhood, one by a Hero like themselves—Thomas

Jefferson—and one by a Prophet, W. E. B. Du Bois, who had grown up just twenty miles or so away in Great Barrington. Jefferson's came from his very last letter, sadly declining an invitation to take part in a 50th anniversary celebration of the Declaration of Independence in Washington, D.C.

"The kind invitation I received from you, on the part of the citizens of the city of Washington, to be present with them at their celebration of the fiftieth anniversary of American Independence, as one of the surviving signers of an instrument pregnant with our own, and the fate of the world, is most flattering to myself, and heightened by the honorable accompaniment proposed for the comfort of the journey. It adds sensibly to the sufferings of sickness, to be deprived by it of a personal participation in the rejoicing of that day. But acquiescence is a duty, under circumstances not placed among those we are permitted to control. I should, indeed, with peculiar delight, have met and exchanged there congratulations personally with the small band, the remnant of that host of worthies, who joined with us on that day, in the bold and doubtful election we were to make for our country, between submission or the sword; and to have enjoyed with them the consolatory fact, that our fellow citizens, after half a century of experience and prosperity, continue to approve the choice we made. May it be to the world, what I believe it will be (to some parts sooner, to others later, but finally to all), the signal of arousing men to burst the chains under which monkish ignorance and superstition had persuaded them to bind themselves, and to assume the blessings and security of self-government. That form which we have substituted, restores the free right to the unbounded exercise of reason and freedom of opinion. All eyes are opened, or opening, to the rights of man. The general spread of the light of science has already laid open to every view the palpable truth, that the mass of mankind has not been born with saddles on their backs, nor a favored few booted and spurred, ready to ride them legitimately, by the grace of God. These are grounds of hope for others. For ourselves, let the annual return of this day forever refresh our recollections of these rights, and an undiminished devotion to them."

Du Bois delivered his remarks at a celebration of his 70th birthday. We shall return to them in due course.

The final course papers were nearly all generational autobiographies, and some of them were extremely moving. Then, once again, I got to see the critiques. Several of them still could not forgive me for meeting every weekday, but they were the exceptions.

"Thanks for the great course. This provided me with a new and unique way of looking at time, history, and the future, which is undoubtedly extremely useful. The movies were, of course, fun. It's a perfect winter study course in that respect. It is a perfect balance of fun and education."

"Overall I thoroughly enjoyed this course. I have never considered really analyzing history from a generational or secular view, and it illuminated details of my personal interactions with relatives. . . You are very good at ramping up discussion and guiding us towards interesting topics and points—which was helpful in our post-movie haze."

"I loved the class, the movies were all interesting (I had not seen the majority of them before), and Strauss and Howe's concept was different, and really cool in their book. I wish they had a regular semester course like this. The only thing I wish was different, is that we had more time to get into discussion . . . I wish you taught here all the time. I would love to take another class with you; you're relaxed and engaging, it's a great combination."

"I feel like what we've learned has changed (slightly at least) how I look at the past and think about the future. I also enjoyed seeing how film characters play out the archetypes. Thanks for the introduction to Strauss and Howe's work."

"I really enjoyed this class. I honestly thought about trying to switch out of it when I found out about how many times it met over winter study, but I am really glad I didn't. . . . It's really been great."

I continued to teach Generations in Film at the War College, although I had to overcome several attempts to kill it on the grounds that it did not fit into any of the established categories within the no-longer Electives Program. But nothing makes me sadder as I look back on my career that I could not make it part of the curriculum at any college or university. The theory of turnings and crises is now proving itself out once again, as political crisis sweeps the whole North Atlantic world, with consequences that no one could possibly foresee in January 2007. It can give everyone a whole new sense of their place in their family and in the world. Yet contemporary academia has no room for it.

The time had come to begin my senior seminar on the Vietnam war. McAllister had strongly urged me to limit it to a dozen students, but 17 signed up, and I took them all. They and I had just one chance to get to know each other and I didn't want anyone to miss it. There were several holdovers, including one of the best students from the fall course, a senior named Brian Van Wyck.

Brian Van Wyck

I met David Kaiser in the fall of 2006 when he was a visiting professor in the History Department at Williams College in Williamstown, Massachusetts. I was a senior majoring in history, and I signed up for David's course entitled "Woodrow Wilson, Franklin Roosevelt, and the Two World Wars." At the time, I had begun researching a senior thesis on Otto von Bismarck's Russian policy and, while my interests always tended toward the other side of the Atlantic, I was intrigued by the course description, particularly as diplomatic history was not a specialty of the Department at the time. As I recall, the course met in Hopkins Hall, not usually a building that hosted classes, in a small room that could get quite warm and stuffy late in the afternoon when the class was held. Nevertheless, from the first class meeting on, discussions were lively and energetic. David seemed particularly enthusiastic to be teaching undergraduates again after years at the Naval War College. What struck me the most about the class at the time was how genuinely interested David was in what students had to say. Though the events, developments, and personages we examined in the class were surely among the most discussed and analyzed in modern American history, David gave all of us the impression that he expected we all could have something genuinely original and valuable to say, provided we read the primary documents closely and carefully.

I enjoyed that first course with David so much that I signed up for the upper-level seminar on the Vietnam War he taught the following semester. In that course, David encouraged us to write our final research papers based on a trove of recently-declassified archival material largely untouched by historians. Producing original arguments without being able to rely on an established scholarly corpus was a challenging and rewarding experience, and David held our work to a high standard which most strove to meet. Particularly in that semester, David and I met frequently to discuss my research project and senior thesis, though the conversations were always wide-ranging, touching frequently on the path David had taken in his career, his advice for me as an aspiring historian, and his observations about the development of the historical profession in American universities, particularly the place of diplomatic history. David encouraged my interest in graduate study while offering a frank assessment of the frustrations and challenges inherent in doing history. Over the years since my graduation, David and I have exchanged occasional e-mails and I've particularly enjoyed reading his perspectives on American politics while studying and researching outside the U.S. Though my research interests as a historian have changed rather dramatically in the interim, the guidance David provided at Williams on issues large and small has contributed to shaping my outlook on the profession and craft of writing history and will continue to do so throughout my career.

∼

The students turned out to be an outstanding group, but were generally innocent of any detailed knowledge of the Vietnam War. Thus I began with the best short history of the conflict,

America's Longest War by George Herring. Then, for the first time in my career, I assigned one of my own books, *American Tragedy*, in its entirety, and spent a couple of weeks on Kennedy and Johnson. For the war itself I decided to use my favorite military history, *The Dynamics of Defeat* by Eric Bergerud, a masterful analysis of the many sides of the conflict based on one key province, Hau Nghia on the Cambodian border. I wanted a book to illustrate how the war had transformed the thinking of so many Americans—particularly younger ones—and I settled on *In Struggle*, a history of SNCC that documented the changes within the civil rights movement starting in the mid-1960s. Lastly, I assigned selections from a wonderful oral history, *The Bad War*. It had gone out of print, but 50 copies were available online, and I didn't want them to miss it. I also had some key documents printed up for them again.

The discussions never flagged and became increasingly animated as the term wore on. Roy Garcia was again a most active participant, sometimes to the irritation of the others, but not for me. Late in the term he announced that he didn't think nations could ever learn from their mistakes, and another bright student exclaimed, "I just can't see the point of thinking that way!" I split the students into teams to research the many press sources available online through ProQuest, including newspaper editorials and columnists from James Reston through Joseph Alsop and Art Buchwald. We also used polling databases again. Many of their parents were anti-war Boomers, and they were shocked to find how deeply most of the country disapproved of the antiwar movement. They proved a very quick study about military issues.

The trouble with Millennials, I had realized in January, was that with rare exceptions, they had a scary trust in authority. One document we studied was a famous meeting in late August 1963, when Rufus Phillips, a junior AID official, argued with McNamara and a general over the strategic hamlet program, which he announced, correctly, was in tatters in much of the country. I asked the students whether they would be more inclined to trust a young person from the field or a senior official, and most of them went with the senior official.

During the first two months of the new term, in February and March, I brought up the issue of my possibly remaining at Williams, first with Bill Wagner, the faculty dean who also happened to be a historian, and then with Chris Waters, who was emerging as the power in the history department. There were some favorable omens. The department was losing two full professors. Regina Kunzel, the chair, was leaving Williams for the University of Minnesota to be with her partner, and another senior historian was becoming a dean. But Wagner held out no hope. Williams, he said, never hired senior faculty except in the most exceptional circumstances. Waters, to whom I showed by teaching evaluations for the first two courses, was somewhat more encouraging. When I met him for lunch, he spontaneously mentioned the shortage of teachers they were facing, and I essentially offered to help. Using a friend's suggestion, I proposed a 3–5 year appointment, which could get me to retirement age. He said he would speak to Regina Kunzel. I ran into her a couple of times over the next few weeks, but she never raised the situation.

On March 8, I wrote her an email, detailing my conversation with Chris about the coming teaching crisis in the history department and my interest in staying to help. I discussed the teaching I had done and the reaction to it, and said that I would also be delighted to teach a course on the great Atlantic crises, from 1774 through 1962 or so, based on the article I had written a few years before. She replied 11 days later that she had spoken to the Dean, and that he had confirmed that they could hire only at the junior level. She thanked me for my contribution in the current year.

I had not discussed any of this with James McAllister, because I did not think it would be fair to involve him in my attempt to stay. He had sold me as a one-year visitor and should not be put in the position of trying to turn me into something more. It wasn't until much later that I learned that Regina Kunzel had never been enthusiastic about bringing in historians of American foreign policy because she regarded the topic as "not what historians do any more."

This news, of course, was a disappointment, but a few weeks later, to my great surprise, McAllister raised the issue of bringing me back for another year as a visitor at some time in the future. I said I would prefer two years to one, but that I was interested.

I finished *The Road to Dallas* that term and made a research trip to Washington to tie up some loose research ends. Meanwhile, James dipped into the Kaplan fund again to bring a distinguished speaker to the campus. At my suggestion he invited George McGovern, who turned out to be hale and hearty in his mid-80s and gave a fine talk to a large crowd. I introduced him at some length, mentioning his military service and his early emergence as a critic of the Vietnam War. I remembered meeting him at a dinner party with my parents in 1966 in Washington, where he calmly and clearly discussed the mistake we were making—one of the first members of the older generation I had heard do that. I also said that in 1972, when he ran for President, he deserved more support from his party and more responsible supporters of his own. He appreciated it. He also met with my class, where we had an excellent Q & A.

The year also allowed me to get to know a giant of the GI generation, James MacGregor Burns, who had founded the Leadership Studies program at Williams which McAllister now directed. His partner, Susan Dunn, a very good and productive historian, also taught in that program, and the four of us had dinner together several times. Burns had written a two-volume biography of Franklin Roosevelt decades before, and a biography of JFK that appeared on the eve of his election as President. He had also run unsuccessfully for Congress himself. We hit it off beautifully. He was now 88 but engaged in a new project, a study of the relationship between Presidents and the Supreme Court. Eventually entitled *Packing the Court*, it appeared in 2009, and surveyed not only the politics but the impact of the court over the whole of US history in just 259 pages. And through it all, Burns remained faithful to the beliefs of his youth, shaped by FDR's battle with the Supreme Court in the mid-1930s: that the Court, which had been a conservative and anti-democratic body for most of its history, should not have the right to overrule acts of Congress. I hope that I will be able to produce work of comparable quality at the same age. Susan Dunn, meanwhile, invited me to a session of her course on Presidents, and I did a generational analysis of George W. Bush.

On April 11 we had a remarkable class discussion about the legacy of the Vietnam War, with the help of critical quotes from all sides of the political spectrum from *The Bad War*. The last four classes were reserved for student presentations, but the discussion was so relaxed and so remarkable that I promised to continue it for a while the next week—"when we might be able to get to the existence of God," I concluded, to loud laughter.

The presentations and the papers that eventually followed were excellent. About half dealt with diplomatic and military issues, the rest with related political or cultural ones. One analyzed the impact of perhaps the three most famous photographs from the war: the burning monk in 1963, the execution on the street of a Viet Cong suspect by a Saigon policeman in 1968, and the burning little girl in 1972. The class met for the last time on May 10. Four students presented 1) a comparison of the SDS and Young Americans for Freedom; 2) a survey of Martin Luther King, Jr., and the war; 3) a brief history of Vietnam Veterans Against the War; and 4) Joseph Alsop and the war. The last came from Emily George, a favorite student, and veteran of Generations in Film—whom I had admitted even though she was only a sophomore. She concluded perceptively that Alsop was in love with JFK, and thus always believed that nothing could have gone wrong if he had lived. We had some more discussion, and then I put up my last slide.

JFK on Happiness

*"Happiness, as defined by the Greeks, is
'the exercise of vital powers along lines of
excellence in a life affording them scope.'"*

August 13, 1963

*". . . . as far as the job of President goes, it is rewarding.
And I have given before to this group the definition of
happiness of the Greeks, and I will define it again: it
is full use of your powers along the lines of excellence. I
find, therefore, the Presidency provides some happiness."*

PRESS CONFERENCE, OCTOBER 31, 1963

"This was obviously one of his favorite quotes," I said. "The
reason I'm putting it up now is that this is what this last year
has been for me.

"I had the odd experience, 30 years ago, of staring my career
at the top. I had four years to find out what I could contribute at
an institution like this one. After that I had one ambition—to
teach at a place I would have enjoyed going to. I don't think I'm
a snob about that—there would certainly be twenty or thirty
schools on that list—but it turned out to be a lot harder than I
thought. I have to thank Prof. McAllister for bringing me here,
because this was the first chance I have had to do it again.

"This has been everything I could have hoped for. You
guys are amazing. You frighten me sometimes—you've been so
ungodly *good* all your lives, and you must have paid a price
for that. You have a couple of problems—you have too much
respect for authority—I've tried to do something about that—
and you don't like to ask for help. You might try to work on
that. But you've put an awful lot into this course. Some of you
were with me at the beginning of the year. You may have been
nervous, but I was more nervous than anyone. I'd been away for
a long time.

"I do wish there could have been more. I know that if students had a vote, I would never have had this problem." (They
were all smiling very warmly by now, and a couple of them
nodded.) But that isn't the way it is. Now I'll be going back
to Newport. My department was started after Vietnam, to try
to make some sense out of the mess we had gotten ourselves
into. Now we have to try to do the same thing again. That's

important, but this, for me, is more rewarding. I just want you to know that, no matter how much you got out of the class, I got more."

They all clapped for about 10 seconds. I stayed all by myself in that room for some time. Then, in the succeeding weeks, it was time for me to read their papers, which were superb. With only one or two exceptions, they were extremely capable writers. And quite a few took the opportunity to say goodbye.

"Thanks for everything, Professor. I've really enjoyed class with you. You've made me think differently about a lot of things. It's really been great."

"I have attached my final paper for this course to this e-mail. I managed to trim the length a little, but it is still a tad on the long side. I hope that is OK. I have really enjoyed this course with you and wish you the best of luck on your trip to France and return to the Naval War College. I'll keep an eye out for your new book!"

"Here's my paper. Again, thanks for a great year, and I wish you all the best."

Thanks so much for this semester. It was truly an awesome class."

One lesson of my career was now clear. As late as the 1950s, the authorities at many major colleges and universities cared enough about the educational experience that their undergraduates would receive to make hiring decisions to improve it. Those days were gone. No one, in any university or any liberal arts college that I know of, was focused on providing high-quality teaching. While some high-quality teachers remained, they had gotten where they were by accident and could not replicate themselves. My own strengths as a teacher were in many ways related to my strengths as a scholar: the breadth of my interests, my openness to new ideas, and my ability to make connections between different eras and different disciplines. But those qualities were disqualifications in 21st-century academia, and my university career could not survive them.

Just as at Harvard, I had taken full advantage of the opportunity, putting everything I had into it and getting at least as much back. Like Bill Fuller at the War College, James McAllister had had the power to make something happen all by himself, and like Bill, he had wanted me, even though when he first contacted me we had never met. John F. Kennedy had brought George Kennan out of retirement in 1961–2 to become Ambassador to Yugoslavia, and I joked with James that he was the JFK of my career. I had proven to myself that I had not been wrong about where I belonged or what I could do. But I had also confirmed that my profession had passed me by.

X

WINDING UP

2008–13

Returning to Newport in the fall of 2007, I found a new curriculum not only firmly in place, but also frozen in stone for the foreseeable future. The various case studies in our two courses were no longer subject to intense annual discussion and revision as they had been in the past, and scholarly credentials no longer counted for much in apportioning departmental responsibilities. The course still offered important opportunities for creativity and self-expression. One case study specifically compared the leaders of two contemporaneous civil wars, Abraham Lincoln in the US and Otto von Bismarck in Prussia and Germany, and I gave a lecture comparing their political leadership during that unit. I used the Strauss and Howe idea of a fourth turning to analyze what they did, and discussed the political effects of the American civil war on Western Europe. But the great period of the S & P Department, I regret to say, was over, largely because history departments no longer turned out the kind of historian that had contributed so much to it in the 1980s and 1990s.

I was more preoccupied with the completion of *The Road to Dallas*, which received excellent editing from Susan Wallace Boehmer of the Harvard Press, supported by Kathleen McDermott, the supervising editor on the project. Unfortunately, the promotion of the book went much less well, and its reception illustrated the pitfalls of taking an individual approach to one of the most politicized historical questions in U.S. history.

The book appeared in early 2008. More than a year earlier, the *New York Times* Sunday book review had devoted long reviews to two new books on the assassination, *Reclaiming History*, by Vincent Bugliosi, and *Brothers*, by David Talbot. Bugliosi and Talbot represented the two major tendencies in assassination books. Bugliosi was a high priest of the Church of the Lone Assassin,[19] while Talbot, a journalist, was on the other hand a typical member of the Church of the Grand Conspiracy. Although Talbot, like never every member of his church, had declined to propose any specific theory of who was guilty or how the conspiracy was executed in *Brothers*, he concluded the book by calling for a Truth and Reconciliation Commission which would presumably fill in the gaps he had left. Both the *Times* reviews were quite respectful. *The Road to Dallas* relied on far more research in the newly opened archives than either of these books, but timing, in life, is everything. When the publicist for Harvard Press contacted the *New York Times* to pitch *The Road to Dallas*, the editor replied that the *Times* had recently devoted a great deal of space to this topic and was not inclined to devote more now. Meanwhile, my book became the target of a campaign waged by the new high priest of the Church of the Lone Assassin, a Washington writer named Max Holland.

Evidently just a couple of years younger than I am, Holland never seems to have attended graduate school, and I am not aware that he ever had a full-time position in journalism. He wrote several works of business history between 1989 and 2002. He apparently became interested in the JFK assassination during the 1990s, and around 1996, he received a large advance from Alfred A. Knopf for a book on the Warren Commission. In 2004 and 2005 he brought out two edited collections of tape transcripts from Lyndon Johnson's oval office relating to the

---

19 To be fair, Bugliosi was less dismissive of some of the key evidence for conspiracy than many of his fellow adherents, agreeing, for instance, that Oswald probably did meet Silvia Odio in Dallas, while denying that the meeting had any significance.

assassination.[20] By that time, he had successfully marketed himself to the media establishment as the "go to guy" on the JFK assassination, whose book was going to blast away all conspiracy theories once and for all. He had also received a $45,000 work-in-progress fellowship for the book in 2001. But by the time *The Road to Dallas* appeared in early 2008, his much-touted book had yet to appear. And despite his reputation as a ferocious researcher, I had never run into him at the JFK collection at Archives II at College Park in all the many weeks I had spent there between about 2002 and 2007.

Holland has frequently spoken on the case and contributed to some cable TV documentaries about it in recent years, and his approach to it has gradually emerged. He has never engaged with most of the important topics the evidence relates to at all. Instead, he has treated the lone assassin conclusion as a given, and suggested, in effect, that only chance and sinister forces have allowed the idea of a conspiracy to become popular. As I write, he has recently published an article arguing that the KGB was solely responsible for Jim Garrison's accusation that the CIA was involved in the assassination (something which, I might note again, I do not believe). He has also been arguing for years that the first of Oswald's three shots was fired several seconds earlier than anyone else ever thought—a contention which, even if it were true, would have no bearing on any of the major controversies surrounding the case.

The publication of *The Road to Dallas* by the Harvard University Press seemed to have shocked Holland profoundly. He began by commissioning a review from a fellow acolyte of the Church of the Lone Assassin, John McAdams, which appeared on Holland's blog, Washington Decoded. McAdams explained why he chose not to believe some of the evidence I cited, while completely ignoring the most important points, particularly the identification of John Martino as the mobster

---

20 This information comes from a 2008 *Washington Post* story, "November 22, 1963." The story says that Holland had received $131,000 in advances, but it is not clear whether that figure refers only to the Warren Commission book or to the others as well.

who evidently organized the assassination himself, admitted it later, and told his family that the murder was going to happen before it took place. One specific point that he raised illustrates how he and the rest of his faith work—and how I work. The day after Ruby shot Oswald, a Brit named John Wilson-Hudson presented himself at the US Embassy in London, and said that he had been detained in Havana in the late summer of 1959, along with an American mobster using the name Louis Santos. He recalled that Louis Santos had been visited by a gangster named Ruby—evidence indicating that Ruby was more than the unknown club owner the Warren Commission portrayed him as. "Louis Santos" was in fact an alias of Tampa mobster and Havana casino owner Santo Trafficante, who was in fact detained at that site—along with mercenary Loran Hall—at that time. McAdams discounted the evidence because another informant had described Wilson-Hudson as unreliable. I believe it for a very simple reason: that we know Trafficante was detained in the facility he identified, *and that we know from other sources that Ruby was in Cuba at that time.* Using arguments like this, McAdams concluded that I had written just another conspiracy book, indistinguishable from hundreds of others—despite, among other things, the not insignificant difference between my book and the others that I thought Oswald was guilty.

Holland promptly picked up that ball and ran with it, writing his own piece in which he argued that since, as McAdams had "shown," my book was indistinguishable from the others, the mystery was how I had managed to "bamboozle" my editors into publishing it. I have been struck in subsequent exchanges with McAdams and Holland at how unable they are to come to terms with what is in *The Road to Dallas*. In 2013, at a joint appearance in Missouri arranged heroically by Professor James Giglio, Holland said that any reader of my book would think there were 40–50 people involved in the assassination conspiracy. I definitely identified only 5. Meanwhile, Holland's own book on the Warren Commission has never appeared.

I am very proud both that I was willing to undertake *The Road to Dallas* and of the result. My work both on Sacco and

Vanzetti and on the JFK assassination has convinced me that it is possible to weigh the evidence on various aspects of complex cases like those and reach a reasonable, probabilistic conclusion. But it is far easier simply to reach one's conclusion at the outset—often for political reasons—and to decide what to believe and what not to believe accordingly. That will always remain a more common method, but I cherish the hope that someday, *American Tragedy* and *The Road to Dallas* might be combined in a volume of the Library of America.

It was now (2008) about thirteen years since I had read *Generations* and then *The Fourth Turning*, predicting a fourth great crisis in American national life sometime in the first 10–15 years of the new century. Many of us thought in the wake of 9/11 that the crisis had arrived in 2001, but as the Bush Administration's policies failed in the Middle East and its incompetence emerged at home, I had come to believe that we had not yet reached the Crisis. The economic and political events of 2008, however, were appropriately momentous, and I was very sad that my dear friend Bill Strauss finally succumbed to his 8-year battle with cancer late in 2007 and did not live to see them. Like my father, who had died earlier in that year, he had thought that Barack Obama might have a remarkable impact on American politics. They were right.

The door to a new Democratic era had already opened in 2006 when the Democrats took control of both houses of Congress. Early in that year, I spoke at a major event at the Kennedy Library, "Presidents and Vietnam," and sat at dinner with Patti, Ted Sorensen and his caregiver (he was nearly blind), General and Mrs. Al Haig, and General and Mrs. Wesley Clark. Sorensen and Clark had agreed that Hillary Clinton had all the major Democratic donors—and therefore, probably, the nomination—locked up. I was not enthusiastic about the candidacy of my most famous contemporary, whose college experience had taken place just a few miles from mine. I was delighted by Obama's strong showing early in 2008 and by the flood of endorsements he received, including those from Sorensen and the Kennedy family. Then came the collapse of the housing bubble, the financial crisis, and the clear evidence that he would win. He campaigned on the need for economic justice, and it seemed that we might indeed be on the verge of another New Deal. For over a year I fell victim to a common disease among Baby Boomers familiar with Strauss and Howe: the belief that their theory means that things will, in the end, turn out just as one had always hoped.

In December 2008, after Obama's resounding victory, I got an awful shock when he announced the appointment of Larry Summers as his chief economic adviser. That was not because of the unfortunate role Summers had played in my own life, but rather because he belonged to the arrogant financial and political establishment which had landed the country in such a mess. So deep was my shock that I really refused to face what this meant for quite some time to come. Yet it became very clear during the first year and a half of the Obama Administration that the new President did not believe that the economic and political system that had been so good to him personally needed fundamental changes. He and his establishment advisers (including his Federal Reserve chiefs) simply did what was necessary to prop up the system as it had evolved under Clinton and Bush, rather than fundamentally alter it. Worse, the President's refusal to start a crusade against economic injustice and the men who had brought us to this pass allowed the Republicans to take the enormous anger in the country and mobilize it against him.

By the middle of 2010, the Affordable Care Act was law, but the rest Obama's agenda was stalled, and the Republicans were clearly on their way to victory in the Congressional elections. Nor had Obama fundamentally re-evaluated George W. Bush's foreign policy, especially in the Middle East. He had re-escalated the war in Afghanistan while pulling out of Iraq, and in later years, he too emerged as another crusader for democracy, with most unfortunate and undemocratic results in Syria and Libya. On July 5, 2010, I published one of my most important essays on historyunfolding.com, entitled "The Regeneracy May not Be Televised." Surveying the many ways in which we remained on the course George W. Bush had set, I speculated that perhaps the great crisis *had* begun on 9/11 after all. Bush had cut taxes twice, embarked on an endless war in the Middle East, and started a drive for energy independence. He had also declared new foreign policy principles proclaiming the right to make war on any state that was developing weapons that the United States did not think it should have. Now, a year into the Trump era, I am even more convinced that Bush did set the country on a new course, and that Donald Trump, Paul Ryan, and Mitch McConnell are simply building on his legacy.

The financial crisis, meanwhile, awakened many new thoughts about history, my own generation, and the place of unusual intelligence in our society today. Our extensive postwar academic establishment, sad to say, had produced a profession of sheep, easily as intellectually conformist as any comparable group from the GI generation. Nowhere was this truer than economics. The macroeconomic concern for full employment that I had been taught as an undergraduate had given way to an unbridled worship of the free market, and all its consequences—including increased inequality of wealth. Worse, the outstanding documentary film *Inside Job* showed how leading economists at Columbia, Harvard and elsewhere had been corrupted by the big banks, producing highly paid academic papers to justify their excesses. Virtually no economist had predicted the greatest financial crash since the Depression—but it turned out that a few lonely souls had.

Michael Lewis, the noteworthy financial journalist who had begun his career in the 1980s with *Liar's Poker*, had been among those who criticized Bill Strauss, myself, and our classmates for complaining about the bonuses paid to the staff of Harvard Management. Lewis never apologized to us publicly after the strategies of those managers turned out to rest upon sand and the value of the endowment fell by ⅓, but he performed a more important service by writing *The Big Short*. It showed how a handful of traders and fund managers had not only predicted the crash but risked their fortunes on their prediction, reaping enormous awards. The book, and the movie that followed, were extremely revealing. Lewis's heroes were not merely iconoclasts—they were nearly all very difficult individuals personally, with symptoms of Asperger's, or, as we say now, of being "on the spectrum." Like me, they had a great respect for data, and like me, they never cared what anyone else thought about their opinion. It occurred to me that their personalities might be a defense against the reaction which unusually smart and courageous people inevitably provoke. I had never had that defense. The testimony of three generations of students within these pages shows, I think that I never sought to impose my opinion on anyone and I was not personally threatened by disagreement. But the same qualities that allowed me to establish such wonderful relationships with students had caused me a lot of pain in my relationship to my profession. I envied the heroes of *The Big Short*, not because of the enormous sums of money they had made, but because real events, verifiable facts, had proven them right— something which, in the nature of a historian's work, cannot happen to him.

Meanwhile, it was time to get to my next book. Thanks in part to my interest in Henry Adams, I have long wanted to write about the politics of the Gilded Age in general and the election of 1884 in particular. That contest pitted the brilliant, charismatic but evidently corrupt Republican James G. Blaine against the young reform Governor of New York, Grover Cleveland. The Democrats—who had not occupied the White House since 1860—confidently expected to beat "Blaine, Blaine, James G. Blaine/The continental liar from the State of Maine," as they called him, but they suffered a terrible shock early in the campaign when Cleveland had to admit that he might have fathered an illegitimate child. "Ma, Ma, Where's My Pa? Gone to the White House, ha! ha! ha!," the Republicans chanted—but Cleveland eked out a narrow victory. I began familiarizing myself with the period, but decided on something else instead.

Three decades earlier, after completing *Economic Diplomacy and the Origins of the Second World War*, I had told May that I would like to look into Roosevelt's strategies during 1941, especially in the last six months of that year. He had been skeptical that much could be added to the existing record, but I had always found that something could. I also wanted to discuss

Roosevelt's leadership during the last great crisis in American national life, to compare it to what Bush and now Obama were doing in the new one.

I tentatively entitled the book "How We Went to War: Franklin Roosevelt and the World Crisis, 1940–41." My agent Christy Fletcher successfully marketed it to a trade house, Basic Books, where Lara Heimert, the head of the Perseus Books division, took it on. Lara and I had a connection. She was a small child when her father, Alan Heimert, was the master of Eliot House, from which I graduated in 1969 and where I became a non-resident affiliate in 1977. More importantly, she had bid unsuccessfully on *The Road to Dallas* as an editor at Yale University Press, losing out to a bigger offer from Harvard. In our first conversation, she commented that she had been surprised by Harvard's rather meager publicity campaign on its behalf. We did not always agree about the shape of the book, but we generally got along very well. A number of other houses declined to bid on the project, and one or two asked what was going to make this book different from all the other books about FDR. Lara knew that it was going to be different because David Kaiser was going to write it.

As usual, I began serious work by going through primary sources that would give me some sense of the entire period under review. These in this case were three diaries by key cabinet members: Harold Ickes, the Secretary of the Interior, who managed to get involved in critical aspects of war planning; Treasury Secretary Henry Morgenthau Jr., who kept careful records of all his contacts with FDR; and Henry M. Stimson, the Republican and former Secretary of State whom Roosevelt made Secretary of War in June 1940. Once again I used a master spreadsheet to enter my notes on all these sources, using headings and subheads to make clear what part of the story they related to. I also began to get a sense of the highly elusive FDR.

The next key step was reading in the "green books," as they are known, the Army's official history of the Second World War. One volume, in particular, *Chief of Staff: Prewar Plans and Preparations*, by Mark Skinner Watson, covered the planning for various possible contingencies in 1940–1, and pointed me towards the archives that I would have to look into myself. Like the JFK collection, they were also at Archives II in College Park, and I once again spent several weeks a year there, taking advantage of the hospitality of Janie Strauss, Bill's widow, and various other family members who continued to live with her. The key collections were the records of the War Plans Division of the General Staff; the conferences of Chief of Staff George Marshall; and corresponding, if much less extensive, records from the Navy Department. I also made two trips to the FDR library. In one of my first major finds, I discovered that FDR, in June 1940, had asked two key Army and Navy planners to discuss a possible situation that might arise during the next year: a continuing conflict with Germany, and possibly Japan as well, waged by the British Navy from ports in the Western Hemisphere, including the United States, after a possible German invasion of Britain. That helped open the door to the real state of mind in Washington in the desperate summer of 1940.

Having lived through wars in Vietnam, the Gulf, and Iraq, today's historians are accustomed to assume that every President simply wants to get into any conflict that is taking place in the world and looks for the opportunity and the excuse to do so. That is how many view Roosevelt's policies in 1940–1, but I discovered something very different. The issue in 1940, with France falling and Britain obviously threatened, was not how to get involved in the war overseas, but how to defend the western hemisphere against the Axis. The first war plans drawn up by the tiny Joint Board of Army and Navy officers aimed to deal with that contingency. In fact, the possibility that the US might face the Axis alone had preoccupied planners since the Munich crisis of 1938. That apparently imminent possibility also convinced the Congress, in June 1940, to double the size of the US Navy—already one of the world's largest. The ships then authorized, however, would not be at sea until 1944 or so, and a desperate situation threatened in the meantime.

The second thing I quickly came to realize was that the problem of preparedness was above all a problem of production. Roosevelt understood this, and beginning in the early summer of 1940 he created a series of new agencies designed to plan a massive expansion of military production, especially of aircraft. His new committees included both business and labor leaders. The mobilization for the war gave New Deal agencies new missions. It also became a great enterprise in which even disadvantaged groups such as Negro Americans (as they were then called) wanted to be involved. The book paid tribute to the spirit and the achievements of the New Deal and the Americans who responded to it. Roosevelt, Stimson, Ickes, General Marshall, and Secretary of State Cordell Hull all belonged to the post-Civil War Missionary generation—the parallel Prophet generation to my own Boom generation. But in contrast to the Boomers, they had set out on a lifelong mission to bring order out of the chaos of the Gilded Age. They knew the world was in a great struggle over values, and they were determined that Anglo-American values would prevail. The Boomers, on the other hand, had given themselves the mission of turning order into chaos—and it showed.

To put what Roosevelt was doing in context, I also returned to some of the issues I had explored as a grad student relating to the policies and strategies of Nazi Germany and Japan. Here I drew upon an enormous secondary literature that had appeared, in waves, over the last six decades. Both Great Britain and the US, I realized, were extremely fortunate that Hitler had not embarked upon a further offensive to the southwest in late 1940, moving through the Iberian Peninsula and into French North and West Africa, after the fall of France. Britain would have been shut out of the Mediterranean and German U-boats would have been in a much stronger position to blockade the British Isles. The Germans might even have threatened Iceland, Greenland, the Cape Verde Islands, the Canaries, and the Azores. But instead, Hitler in late 1940 turned to his real goal, the attack on the Soviet Union. Meanwhile, the Japanese in the fall of 1940 definitely threw in with Hitler and the Nazis when they signed the Tripartite Pact with Germany and Italy. All three powers promised to go to war against the US if the US became involved in war either in Europe or Asia. The Magic intercepts—the Japanese diplomatic documents which US Naval intelligence had begun to break in 1940—had now been published, and I read them carefully. They had informed Roosevelt, Stimson, Marshall and CNO Admiral Stark the Japanese had every intention of keeping this promise, and that there was no hope, therefore, of keeping Japan out of a war with Germany.

It became clear during my research that even though FDR secured the passage of the Lend-Lease Act in early 1941—allowing for new increases in military production to make shipments to Britain and other allies—he most definitely did *not* yet want to enter the war then, although some of his advisers did. The turning point came in late June, when Hitler attacked the USSR. Not only did FDR insist, against the almost unanimous advice of his advisers, on providing weapons to the Soviets, but he also asked the War Department to determine how many troops and how much production would be necessary to *defeat* (not defend against) *all* the possible enemies of the US. The War Plans Division finished the job in September, calling it the "Victory Program," and anticipated the eventual size of our forces very accurately. In what became the climax of the book, on December 9, 1941—two days after Pearl Harbor—Stimson asked William Knudsen, the General Motors CEO who had come to Washington to supervise war production, if the country could meet the production targets of the Victory program by July 1, 1943. "We can't," said Knudsen—"but we can meet them by July 1, 1944." Two days into the war, Roosevelt's men could predict the date at which the final offensives against the Germans and Japanese would begin.

In the midst of my research, I ran across a familiar name: Roger Merriman, the professor (also from the Missionary Generation) who had taught History 1 (really Western Civ) to parts of three generations of Harvard undergraduates, including both FDR and John F. Kennedy, for about 40 years. In his last lecture in May 1941, he once again expressed his view of history: that it was divided into periods of greater freedom, and greater authority. This was the idea that John Clive, another Harvard professor, had ridiculed at the History Department retreat in the 1970s, after I said that the monographs generated by the historical profession should be used to create better syntheses.

But Merriman had been right—and he didn't realize in 1941 that a great era of authority was reaching its peak, only to begin to collapse about 25 years later. In 2000 I had concluded *American Tragedy* with a prediction of a coming crisis in American life, and I concluded *No End Save Victory* with a discussion of Obama's failure to do what FDR had done, mobilize the nation, and get us back on a sounder path.

Given the intensity of the year I had spent at Williams, I could not give up on the idea of returning to a college or university department again. At some point, I wrote my old friend Alan Brinkley, who had become the Provost at Columbia, speculating that I might try to find a wealthy donor who might create a chair that I could occupy at his favorite college or university. Alan replied that he did not know of a single school that would allow a donor to make such a choice. I also wrote a Harvard administrator named Susan Lewis, who had administered the freshman seminar program 30 years earlier and now ran the core curriculum. I talked about the innovative teaching I did done and asked if there were any schools that would hire someone based on the educational contribution that he could make. She replied in the negative. Lacking other options, I wrote letters about a variety of jobs from 2007 through 2011. Two of them stand out for what they revealed about the process in the new century.

I could not resist the first position for personal reasons. It was a senior position at Claremont McKenna, in Claremont, California—right next to Pomona, where my older son had graduated in 2001. The setting, nestled below the San Gabriel Mountains, was quite spectacular, and I was sure that Patti and I could get used to southern California weather. The job called, unfortunately, for an intellectual historian, but I wrote an exploratory note to Jonathan Petropoulos, the search committee chair. It turned out that I had stumbled upon someone who knew quite a bit about me and who liked the idea of having me as a colleague. A copy of *Politics and War*, he reported, was sitting before his eyes on his bookshelf as he typed his response. He was however concerned that I would not fit the job description. I was immediately reminded of the job at Reed College, a similar institution, in 1977–8, and I told him the story of my failure to get considered for that one because it had called for an early modern historian. I wondered whether the candidate they selected had contributed as much to their college as I might have. He immediately invited me to apply, but I was eliminated in the first go-around without an interview. That was that.

The second episode was in a way even more revealing. Some years before, pursuing my avocation as a cyclist, I had struck up a conversation with another rider on a Sunday ride hosted by the Narragansett Bay Wheelmen, the Rhode Island cyclists' club. He turned out to be a history professor at Brown named Ken Sacks, an exact contemporary of mine, and a relatively versatile intellect who had begun his career as an ancient historian and later written a book on Emerson. We took a number of club rides together, and I met him for lunch at least once. Now his department listed an opening for a senior professor, and the desired fields included "the Atlantic world." Having now published my article, "The Great Atlantic Crises, 1774–1962," on the politics of the United States and the major western European states, I thought I might qualify. And were I to get the job, I would not even have to move.

Ken replied politely but firmly to my email. Implying, as departments often did, that even being considered for a position would be an honor and inviting me to apply, he made clear in no uncertain terms that I had no chance. He explained, more bluntly than anyone ever had before, why I had almost never gotten any serious consideration for a job. Departments, he wrote, only got the authorization to create a position by convincing deans that they had a particular gap that they simply had to fill. As a result, their selection had to be a perfect fit for that gap—something which an historian of my breadth of interests could never be. And to the Brown history department, he said, "the Atlantic World" meant—slavery. I did not apply, and I never saw or spoke to him again.

In academia at large, it was now fashionable to argue that "the culture wars are over," perhaps because one side had evidently won. Some observers still put developments in historical perspective.

In 2009, *Academic Questions*, the journal of the National Association of Scholars, published a remarkable article by a historian named Ricardo Duchesne, "The World Without Us." "The liberal idea that human history could be comprehended as a rational process having an intelligible order, which could be described in terms of successive stages of cognitive/technical and moral knowledge," it began, "commanded wide credence in the West from the Enlightenment until the 1960s." This idea was behind the spread of western civilization courses in American colleges and universities towards the middle of the twentieth century. But such courses had become unfashionable in the 1960s, thanks in part to disillusionment with the Vietnam War and other aspects of modern civilization, and also to a general distaste for required courses of any kind. That, however, was not all. "From the 1960s forward," Duchesne continued "the notion of sustained progress in human history came under increasing and continuous criticism by scholars interested in the causes of persistent poverty in the third world." And the idea of western civilization as the leading edge of human development gave way before the turn of the century to a new idea of world history, centered on the story of how the western Europeans established hegemony over the rest of the world, and on the heroic resistance of other continents. The new world history frequently argued, in addition, that there was nothing unique about the cultural, economic and political achievements of the West. These forms of world history replaced western civ at many colleges and universities, including Carnegie Mellon, where Peter Stearns put the change through in the late 1980s. These developments were further milestones in the erosion of the modern western intellectual tradition, and I am convinced that they are now having serious political effects, as well.[21] Those who no longer believe that the western tradition embodied progress have no reason to continue it or enhance it.

---

21 Ricardo Duchesne, "The World Without Us," *Academic Questions*, 22(2009), pp. 138–176.

On June 3, 2009, my ex-wife Cathy forwarded me a brief news story. Ernest R. May, my adviser, had died at the age of 80. It turned out that he had succumbed to a post-operative infection after what appeared to be relatively minor cancer surgery. Several generations of his students congregated for his memorial service some weeks later, and I had a nice breakfast meeting with Sam Williamson. Remembering the impact I had had ten years earlier at his seventieth birthday observance, I offered to speak, but was not invited to do so. On my way to the event, I ran into Patrice Higonnet, who immediately recognized me and struck up a conversation. He said spontaneously that he did not remember the details of the conflict we had had over my future many years ago, but he hoped I could understand that his behavior simply reflected some of the darkness that lurks in all our souls. I did not offer absolution but simply remarked that the episode had been particularly sad because we had been friends. I also saw both Niall Ferguson and Erez Manela, who had been hired instead of myself some years earlier, and introduced myself to Manela, with whom I had crossed swords on H-Diplo.

At the memorial, I learned for the first time that May, like both of my own parents, had lost his mother in sudden and shocking fashion when he was still a child—in her case, in a car accident. He too had evidently suffered from PTSD all his life, explaining his noteworthy reserve, and perhaps his equanimity at the trauma he had helped put me through. At the time of his death May was still teaching, but he had dropped all affiliation with the History Department and was now full time at the Kennedy School of Government, Sometime later I discussed him with a contemporary of his, a mutual friend, who told me that May had recently expressed some regrets to him that he, May, would not leave more great works of history behind him.

I did some financial planning with the help of my accountant, and concluded that I could comfortably retire and move back to the Boston area at last after 2013 when I would turn 66. James McAllister and I briefly discussed bringing me back to Williams in 2011 for two years, but that did not work out. I made rapid progress on *No End Save Victory* thanks to the reduction in the teaching load at the War College, and I managed to keep Generations in Film in the curriculum despite periodic attempts from administrators to kill it. These last years were also noteworthy because Admiral Phil Wisecup took over as President of the War College. He had been a student in my seminar and a member of the very first iterations of Generations in Film in 1997–8, and he had never stopped thinking about Thucydides, Strauss, and Howe. I knew my elective was safe as long as he was around.

Phil Wisecup

I first met David Kaiser in March of 1997 when I came to the Naval War College right out of command of a destroyer in San Diego. He introduced me to the "Fourth Turning"—the work of Strauss and Howe—which I have continually discussed with young officers since my time with him now almost twenty years on. I'm pretty sure we met one of the authors during a visit he organized to the War College. This also put me onto Nathaniel Hawthorne's "twice told tales" and his short story "the gray champion"—which I had never read before reading *The Fourth Turning*.

He was also the professor who first introduced me to Thucydides. Some years later, coming right off of command of a destroyer squadron deployed after 9/11, I was a CNO fellow at the CNO Strategic Studies Group when the decision was made to go into Iraq. My first thought (and I vividly remember this) was about the Athenian decision to go to Syracuse, and I hoped our decision wouldn't turn out to be an "overstretch" with such catastrophic results. So Professor Kaiser's lessons and the discussions we had in his classroom penetrated my thought processes deeply.

My son will graduate from college in a few months with degrees in classics and international relations. He wants to be a Navy SEAL. He is a stoic. I also know now having read classics, that my father, a career educator, was also a stoic. My son's decision to move into classics was not by accident. He and I discussed it often. As a young teenager when I was president of the War College as a flag officer, he actually met people like David Kaiser and his colleagues in the Strategy and Policy Department, and the spouse of one of David's colleagues taught him Latin. Together we read many of the same books as he took his courses in college—to the betterment of us both. I can only thank Professor Kaiser, who was an enlisted soldier in the Vietnam era, for introducing me to the classics in general, and Thucydides in particular.

Professor Kaiser's influence on my thinking represented the best of what the Naval War College hoped to achieve—to teach officers how to think critically about the complex problems they face. I can honestly say that Professor Kaiser had the desired effect on my thinking—not only did he ignite a desire in me to see things differently, and not to blindly accept the status quo, but the end result was it made me a better leader, a better father, and better person. I took this skill to NATO, to sea, to the strategic studies group, to the White House situation room, and into my years as a flag officer. Who could ask for more? He helped me look always for a different way to see things—and this comes through in all his own writing as well. We were lucky to have him as a professor.

$\sim$

Phil was one of two students of mine in my years at NWC who reached general officer rank. In 2009–10 I was fortunate enough to have an outstanding Army Colonel named Mark Stock, who was between command tours and whom I really expected to become a general. That did not happen, but we remained in touch, and he kept me posted on what he was doing as well.

Mark Stock

I met Dr. David Kaiser in the fall of 2009 in Newport Rhode Island. His influence would have a positive and fundamental impact on my approach to serving as a senior military leader dealing with complex and challenging strategic issues.

An Army Lieutenant Colonel with 20 years of service, I was selected to attend the Naval War College, a professional military education program that provides students with graduate-level preparation for higher responsibilities as senior officers. Having spent 18 of the past 24 months deployed to Iraq and Afghanistan, I was looking forward to a relaxed educational experience. Although I had always enjoyed and thrived in academic environments, my personal goal for the year was to reconnect with my family and recharge my batteries for the next inevitable deployment. I assumed this meant reduced, or even minimal, effort in my studies. This assumption did not survive contact with Dr. Kaiser, the professor who led my Strategy and Policy seminar.

The Strategy and Policy Course was the highlight of my Naval War College experience. The course is designed to teach students to think strategically. It adopts an interdisciplinary approach to strategy, drawing on history, political science, international relations, and economics. It integrates those academic perspectives with critical military factors. The result is a coherent frame of reference to analyze complex strategic problems and formulate strategies to address them. It requires a very talented and nuanced teacher to lead and facilitate this ambitious curriculum. I was both lucky and privileged to have David Kaiser at the helm of my seminar.

A thoughtful and unpretentious man, Dr. Kaiser did not immediately strike me as anything special. But over the first weeks of the course, it became clear to me that David was both a gifted instructor and powerful intellect. A historian by inclination and education, he provided much-needed perspective to classroom discussions. Additionally, his deep knowledge and appreciation of the subject matter served to inspire the class to strive for excellence.

A typical class at the Naval War College is composed of a dozen or more military and civilian leaders with strong personalities and firm opinions that have been shaped by decades of life experience. Discussion and analysis of military and political events often generated fierce and occasionally partisan debate. Dr. Kaiser deftly guided these engagements with probing questions, historical examples, and personal experience. His approach exposed and challenged weak augments, sharpened the discourse and generated a powerful learning environment. It was not about imparting the wisdom of the teacher to the student but leveraging the decades of varied professional student experiences to generate and provoke thought and contemplation. It was shared learning, and it was very effective.

Most importantly, David expected and received the best from each student. His personal engagement, enthusiasm for the subject matter and incisive questioning drove me to read more deeply, prepare more thoughtfully and write more concisely and clearly. Despite my initial desire to devote a nominal effort to my academics, I found myself more engaged than ever. I wanted to do my best, and I did not want to disappoint Professor Kaiser. The result was a rewarding and fulfilling trimester of studies that have served as a foundation of for my actions during the second decade of the century. Both of these outcomes I attribute to Dr. David Kaiser.

∼

By 2011–12 I was ready to go. I was also ready to close another chapter in my professional life, my long involvement on the H-Diplo email list. On October 7, 2011, I made the following post on it.

> "In 1994 or 1995 I made my first post on H-Diplo, and I have certainly been "one of the most active post-ers—perhaps, indeed, the most active—for the last 17 years. This was, at the outset, a rare and rewarding opportunity for personal expression within a very lively intellectual environment. It has also been a forum within

which changes within the historical profession could be observed. Sadly, many vital aspects of the list have changed. Although the American historical profession was well into its great and disastrous transformation by the mid-1990s, it was still in a transitional phase. Many posters in those days had been born well before the Second World War. Nearly every university or liberal arts college still included in its history department at least one genuine specialist in American diplomacy, and very possibly, a scholar of European diplomacy as well. They had been trained to address, research, and study great questions of war and peace, and they had done so. They took their own and others' opinions on those questions very seriously, and they enjoyed discussing these questions in a frank, if generally friendly spirit. I myself belonged, I can now see, to the dying days of that tradition, having earned my Ph.D. in 1976. By 1991 the vagaries of the historical profession had landed me here at the Naval War College. The internet in general, and H-Diplo in particular, arrived just in time for us to take advantage of it, and for some time, we did.

"Those who take the time to go through the H-Diplo logs in the mid- and late 1990s will find, I think, a record of extraordinary intellectual vigor and curiosity. We had very long debates on major historical questions, including the decision to drop the atomic bomb, the origins of the Korean War, the reason that Pearl Harbor was such a surprise, and many more. In 2002–3 we had a long and heated discussion about the forthcoming war in Iraq. We were also joined, from time to time, by non-historians who brought something different to the discussions. The prominent neocon David Horowitz posted for an extended period. The convicted spy Morton Sobell appeared briefly at one point to proclaim his innocence—a position he has now recanted. Most importantly of all, perhaps, the historians and political scientists who posted regularly did not feel bound to confine their comments to their research specialties. We had been taught that historians have opinions on every major question, and we expressed them. Of the historians who made the list go in those days, only two seem to be left: Ed Moise and myself. And we appear much less frequently than we did then.

"Later in the 1990s, if I am not mistaken, H-Diplo became the site of a series of very heated discussions about postmodernism, whose value I and some others sharply questioned. It was now clear that history was at a serious turning point indeed. I had been taught that historians used the fullest possible documentary record to make the best judgments they could about what actually happened. Now a new view was taking hold: that arguments about knowledge, as Joan Scott put it in a celebrated article, were about the interests of groups, not the opinions of individuals, and that everyone was free to reshape the past based in large part on identity politics. The arguments over this position raged for several years and I think they were intellectually productive. They have however now died down, as a younger generation that grew up with postmodernism has come to the fore.

"Indeed, it seems that H-Diplo is no longer a discussion forum—it is an online journal. I do not in the least mean to slight the work of the moderators who have done a thankless job very well for all these years. The trouble is with the posters, not the moderators. A new view of history has triumphed, one which indeed denies the existence of any single truth. (I am not suggesting that truth is ever easy to find, but I do believe it exists and is well worth looking for.) Everyone, it seems, is entitled to his or her own small plot of intellectual land, within which he or she can develop a particular variety of history. A general non-aggression pact among the practitioners prevails. The idea that certain books are superior in research, argument, or scholarship to others has become most unfashionable. Dissent from these views has not in fact died out, but it has shrunk to the point that it can safely be ignored. I recall that sometime in the 1990s I tried to start a thread entitled, "What Makes a Great Historian?" I put forward some ideas of my own, but that post never drew a single reply of any kind. That question, however, has continued to interest me deeply, and that is probably the reason why I am now well into my seventh book, each of them on a very different topic from all the rest. It has occurred to me, by the way, that several of my favorite historians, including Henry Adams, W. E. B. Du Bois, Charles A. Beard, and Luigi Albertini, had either a fleeting involvement in the academy or none at all. Perhaps there is a lesson there too.

"The last time that I made a post questioning the conclusions of a book that had been the subject of a roundtable; I received six emails within 24 hours thanking me for what I had said. I asked each correspondent to think about posting their views on the list. Not one of them did. That is another feature of the current historical profession: historians (and political scientists) are afraid to take a stand. Having grown up with the idea that history is controversy, I am very sad about that. More recently, in a perfectly friendly spirit, I raised a serious question of fact arising from another roundtable. No one responded publicly or privately to that one. I am quite certain they would have 15 years ago.

"I would like to close with two broader comments. First of all, it is a paradox that serious archival work involving exhaustive research has fallen out of fashion at a moment when the opportunities to do it are exploding. The digitization of history is a godsend to historians. The ProQuest historical newspaper database, for instance, could allow historians to write political history of a kind that would have been impossible in earlier ages. Other aspects of computer technology, particularly the excel spreadsheet, have enabled me, in my last project and in my current one, to collect, store, and organize data on a hitherto undreamed-of scale. I regret that I have had no opportunity to pass these new techniques on to younger generations of historians. On several occasions I asked friends in history departments if I might give a presentation about them, but that never happened.

"My second point involves the relationship of the historical profession to politics. It is commonly asserted that left-wing politics dominate the academy and the historical profession, and in a sense that is surely true. Yet I am convinced, as a lifelong student of American politics, that the changes in the academy have benefited the political right far more than the political left. Because the historical profession is no longer interested in the doings of the rich and powerful, but only in the lives of the marginalized, universities have turned out a generation of undergraduates lacking the intellectual tools to understand the world around them. One cannot understand the great crisis the United States and the world are now passing through without detailed knowledge of the American Civil War, or the Depression and the Second World War, but such knowledge is increasingly unavailable on college campuses. And because we do not understand those crises, we have been, to date, almost completely unable to cope with this one in a useful manner. The right has never lost interest in American politics and in how things actually work—and it shows.

"H-Diplo probably made me better known within the historical profession than anything, I have written. (My books made me better known outside it, of course.) I made more than a few friends here, and I know that many people found things I said useful and encouraging. (I would warn them against believing, however, that ideas like mine have any place in contemporary history departments.) I am continuing to write the kind of history I believe in, and I am sure that I will do so for a long time to come. I also have an additional year of teaching at an excellent liberal arts college, where I know from recent experience that the students want what I have to offer, to look forward to. After that, however, my professional career—not my writing career—will come to an end. I shall try to keep the best historical traditions alive, and I am very satisfied with what I will have left behind.

"This will be my last post on H-Diplo.

Sincerely yours,

David Kaiser"

Writing now in 2017, I looked back at H-Diplo online to see what was happening there. On July 28 the list published a roundtable on a new book by John M Schuessler, *Deceit on the Road to War: Presidents, Politics and American Democracy,*" dealing with the ways in which Franklin Roosevelt, Lyndon Johnson, and George W. Bush misled the public to involve the United States in war. Not a single historian or political scientist has seen fit to comment on the roundtable.

The last iteration of Generations in Film featured an interesting Navy captain named Michael Junge, who was already familiar with Strauss and Howe and their implications for Navy management. By now the course had allowed many students to write autobiographical papers that went into subjects that had probably never shared with any one in authority before. I still have copies of many of them, but I cannot quote. Michael then became a member of my last S & P seminar in the spring of 2012. He wrote one of the best papers I had ever received on George F. Kennan's and Paul Nitze's views of the Cold War. Then he told me something that moved me almost to tears. He had been assigned to the NWC faculty—and he intended to take over teaching Generations in Film. He did—but as it turned out, he didn't have the necessary clout to keep it going for long.

Michael Junge

In the summer of 2011, my family and I moved from Washington, DC to Newport RI. As an active duty naval officer I had orders to teach at the Navy's Command Leadership School—a job I first became interested in almost a decade earlier. I was escaping the Pentagon, DC traffic, and looking forward to focusing on leadership—both studying and teaching it.

As often happens, unforeseen events intervened. I stayed in Newport, but became a student at the US Naval War College. In 2002 I graduated from the USNWC's College of Distance Education, so I already had a degree. I was now chosen not because I wanted to go, but because my community in the Navy was short on attendance—and I was local and met a desired demographic. I didn't want to go and repeat something I'd already done. The Navy didn't care.

The War College teaches in thirds, trimesters rather than semesters. My first trimester put me Joint Maritime Operations. Joint Maritime Operations was something of a nose to the grindstone class and did not fit my idea of education. Since I didn't want to be there, to begin with, I wasn't a particularly attentive student. After a while I stopped reading—but still participated. Then I played with the class to see how far I could derail discussions, still on topic but tangential. My approach to class is not something I am particularly proud of, but something I did and have to accept and admit to. That behavior is also an important part of how I came to meet, learn from, know, and admire Dr. David Kaiser.

At the War College students are allowed very little personal choice. The one-course students can choose is in the elective program. In my bitter first trimester, I took an elective that was neither illuminating nor interesting. For the second trimester, I took David's class on "Generations in Film"—an innovative idea that combined film depictions of American life with Neil Howe and Bill Strauss's generational theory. I already had one of Strauss and Howe's book—was exposed to it my first time at the Navy's Command Leadership School, and thought I had a way to regain my interest.

I vividly recall the first day of class. David provided some introduction to Strauss and Howe and showed a clip from *It's a Wonderful Life*. In the clip, George Bailey's father is asking George to stay and run the town bank, but George has other ideas. David asked us what we saw in the conversation and I, being generally frank, candid, and outspoken, called the elder Bailey "selfish."

David took exception to my characterization, and we danced the argument back and forth for a while. Later, far, far later, I realized that our differences in opinion lay entirely in our own generational lenses. David, a Baby Boomer, saw the elder Bailey as asking George to put the town's needs ahead of his personal desires. I, from Generation X, saw the elder Bailey seeking to preserve his own legacy by guilting his son into taking over. At the time I didn't understand, but now I see that both perspectives are correct. Which is part of the genius of Strauss and Howe.

As the trimester went on, I became more and more fascinated with the depths of the theory and the use of film to describe American life. There's some challenge in that. For it to work well, the films need to be contemporary to the time and generation they portray. A case in point is *The Bad News Bears*. The original film with Walter Matthau and Tatum O'Neill showcases the generations of their time, in their contemporary setting. The Billy Bob Thornton remake fails because it took the generational behavior of one generation and forced it into a different generational genre. Millennial kids just don't act like Xer kids did. The world is different, for all the reasons Strauss and Howe explained.

I found myself in David's Strategy and Policy class during the spring (and final) trimester. As part of my changed assignment I anticipated continuing on as a faculty member in S&P, and I figured I could do far worse than learn more from David.

So, I altered my in-class behavior from my first trimester. First, I respected David too much to derail class. Second, there were classmates in the seminar who were reticent to speak, but had important insights that they would mutter sotto voce. Rather than drown those students out, I settled back and tried to get them to speak. And it worked, but I erred in not telling David what I was doing.

When David began the trimester, he read us a section of Clausewitz normally ignored by historians. David referred to it as the beginning of net assessment, because Clausewitz uses it to make the point that every actual war is in some sense unique and has to be understood in its own terms.

In Strategy and Policy, students write two papers addressing specific questions assigned by the faculty. My second assignment concerned comparing the words of Cold War strategists, George F. Kennan and Paul Nitze. Starting with Clausewitz's idea of net assessment I dissected both author's language, Kennan's famous X Article and Nitze's NSC-68.

I was eventually assigned to stay at Newport and teach, but unfortunately, an assignment to Strategy and Policy did not pan out. I went to teach in the very department I'd been such an inattentive student—Joint Maritime Operations. It was only a year, and I expected to move on as soon as that year was done, if not sooner.

But, in that one year, I had one request. David retired, and no one was slated to pick up his elective—a popular class taught consistently for a decade and a half. I asked, and was allowed, to continue his elective. Something that remains a highlight of my time in Newport.

As had happened twice before, the Navy changed plans, and I am now in my fifth year of that one-year assignment to JMO. I only taught "Generations" one semester before the bridge between myself and the electives coordinator was torched, from both ends, and while I remain an adherent and proponent of Strauss and Howe, I no longer teach their theory.

However, I do remain in contact with David Kaiser—somewhat sporadically, even though he only lives a few hours away. That contact, however, is the only consistent contact I have with any of my War College professors (except for the one I now work with in JMO.) David became one of my role models in teaching—not just in the classroom but outside the classroom. David's example reminded me to find an area I liked, and believed in, to teach it and write on it. To stick to it, even when that was difficult. I am now writing my dissertation, also a path David helped me move towards, and look forward to someday reinvigorating the "Generations in American Life" elective and ultimately blending Strauss and Howe with my generally completely unrelated dissertation.

[Michael also wrote me a handwritten note at the end of that year. "Your achievements combined with your intellect would have been hubris in a person of lesser character," he wrote. "Instead you have taken our humility and turned it into an asset that allows any student to question your assumptions—and in doing so, learn!"]

My final lecture took place at the outset of the senior course unit on Vietnam, which I had finally won a battle to revise. The lecture surveyed the policies of different US Administrations towards the third world during the Cold War, from Truman through Reagan. My last teaching partner, Rob Krivacs, helped me produce a series of maps of the world that showed third world nations shifting back and forth over the decades from the US orbit into the Communist one, and out of it. The lecture identified various different strategies different Administrations had tried, including the overthrow of unfriendly governments (and occasionally friendly ones) through covert action; the provision of security assistance; diplomacy to lure nations like Egypt or China out of the Soviet orbit; and the deployment of troops, as in Vietnam. I gave the highest marks to the diplomatic strategy. The lecture is posted on YouTube, and this time—unlike at Harvard—I said exactly what I wanted to say—especially at the very end. But my hope that I might return to Newport to give it again was never fulfilled.

Patti's and my return to Williams took place in an atmosphere of considerable stress. In the spring we had found an excellent two-story condo in Watertown, which remains our home today, but our Jamestown house had not yet sold when we left. We did find a buyer several months later, although it took about another year to close the deal. As a result, in

2012–3 I had the responsibility for three different properties: the Jamestown house, the new Watertown one, and the faculty housing we were assigned at Williams. That, however, was not all. In 2006 I had returned joyfully to college life with the hope that the return might last out my career. Now I was going back to yet another place that had declined to make further use of my services, knowing that this year would bring my full-time teaching career to an end. Stress increased still further when, incredibly, it seemed in September of 2012 that the tumor that had first been diagnosed six years earlier might have recurred. The suspicious bump I had under the skin of my abdomen in almost exactly the same place led to several appointments at Dana Farber. It fooled the radiologist who did an ultrasound, leading to a biopsy. But by the time of the biopsy, it was clear that it might easily be nothing but an infection probably brought about by a tick bite. So it was, and it was easily dealt with.

I had decided to give the same two courses in the fall and spring term—Wilson, Roosevelt, and the Two World Wars in the fall, and the seminar on Vietnam in the spring. But this time Patti and I wanted to spend December and January in Watertown, and I did not volunteer to do Generations in Film as a winter study course. I was also a bit taken back when James McAllister told me that the incumbents of the Stanley Kaplan chair were no longer affiliating with the history department. Even though I had endured 36 years of frustration trying to get college history departments interested in what I could do—including that one—I still could not shake the feeling that that was where I belonged. I felt a bit like George Kennan when he rejected John Foster Dulles's 1953 suggestion that he join the CIA—he had given his life to the State Department, and if he was not wanted there, he did not want to remain in government. But I knew James McAllister had good reasons for the change. What really saddened me was that my courses would not even be listed as history courses, and that inevitably had a negative effect on enrollment, particularly in the seminar, which had about 1/3 the members that I had had in 2007.

Only six years had passed, but Williams was clearly a somewhat different place. Political correctness was now omnipresent, spread in a steady stream of emails to the whole campus from the dean's office. In the previous year a controversy had erupted, leading to at least one day of meetings, when a graffiti, "All niggers must die," was discovered on campus. In the course of the year a very level-headed student whom I totally trusted told me that he had attended a meeting in which a black student had admitted that she had written it. This year, the dean sent another anguished message about the hurt feelings of marginalized students after another graffiti, "All beaners must die," was discovered—followed a day later by another email explaining the definition of "beaner." More seriously, I came across a good deal of evidence, both personal and anecdotal, that the intellectual quality of Williams students was becoming much more erratic. Many were still excellent, and I rapidly connected with them yet again. But a significant minority had clearly found their way to the campus for other reasons, including their athletic ability, or their family's wealth, or their family's status within a foreign country. Williams had the highest per-student endowment of any college in the country, but it had not used it to make the school any more affordable than any other elite institution.

The fall course went well, particularly since the second half—on FDR—involved the material I was in the final stages of writing up for *No End Save Victory*. Its most remarkable student was a senior, Annie Dear, who made a key contribution to that book. In an excellent paper based upon polling data that was now available online, she showed that while a majority of Americans opposed immediate entry into the war right up until Pearl Harbor, a large majority also accepted that war was inevitable. I incorporated that into the book, with an appropriate acknowledgment in an endnote, and two years later I presented her with a signed copy in person. I introduced the students to the idea of the Fourth Turning, and my most intense moment of the year occurred one day after class when a freshman from the west coast eagerly accosted me. On a visit home, he had discovered that someone had given him a copy of *The Fourth Turning* some years before, and he had eagerly read it from start to finish on the plane back. We talked for a while about it, leaving me near tears in frustration at all the other students like him I might still reach if I were given a chance.

The spring course had 9 students. One, a junior named Anna Barnes, immediately stood out. In an early discussion of the Kennedy Administration, I mentioned my father's ambassadorial appointment and my own frustration at having to leave for Africa. She immediately volunteered that something similar had happened to her at a similar age, and asked if I had ever gotten over my anger. I said, not really, and she said the same. This was very unusual for a Millennial—I had commented six years earlier during Generations in Film that they would have to be waterboarded to say anything negative about their parents. Anna was very involved in theater and extremely annoyed by some of the postmodern interpretations and recasting of plays that she was encountering. She eventually wrote a fine paper on how Vietnam had changed American films—moving action pictures from the battlefield to the world of fantasy. The research papers included several on diplomatic topics and one by a Korean-American who analyzed South Korea's role in the conflict. Another paper analyzed the emergence of black nationalism within the civil rights movement.

Anna Barnes

I arrived at Williams thinking that I was going to be a History major. After a rewarding, but difficult, tutorial on World War One, I realized that the history department wasn't for me and found my way into the political science department instead. Professor Kaiser's class, which I took my junior spring, was particularly recommended to me by my Political Science advisor, Jim McAllister—a great professor in his own right who also did the school an invaluable service by bringing in some of the most interesting people I've ever met as guest professors.

Although I wasn't due to take a senior seminar for another year, McAllister encouraged me to take David's course on the Vietnam War and the Vietnam Era. The previous year, I had taken a course on the Vietnam War that McAllister co-taught with guest professor Mark Lawrence; in the course of that semester, I discovered that I'd much rather write about *The Quiet American* than stare at troop movements, so McAllister thought that Professor Kaiser's focus on the broader cultural and political context of the period would be especially exciting for me. He couldn't have given me better advice. I had previously focused on International Relations because American Politics annoyed me—six years in blindly, belligerently blue Boulder, Colorado, followed by two years in blindly, belligerently red Fort Worth, Texas left me with a decided distaste for anyone who felt passionately about current events in my own country. Professor Kaiser's course used the lens of the Vietnam War to explain American political history in the twentieth century, providing me with a context to understand not only the Vietnam War, but everything that's happened in American politics since. In addition to this, I had the opportunity to write one of the most fun research papers I undertook at Williams—a comprehensive survey of popular movies from 1965–1980. Professor Kaiser's course played an invaluable role in shaping my view of American politics—and American movies—and how they came to be the way they are today.

∽

Early in the spring, McAllister organized a conference centering on John Lewis Gaddis's new biography of George F. Kennan, and I contributed a short talk on Kennan's view of the importance of law in international politics. One of the other conferees came from the BU history department, and at lunch, I told him about Generations in Film and my hope to find a home for it at some Boston area university. "I'd like to take that course!" he said enthusiastically. But when he passed the idea along, his chairman replied that it would be difficult to budget for it. I reminded him that I had said that I would do it for nothing, and I meant it. In the succeeding years, I approached at least three different departments about it, but without the slightest result. It seems that course may never be given again.

My last class would take place on May 9. Several days earlier, I wrote an email to four of my favorite students from the fall term. I said that every term there were a few people who, for whatever reason, made things memorable. I talked a little about my career and how glad I had been to be here, very much along the lines of what I planned for the last class. One of them got back to me, and we met for lunch.

The last class began with two presentations by the two weakest students, who had taken the most time during the term. Then, I went into an extended discussion of the long-term impact of Vietnam. I began with a survey of Cold War and post-Cold War foreign policy, talking about the reforms of the intelligence agencies under Ford and Carter, and then Reagan's revival of the confrontation with the Soviets—but without any new military involvement in the Third World. Then I talked about the collapse of Communism, explaining it in Soviet generational terms. And I asked them about inspirational Presidents. I said Kennedy had inspired my generation, and that Reagan, as I came to understand at NWC, had inspired a great many Gen Xers. Had Obama inspired them? There was a long silence. "Yes," said one of the strongest students—"until he was elected." They pretty much all agreed that he had been a disappointment. I praised George H. W. Bush for his handling of the windup of the Cold War, said relatively little about Clinton, and then talked about George W. Bush as a typical Boomer and someone who thought he could have everything just by wishing for it. And then we talked about how Obama had changed some things, but not others.

And that led me into a discussion of the future. I pulled out the story I had found this year about the last lecture given in May 1941, before 1000 Harvard undergraduates, by the legendary Roger Merriman, who had taught European history from the fall of Rome to the present for 40 years. I said such courses were standard in those days, but they confirmed that none of them had had one like it. I mentioned that western civilization has pretty much been replaced by world history, which is usually taught as the story of how western civilization oppressed the rest of the world. Merriman explained in his last lecture, as he always did, that every historical development produced a reaction, but that even after the reaction civilization had progressed a step forward. Anarchy in the Middle Ages and religious wars had given way to strong monarchies in the 17th and 18th centuries, then to the French Revolution. Laissez-faire in the 19th century had given way to economic regulation in the 20th. And so on. And to drive the point home, Merriman hung his pocket watch on the blackboard and got it swinging back between liberty and security. I mentioned that back in 1979, when I heard an older faculty member at Harvard tell that story, everyone had laughed at how funny it was, but that now it seemed Merriman was having the last laugh. What I did not tell them was that, in a saner world, I could have been the Merriman of the last 35 years.

Continuing, I said that the reaction of the Boom generation against the world they were born into was inevitable, but that I was convinced that Vietnam had made it a lot worse because it gave us the license to believe that everything our parents had ever said was wrong. As I had tried to express at the end of *American Tragedy*, which I had asked them to review for today, the story of the war still hurt so much for me because at the moment it began our institutions seemed to be working so well, and they had never worked so well again. And I said that we had been tearing down our parents' achievements ever since. To drive the point home, I showed two clips from *Wall Street*, the first of Charlie Sheen getting wise advice from Lou (Hal Holbrook), the GI stockbroker who represents Oliver Stone's own father, and then the scene in which he meets Gordon Gecko. Most of them, to my amazement, had never seen the movie. It made an impression. I talked about the decline of authority and the over-emphasis on freedom. I said I knew that up until now, they had gotten where they were by following the rules and doing what was expected of them. I certainly didn't hold that against them, but I said that I sincerely doubted that society as we have known it could survive if we didn't recover some of the virtues of sacrifice and common purpose that have been lost, and, in effect, move more towards security and away from total liberty. One of them said he was most worried about the environment. I said that yes, it's possible that climate change could make things so bad that we would have to respond. That led to some further discussion. I urged them all to do what they could to make any institution they became involved in work better, and endure, and represent something bigger than itself. I cited my son Tom's middle school as an example of such an institution. I said that although it had very strict discipline, it was clear that every kid in the school was delighted to be there.

And then I referred to my prepared remarks at the end.

"Fifty-two years ago," I said, "I had learned I was going off to Africa, and I had to learn French within three or four months." And the first piece of literature I remembered reading was a story by Léon Daudet called La dernière classe—the last class. And to my utter amazement, Hiu Jin Shu, who also signs herself Eugene, the Korean-American, smiled and said she knew the story—that it was very popular in Korea. I explained that it was about a little boy in Alsace in the 1870s going to school one morning. His teacher asked him to recite the day's French lesson, and he was unprepared and couldn't do it. He was filled with shame. Then the teacher announced that this was the last time they would be seeing him, because the Germans were taking over the school the next day and all future instruction would be in German. He pleaded with them to keep up their French. Eugene explained that the Koreans had gone through something similar under the Japanese.

"Well," I said, "this is my last class. I don't think it will be my last class ever, but it is my last class as a full-time faculty member." And I sketched out my career—that it had started out, 37 years ago, at the top, and that I had found out how much impact I could have in a certain kind of institution—very simply, the kind that I would have wanted to attend myself. That had lasted only four years, and I had been determined to make that happen again, somewhere. But I had never been able to do that except in 2006–7 here at Williams and then again this year. That was all thanks to James McAllister (they all immediately smiled and nodded when I said that), who cared about the education the kids got and who had guts. Those were very rare qualities nowadays, I said. I think I forgot to say, this time, how much it meant to me to have had that chance just to prove to myself that I hadn't been dreaming about what it would be like. I said what I was doing today was what I had been doing all along: expressing fascination for the past in itself, but also trying to see how it related to the present and the future. That is why Strauss and Howe, two amateurs, had come to mean so much to me. And I did not mention that I had tried and failed to make it last longer six years ago. I did say that, sadly, there was no market in today's world for what I could do in a college classroom.

And then, I said that I did not expect any of them to go into academia—they were too smart. But one of them is, in political science, and he may do well, for a variety of reasons. But, I said, some of you may fall in love with what you do. That's great; but it can also cause you a lot of pain. And to sum that up, I said, I was going to read from the end of *Ball Four*. I explained who Jim Bouton was, an aging pitcher who had written a diary of the 1969 season, in which he thought he had revived his career, and I read the very last passage of the book.

"When I took a cab to the airport in Cincinnati [after the season was over], I got into a conversation with the driver, and he said he'd played ball that summer against [long-time big leaguer] Jim O'Toole. He said O'Toole was pitching for the Ross Eversoles in the Kentucky Industrial League. He said O'Toole is all washed up. He doesn't have his fastball anymore, but his control seems better than when he was with Cincinnati. I had to laugh at that. O'Toole won't be trying to sneak one over the corner on Willie Mays in the Kentucky Industrial League.

"Jim O'Toole and I started out even in the spring. He wound up with the Ross Eversoles and I with a new lease on life. And as I daydreamed of being Fireman of the Year in 1970, I wondered what the dreams of Jim O'Toole are like these days. Then I thought, would I do that? When it's over for me, would I be hanging on with the Ross Eversoles? I went down deep, and the answer I came up with was yes.

"Yes, I would. You see, you spend a good piece of your life gripping a baseball, and in the end, it turns out that it was the other way around all the time."

They nodded, and nearly every one of them thanked me very warmly. I cleaned my office and office computer out after class. Later in the evening, I set out for the library to return one more book. I ran into one of them who said my closing was very inspirational. And then in the library, I saw another of the four students from the fall whom I had written. Without a word, we threw our arms around each other for a brief hug.

XI

THE CRISIS IN HISTORY

The tempo of history has quickened in the five years since I left Williams. While I and the other participants in the Fourth Turning Facebook page were quite convinced by 2013 that we were in the middle of the great crisis Strauss and Howe had predicted twenty years earlier, none of us foresaw the complete collapse of the American political order that the election of Donald J. Trump represents. And that leads me to another conclusion about our recent history and its relation to the course of my career. The collapse of the historical profession which I witnessed firsthand is, I am convinced, quite connected to the broader decline of public life in the United States, and the threatened collapse of American society. Like our grandparents and our parents, we too are living through world-historical events, but this time they are characterized by entropy rather than achievement.

A new set of ideas about power and group identity now dominate not only the discipline of history and the rest of the humanities, but also the general atmosphere on almost every campus of the nation. Those ideas see us all not only as defined by our gender, race, sexual orientation, and perhaps religion, but also as carrying with us all the guilt or shame that goes with membership in an oppressor or oppressed group. Not only are the thoughts and feelings of women, nonwhites, and LGBTQs treated as sacrosanct, but whites (and white males in particular) are taught not to trust their own thoughts and feelings on sensitive issues. These new habits are completely at odds with the earlier vision of academics as *individuals* examining sources with all the impartiality they can muster in an effort to discover the truth about some aspect of the human experience. Indeed, they actually teach young people that their individual thoughts and experiences are secondary to their demographic characteristics in determining what they feel and think. This has almost completely destroyed the academic tradition in which I first grew up, and replaced it with a sterile intellectual environment.

When I taught *Twelve Angry Men* as part of Generations in Film, I would always acknowledge that all twelve characters were white men. But rather than imply that being white conferred virtue, the movie instead taught that being a just, good person had nothing to do with being white or nonwhite, or male or female. The white men ran the gamut from tolerant to bigoted, from reasoned to emotional, and from foolish to wise. The same point can be extended to the whole of western history. Until 2008, at least, no one ever voted for a presidential candidate in the United States *simply because he was a white male*. All major candidates in the general election were white males, and race and gender, therefore, could not help a voter make a choice. In the same way, white males could be found on both sides of every controversial historical question in American history, including those having to do with race. And I am touching here on one of the aspects of my teaching that students remembered most vividly nearly forty years after the fact: my insistence that the particular individuals who made decisions on questions of war and peace made an enormous difference to everyone concerned.

The escalating tensions on campus surrounding free speech and the sexual assault controversy, indeed, have forced me finally to confront some difficult questions. Thirty years ago at Carnegie Mellon, I introduced Alice Miller into my War and Revolution course to explain the behavior of Nazis and Stalinists. She argued that many of these men (and, at times, women) were acting out their hatred for their own abusive parents against Jews, Kulaks, the mentally ill, or the bourgeoisie—and she convinced me that she was right. Having just read *Unwanted Advances* by the Northwestern Professor of Media Studies Laura

Kipnis—who was the subject of a Title IX investigation because she criticized proceedings against another professor in print—I have concluded that I must not shrink from applying the same analysis to today's ideologues. Campus activists, individual undergraduates and grad students, and university bureaucracies enforcing new norms are turning on certain students and faculty with a ferocity that simply cannot be explained by anything that those unlucky people did. They are also consigning not a few white male faculty and students to a moral hell merely by virtue of their supposedly inherent racial and gender characteristics in a manner all too familiar from 80 years ago. The hatred they are venting, it seems to me, must really be aimed at people from their own personal emotional universe. Unfortunately, as historical examples also show, no one else can make ideologues recognize these things about themselves.

In the new moral view of the universe that has spread over nearly all our campuses during the last few years, no one who has ever held power can escape moral opprobrium—and one of the punishments for their supposed crimes is to be ignored. That is the main reason, I think, why so little academic history now deals with the men—and women—who have had the most impact on how we all live, in politics and in economic life. Since power is evil, virtue only emerges among the marginalized—and they, therefore, become the proper objects of study. Western Europe and the United States are also increasingly suspect as the home of the world's dominant civilization over the last few centuries. All this has had an enormous impact on what is studied, and not studied, in history departments today.

To illustrate this point, let us take a look at recent Ph.D. dissertations in two leading departments, Yale and Columbia. The Yale history department's web page allows us to look at all the dissertations completed during the five years 2011–15. Out of these 121 dissertations—an impressive number—only 35 have even a tangential relationship to politics, government, or diplomacy, and none of them specifically focuses on the political history of a specific nation during a given time period, much less the origins of a particular war. The most traditional is a study of John Quincy Adams's attitudes towards foreign policy, whose author, Charles Edel, now teaches in my old department at the Naval War College. Most of them are much too narrow to arouse any interest outside the historical profession. Columbia, by contrast, lists 68 dissertations in progress of which 19 have some tangential relationship to politics. But none of these dissertations—at either Yale or Columbia—deals specifically with a major political event or even focuses directly on what a government does. I did not, for example, see a single dissertation relating to any aspect of the domestic or foreign policies of the Reagan Administration—and that administration is as distant in time from us now as the Second World War was when I was in graduate school. A few citations of typical dissertation topics would indicate what kinds of topics are fashionable at the moment, but I do not want to embarrass any of the young men and women who are trying to make their way in the world simply by doing what they have been taught.

One of the saddest developments in higher education over the last 50 years is the collapse of the distinction between undergraduate and graduate education. In the mid-1960s everyone understood that while academics had to specialize rather narrowly, especially when writing their dissertations, undergraduate courses required a broad view. That is no longer the case, and academics now generally use the same approach in the classroom that they use in their research. That is undoubtedly why the popularity of history courses has fallen off so badly. Nor is this all. As recently as a decade ago, many major history departments featured one or two very popular courses on traditional topics which drew a large percentage of the total departmental enrollment. But they were generally taught by faculty from the Silent or early Boom generations, and those faculty are now retired, taking their courses with them. Seventeen years have passed since I wrote my first piece for *Academic Questions*, "My War with the AHA," about my disputes with the American Historical Association. "I am sure the kind of history that the AHA now encouldges is destined to wither and die," I wrote, "largely because it has nothing to contribute to society at large, and it seems quite possible that the AHA itself will wither and die along with it." To judge from university course enrollments, the first half of that prediction has rapidly come true. The situation has become sufficiently serious for Professor Fredrik Logevall of Harvard to co-author an op-ed in the *New York Times* in August 2016, "Why did We Stop Teaching Political History?" "American political history as a field of study has cratered," the authors wrote. "Fewer scholars build careers on studying the political process, in part because few universities make space for them. Fewer courses are available, and fewer students are exposed to it. What was once a central part of the historical profession, a vital part of this country's continuing democratic discussion, is disappearing."[22]

Present-day historians would undoubtedly argue that the changes I have just been describing represent progress, a welcome shift in attention from white males and the civilization they created to the rest of society and the rest of the world. But they cannot argue with the catastrophic decline in the place of history on campuses that has resulted from these changes. When I arrived at Harvard in the fall of 1965, the History Department had just awarded undergraduate degrees to about 273 Harvard and Radcliffe undergraduates, or about 18% of the total senior class. Most of the courses offered by the department dealt with the national histories of the United States and the major European nations, although every continent was well represented in the course catalog. 14 years later, in 1979, when I was on the faculty myself, the number of history majors had fallen by about 50%, but still reached 142 students, about half of whom probably wrote senior theses. But by 2018, the number of history majors had fallen to just 43. What is rather striking is the failure of the number of faculty in the department to drop in proportion to the number of students that it now taught. In 1979 I was one of 40 full-time faculty—about one per every 3.5 history majors. Fourteen years earlier I suspect that the number of full-time faculty members was about the same, meaning that in 1965, there were about 7 history majors for each full-time

---

22 https://www.nytimes.com/2016/08/29/opinion/why-did-we-stop-teaching-political-history.html?_r=0

faculty member.[23] Today the History Department includes 47 full-time faculty *or about one per history major.* Their workload must have dropped a great deal. Lecture courses ruled the college in the 1960s, they have become extremely rare. Small group courses—which are much less demanding for faculty and students alike—are now the rule.

The same pattern has occurred, albeit a bit less dramatically, at other major institutions. Columbia in 1965 had about 76 history majors out of 569 graduating seniors, taught by 32 permanent faculty members. By 2016 the graduating class had doubled to 1135, and the history faculty had increased to 67 permanent members, but only 68 history majors graduated. Swarthmore in 1966 graduated 33 history majors, taught by just 7 full-time faculty, out of 238 graduating seniors. The senior class in 2017 totaled 294, and the history department now had 10 permanent faculty, but only 22 history majors graduated—many of them double majors. 9 full-time history faculty at Wellesley taught 53 graduating majors in 1965, out of a class of 381 students. By 2017 the number of graduating seniors had reached 547 and the history faculty 14, but only 12 history majors received diplomas—less than one per faculty member. As I had found at Williams, the fields in which faculty have increased, including gender history and the history of third world nations, evidently have very little appeal to undergraduates.

The eclipse of history within leading colleges and universities has undoubtedly had an impact on the tastes of the reading public as well. As recently as the 1980s, books like Robert Caro's biographical volumes on LBJ, Doris Kearns Goodwin's on the Kennedys and the Roosevelts, and even Paul Kennedy's on the great powers stayed on the best-seller lists for months at a time. But the market for books like those seems to have come mostly from the GI and Silent generations, who have largely died off. Not even Caro or Goodwin enjoys anything like the kind of

---

23 Unfortunately, I could not find definite data for 1965 faculty numbers. I have not been able to get comparable data from other institutions, including Stanford, UC Berkeley,and the University of Chicago.

sales that they used to. And the change in popular taste has also had an impact on my own career as an author.

American Tragedy, which appeared in 2000, was widely reviewed and must have sold more than 20,000 hardcover copies. *The Road to Dallas* appeared 8 years later and was hardly reviewed at all, but it sold 15,000 copies very quickly before sales came to a halt. *No End Save Victory: How FDR Led the Nation into War* appeared in the spring of 2014, and received very favorable reviews in the *Washington Post*, the *Wall Street Journal*, and *The New York Times*—in some respects the best track record of any of my books. But it sold less than 9,000 hardcover copies. I spoke about it at the FDR Library's annual book fair—a wonderful occasion—and that talk was broadcast on C-Span, but it had far less impact on my Amazon ranking than a similar talk about *American Tragedy* in 2000 had when it was broadcast by the same network. All the other non-fiction writers that I know report that their sales have fallen off, and one even contributed the horrifying datum that a long-awaited invitation to appear on *Fresh Air* with Terry Gross did almost nothing for his book's Amazon rank.

The shift in historical focus from governments, laws, great political movements, and wars on the one hand, to marginalized groups, remote borderlands, and linguistic issues on the other, has also, in my opinion, had a profound and disastrous impact on American politics. This was the subject of another article I wrote for *Academic Questions* after leaving academia, "How Postmodern Historians Helped Cripple the American Left," which appeared in 2015.[24] The new kind of history, I wrote, "is much more focused upon how the past has supposedly been viewed, and how it might be viewed differently, than upon the past itself. History is seen less as a contest among actual political entities—using armies, ideologies, and economic power to expand and contract—than as a struggle of viewpoints, of hegemonic ideas, always contested by marginalized groups. It is as if the political world has been reduced to an academic

---

24 David Kaiser, "How Postmodern Historians Have Helped Cripple the American Left," *Academic Questions*, vol. 28 (February 2015), pp. 66–72.

department riven by clashes between competing worldviews. Concepts such as citizenship, memory, gender, and sexuality are weapons deployed in an endless struggle between hegemonic views—essentially, the values that made Western civilization what it was around 1965—and marginalized alternatives." I might have added that many new historians claimed authority by virtue of their identification with one or more marginalized groups. And all this, as we have seen, has vastly reduced the popularity of history within colleges and universities and cut off the profession from society at large.

As a result, the influence of historians upon politics during the current saeculum, or 80-year period in American life, that began in 1945, has been infinitesimal in comparison to its influence in the years 1868–1945. Historians in that era, led by Charles A Beard, focused on the relationship between the state and society, especially in the economic sphere, and saw the drama of American history as a struggle for economic equality. They, therefore, contributed to the great achievements of the New Deal era and its aftermath. Today, both history departments and campuses generally are obsessed with the status and feelings of women, minorities, and LGBTQs. While this has helped secure equal rights for these groups over the last half century, it has also allowed the enormous growth of corporate power in the US and the wider world to proceed unchecked, without any countervailing intellectual influence from universities.

I appreciate that the National Association of Scholars gave me the chance to publish these findings, but I am sad to say that that organization, as I first came to know it in the 1990s, has been another casualty of the age we live in. In the 1990s in particular, a number of older academics published excellent, courageous articles in its journal, protesting current trends in academia. Now most of them and those who read them are dead or retired. The membership of the organization has obviously declined, and it can no longer survive on its membership dues. It, therefore, raises a great deal of money from right-wing foundations, and it has allowed them to influence its activities. Opposition to the "sustainability" movement on campus, and even skepticism about global warming, have become hallmarks of its publications and its activities in the public sphere. It too has felt the impact of the partisanship of our age.

That, however, is not all. Today's young people have grown up in a wretched era of American politics, marked by an increasing influence of great wealth, extreme partisanship (which occurs in any great crisis or Fourth Turning), a Congress that rarely manages to address real problems, and a decline in respect for objective truth. And because they have not had the opportunity to study the careers of Jefferson, Lincoln, Theodore Roosevelt, Wilson, Franklin Roosevelt, Kennedy and Johnson, and other Presidents in detail—to say nothing of other influential figures like Henry Clay, George Norris, William Jennings Bryan, and many more—they have no idea of what a robust political order looks like and little conception of what the government has been able to accomplish at different times. The election of Donald Trump represents the greatest collapse of the American political order since 1860, and it would not have happened, in my opinion, if Americans had not almost completely lost any real understanding of and reverence for their political tradition and what it has been able to accomplish in the past. The historical profession bears an enormous responsibility for the loss of that great American heritage.

William Strauss and Neil Howe's new perspective helps us understand what is happening because of the long-term patterns they saw. The breakdown of consensus, the increase in partisanship, the growth of nativist feeling and our disagreements over basic facts, they showed, are all recurring themes of previous crises that the nation has managed to surmount during the civil war and in the era of Franklin Roosevelt. To do so, however, both Lincoln and FDR had to recognize that the old order they had grown up with was dead and that they had to build, and explain, a new one. In our own time, the Democrats have essentially been content with the status quo, and Barack Obama believed that he merely had to tinker with our economic system a bit to get the country behind him. The Republicans, on the other hand, have been pushing for the death of the New Deal order since at least the 1980s and have put forth a much clearer alternative vision, however misguided it may be. Because they have welcomed and worsened the crisis in our politics, their ideas are coming out on top.

The significance of Strauss and Howe emerged again late in 2016 when Donald Trump first appointed Steve Bannon to direct his campaign and then brought him into the White House as chief strategist. I had met Bannon in 2009, when he called me from his office at Citizens United in Washington to ask to interview me for a documentary film he was making, entitled *Generation Zero*. He was very interested in the ideas of Strauss and Howe, equally convinced that the nation was in the midst of the great crisis they had predicted, and eager to talk about their ideas with someone else who was also familiar with him. I must admit that I did not understand exactly what I was getting into, but Bannon was both personable and professional during the interview, which we both enjoyed very much. I certainly had no idea that the man I was talking to might one day sit at the right hand of a US President, and I doubt that he did either. One off-camera exchange stuck in my memory. Bannon noted that the previous Fourth Turnings—the American Revolution, the Civil War, and the FDR era—had all involved a major war and that those wars had been steadily getting bigger. He clearly believed, and would have loved to have me say on camera, that the current crisis was going to involve a conflict at least on the scale of the Second World War. But I did not believe that and would not say it. His use of my interview in the eventual film—a very educational one in light of recent events—was perfectly fair.

When Trump appointed Bannon to the White House, I immediately told this story on historyunfolding.com, and enjoyed a heady few months of fame as a result. I was interviewed by publications in the US, France, and Germany, and appeared in a *Frontline* documentary about Bannon and in an NPR radio interview by Christopher Lydon. All this also created a flurry of interest in Strauss and Howe, and *The Fourth Turning* rose significantly in the Amazon rankings and was soon prominently displayed in various Barnes and Nobles. But despite the events that have transformed the country since 2008—if not 2001—the theories still have failed to win any acceptance in the major media, much less in academia. In 2014 the reviewers of *No End Save Victory* were uniformly negative about my use of the theory, and I tried without success in 2015 to place a long piece on the current crisis in American life in major print and online outlets. Thanks in part to our higher education system, the capacity to think in 80-year periods of history only exists among those lucky enough to have discovered Strauss and Howe on their own. More are doing so. Tens of thousands of copies of *The Fourth Turning* have sold since Donald Trump was inaugurated.

Amidst the press comment on Bannon, Strauss and Howe, a few commentators seemed to suggest that those two authors were in some sense *responsible* for Bannon, but that is absurd. The recurring crises in our history—the fourth turnings—were not *advocated* by Strauss and Howe, they were simply *identified* by them. It was inevitable that the new American order created by the New Deal and the Second World War would be challenged in the 1960s and 1970s, that it would unravel in the 1980s and 1990s, and that new political movements would fight to define the shape of a new America in the first two decades of the new century. What has given Republicans an edge is there utter lack of any commitment to the dying old order, which some of the most important among them never accepted in the first place. In May of 1963, addressing the Harvard Young Republican Club, Barry Goldwater announced, "Our generation has gotten the country into trouble, and we want you to get us out."[25] And as Goldwater's GI generation faded from the scene and Silents and Boomers took over, his ideas became mainstream—or even centrist.

Great historians, I often say, do not argue with history. Most historians today would argue that the American High of 1945–64 perished because it paid too little attention to the rights of minorities, women, and gays. With this, I do not agree. That was, in fact, the era of greatest progress in civil rights for black Americans, and there was no reason why women could not have

---

25 http://www.thecrimson.com/article/1961/5/3/goldwater-calls-new-frontier-policy-throwback/

been admitted into the workplace on equal terms within its framework. Attitudes towards sexual orientation would eventually change at their own pace. But the discipline, the respect for authority, and the sense of common purpose that dominated that era sparked a great rebellion among my own generation that has continued for decades. While left-wing Boomers overturned social norms, right-wingers destroyed the New Deal economic order. As a result, the American government that did so many remarkable things at home and abroad during the middle third of the twentieth century is now a shadow of its former self. I found at Williams College that today's youth will respond to inspiring accounts of the past, but almost no one is providing them. We must accept this as part of the rhythm of history—but that does not mean that these changes have left us better off, or that we will not need a rebirth of the older virtues to maintain prosperity and our political system, and perhaps even our nation itself.

The record of modern western civilization (including its interaction with the rest of the world) which historians made in the 19th and 20th centuries remains a monument to the human spirit. The great works of historians like Henry Adams, Allen Nevins, Luigi Albertini, Leopold von Ranke, Pieter Geyl, Fritz Fischer, and many more, remain, for me, some of great achievements of our civilization, equal in their way to the renaissance architecture of Italy, the music of classical Vienna (which has always played an enormous role in my life as well), and the literature of Britain or France. Someday a new renaissance will rediscover them. I have tried to add to that tradition, and at times I feel that I have been successful.

Having retired in 2013, I embarked upon a second baseball book, using new methodology to identify and analyze the game's greatest players and teams since 1901. Entitled *Baseball Greatness*, it appeared in early 2018. Its major conclusion had broader relevance. Out of more than 20,000 men who have played major league baseball since 1901, I identified about 100—0.5 per cent—who were much, much better than anyone else. I am convinced that the same situation prevails in any complex field of human endeavor. The beauty of baseball is that we can actually measure that superiority—and thus, those who possess it are appropriately rewarded. Now it is time for my next book—a long-planned study of the politics of the Gilded Age, focusing on the presidential election of 1884, in which Grover Cleveland (D) defeated James G. Blaine (R). Cleveland's victory—the first by a Democrat since 1856—helped to pull the country back together after the Civil War. That will again become the task of our political leadership in the next couple of decades.

Sometime in the fall of 1971, during my first term in graduate school, my fellow student Diana Pinto went to see our teacher Franklin Ford to discuss her future in the historical profession and its frustrations. "You have to love history," he replied simply. I did, I always had, and I still do. The testimony of my various students in these pages show how that love spread through every class I ever gave and enriched many other lives as well. That is why I believe I was the lucky one, luckier than any of the postmodernists and Brits who fill the ranks of history departments at our most prestigious colleges and universities today. My rewards were greater. No one could take them away.

In June of 2017, my wife Patti Cassidy organized a 70th birthday party for me. The guests included friends, family, and two one-time students. A few guests spoke, and in the end, I took the floor myself. After paying tribute to her and to my sons, I picked up one of my favorite texts.

W. E. B. Du Bois, whom I had discovered in the 1990s, is in some ways even more of a kindred spirit than Henry Adams. Since Du Bois was born in 1868, his life stood in exactly the same relation to the Civil War as mine did to the Second World War. He was born in western Massachusetts and, like me, earned undergraduate and graduate degrees at Harvard. He also studied in Germany and clearly felt himself to be a part of a North Atlantic civilization, as I did. He too dreamed of an academic career but was disappointed. In my case the obstacles came from changes in my profession; in his, as he explained in his autobiography, *Dusk of Dawn*, they came from the opposition of one man, Booker T. Washington, who made sure that no college, black or white, would hire Du Bois, who was contesting

Washington's leadership and his extremely moderate approach to civil rights. Du Bois nonetheless eventually wrote and published a great work of history, *Black Reconstruction*, showing for the first time that the mixed-race Reconstruction governments had given the southern states the first real governments they had ever had and detailing how they had been overthrown by terror. So unpopular was this view in the 1930s that the *American Historical Review* declined to review it. The same fate has befallen my last three books: *American Tragedy*, *The Road to Dallas*, and *No End Save Victory*. So it goes.

Du Bois ended an autobiographical work, *Dusk of Dawn* with remarks that he delivered in 1938 at a party for *his* 70th birthday. He lived another 25 years—dying literally on the eve of the great March on Washington in 1963, which I attended—and in 1960, at 92, he recorded two long interviews. They show that his intellectual capacity was perfectly intact. I hope to equal him in that regard. I have used these remarks in the last class of *Generations in Film* both at Williams and at the War College to embody the Prophet archetype to which he and I both belong. I also read them at the memorial of my great contemporary, Bill Strauss. I have never hesitated to quote someone else's words when they have expressed my thoughts better than I ever could. So it is now, in this case, as I conclude this history.

"I have been favored among the majority of men in never being compelled to earn my bread and butter by doing work that was uninteresting or which I did not enjoy or of the sort in which I did not find my greatest life interest. This rendered me so content in my vocation that I seldom thought about salary or haggled over it. . . . I insist that regardless of income, work worthwhile which one wants to do as compared with highly paid drudgery is exactly the difference between heaven and hell.

"I am especially glad of the divine gift of laughter; it has made the world human and lovable, despite all its pain and wrong. I am glad that the partial Puritanism of my upbringing has never made me afraid of life. I have lived completely, testing every normal appetite, feasting on sunset, sea and hill, and enjoying wine, women and song. I have seen the face of beauty from the Grand Canyon to the Great Wall of China; from the Alps to Lake Baikal; from the African bush to the Venus of Milo.

"Perhaps above all I am proud of a straightforward clearness of reason, in part a gift of the gods, but also to no little degree due to scientific training and inner discipline. By means of this I have met life face to face, I have loved a fight, and I have realized that Love is God and Work is His prophet; that His ministers are Age and Death.

"This makes it the more incomprehensible for me to see persons quite panic-stricken at the approach of their thirtieth birthday and prepared for dissolution at forty. Few of my friends have openly celebrated their fiftieth birthdays, and near none their sixtieth. Of course, one sees some reasons: the disappointment at meager accomplishment which all of us to some extent share; the haunting shadow of possible decline; the fear of death. I have been fortunate in having health and wise in keeping it. I have never shared what seems to me the essentially childish desire to live forever. Life has its pain and evil—its bitter disappointments; but I like a good novel, and in healthful length of days, there is infinite joy in seeing the World, the most interesting of continued stories, unfold, even though one misses THE END."[26]

---

26 W. E. B. Du Bois, excerpt from *Dusk of Dawn: An Essay Toward an Autobiography of a Race Concept* (New York: Harcourt, Brace World, 1940). Copyright Harcourt Brace 1940. Reprinted with the permission of The Permissions Company, Inc., on behalf of The David Graham Du Bois Trust.

INDEX

9 781732 874503